# TAXING
## CHOICE

# Independent Studies in Political Economy

# TAXING
# CHOICE

## The Predatory Politics of Fiscal Discrimination

### William F. Shughart II
*editor*

**With a Foreword by**
**Paul W. McCracken**

**Transaction Publishers**
New Brunswick (U.S.A.) and London (U.K.)

This book is printed on acid-free paper that meets the American National Standard for Permanence of Paper for Printed Library Materials.

Library of Congress Catalog Number: 97-13662
ISBN: 1-56000-303-0 (cloth); 1-56000-931-4 (paper)
Printed in the United States of America

Library of Congress Cataloging-in-Publication Data

Taxing choice : the predatory politics of fiscal discrimination / edited by
    William F. Shughart II ; foreword by Paul W. McCracken.
        p. cm.
    Includes bibliographical references and index.
    ISBN 1-56000-303-0 (cloth : alk. paper)
    1. Excise tax—United States.  2. Taxation—Political aspects—United
States.  I. Shughart, William F.
HJ5707.U5T39  1997
336.2'00973—dc21                                              97-13662
                                                                  CIP

**The Independent Institute** is a non-profit, non-partisan, scholarly research and educational organization that sponsors comprehensive studies on the political economy of critical social and economic problems. The politicization of decision making in society has largely confined public debate to the narrow reconsideration of existing policies. Given the prevailing influence of partisan interests, little social innovation has occurred. In order to understand both the nature of and possible solutions to major public issues, The Independent Institute's program adheres to the highest standards of independent inquiry and is pursued regardless of prevailing political or social biases and conventions. The resulting studies are widely distributed as books and other publications, and publicly debated through numerous conference and media programs.

Through this uncommon independence, depth, and clarity, the Independent Institute pushes at the frontiers of our knowledge, redefines the debate over public issues, and fosters new and effective directions for government reform.

# Contents

# Foreword

This century saw the epic struggle between the liberal, market-organized economic system and the state-managed economic order resolved in favor of the former. With the disintegration of the USSR and the shift in China toward more activity through a private sector, the century has delivered its verdict about a so-called planned economy, and it is not a favorable one for those who saw the route to progress through government management of economic life. Yet for much of this century, it is not amiss to point out, the prevailing orthodoxy in the intellectual community tended toward "the primacy of politically directed social planning."[1] History's verdict is now in. Reliance on politically directed social planning to achieve economic progress is a losing strategy. Indeed, logic was always on that side of the case, but logic often has hard going against views that seem to take on the mantle of quasi-religious beliefs.

In view of this it is remarkable that we continue to see an expanding "socialization" of economic life in countries with liberal, market-organized economic systems. A crude measure of this is simply the share of the national income channeled through the public sector either via taxation or government borrowing (or alternatively government expenditures as a percentage of gross domestic product). The disappointing results of thus socializing a substantial proportion of economic activity certainly do not reflect any lack of trying. The higher income countries of the world during the last three decades have seen large increases in the public sector's preemption of national income and output. While the ratio of government spending to GDP still varies widely, by the 1990s this ratio for the group was approaching 50 percent, and during these thirty years it had almost doubled.[2] For the U.S. and Japan in 1993 government spending was equal to somewhat over 34 percent, but these two countries were at the low end. For many European countries government spending is now 50 percent or more of GDP, and for Sweden it is now over 70 percent. And not surprisingly public sector employment in Sweden has accounted for all of the increase in Sweden's total employment in recent years.[3]

The expenditure side of the budget is not, of course, a full measure of the public sector's displacement effect on the economy. Another source is the growth of regulation. That is always a politically attractive alternative to running things through budgets since then the government does not have to explain the fiscal results that might arouse the citizenry. While the displacement

ix

effects from regulations are not easily "added up," two things are clear. First, by any measure the volume of regulatory activity has increased sharply in recent years. Regulatory spending at the Federal level in real terms has been increasing at a rate that is at least double the increase in our real GDP. And other volumetric measures show a broadly similar trend.

Second, the "cost" of this in terms of the drag on productivity and improvement in real income has been substantial. One estimate suggests that real national output would be 30 percent higher today if the regulatory expansion beginning in the 1960s had not occurred. [4] In any case, we do know that there was a sharp decline in the rate of growth in real incomes after the early 1970s. It is reasonable to assume that the sharp increase in Federal regulatory activities played a role in the economy's more anemic productivity performance. The economic costs can be finagled out of the budget, but they cannot be finagled out of the economy. They will show up somewhere.

Another politically attractive way for government to intrude on the size and the shape and character of the private sector is through selective taxes. For one thing this puts more money in the government's till, and governments are always yearning for yet more revenue. Moreover, many of these seemingly can be justified on the basis that they tax things not really good for people. So it is all and heaven too—a forced reduction in people's propensity to err, and more revenue.

In a sense the use of selective taxes thus fits the contemporary philosophy that the route to the good social and economic order is to blueprint this good society and then use the instruments and power of government to implement the blueprint. (This contrasts sharply with that of basic liberalism—which sees the role of government to establish a stable framework or structure, within which the optimum pattern will emerge naturally as people give expression to their preferences and knowledge and creativity.) The role of selective taxes and the criteria which should guide their use—these are issues that deserve much more analysis than they have received in recent years, and that is the objective of this volume. It comes along none too soon since far more is involved here than such phrases as nuisance taxes or sin taxes might seem to imply.

One more quick point. If we live in a democracy where the people always have the ultimate power to vote the rascals out, is there really an issue here? Is what we have simply the preferences of the people being given expression through the normal workings of the democratic process?

After the perceptive work of James Buchanan and his colleagues, we know that things are not quite that simple. Each new program enlarging the public sector creates two new interest groups. One is the beneficiaries of the program; the other is the bureaucracy that develops to run it. And even if it is inimical to the welfare of citizens generally, the political power of, strongly focused interest group is apt to determine the outcome.

The cause of good public policy is not, however, lost. By some mysterious process once people are informed they can and do move policy in a constructive direction. This volume will contribute to that congealing process for an issue of public policy now needing and beginning to receive more attention.

Paul W. McCracken
Edmund Ezra Distinguished
Professor Emeritus
Graduate School of
Business Administration
University of Michigan

## Notes

1. Zbigniew Brzezinski, "The Grand Failure" (Scribners, 1989), p. 11.
2. "OECD Economies at a Glance: Structural Indicators" (Organization for Economic Cooperation and Development, 1996), pp. 100–1.
3. Sherwin Rosen, "Public Employment and the Welfare State in Sweden", Journal of Economic Literature, June 1996, pp. 729–31.
4. Richard K. Vedder, "Federal Regulation's Impact on the Productivity Slowdown: A Trillion-Dollar Drag" (Center for the Study of American Business, Washington University, July 1996), p.13.

# Preface

Nineteen eighty-four arrived ten years behind schedule. But writing nearly half a century ago, George Orwell should be forgiven for missing by only a decade widespread acquiescence to the big lie as a means of acquiring and maintaining control of the levers of political power. Neither did he foresee slogans like "Decade of Greed" being used in place of "War is Peace" as electioneering mantras whose endless repetition would cause voters to disbelieve their own experiences, allowing a presidential candidate to manufacture the notion that the Reagan-Bush years witnessed the worst economy since the Great Depression.

A similar disregard for the truth characterized much of the rhetoric in the "historic" health care reform debate raging just a few years ago. A crisis of epic proportions, in large part caused by uncontrolled cost inflation in federal Medicare and Medicaid programs, was sold by the Clinton administration as evidence of the need for a much more extensive governmental role in health care delivery. Fortunately, no one at the time was convinced to buy.

Rhetoric likewise replaced reason in public discourse on the various schemes for financing health care reform. The most talked about of these were the "compromise" plan to triple the federal excise tax on cigarettes and Senator Moynihan's proposal to raise taxes on handgun and handgun ammunition sales dramatically. Both of these financing strategies were justified on the basis of trumped-up claims that the consumers of these products impose huge "external" costs on society. Apparently unembarrassed by the weakness of the scientific evidence supporting such claims to begin with, proponents of using excise taxes to finance health care reform went on to concoct multibillion-dollar estimates of these social costs by, among other gimmicks, supposing that if someone dies prematurely, society "loses" the goods and services he would have produced and the taxes he would have paid during the remaining years of normal life expectancy. It is as if society is entitled to all of the citizen's produce, a proper share out of which he has ungratefully cheated the tax collector by going to an early grave.

This same sort of disinformation is increasingly being used to justify taxing all manner of products and regulating all types of even remotely objectionable behavior. The list of the traditional sins of smoking, drinking, and gambling is relentlessly being expanded to include cooking outdoors, wearing perfume, eating snack foods, buying expensive cars or yachts, bearing arms, and on and on.

For example, one of the more bizarre of all excise taxes may be the soft drink tax. It might appear at first blush to even the most cynical tax enthusiast that this is nothing more than a punitive tax levied on an industry that can afford it because it produces a lot of visible products on which small levies can generate substantial revenue. However, while goliaths like Coke and Pepsi may present large, fertile targets for tax purposes, legislators are actually penalizing local community bottlers and their employees, small business retailers, and the consuming public, especially the most disadvantaged, to whom soft drinks are nothing more than a harmless, inexpensive pleasure amidst life's hardships.

Fifteen years ago, the Federal Trade Commission was tagged with the title "national nanny" for attempting to regulate the advertising of children's ready-to-eat cereals. Media commentators at the time were properly scornful of the idea that a government agency is competent to lecture parents on what they ought to let their kids eat for breakfast. But the arrogance of Jimmy Carter's FTC pales in comparison to the nearly hysterical propaganda of today's lifestyle dictators who demand that government legislate a smoke-free, fat-free, caffeine-free, gun-free, politically correct society, regardless of the individual freedoms that must be sacrificed in the process.

Hence, when David Theroux of the Independent Institute asked whether I might be interested in putting together a volume to explore the purposes and effects of tax policy in regulating consumption choices, I eagerly accepted. Let me here acknowledge the Independent Institute's financial sponsorship and David Theroux's encouragement along the way. Pam Brown read the entire manuscript and made many useful suggestions for improving the final product. Helpful comments were also provided by the participants in the Independent Institute conference "De-Taxing America? Alternatives to Predatory Politics," held on 13 July 1995 at the Willard Hotel in Washington, D.C. I also wish to thank the Institute's Theresa Navarro, for ably carrying out the myriad administrative details necessary to engage the volume's contributors and to keep them on schedule, and Harrison Shaffer, for handling the publication arrangements professionally and expeditiously. Finally, I am grateful for the continuing support generously provided by the Self family of Marks, Mississippi, without which this and many other academic projects would not have been possible.

All of us make choices that are reproachable. After all, as Lucretius observed long ago, "what is food to one man is poison to another." Starting as a college freshman, I smoked cigarettes for twenty-eight years; after quitting four years ago, I still enjoy an occasional cigar or pipe. I drink beer and wine religiously to promote coronary fitness. Surely I have other politically incorrect habits as well. To paraphrase another former smoker, whose observations are quoted by Alexander Volokh in a recent issue of the Competitive Enterprise Institute's *CEI Update*, I hope my two sons never smoke. I also hope they never ride motorcycles, skydive, bungee jump, or become Democrats. But more than anything else, I hope they do not grow up thinking that choices such as these should be made by anyone but themselves.

William F. Shughart II

# Introduction and Overview

## William F. Shughart II

Mr. BUNNING: The administration claims it wants to tax smokers to make them pay for part of the new [health care] system, raising about $105 billion over 5 years of the $730 billion of the total cost. If revenues from taxing cigarettes decline, do you think the administration would consider taxing other like substances like caffeine, cholesterol, salt, sugar, alcohol?

Mrs. CLINTON: If there is a way that you can ever come up with to tax substances like the ones you have just named, we will be glad to look at it. (U.S. House 1993, 49–50)

Mrs. Clinton apparently failed to appreciate the humor in Mr. Bunning's question. In fact, her voice turned "momentarily snappish," according to the *New York Times* (Clymer 1993, A-1). As well it should have. Carried to its logical extreme, the notion that any product or lifestyle choice that even remotely contributes to health care costs should be taxed to help finance public spending in this area would leave nothing untaxed.

In the First Lady's defense, it should be said that she rose to the challenge by distinguishing tobacco taxes from the alternatives put forth by the Republican congressman from Kentucky on two grounds. To begin with, she did not think that any of Mr. Bunning's proposals could be "realistically implemented." Second, she asserted that when used in moderation, none of the other substances he listed has been proven to have the same kinds of detrimental health effects as tobacco.[1]

Mrs. Clinton's testimony drew a standing ovation from members of the House Committee on Ways and Means, and rave reviews from the press. Although it has come and gone, the administration's plan for universal health insurance coverage that, in the president's words, "no one can ever take away," financed partly by tripling the federal excise tax on cigarettes, carried a great deal of emotional appeal. But, to paraphrase George Stigler, emotion is not what public policy should live by or on. The proposition that smokers, drinkers, and others consume disproportionate shares of society's scarce health care resources and, hence, should be singled out to bear disproportionate shares of the cost of supplying them will simply not stand scrutiny.

Taxes are popularly viewed as unpleasant sacrifices necessary for meeting government's revenue needs. But as the "historic" health care reform debate

1

of 1994 illustrates, taxes are often utilized to restrict private consumption choices. The tax collector for the welfare state has become a scold who wants to force individuals—for their own good, of course—to conform to a particular pattern of behavior and, increasingly, of thought. The extent of this social-engineering application of the tax code is largely misunderstood by the general public. Even those citizens who keep informed about local and national affairs underestimate the frequency with which taxes are selectively imposed to restrict the range of voluntary choice and to reward special-interest groups.

This book explores the economics and *politics* of selective excise taxation. While excise taxes are, at least in theory, designed to create incentives for consumers to take account of the costs their consumption choices impose on others, they are also a tool that can be used strategically to restrain competitive market forces and wealth creation. A tax on alcohol, which curtails the consumption of a product whose abuse is linked to highway fatalities, is also a tax that can be structured to benefit brewers at the expense of vintners. Taxes on executive salaries in excess of $1 million or on the purchase of "luxury" goods like furs and yachts, which redistribute income away from "overpaid" corporate management and the "rich," are also taxes on effort and the accumulation of wealth.

Evidence that pressure-group politics underlies the push for selective excise taxation is provided by the historically wide variety of goods and services on which such taxes have been imposed. Automobile tires, local and long-distance telephone calls, chewing gum, oleomargarine, theater tickets, luggage, carbonated soft drinks, and phosphorous matches are a few among the scores of products that have been singled out for taxation by special-interest groups seeking competitive advantages, bureaucrats seeking revenue, or both. Hence, while "social cost" rhetoric has come to dominate the public-policy debate, ordinary political forces are frequently at work.

## Social Costs versus Private Costs

Social-cost arguments are increasingly being brought to bear to justify the use of selective excise taxes (and other of the state's police powers) to regulate the consumption of an expanding list of goods and services to which anyone, anywhere, objects. A neo-Puritan ethic is on the rise, seeking to restrict or prohibit smoking, drinking, driving, outdoor cooking, movie theater popcorn, and anything on the menu at Chinese and Mexican restaurants, along with myriad other commercial products and activities that on the weakest of scientific evidence can be claimed either to adversely affect human health or to harm the environment.

Like the Clinton administration's forsaken health care reform financing proposal, these calls for government action assume that the consumption or use of certain products imposes costs on society that the consumers do not themselves bear and which they consequently do not take into account when making decisions about how much to consume. Smokers, for instance, fail to consider the adverse effects of exposure to environmental tobacco smoke on the well-being of nonsmokers. Consumers of movie theater popcorn do not consider the tax revenue that will be lost if they die prematurely because of the extra fat and salt they've voluntarily added to their diets. And so on.

The conventional wisdom is that government intervention is required to align private costs more closely with social costs. Short of banning smoking or popcorn eating outright, a selective excise tax on tobacco or movie theater popcorn accomplishes this purpose by raising the politically incorrect product's price and providing consumers with incentives to curtail their purchases. This reduction in purchases, in turn, reduces the socially objectionable by-products of consumption. Moreover, the unrepentant consumers who continue to smoke and eat popcorn at the higher after-tax prices are thereby forced to help pay for the costs they persist in imposing on the rest of society.

The meddlesome preferences that underlie puritanical urges to regulate the lifestyle choices of others clash with the revenue-raising potential of selective excise taxes. Government policy toward alcohol and other drugs, historically considered among the most evil of substances, has consequently been locked into a regulatory cycle of tax and taboo. Moral indignation leads to prohibition, which provides psychic benefits to Baptists who preach abstinence on Sunday morning and monetary benefits to bootleggers who supply their liquor on Saturday night (Yandle 1983). The gangsterism and widespread disobedience of the law that predictably follow bring calls for repeal, and the cycle begins anew.

Support for legalization is buttressed by the revenue-generating power of taxes on "sin." Indeed, Franklin Roosevelt's pledge to repeal the Eighteenth Amendment was openly mercenary (Johnson and Porter 1973, 332). Because the Great Depression had reduced incomes (and, hence, income tax receipts) dramatically, Congress was desperate for the revenues that would be generated by legalizing and taxing liquor sales (Boudreaux and Pritchard 1994). According to one contemporary wag, the theme of the Democratic party's 1932 election platform was that "if only given the chance, Americans might drink themselves into a balanced budget" (Leff 1984, 31).

The tension between the regulatory and revenue-raising objectives of selective taxes is an enduring theme in the formulation and execution of public policies toward politically incorrect products. Is it somehow "better" to ban the possession and sale of certain substances outright, thereby shifting transactions to the underground economy? Or should transactions involving these substances instead be legalized and taxed?

The costs and benefits of these two alternative public-policy approaches for dealing with politically incorrect products are addressed thoroughly in the following chapters. The method of analysis is grounded in the principles of public choice. Most of the contributors to the book are economists. Some also have training in the law, but each of them is versed in the Virginia school of political economy, which insists that *all* decision makers, in or out of government, are guided by their own personal self-interests. As it does in other domains where politics and economics interact, the Virginia school approach moves the debate about the regulation of "sinful" products away from sterile derivations of "optimal" tax rates computed and levied by benevolent government officials interested only in maximizing some fuzzy notion of what is best for "society," toward a consideration of the ordinary political forces that actually shape public policy in this area.

## The Plan of the Book

*Taxing Choice* is organized into four main parts. Following this introduction, chapter 1 provides a summary and critique of the standard economic arguments used to justify the taxation of "sin." The first of these is the Ramsey rule, which contends that the selective taxation of politically incorrect products is a nearly ideal method of public finance. This is because such taxes have little or no impact on consumption and, hence, impose minimal welfare losses on society. More recently, taxes on politically incorrect products have been justified either as "user fees" or as ways of correcting the negative externalities ("social costs") associated with their consumption. However, given the inherently regressive and discriminatory nature of selective excise taxes, the chapter concludes that one must look to politics, not economics, to explain why they persist.

The next two chapters place selective taxation in historical perspective. Brenda Yelvington provides a broad overview of the history of selective excise taxes in the United States. Her chapter contributes detailed information on the amount of revenue raised by these taxes over time, beginning with the infamous whiskey tax of 1791, and continuing through the Clinton administration's recent excise tax proposals. Yelvington's chapter highlights both the role played by excise taxes in financing wartime spending and the broad range of products that have been subject to excise taxation since the New Deal. Adam Gifford, Jr., then looks more closely at three historical episodes involving the use of selective excise taxes to regulate behavior. Two of these, the colonial stamp tax and the whiskey tax, illustrate the tendency for such policies to alternate between revenue-raising and regulatory phases. The third episode, the tax on oleomargarine enacted in 1886, shows how the political process can be manipulated by powerful special-interest groups—the dairy industry, in this case—to obtain benefits for themselves at the expense of consumers and competitors.

Part II explores the predatory politics of excise taxation. In chapter 4, Randall Holcombe sets the stage by developing a model that explains how selective excise taxes emerge in a political marketplace where competing pressure groups lobby for wealth transfers in their own favor. Selective excise taxes are politically popular in such a setting precisely because their burden falls more heavily on some groups than on others. Those groups who will bear the burden of a particular excise tax have an incentive to lobby their legislative representatives to prevent the tax from being enacted, or to reduce or repeal existing taxes. Those groups who will benefit from the revenue generated by the tax have an incentive to lobby their legislative representatives to see that the tax is imposed. An excise tax that is paid by half the population maximizes the legislature's political support in Holcombe's model, but it also maximizes the social-welfare losses associated with taxation. Evidence drawn from a number of sources, including taxes on carbonated soft drinks, the recently reenacted federal excise tax on airline tickets, and state cigarette excise taxes, provides support for chapter 4's general conclusion that rent seeking by politically powerful special-interest groups is the key to understanding excise tax policy.

In chapter 5, Dwight Lee argues that the user-charge and social-cost justifications for selective taxes have in many cases been invoked as pretexts to overcome taxpayer resistance to what would otherwise be plainly seen as highly regressive and discriminatory revenue sources. Moral zeal for the virtues of temperance, reinforced by proposals to earmark tax receipts to alleviate the wages of sin, helps generate the political support necessary for enacting selective excise taxes. Besides supplying political camouflage, tax earmarking provides benefits to legislators by freeing general-fund appropriations for use elsewhere in the budget.

Thomas DiLorenzo furnishes a chilling example of such political subterfuge in chapter 6. He examines California's Proposition 99, a 1988 ballot referendum that tripled the state's excise tax on cigarettes (from ten to thirty-five cents per pack) and earmarked much of the additional tax revenues for financing the activities of a coalition of antismoking groups. DiLorenzo shows how Proposition 99 funds have been used systematically to benefit state government bureaucracies and activist nonprofit organizations, with little or no discernible impact on the public's health.

Part II closes with a chapter by Gary Anderson that focuses on bureaucratic incentives to explain why a regime of selective excise taxation, designed initially to raise revenue, gradually evolves into one of regulating consumption and, ultimately, into outright prohibition. Prohibition, after all, requires that tax revenues be sacrificed. But insofar as prohibition demands ever-larger law enforcement budgets and ever-larger numbers of law enforcement personnel, politicians and bureaucrats may rationally support a policy that on the surface seems inconsistent with revenue-maximizing objectives. Anderson illustrates his argument with examples taken from America's embryonic public policies toward narcotics and its "noble experiment" with alcohol prohibition. More recent proposals to dramatically increase taxes on tobacco and handgun ammunition are also considered in this light.

Part III looks more closely at the purposes of specific excise taxes and their effects on "sin." In chapter 8, Mark Thornton provides a detailed social and political history of prohibitionism in the United States. He sees strong parallels between the temperance movements of the eighteenth and nineteenth centuries and contemporary antitobacco and antidrug crusades. Next, Bruce Benson and David Rasmussen present an economic anatomy of the "war on drugs." They supply theory and evidence suggesting that the heavy emphasis placed on drug law enforcement beginning in 1984—a shift in philosophy reinforced by the enactment of civil forfeiture laws, which allow police to share in the proceeds from selling assets seized in the course of drug arrests—had a number of perverse consequences. Chief among these are overcrowded prisons, greater participation by juveniles in the drug trade, and increases in non-drug-related crimes. Benson and Rasmussen attribute these social costs in large part to the bureaucratic incentives created by asset forfeiture laws that operate much like a lump-sum tax on drug crime, and they see no evidence that the war on drugs has produced any benefits in the form of reductions in drug use or drug-related criminal activity.

Chapters 10 and 11 turn our attention to alcohol taxes. Richard Wagner challenges the social-cost justification for higher taxes on alcoholic beverages. He argues that while a case can be made that drunk driving imposes substantial costs on third parties, taxation is an inappropriate policy response for internalizing this externality. A tax on alcohol designed to force consumers to take account of the social costs associated with drunk driving punishes the many innocent individuals who drink in moderation for the damages caused by the dipsomaniacal few. Wagner suggests that alternative policies, such as imposing stiffer legal penalties on drunk drivers and securing compensatory restitution for their victims, are superior to the standard tax approach, which does not discriminate between responsible and irresponsible alcohol consumers.

In chapter 11, Paula Gant and Robert Ekelund, Jr., use evidence from the 1990 federal excise tax increase on alcoholic beverages, enacted as part of President Bush's calamitous budget deal, to show how differential tax rates affect alcohol consumption and, hence, the social costs of intemperance. The brunt of the 1990 tax increase fell on wine, making it more expensive relative to beer and distilled liquor. Specifically, wine taxes increased more than fivefold, while beer taxes doubled and liquor taxes rose by less than 10 percent. This change in relative tax rates predictably caused consumers to increase their purchases of beer and liquor, substituting these alternative alcoholic beverages for the now relatively more expensive wine. As a result, Gant and Ekelund suggest, the tax increase may have actually increased the social cost of alcohol use insofar as wine consumers tend to have more responsible attitudes toward drinking and driving than their beer- and liquor-drinking counterparts.

Part III ends with Richard Vedder's chapter on cigarette taxes. He highlights a particular consequence of excise taxation in a world with borders, namely the propensity of consumers to shift their purchases to lower-tax jurisdictions. Evidence from the states suggests that these cross-border effects place a binding constraint on any one government's ability to raise additional revenue by raising tax rates. Revenue is lost not only because consumers cross borders to make their purchases, but also because higher tax rates raise the rate of return to smuggling and other tax-avoidance activities. Both the Canadian experience (where it is estimated that prior to a major tax reduction in February 1994, contraband accounted for 40 percent of the cigarettes consumed nationwide, and perhaps as much as 75 percent of those consumed in Quebec) and the recent growth of cigarette smuggling along the California-Mexico border should give pause to supporters of proposals to increase the federal excise tax on cigarettes or to selectively tax soft drinks and snack foods at the state level.

Constitutional issues related to the taxation of "sin" are raised in part IV. In chapter 13, Jonathan Macey examines the purposes and effects of taxes applied to financial transactions in the economy, including limits on the tax deductibility of corporate "greenmail," executive salaries in excess of $1 million, and so-called golden-parachute payments to managers who lose their jobs in the wake of mergers and acquisitions. He concludes that these taxes reduce the efficiency of capital markets and, hence, interfere with their ability to reallocate scarce productive resources from less highly valued to more highly valued uses. All that is gotten in return for these restrictions on the rights of business owners and managers is the fulfillment of dubious egalitarian goals.

Bruce Kobayashi next explores how taxes and other restrictions on the sale of firearms and firearm ammunition have been used by special-interest groups to weaken the Second Amendment piecemeal. Indeed, Kobayashi argues that a piecemeal approach offers a clever way for gun control advocates to achieve broad restrictions on firearm ownership at low political cost. Recognizing the constitutional challenges likely to be triggered by attempts to enact sweeping gun control laws, proponents of restricting the private ownership and use of firearms have lately begun lobbying for taxing rather than banning the sale of guns and ammunition. Moreover, given the likely political hurdles to be faced in passing general tax legislation (as opposed to imposing taxes on selected types of guns and bullets), these same gun control advocates have pushed for achieving a similar goal through the courts by arguing in favor of imposing strict liability on the manufacturers, distributors, and even retailers of firearms.

Hence, while advocates of gun control would prefer broad-based federal restrictions on the private ownership of firearms, a piecemeal approach offers a number of political benefits, according to Kobayashi, including opportunities to expand their scope administratively after passage or to argue for more sweeping restrictions when the more narrowly tailored ones predictably fail to produce the intended outcomes. Kobayashi then goes on to expose the flaws in the reasoning used nowadays to justify the selective taxation of firearms. He shows that the economic framework explicitly adopted by gun control advocates for debating the issue, namely that taxing firearms would increase social welfare by forcing gun purchasers to internalize the externalities associated with bearing arms, misapplies the economic model by failing to distinguish between legal use and misuse. Moreover, Kobayashi argues, selective taxes of this sort may have effects opposite of those intended. Finally, he addresses the broader constitutional issues raised by the gun control debate, pointing out that the central question before society has less to do with the ability of law-abiding citizens to protect themselves against criminals than with their capacity to fend off attacks on their liberty by an ever more intrusive central government.

Civil forfeiture laws, once confined to customs violations and piracy, are the subject of chapter 15. Donald Boudreaux and Adam Pritchard trace their history, arguing that the growing use of asset seizures in drug law enforcement activities violates the Eighth Amendment's excessive-fines clause. They also suggest that by merely labeling these actions as "civil" in nature, an overreaching government is able to prosecute individuals without abiding by the constitutional restrictions designed to protect the rights of the accused in criminal proceedings.

In the book's final chapter, Gordon Tullock breathes a puff of fresh air into the contentious debate about smoking. He argues that politics and junk science have transformed what would otherwise be a mild problem of externality, often resolved privately by smokers and nonsmokers in mutually satisfactory ways, into publicly orchestrated campaigns of propaganda against smoking and harassment of smokers. The irony, of course, is that tobacco tax revenues will go up in smoke if these campaigns are successful.

Tullock's chapter brings one of the book's central themes full circle. There is a fundamental tension between the revenue-raising and regulatory goals of selective excise taxes. Politicians and policy makers cannot have it both ways. But in fact, this conflict is more apparent than real. The objective of discouraging "sin" is at bottom just a handy political pretext for pushing back the limits of taxpayer resistance to feeding government's insatiable revenue appetite. Without the cloak of moral indignation about immoderate smoking, drinking, and gambling, these taxes would be revealed for what they are: revenue sources that, because they are both discriminatory and regressive, violate the most basic principles of tax fairness.

The desire to meddle has no rational stopping point. Lest those upright citizens who neither smoke, drink, nor gamble think that taxes on choice are a small price to pay for encouraging moral behavior among the weaker willed, Mrs. Clinton's testimony before the House Committee on Ways and Means should serve as a wake-up call. Just remember: "If there is a way that you can ever come up with to tax substances like the ones you have just named, we will be glad to look at it...."

## Note

1. Mrs. Clinton presumably misspoke when she stated that "tobacco, insofar as we are aware, is the only substance that if used correctly as directed has these health care *benefits*. Neither alcohol nor caffeine or the others if used in moderation or in small amounts are proven to have the same kind of effects" (U.S. House 1993, 50; emphasis added). Mrs. Clinton's summary of the scientific evidence is overly broad, however. One of the major defects in the research on the links between smoking and health is the absence of attempts to derive conventional dose-response relationships that distinguish between the physiological effects of moderate and immoderate tobacco use. As Mrs. Clinton's remarks imply about alcohol, caffeine, and other possibly harmful substances, the dose does in fact make the poison.

## References

Boudreaux, Donald J., and Adam C. Pritchard. 1994. "The Price of Prohibition." *Arizona Law Review* 36 (spring): 1–10.

Clymer, Adam. 1993. "Clinton's Health Plan: Hillary Clinton, On Capitol Hill, Wins Raves, If Not a Health Plan." *New York Times*, 29 September.

Johnson, Donald B., and Kird H. Porter. 1973. *National Party Platforms, 1840–1972*. Urbana-Champaign: University of Illinois Press.

Leff, Mark H. 1984. *The Limits of Symbolic Reform: The New Deal and Taxation, 1933–1939*. New York: Cambridge University Press.

U.S. House. 1993. Committee on Ways and Means. *The President's Health Care Reform Proposals: Hearings Before the Committee on Ways and Means*. 103rd Cong., 1st sess. 28 September.

Yandle, Bruce. 1983. "Bootleggers and Baptists." *Regulation* 7 (May-June): 12–16.

# Part I

# The Political Economy
of Excise Taxation

# 1

# The Economics of the Nanny State

*William F. Shughart II*

Recent proposals to pay for national health care reform by raising existing federal excise taxes—or by levying new ones—seek legitimacy in the language of economists. Terms like "social cost" and "user fee" have become the accepted pretexts for selectively taxing the consumers of alcohol, tobacco, firearms, and other politically incorrect products in order to finance the creation of new government entitlement programs promising benefits to all.

Selective excise taxes are nothing new, of course. After all, they gave their names to the Boston Tea Party and the Whiskey Rebellion. Customarily imposed as wartime emergency measures, federal excise taxes nowadays apply to a wide variety of products, including automobiles retailing for $30,000 or more, heavy truck tires, gasoline, coal, certain sporting goods (fishing tackle, firearms, and shells), local and long-distance telephone calls, alcohol, tobacco, airline tickets and, until recently, yachts. State and local governments likewise selectively tax gasoline, alcohol, and tobacco products, and they have lately taken the lead in taxing carbonated soft drinks.

There are three common economic justifications for resorting to selective excise taxes as means of public finance. One is the so-called *Ramsey rule* for minimizing the excess burden of taxation: A benevolent government, motivated by the goal of raising tax revenues at the lowest possible social cost, would levy taxes on products in inverse proportion to their elasticities of demand. Relatively high alcohol and tobacco taxes, for instance, have been rationalized on the basis of the Ramsey rule because consumers' relative insensitivity to price increases, at least in the short run, prevents the welfare losses imposed on them from greatly exceeding the amount of the tax.

Second, selective excise taxes can serve as ersatz *user fees* when their proceeds are dedicated to financing the construction and maintenance of public goods or the provision of public services from which the taxpayers themselves directly benefit. The federal excise tax on gasoline, some of whose revenues are earmarked for the Highway Trust Fund, is often justified on

13

these grounds, for example. More recently, this reasoning has been extended to justify the taxation of alcohol, tobacco, and firearms on the grounds that the purchasers of these products place disproportionate burdens on the public sector's social services and health care resources.

Finally, selective excise taxes can be viewed as *corrective taxes* when they are levied on products whose consumption generates negative externalities. In such cases, the tax can be thought of as a penalty that helps curtail the production of the externality by forcing individuals to take account of the costs their consumption choices impose on others, as a way of raising revenue for the purpose of compensating those who are harmed by the externality, or both. Environmental tobacco smoke, drunk driving, and drug-related shootings are examples of the negative externalities associated with the consumption of politically incorrect products, and are frequently used to justify selective taxation.

This chapter examines each of these economic justifications for excise taxes in some detail. Two conclusions are drawn from the discussion: First, while such levies can be defended with economic reasoning in a few isolated cases, there are no general grounds on which the existing panoply of selective excise taxes can be justified. Second, because of their inherently regressive and discriminatory natures, one must look to politics, not economics, to explain why selective excise taxes persist.

## Selective Taxes and the Ramsey Rule

Selective excise taxes, including those levied on politically incorrect products, are something of a mystery of public finance. Because they tend to be regressive, falling disproportionately on consumers at the lower end of the income distribution, they violate the principle of tax fairness known as vertical equity, which states that tax liabilities should rise along with an individual's ability to pay.[1] Because they are discriminatory, falling on the consumers of some products but not others, they violate the principle of tax fairness known as horizontal equity, which states that individuals with equal abilities to pay should face equal tax liabilities.

The mystery is that despite violating the equity standards accepted by most students of public finance, selective excise taxes continue to be levied by governments at all levels. Fairness does not explain their use. Neither does revenue. In fiscal year 1993, for instance, excise tax receipts accounted for less than 5 percent of total federal tax collections.[2] While this figure is considerably higher at the state level,[3] revenue raising is clearly not the only reason selective excise taxes are imposed.[4]

### Taxes and Product Attributes

Excise taxes reduce the output of the taxed commodity, raise its price, and modify its attributes (Wagner 1983, 259). Social welfare is consequently affected in two ways when a particular product is singled out for taxation.

Consider the impact of a selective excise tax on a product's characteristics. All goods are bundles of attributes, most of which can be varied by varying some aspect of the production process. Cigarettes, for instance, can be long or short, be filtered or unfiltered, and have brown or white paper wrappers. The tobacco they contain can be blended to be strong or mild, to be harsh or smooth, and to deliver more or less tar and nicotine. Distilled spirits can vary in age and alcohol content, gasoline can have higher or lower octane ratings, and so on.

Excise taxes, which by definition are levied on a per unit basis, affect the relative prices of a product's assorted attributes and, hence, tend to change the mix of characteristics that will be supplied, accentuating those receiving favorable tax treatment. This observation is a straightforward application of the Alchian and Allen theorem (1967, 63–64), which shows how fixed costs can affect the relative prices of low- and high-quality products.

To illustrate, suppose that prior to the imposition of any tax, short (80-millimeter) cigarettes sell for $1.00 per pack of twenty cigarettes, while long (100-millimeter) cigarettes sell for $1.25 per pack. One way of comparing these prices is to calculate that the pretax price of tobacco sold in the form of cigarettes is .0625 cents per millimeter (or 6.25 cents per 100 millimeters). Ignoring the filter, a pack of twenty short cigarettes contains 1,600 millimeters of tobacco, while a pack of twenty long cigarettes contains 2,000 millimeters of tobacco.

Now suppose that an excise tax of twenty-five cents per pack is imposed on all cigarettes, short or long, and, as a first approximation, assume that the full amount of the tax is passed on to consumers in the form of higher prices.[5] Short cigarettes now sell for $1.25 per pack and long cigarettes for $1.50. The tax causes the price of short cigarettes to increase to slightly more than .078 cents per millimeter (7.8125 cents per 100 millimeters). The price of long cigarettes has likewise increased, but to only .075 cents per millimeter (7.5 cents per 100 millimeters). Thus, while the excise tax has increased the prices of all cigarettes and fewer of them will therefore tend to be sold overall, long cigarettes have become cheaper relative to short cigarettes. Other things being the same, consumers will rationally want to buy more of them after the tax has been imposed than before, and cigarette manufacturers will respond to this demand. We therefore expect to observe relatively more long cigarettes being bought and sold as a result of the excise tax.

There are many more examples of the impact of excise taxation on product attributes that the Alchian and Allen theorem helps to illuminate. For instance, the substantially higher alcohol and tobacco taxes levied in much of the rest of the world explain why brands sold outside the United States tend to be more potent (have higher alcohol and nicotine contents) than their domestic counterparts. Zero-tolerance drug law enforcement policies, which make no distinction between illicit substances on the basis of quantity or their psychophysiological effects, likewise predictably shift market transactions away from bulky, less potent drugs (such as powdered cocaine) in favor of more compact and powerful substances (such as crack cocaine).

Consumer welfare is reduced as a result of tax-provoked changes in product characteristics in the sense that the value buyers place on the additional attributes is less than the increase in price that occasions their supply. After all, had consumers been willing to pay more for longer cigarettes, stronger alcoholic beverages, or higher-octane gasoline than it costs to produce them, these characteristics would have been supplied in the absence of the tax. Put differently, if the price-attribute combinations available to consumers were optimal prior to the tax, they must be suboptimal after the tax is imposed.

### Taxes and Social Welfare

Social welfare is adversely affected in an even more fundamental way when an excise tax is imposed. Because the tax reduces the output of the taxed product and raises its price, consumers respond by shifting their purchases toward less highly valued alternatives. The value consumers attach to the units of the good the tax forces them to forgo must be greater than the value of the alternatives to which they turn; if not, they would have rearranged their purchases in favor of these alternatives beforehand. The owners of any specialized inputs used in the taxed good's production are likewise made worse off. As the output of the taxed good declines, some of these inputs either become unemployed or are forced to transfer to less highly valued uses. Their owners accordingly command lower incomes. Hence, the welfare of both consumers and producers is reduced as a result of the tax.

The lion's share of the value of this welfare reduction is transferred to the government in the form of tax revenue—income that would have been spent to purchase the product and to compensate the owners of specialized inputs is remitted to the tax collector instead. In addition, because the tax inserts a "wedge" between the amount paid by the consumer and the after-tax amount received by the producer, a "deadweight" welfare loss is also imposed on society. This loss is called a deadweight loss because its value is transferred away from market participants but is not captured by the government or anyone else. The deadweight welfare loss is also referred to as the "excess burden" of the tax because it represents the amount by which the value of the welfare losses imposed on producers and consumers exceeds the revenue collected by the tax authority. But no matter what this social-welfare cost may be called, it is the value (measured in terms of opportunities sacrificed) of the units of output not produced or consumed as a result of the tax.

The excess burden of a tax, it is important to emphasize, has nothing whatsoever to do with the administrative costs of collecting it, which are fairly modest in most cases, typically estimated to be on the order of 5 percent or less of the revenue raised. Neither does the excess burden have anything to do with taxpayers' direct or indirect costs of compliance, including filling out tax forms, remitting tax payments, and so forth. "Excess burden" instead refers to the welfare cost associated with tax-induced changes in behavior— the influence of the tax on the consumption and production decisions of individuals and firms. These costs are not insignificant: one study (Ballard, Shoven, and Whalley 1985), for example, estimated the social-welfare cost of the U.S. tax system as a whole to be on the order of thirteen cents to twenty-four cents per dollar of revenue raised, figures that translate into a total cost to the economy amounting to about 5 percent of GNP (Holcombe 1988, 173).

Efficiency, along with equity, are the normative standards most often used by public-finance economists to evaluate alternative tax systems. In the context of taxes, efficiency is measured in terms of the cost per dollar of revenue raised, where "cost" includes both the direct costs (administration and compliance) and the indirect costs (excess burdens) of the taxes.

A selective excise tax, as we have seen, causes the consumer to substitute away from the taxed good. Indeed, it is this substitution effect that is responsible for the excess burden of the tax. Other things being the same, this excess burden will be greater the greater is the reduction in the consumer's purchases. In other words, the more responsive consumers are to a change in the taxed good's own price—in the jargon of economists, the more elastic is the demand for the taxed good—the greater will be the excess burden of the tax.

*The Ramsey Rule*

The relationship between the elasticity of demand and the excess burden of a tax was derived formally by Frank Ramsey (1927). The Ramsey rule states that in order to minimize the excess burden of raising a given amount of tax revenue, taxes should be placed on goods in inverse proportion to their elasticities of demand. A benevolent government interested in maximizing the efficiency of the tax system should, according to Ramsey, impose relatively high tax rates on goods having relatively inelastic demands, and vice versa.

The Ramsey rule thus provides an intellectual justification for the selective taxation of goods such as alcohol and tobacco, whose consumers are relatively unresponsive to increases in price. But the justification is incomplete for a number of important reasons. For starters, neither Ramsey himself nor anyone since has produced a testable model of tax policy making that explains why government would be motivated to maximize the efficiency of the tax code in the first place. Indeed, the modern public-choice literature shows that models of political behavior based on the assumption of self-interest have greater explanatory power than public-interest models. Second, the Ramsey rule assumes that government's objective is to select a set of taxes and tax rates that raise a predetermined amount of tax revenue at the lowest possible cost. The Ramsey rule no longer applies if government pursues some other goal, such as maximizing the amount of tax revenue it collects. The revenue-maximizing set of taxes and tax rates is unlikely to be the same as the Ramsey-optimal set.

Ultimately, of course, the Ramsey rule fails as a matter of logic in the case of sin taxes. Along with other sumptuary taxes, sin taxes comprise a category of taxes whose regulatory effects are thought desirable on ethical or moral grounds. The underlying rationale for such taxes is that taxation will discourage the consumption of goods or services that the majority finds objectionable. But the Ramsey rule singles out products to be taxed precisely because taxation's impact on consumption is minimal. Hence, the regulatory and revenue-raising justifications for sin taxes work at cross-purposes.[6]

Nowhere is the underlying tension between those who support selective excise taxes to discourage the consumption of sinful products and those who support them as efficient revenue raisers more apparent than in the recent health care reform debate. Proponents of increasing taxes on tobacco, firearms, and other politically incorrect products to finance federal health care reform were placed in the position of arguing that such taxes would help reduce the consumption of these products—but, it was hoped, not by too much.

## Selective Taxes as User Fees

*Benefits received* stands on a par with *ability to pay* as one of the overarching principles of tax policy. The benefits principle of taxation rests on the premise that individuals who consume the greater part of the benefits of the goods and services provided by the public sector should bear the greater part of the cost of financing the provision of these benefits. Reasoning of this sort is used to justify a number of selective excise taxes, including the federal excise tax on gasoline, some of whose proceeds are earmarked for the Highway Trust Fund, and the recently reenacted federal excise tax on airline tickets, whose proceeds are earmarked for the Airport and Airway Trust Fund. The revenue generated by these taxes is used to build and maintain roads, bridges, air traffic control facilities, and other infrastructure from which the taxpayers themselves directly benefit. The user fee character of these taxes is reinforced by the facts that they can be avoided in principle—those who do not benefit are not required to pay—and they vary directly with the taxpayer's intensity of use of the publicly financed good.

Knut Wicksell ([1896] 1958), in fact, envisioned a tax system composed entirely of earmarked taxes.[7] He recommended that every government spending program be tied to a specific revenue source. In other words, on all matters requiring the outlay of public funds, voters would be presented with a fiscal package containing a spending proposal and a tax dedicated to financing it. Each voter then has the opportunity to decide whether to accept or reject the package according as the program's expected pro rata benefits are greater or less than its expected pro rata tax costs. If, in addition, a qualified majority approaching unanimity is required to secure enactment of the spending proposal, fiscal decisions will generally be efficient in the sense of approximating the "correct" quantities of public goods and services.

Most important, though, if a spending program's expected tax costs exceed its expected benefits for enough voters so that a qualified majority in favor of the fiscal package is not achieved, the tax is rejected along with the public good or service to which it was tied. Because tax revenues can be raised only in support of specific government spending programs that pass a benefit-cost test, once a proposal has been disapproved, the dedicated revenue source cannot be redirected to create another new spending program or to expand an existing one. As such, under Wicksell's plan taxpayers will not in general be obliged to finance the provision of public goods and services for which costs exceed benefits.

This efficiency property of earmarking breaks down in a world of general-fund financing, where taxes and public expenditures are not directly related and where, moreover, taxing and spending decisions are made not by the voters themselves but rather by their politically self-interested legislative representatives. This is especially true in a geographically based representative democracy, where politicians striving to maximize their probabilities of reelection have strong incentives to engage in pork barrel, that is, to support programs and policies whose benefits accrue disproportionately to their constituents but whose costs are borne disproportionately by voters in other legislative districts.

Proposals to establish a new revenue source (or to dedicate an existing one) for the purpose of financing an ongoing spending program fail to prevent public goods and services from being supplied in nonoptimal quantities, because of revenue substitution possibilities within the overall public budget. In such cases, "earmarking" becomes a political smoke screen for raising taxes to finance programs or policies that would not pass a benefit-cost test if voted on separately.

Suppose, for example, that a government highway program is currently being financed with $1.00 in general-fund appropriations. A proposal is advanced to raise the excise tax on gasoline by $1.00 and to earmark the additional tax revenue for financing road repairs. If the proposal is enacted, a likely outcome is that the $1.00 in existing general appropriations will simply be shifted elsewhere in the budget. Politically self-interested legislative representatives will rationally reallocate the general-fund revenues freed up by the earmarked tax to finance new programs or expand existing ones in ways that enhance their probabilities of reelection, benefiting themselves at the expense of the taxpayers. Most empirical studies in fact suggest that earmarked tax revenues are fungible to a fairly high degree. Borg and Mason (1988), for instance, find nearly dollar-for-dollar substitution between earmarked state lottery revenues and general-revenue appropriations for public education.[8] Becker and Lindsay (1994) likewise find that state legislatures tend to reduce budgetary appropriations for higher education whenever schools raise more money from private sources.

The user fee rationale for selective excise taxes also breaks down as the ultimate use of the funds becomes more and more remote from the taxed activity that generates them. To reiterate, a user fee can in principle be avoided by nonusers and, moreover, varies directly with the taxpayer's intensity of use. A "user fee" that does not satisfy these two conditions is simply a tax going under another name. Hence, calling selective taxes user fees simply because their proceeds have been earmarked for some specific purpose perverts the meaning of the term.

Consider proposals to dedicate some or all of the revenue generated by proposed increases in federal alcohol and tobacco taxes to fund health care reform. Certainly alcohol and tobacco consumers benefit from programs like Medicare and Medicaid, but so do many people who do not consume these products. A "user fee" that applies only to some users is plainly discriminatory. On the other hand, large numbers of alcohol and tobacco consumers do not utilize Medicare or Medicaid; hence, earmarking their tax payments to help fund these programs forces them to pay for benefits they do not receive.

Despite its superficial appeal, the user fee concept does not stand scrutiny as a justification for selective taxes (Lee 1991). This conclusion is strengthened by considering the highly regressive incidence of these taxes.[9] Federal health care reform was marketed as an entitlement program for the middle class. Yet the consumers of alcohol and tobacco are disproportionately young and poor. As such, proposals for earmarking selective tax revenues to finance government health care programs are political ruses that serve to disguise a transfer of wealth from the lower end of the income distribution to the middle.

## Selective Taxes as Corrective Taxes

The assertion of market failure is one of the leading justifications underlying proposals to increase existing selective taxes or to enact new ones. "Market failure" refers to situations in which freely functioning private market institutions "fail to sustain 'desirable' activities or to estop 'undesirable' activities" (Bator 1958, 351). Such situations arise when the benefits or costs of an activity at the level of the individual diverge from the benefits or costs of that same activity at the level of society, that is, when the economic agents interacting in an unfettered market do not bear the full social costs—or cannot capture the full social benefits—of their own decisions or choices.

Where externalities, or spillover effects, exist, private market institutions may produce "too little" of some economic goods, such as education, charity, and inoculation against communicable diseases, and "too much" of some economic bads, such as litter, air pollution, and acid rain. Private markets may be completely unable to supply certain "public goods"—national defense, for example—that, once produced, are freely available to all, including individuals who have not helped to pay for them.

The particular assertion of market failure of concern to the proponents of selective tax increases is one of negative externality, of social costs in excess of private costs. Here the argument is made that the consumption of certain products, such as alcohol and tobacco, imposes costs on society that the consumers do not themselves bear and which they consequently do not take into account when making decisions about how much to consume. Alcohol and tobacco consumers therefore tend to drink and smoke more than is optimal from society's point of view, and government intervention is accordingly required to help align private costs with social costs. An excise tax accomplishes this purpose by forcing consumers to internalize the externality. The market price increase that follows the imposition of a selective excise tax encourages consumers to curtail their purchases of politically incorrect products, and this reduction in purchases, in turn, reduces the production of the socially undesirable by-products of consumption. Moreover, the revenue generated by the tax can be used to compensate those who bear whatever external costs remain.

The corrective tax rationale for selective excise taxation rests on the premise that there are significant social costs associated with alcohol and tobacco consumption that continue unremedied under existing public policies and, additionally, that government intervention can reduce or eliminate these residual externalities cost-effectively. Estimates reporting substantial drinking- and smoking-related workplace productivity losses and extra demands on society's scarce health care resources are commonly presented as evidence of the need for further selective tax increases.

Typically, however, these estimates are biased upward by erroneously counting private costs as social costs. Consider productivity losses. If it is in fact true that alcohol and tobacco consumers are absent from work more often or are less productive on the job than their abstemious colleagues, then they themselves bear the costs of their own consumption choices. More frequent work absences and lower on-the-job productivity translate into smaller wage increases, less attractive job assignments, and slower rates of career advancement. At the extreme, employees who are unable to perform their duties satisfactorily for any reason, including alcohol and tobacco use, will lose their jobs.

At any rate, the employee personally bears the costs of his or her own consumption choices in the form of lost income. Put differently, "society" is fully compensated for the output the employee would have produced if he or she had not been absent from work or had been more productive while on the job. If smokers or drinkers produce less, they will be paid less. There is no externality left to internalize.

This theoretical reasoning is bolstered by evidence suggesting that individuals' health status has a significant impact on their labor market earnings. Indeed, the authors of one study (Chirikos and Nestle 1985) have concluded that there is considerable empirical support for the proposition that persistent health problems adversely affect workers' employment and earnings prospects. They found that both white males and white females who experienced chronically poor health over a ten-year period earned significantly lower wages than their counterparts who remained healthy. Adjusted for differences in labor force participation rates, healthy men earned 11 percent more and healthy women earned 12 percent more than individuals of the same sex whose health was poor.

In a related study, Mullahy and Sindelar (1991) reported evidence showing that alcoholism adversely affects individuals' income-earning potential, although the magnitude of the effect varies substantially, depending on such factors as the worker's sex and the point in his or her career where drinking becomes a problem. The inverse relationship between alcohol use and income is apparently dominated by the significantly lower productivity of those workers who abuse alcohol most heavily. While the jury is still out on the effects, if any, of moderate alcohol use,[10] the weight of the evidence points to the conclusion that workers bear the costs of their own lifestyle choices.

The corrective tax rationale for imposing additional sin taxes has recently been extended to include estimates of the costs borne by nonsmokers on account of exposure to tobacco smoke in the workplace. For example, the Environmental Protection Agency attributes 3,000 lung cancer deaths each year and numerous respiratory illnesses in nonsmokers to contact with coworkers' cigarette smoke. The productivity losses associated with extra sick days and premature disability or death resulting from nonsmoking employees' exposure to tobacco smoke on the job, as well as the direct costs of treating the respiratory illnesses of nonsmokers, are counted as part of the social costs of smoking.

Again, however, most of these "social costs" are private costs. It has long been recognized that wage rates adjust in competitive labor markets to reflect differences across a wide range of job characteristics, including geographic location, security of employment, and degree of risk to workers' health and safety.[11] Consequently, even if, as the government claims, it is true that exposure to environmental tobacco smoke in the workplace is harmful to nonsmokers, economic theory predicts that such costs will be reflected in the relative wages of smoking and nonsmoking employees. The wages of nonsmokers will rise relative to those of smokers to compensate them for whatever additional health risks or unpleasantness they bear on account of their employer's workplace smoking policy, the wages of smokers will fall relative to those of nonsmokers to compensate the employer for whatever additional health care, fire insurance, or cleaning costs are attributable to smoking in the workplace, or both. While the direction of the relative wage adjustment in any particular case depends on factors such as the specific terms and conditions contained in the employer's smoking policy and the mix of smokers and nonsmokers in the given workplace, the costs of smoking are internal to the firm.

The scope for voluntary agreements that internalize externalities in mutually satisfactory ways is quite extensive (Coase 1959, 1960; Cheung 1973). Private bargains are especially likely to be struck when the interests of smokers and nonsmokers come into conflict in the workplace, because negotiations to resolve property rights disputes take place in a small-numbers setting and, in many cases, institutions such as labor unions and grievance procedures are already in place to govern the relationships both among the employees themselves and between the employees and their employer. In addition, the firm's owner has a strong incentive to see that the most cost-effective solution to the externality problem is adopted (Shughart and Tollison 1986).

The foregoing discussion notwithstanding, a role could still be found for a corrective tax policy if individuals are poorly informed about the possible health risks associated with alcohol and tobacco use. Recently, however, accumulating evidence has suggested that the reverse is true. Viscusi (1990), for instance, investigated the impact of risk perceptions on tobacco consumption. He concluded from extensive survey data that "both smokers and nonsmokers greatly overestimate the lung cancer risk of cigarette smoking."

Viscusi's findings are consistent with a large number of studies indicating that human beings have a general propensity to overestimate risks. This propensity is apparently attributable to a number of factors. First, Viscusi and other researchers have presented evidence suggesting that risks are frequently overestimated when the true probability of the event occurring is low,[12] as it is in the cases of developing lung cancer from exposure to environmental tobacco smoke or of being involved in a drunk-driving accident. A bias toward overestimating the risks associated with low-probability events is not due to any systematic error on the part of individuals, but rather is explained by "a rational Bayesian learning process in which one revises one's prior beliefs toward the truth" (Viscusi 1990, 1260).

Second, the potential health hazards of tobacco and alcohol consumption are highly publicized. The evidence suggests that the risks of highly publicized events are commonly overestimated (Combs and Slovic 1979; Lichtenstein et al. 1978). Third, the warnings dispensed about the possible health hazards of smoking and drinking indicate a risk but not its magnitude.[13] Failure to communicate information on actual risk levels has been shown to cause an upward bias in individuals' risk perceptions. In a study of perceptions of the hazards associated with radon exposure, for example, subjects given a one-page fact sheet listing the potential health hazards, but not the magnitudes of the possible risks, exhibited an excessive demand for additional information and testing by licensed technicians (Smith and Desvousges 1990).

In short, lack of information about the possible health effects of smoking and drinking cannot legitimately be used to justify imposing corrective taxes on these products. If anything, the evidence on risk perceptions suggests that individuals consume less of these products than warranted by the actual health hazards to which they are exposed and, hence, that a subsidy to help offset consumers' misperceptions would be a more appropriate public policy.

Even if consumers were making fully informed decisions about alcohol and tobacco use, though, negative externalities might still justify proposed increases in federal excise taxes to finance health care reform if it could be shown that the external costs associated with drinking and smoking exceed levels reimbursed by current tax rates. Generous estimates of the social costs of smoking, which eliminate some but not all of the double-counting errors of earlier studies, place the net external cost at about thirty-three cents per pack, a figure that is significantly less than the combined federal and state excise taxes levied in most jurisdictions, which currently average fifty cents per pack (Gravelle and Zimmerman 1994).

Whether alcohol is likewise overtaxed at present is less clear. While some researchers (e.g., Manning et al. [1991] and Grossman et al. [1993]) suggest that negative spillover effects (associated mainly with drunk driving)[14] justify significant increases in alcohol taxes, double-counting of private costs and failure to make adjustments for the beneficial effects of moderate alcohol consumption remain as problems for these studies (see chapters 10 and 11 of this book). Certainly, sufficient questions remain as to the magnitude of the social costs of alcohol consumption to give pause to those who would propose increasing alcohol taxes on this basis alone. This is especially true given that such taxes penalize large numbers of prudent drinkers in order to reduce the negative spillover effects generated by a comparatively small number of alcohol abusers (Heien and Pittman 1993).

## Concluding Remarks

Sumptuary taxes originated in the Middle Ages when laws were passed "attempting to fix what kinds of clothes people might wear and how much they might spend" (Tuchman 1978, 19).[15] In modern times they have chiefly been tools for regulating the traditional "sins" of drinking, smoking, and gambling. Such levies are justified as ways of penalizing sinners and thereby discouraging the commission of sin. The fact that these taxes also raise revenue is in theory of secondary importance to the promotion of virtue.

But revenue is never inconsequential to government in practice. Alcohol and tobacco taxes contribute billions of dollars that cannot easily be replaced to public treasuries. And because government's appetite for revenue is insatiable, the goal of discouraging consumption rapidly loses its appeal. Indeed, as evidenced by the recent wave of adoptions of legalized casino and riverboat gambling by the states, government is not above promoting sin when it is in its interest to do so.

Other rationales for imposing sin taxes must accordingly be found. One of these justifications—the Ramsey rule—turns the orthodox reasoning on its head. It argues that selective taxes are ideal elements of an efficient tax system precisely because they have little or no impact on consumption and, hence, impose minimal excess burdens on society. More recently, taxes on politically incorrect products such as alcohol and tobacco have been justified either as user fees or as ways of correcting the negative spillover effects associated with their consumption. But both of these rationales, while cloaked in the language of economists, are fundamentally mistaken in their economic reasoning.

The fact of the matter is that government has no interest in designing an efficient tax system, in setting optimal user fees, or in correcting externalities cost-effectively. Government's objectives are more self-interested and more short-sighted. Just as pork barrel offers a higher marginal political payoff to the politicians and policy makers who determine spending policy than projects whose benefits are more widespread, so can revenue be raised at lower marginal political cost by selectively taxing "sin" than by levying broader-based taxes. The terms "user fee" and "corrective tax" are simply convenient pretexts for raising revenue in ways that would otherwise be seen for what they are, namely highly discriminatory and regressive taxes.

### Notes

1. "Cigarette taxes are strikingly regressive" (Viscusi 1994, 13). See Shughart and Savarese 1986 for a summary of the evidence on the regressivity of excise taxes in general and taxes on tobacco and alcohol in particular.
2. See Office of Management and Budget 1994. In fiscal year 1993, excise taxes accounted for just over $48 billion (4.2 percent) of the $1,135 billion in total tax revenue collected by the federal government (excluding customs duties).
3. Selective sales and gross-receipts taxes, a category that includes taxes on motor fuels, public utilities, tobacco products, insurance, alcoholic beverages, pari-mutuel betting, and amusements, generated over 16 percent of the total tax revenue collected by the typical state during the late 1980s. This figure varies considerably, however, ranging from a low of seven-tenths of 1 percent (Alaska) to a high of nearly 37 percent (Nevada). On average, taxes on motor fuels account for about 40 percent of the selective sales and gross-receipts tax take at the state level of government. See Council of State Governments 1990, 331–34.
4. This point is made by Buchanan and Flowers (1980, 427), who go on to state that discriminatory "taxes such as these could rarely, if ever, be approved initially were it not for the nonrevenue aspects."
5. The incidence of the tax—the amount of the tax actually paid by consumers and producers—depends on the relative elasticities of market demand and supply.

Assuming that the full amount of the tax is shifted forward to consumers is equivalent to assuming that the demand curve is vertical (perfectly inelastic) or, equivalently, that there are no substitutes for the taxed product. More generally, the burden of an excise tax will be shared by consumers and producers (more correctly, the owners of inputs used in the production process), with the burden tending to fall more heavily on the side of the market that is relatively unresponsive to the tax-induced increase in price. Shughart, Tollison, and Higgins (1987) derive the conditions under which an input's owner would benefit from an excise tax on output.

6. This conflict may be more apparent than real when considered in light of models of "rational addiction" (Becker and Murphy 1988). An addictive good, by definition, exhibits first-order serial correlation—consumption this period is positively correlated with consumption next period. While the demands for such goods may be fairly inelastic in the short run, in the long run consumers may be no less sensitive to changes in their prices than they are to those of other goods. This conclusion follows because any adjustment to a change in the price of an addictive good in the current period carries over to all future periods. For evidence that the demands for alcohol and tobacco are indeed fairly elastic in the long run and, hence, that taxes on these products may not be justifiable on grounds of low excess burden, see Grossman et al. (1993) and Becker, Grossman, and Murphy (1994).

7. See also Buchanan (1967, 72–87), and Buchanan and Flowers (1980, 77–79).

8. Thomas Jefferson thought that state-run lotteries were an ideal tool of public finance because they represent a "tax paid only by the willing." The lottery-as-implicit-tax reasoning, attributable to Brinner and Clotfelter (1975), is summarized in Jackson, Saurman, and Shughart (1994).

9. Anderson, Shughart, and Tollison (1989) present evidence from the states suggesting that governments tend to rely more heavily on regressive consumption taxes as revenue sources where the interests of low-income voters carry less weight in the political process.

10. Berger and Leigh (1988), for instance, found evidence suggesting that employees who consume alcohol are paid higher wages than their abstemious but otherwise comparable coworkers. As the researchers point out, however, this somewhat surprising result may be due to data limitations and not to any inherent benefits of alcohol consumption. In addition, alcohol consumption in general and drinking on the job may affect wages differently. This is a distinction Berger and Leigh allude to by attributing their findings to the possibly beneficial effects of moderate alcohol consumption during nonworking hours.

11. Adam Smith ([1776] 1937, 100) provided what was perhaps the first statement of the theory of compensating wage differentials when he observed that "the most detestable of all employments, that of public executioner, is, in proportion to the quantity of work done, better paid than any common trade whatever."

12. See, for instance, Lichtenstein et al. (1978), Viscusi (1985), and, especially, Viscusi and Magat (1987).

13. For example, the current warning label on alcoholic beverages states:

> ACCORDING TO THE SURGEON GENERAL, WOMEN SHOULD NOT DRINK ALCOHOLIC BEVERAGES DURING PREGNANCY BECAUSE OF THE RISK OF BIRTH DEFECTS. CONSUMPTION OF ALCOHOLIC BEVERAGES IMPAIRS YOUR ABILITY TO DRIVE A CAR OR OPERATE MACHINERY, AND MAY CAUSE HEALTH PROBLEMS.

14. Although highway accidents involving drunk drivers are commonly accepted as the chief social cost associated with alcohol consumption, it is by no means clear

that a Pareto-relevant externality exists in this case. Sober individuals choose to drive rather than walk or take a bus by weighing the benefits and costs of automobile travel, and the costs include the (small) probability of being hit by a drunk driver. Because these costs are taken into account *ex ante* in decisions to drive, and perhaps are borne in part by responsible vehicle operators who exercise greater care at times when more drunk drivers are likely to be on the road, the social costs of alcohol consumption may be smaller than previously thought.

15. Despite fines and intrusive searches and seizures, medieval bureaucrats were no more successful than their modern counterparts: "The sumptuary laws proved unenforceable; the prerogative of adornment, like the drinking of liquor in a later century, defied prohibition" (Tuchman 1978, 20).

## References

Alchian, Armen A., and William R. Allen. 1967. *University Economics*. 2nd ed. Belmont, Calif.: Wadsworth.

Anderson, Gary M., William F. Shughart II, and Robert D. Tollison. 1989. "Political Entry Barriers and Tax Incidence: The Political Economy of Sales and Excise Taxes." *Public Finance* 44:8–18.

Ballard, Charles L., John B. Shoven, and John Whalley. 1985. "The Total Welfare Cost of the United States Tax System: A General Equilibrium Approach." *National Tax Journal* 2:125–40.

Bator, Francis M. 1958. "The Anatomy of Market Failure." *Quarterly Journal of Economics* 72:351–79.

Becker, Elizabeth, and Cotton M. Lindsay. 1994. "Does the Government Free Ride?" *Journal of Law and Economics* 37 (April): 277–96.

Becker, Gary S., Michael Grossman, and Kevin M. Murphy. 1994. "An Empirical Analysis of Cigarette Addiction." *American Economic Review* 84:396–418.

Becker, Gary S., and Kevin M. Murphy. 1988. "A Theory of Rational Addiction." *Journal of Political Economy* 96:675–700.

Berger, Mark C., and J. Paul Leigh. 1988. "The Effect of Alcohol on Wages." *Applied Economics* 20:1343–51.

Borg, Mary O., and Paul M. Mason. 1988. "The Budgetary Incidence of a Lottery to Support Education." *National Tax Journal* 41:75–85.

Brinner, R. E., and C. T. Clotfelter. 1975. "An Economic Appraisal of State Lotteries." *National Tax Journal* 41 (December): 395–404.

Buchanan, James M. 1967. *Public Finance in Democratic Process*. Chapel Hill: University of North Carolina Press.

Buchanan, James M., and Marilyn R. Flowers. 1980. *The Public Finances: An Introductory Textbook*. 5th ed. Homewood, Ill.: Richard D. Irwin.

Cheung, Steven N. S. 1973. "The Fable of the Bees: An Economic Investigation." *Journal of Law and Economics* 16:11–33.

Chirikos, T. N., and G. Nestle. 1985. "Further Evidence on the Effects of Poor Health." *Review of Economics and Statistics* 67:61–69.

Coase, Ronald H. 1959. "The Federal Communications Commission." *Journal of Law and Economics* 2:1–40.

———. 1960. "The Problem of Social Cost." *Journal of Law and Economics* 3:1–44.

Combs, Barbara, and Paul Slovic. 1979. "Newspaper Coverage of Causes of Death." *Journalism Quarterly* 56:837–43.

Council of State Governments. 1990. *The Book of the States*. 1990–91 ed. Lexington, Ky.: Council of State Governments.

Gravelle, Jane G., and Dennis Zimmerman. 1994. *Cigarette Taxes to Fund Health Care Reform: An Economic Analysis.* CRS Report for Congress 94–214 E. Washington, D.C.: Congressional Research Service.

Grossman, Michael, Jody L. Sindelar, John Mullahy, and Richard Anderson. 1993. "Policy Watch: Alcohol and Cigarette Taxes." *Journal of Economic Perspectives* 7:211–22.

Heien, Dale M., and David J. Pittman. 1993. "The External Costs of Alcohol Abuse." *Journal of Studies on Alcohol* 54 (May): 302–7.

Holcombe, Randall G. 1988. *Public Sector Economics.* Belmont, Calif.: Wadsworth.

Jackson, John D., David S. Saurman, and William F. Shughart II. 1994. "Instant Winners: Legal Change in Transition and the Diffusion of State Lotteries." *Public Choice* 80 (September): 245–62.

Lee, Dwight R. 1991. "Environmental Economics and the Social Cost of Smoking." *Contemporary Policy Issues* 9 (January): 83–92.

Lichtenstein, Sarah, Paul Slovic, Bernard Fischhoff, Mark Lyman, and Barbara Combs. 1978. "Judged Frequency of Lethal Events." *Journal of Experimental Psychology: Human Memory and Learning* 4: 551–78.

Manning, Willard G., Emmett B. Keeler, Joseph P. Newhouse, Elizabeth M. Sloss, and Jeffrey Wasserman. 1991. *The Costs of Poor Health Habits.* Cambridge: Harvard University Press.

Mullahy, John, and Jody L. Sindelar. 1991. "Gender Differences in Labor Market Effects of Alcoholism." *American Economic Review Papers and Proceedings* 81:161–65.

Office of Management and Budget. 1994. *Budget of the United States Government, Fiscal Year 1995.* Washington, D.C.: U.S. Government Printing Office.

Ramsey, Frank P. 1927. "A Contribution to the Theory of Taxation." *Economic Journal* 37:47–61.

Shughart, William F. II, and James M. Savarese. 1986. "The Incidence of Taxes on Tobacco." In *Smoking and Society: Toward a More Balanced Assessment,* edited by Robert D. Tollison, pp. 285–307. Lexington, Mass.: Lexington Books.

Shughart, William F. II, and Robert D. Tollison. 1986. "Smokers versus Nonsmokers." In *Smoking and Society: Toward a More Balanced Assessment,* edited by Robert D. Tollison, pp. 217–24. Lexington, Mass.: Lexington Books.

Shughart, William F. II, Robert D. Tollison, and Richard S. Higgins. 1987. "Rational Self-Taxation: Complementary Inputs and Excise Taxation." *Canadian Journal of Economics* 20:527–32.

Smith, Adam. [1776] 1937. *An Inquiry into the Nature and Causes of the Wealth of Nations.* Edited by Edwin Cannan. Reprint, New York: Modern Library.

Smith, V. Kerry, and William H. Desvousges. 1990. "Risk Communication and the Value of Information: Radon as a Case Study." *Review of Economics and Statistics* 72:137–42.

Tuchman, Barbara W. 1978. *A Distant Mirror: The Calamitous 14th Century.* New York: Alfred A. Knopf.

Viscusi, W. Kip. 1985. "A Bayesian Perspective on Biases in Risk Perception." *Economic Letters* 17:59–62.

———. 1990. "Do Smokers Underestimate Risks?" *Journal of Political Economy* 98:1253–69.

———. 1994. "Cigarette Taxation and the Social Consequences of Smoking." National Bureau of Economic Research Working Paper No. 4891. October. Cambridge, Mass.

Viscusi, W. Kip, and Wesley A. Magat. 1987. *Learning About Risk: Consumer and Worker Responses to Hazard Information.* Cambridge: Harvard University Press.

Wagner, Richard E. 1983. *Public Finance: Revenues and Expenditures in a Democratic Society.* Boston: Little, Brown & Co.

Wicksell, Knut. [1896] 1958. *Finanztheoretische Untersuchungen.* Jena: Gustav Fischer. Reprinted as "A New Principle of Just Taxation." In *Classics in the Theory of Public Finance,* edited by Richard A. Musgrave and Alan T. Peacock, pp. 72–118. Reprint, London: Macmillan.

# 2

# Excise Taxes in Historical Perspective

## *Brenda Yelvington*

President Bill Clinton brought the subject of sin taxes to the fore once again with his 1994 health care reform proposals. The sin tax he would have most liked to increase was the tax on cigarettes. Taxes on articles of consumption like the cigarette tax are really nothing more than garden-variety selective excise taxes, which have been a part of the U.S. tax code since 1791. It is the characterization of the consumption of the item that leads politicians to refer to certain excise taxes as sin taxes. *Webster's New World Dictionary* defines *sin* as "a wrong or fault." The Clinton administration used the word to refer to consumption of an item that is considered detrimental to an individual's health (U.S. House 1993, 35).

This chapter summarizes the history of the excise tax in the United States, beginning shortly after the American Revolution's end. The discussion covers both the specific types of excises levied on the American public and the reasons particular items of consumption have been chosen for taxation. The reaction of taxpayers to the first excise tax, which erupted into the Whiskey Rebellion of 1794, serves as the chapter's point of departure.

Excise taxes subsequently became important revenue sources during most of the major wars in U.S. history. The War of 1812, the Civil War, World War I, World War II, and the Korean War were all financed in part by raising existing federal excise taxes and imposing new ones. These levies were customarily scaled back or repealed at the conclusion of hostilities. An exception to this wartime-emergency-only rule occurred during Franklin Roosevelt's administration. His New Deal excise taxes are considered following the discussion of the war taxes.

While excise taxes have contributed revenues throughout U.S. history, they declined sharply in importance after 1913 when the federal income tax came into being. Following an evaluation of the passage of the income tax on the role of the excise tax in public finance, the purposes and effects of selective excise taxes in the postwar economic environment are reviewed. Particular attention is paid to the reasons underlying the 1980 windfall-profits tax—possibly the most significant recent development in the history of excise taxation.

The chapter concludes with a brief summary of the Clinton administration's selective tax proposals, along with the alternative compromise plans proposed in the House and Senate. Although only modest increases in selective taxes were ultimately enacted in 1994, the resemblance between contemporary rhetoric and the reasons advanced to justify excise taxes earlier in American history is striking.

## The Origins of the Excise Tax

In order to understand the origins of the current system of federal excise taxes, one must begin with the American Revolution. The colonies incurred large war debts in the six years it took them to win independence from Britain (Forsythe 1977, 17). Because taxation without representation was at the heart of colonial grievances against the British government, it is understandable that the newly formed Congress was not given the power to tax under the Articles of Confederation ratified in 1781 (C. Adams 1993, 308; Forsythe 1977, 14). All taxing power was to remain at the state level, where property taxes were the primary revenue source.

When the federal government needed money, a requisition was made upon the states based on real-property (land) values.[1] This system might have worked, but the states themselves were in desperate financial trouble (C. Adams 1993, 308).[2] Periodic requisitions on them consequently produced little revenue for the federal government, and its inability to raise funds directly through taxation made promises to refund the war debts ring hollow. In fact, at one point, Congress was unable even to pay the interest on the debt. Charles Adams (1993, 308) states that "without money, the Congress became the laughingstock of the new nation," a reputation some might think it has yet to live down.

When delegates to the Constitutional Convention assembled in Philadelphia in 1787, "everyone now agreed the federal government must be able to tax" (C.Adams 1993, 309). Hence, the first power granted to the new Congress in the Constitution adopted in 1789 was "to lay and collect Taxes" that were "uniform throughout the United States." The federal government was given this power "in order to pay the debts and provide for the common defense and general welfare of the United States." Congress initially raised revenue through import tariffs, which were also protectionist in nature.[3] Tariff revenues were not enough, however. Prodded by Alexander Hamilton, Congress began to consider the first internal tax.

### The First Excise Tax (1791)

Shortly after taking office in 1788, George Washington appointed Alexander Hamilton as his secretary of the treasury (Kirshon 1989, 202). Hamilton was a New York lawyer and banker who favored a strong central government (Kirshon 1989, 191). He devised a fiscal plan to establish sound credit for the new nation (Kirshon 1989, 204). At the heart of the plan was the refunding of the Revolutionary War debts. In order to raise the revenues necessary for achieving this goal, Hamilton supported the adoption of an internal excise tax, thus becoming the father of the sin tax.

In 1790, Hamilton, following Adam Smith's *Wealth of Nations,* proposed that an excise tax on whiskey be enacted (Forsythe 1977, 39; C. Adams 1993, 315).[4] Excise taxes had historically been unpopular. When a temporary excise tax was levied in England in 1641, for instance, riots broke out. In 1734, another proposal for an excise tax was defeated in the House of Commons (Forsythe 1977, 39). Indeed, in his well-known eighteenth-century *Dictionary of the English Language,* Samuel Johnson defined *excise* as "a hateful tax levied upon commodities, and adjudged not by common judges of property, but by wretches hired by those to whom the excise is paid."

Indeed, one might not go too far wrong speculating that the excise tax, which ultimately was imposed in England on a variety of items, including liquor, tea, coffee, soap, and salt (C. Adams 1993, 254), was one of the main forces that drove immigrants to America. Only a few years after the Revolution, however, Congress was contemplating inflicting this hateful tax on the new nation.

Whiskey was a convenient commodity to be singled out for the new excise tax. Hamilton thought the consumption of whiskey to be a luxury and, moreover, to represent a threat to the nation's virtue. In Hamilton's words, "the consumption of ardent spirits particularly, no doubt very much on account of their cheapness, is carried on to an extreme, which is truly to be regretted, as well in regard to the health and the morals, as to the economy of the community" (Cooke 1964, 34). In answer to those who opposed the whiskey tax, Hamilton argued that import duties had been extended as far as the interests of trade would allow (H. Adams 1884, 45).

The first law imposing an excise tax in the United States was approved on 3 March 1791. A permanent tax on whiskey (distilled spirits) was passed in the House by a vote of 35 to 21 on 8 May 1792 (H. Adams 1884, 45). Henry Adams contended that many of those who voted for the tax were opposed to excise taxes in principle and, had the tax been extended to any article of consumption other than whiskey, it is doubtful that the tax would have passed.

## The Whiskey Rebellion of 1794

The whiskey excise tax levied a duty of seven cents per gallon on spirits distilled from materials produced in the United States (whiskey) and ten cents on spirits distilled from foreign materials (rum; H. Adams 1884, 46). New England's whiskey manufacturers were apparently able to shift the lion's share of the tax forward to consumers. However, farmers in western Pennsylvania, Maryland, Virginia, and North Carolina, for reasons given below, were forced to shoulder the tax directly (Ratner 1942, 27; Paul 1954, 6). Adding to the general discontent with the new tax, many opponents of the whiskey tax (especially the farmers) believed that its adoption helped legislators avoid raising property taxes—taxes that would have hit the well-off New England area much harder than western and southern farmers with proportionately more undeveloped land.

The farmers in Pennsylvania rebelled. In their view, whiskey was not a luxury item. Rather, it was the basic medium of exchange in a largely barter economy (Weisberger 1991, 22). While the tax of seven cents per gallon might not have seemed excessive to Alexander Hamilton, it had to be paid in scarce hard currency. It was a common practice among farmers in western Pennsylvania to grow rye, distill it into whiskey, and then transport the whiskey across the mountains to Philadelphia (C. Adams 1993, 317), where it was then sold or exchanged in barter transactions. The grain from which the whiskey was distilled was itself too bulky for transporting—wagon roads either did not exist or were impassable (Weisberger 1991, 22).

The enforcement of the whiskey tax was delegated to private tax collectors enlisted under a tax-farming system.[5] The collectors, who had the authority to enter cellars and barns to search for bootleg whiskey, received 4 percent of their take (Weisberger 1991, 22). The more whiskey the collectors found, the more income they earned. Given the incentives for vigorous law enforcement created by the tax-farming system, it is not surprising that most collectors were hated and that some were tarred and feathered.

Encouraged by his treasury secretary, President Washington took a strong stand against the tax revolters. After giving the farmers two warnings, Washington called out 12,500 militiamen to enforce the new government's tax law (Kirshon 1989, 212). Washington actually led the troops in the field (C. Adams 1993, 319). A military confrontation was averted at the last minute, though. The rebels surrendered, and an antitax committee signed a "solemn promise" to submit to all U.S. laws in the future in exchange for pardons of any past offenses (Weisberger 1991, 23). No farmers went to jail.

The events surrounding the first sin tax are important for several reasons. First, the new government demonstrated its ability to enforce the law. Second, taxpayers displayed their willingness to fight what they believed were unjust taxes. Third, and possibly most important, Congress discovered a new source of revenue—the selective excise tax. It had been proved that taxes on articles of consumption could be successfully imposed if the articles themselves were portrayed as luxuries or if their use were pronounced harmful to individuals or the economy as a whole.

*Excise Taxes Following the Whiskey Rebellion*

The tax on whiskey opened the door for additional excise taxes on "luxury" items. A similar tax was imposed on carriages in 1794 (H. Adams 1884, 48).

The 1794 excise tax system was later expanded to include duties on the sale of certain liquors, the manufacture of snuff, the refining of sugar, the proceeds of auction sales, and the purchase of salt (H. Adams 1884, 48–49). Not all of these levies could of course be justified on the grounds that they represented taxes on luxuries or on products harmful to individuals. Congress had seemingly gone far beyond Hamilton's original plan by setting up an elaborate system of excise taxes whose chief purpose was to increase government revenues.

This objective was not met, however, largely due to the high cost of collection (Forsythe 1977, 50). In addition, the excise taxes were extremely unpopular with the voting public. Using the abolition of internal taxes as one of his key campaign promises, Thomas Jefferson became president of the United States in 1801. With the exception of the tax on salt, Jefferson eliminated the excises in 1802 (Pechman 1987, 305). The salt tax was repealed in 1807 (Paul 1954, 6).

## From Sin Taxes to War Taxes

History reveals that with the exception of the period following the Great Depression, federal excise taxes were predominantly enacted as wartime emergency measures. The majority of the taxes were customarily repealed when hostilities ended.

### The War of 1812

In 1812, the United States again found itself at war with Britain. Congress was at first hesitant to enact internal taxes to help finance the war effort. Customs duties were doubled, but the war's adverse impact on international commerce caused revenues from this source to actually decline by half in 1813 (Forsythe 1977, 58). Congress soon realized that it would be virtually impossible to rely on tariff revenues alone to pay for the war.

In August 1813, new excise taxes were approved by Congress. The tax structure was similar to that imposed under Alexander Hamilton's financing plan, and included excise duties on carriages, sugar refining, and distilled spirits. There was one major difference between the excise taxes of 1813 and their predecessors, though: the 1813 taxes were presented to the public as war taxes. In fact, the taxes were explicitly highlighted in italics in the body of the legislation as *war taxes* and were automatically to be repealed within one year following the end of the war (H. Adams 1884, 58).

The method of collection during this second period of excise taxation likewise departed from earlier precedent. Tax farmers were replaced by tax collectors who were required to be "respectable freeholder[s] and reside in the district" (H. Adams 1884, 60). In addition, the states were permitted to collect and pay directly into the Treasury the amounts assigned to them. A re-

TABLE 2.1
Excise Tax Collection Costs, 1795–1801 and 1814–1816

| Year | Actual Revenues Collected (Dollars) | Cost of Collection (Dollars) | Cost of Collection (Percent) |
|---|---|---|---|
| 1795 | 337,755 | 84,943 | 25 |
| 1796 | 474,289 | 88,585 | 19 |
| 1797 | 575,491 | 86,098 | 15 |
| 1798 | 644,733 | 119,890 | 18 |
| 1799 | 779,136 | 129,912 | 16 |
| 1800 | 806,396 | 103,785 | 12 |
| 1801 | 1,048,033 | — | — |
| 1814 | 1,910,995 | 148,991 | 7.8 |
| 1815 | 4,976,529 | 279,277 | 5.6 |
| 1816 | 5,281,111 | 253,440 | 4.8 |

Source: Henry Adams (1884, 65).

duction of 15 percent of the total due was granted to each state for performing the collection service (H. Adams 1884, 68). In 1814, seven states took advantage of this tax reduction opportunity.

The costs of collecting the excise taxes enacted in 1813 were in fact much lower than those associated with the earlier internal-tax levies. Some comparative collection cost figures are shown in table 2.1.[6] The average cost of collecting taxes had been 17.5 percent of revenues for the period of 1795–1800; the comparable figure was 6 percent during the War of 1812.

What caused such a dramatic decline in the cost of collecting taxes just eighteen years after the infamous Whiskey Rebellion? According to Henry Adams, it was not due to a more efficient tax collection system. Adams instead attributed the large differences in collection costs to other factors. First, he argued that there was greater public enthusiasm for the War of 1812 and, hence, a greater willingness to pay taxes to help finance it, than there had been to help extinguish old Revolutionary War debts during the relatively peaceful mid-1790s. Second, the temporary nature of the war taxes—they were in fact repealed in 1817—made them more palatable. Adams suggested that these observations should bring "again clearly to our view how important an element is public sentiment in the working of all revenue systems" (H. Adams 1884, 67).

After the War of 1812, the tariff regained its position as the federal government's primary source of revenue. Washington's expenses were chiefly defrayed by customs duties, supplemented occasionally by the sale of public lands or the issue of Treasury notes (Smith 1914, 1). During the period of 1817 to 1857, the government usually ran a budget surplus. Any revenue shortfalls that occurred were covered by balances held over from previous years. There was no need for any form of internal taxation.

## The Civil War

Ratner (1942, 80) calls 1862 and 1863 "the darkest period in the financial history of the federal government." At the Civil War's outbreak, the government relied chiefly on borrowing as a method of finance. Collections of customs duties were at a standstill, largely due to the interdiction efforts of the Confederate Navy (Ratner 1942, 82). By 1861, the federal government collected only $1.00 in taxes for every $8.52 it borrowed (Kirshon 1989, 367).

The Union's financial crisis called for drastic measures. President Lincoln signed the Internal Revenue Act of 1 July 1862 on the day Congress passed it (Paul 1954, 9; Ratner 1942, 73). This legislation was the most comprehensive tax measure enacted in the seventy years since the nation's first revenue act in 1791. The 1862 act provided for the first tax on income ever put into operation in the United States.[7] In addition, the act imposed an inheritance tax and included all of the excises, license fees, and stamp duties levied by the federal government during the War of 1812 (Paul 1954, 10).

But the Internal Revenue Act of 1862 went further. The list of items subjected to federal excise taxes was expanded. Every manufactured article was taxed, and rates of 1.5 percent and 0.3 percent were applied to the gross receipts of railroads, ferryboats, steamships, toll bridges, and advertisers (Paul 1954, 10). The 1862 act also covered a broader range of legal documents and financial transactions than the taxes of 1813.

As the federal government's revenue needs continued to grow, Congress demonstrated its willingness to raise excise taxes sharply. In the Internal Revenue Act of 30 June 1864, tax rates on distilled spirits were raised from twenty cents to $1.50 per gallon. Subsequent increases in the alcohol tax resulted in 1865 in a top rate of $2.00 per gallon, which was ten times the original cost of the product (Paul 1954, 13). Other increases included the tax on loose tobacco, which more than doubled, and the tax on cigars, whose maximum rate jumped from $3.50 per thousand to $40.00 per thousand.

As had been done following the War of 1812, the majority of the Civil War excise taxes were rescinded by Congress, with legislation passed in 1867 and 1870 (Ratner 1942, 116, 124). However, the liquor and tobacco taxes remained in place and became permanent fixtures of the federal revenue system (Pechman 1987, 305). A definite precedent had nevertheless been established for federal excise taxes. No longer were such taxes justified solely as ways of protecting the country's health and morals. Rather, excise taxes were rationalized as patriotic ways of raising additional revenues during wartime emergencies.

*World War I*

The country again found itself in financial straits during World War I. Although the Income Tax Act of 1913 was in place, it was new and the revenues it generated were not sufficient to make up for declining tariff collections.

Congress once again turned to the excise tax. The War Revenue Tax Act of 22 October 1914 brought back the Civil War excise taxes and greatly expanded the list.[8] Federal excise taxes were levied on manufacturing, theater admissions, telephone calls, and retail sales of jewelry, toilet preparations, luggage, and chewing gum (Pechman 1987, 305; Ratner 1942, 342). With the exception of the tobacco, liquor, and stamp taxes, the World War I excises were repealed afterward by the Revenue Act of 1924 and the Revenue Act of 1928 (Ratner 1942, 416, 432).

*World War II*

During World War II, the excise taxes still in effect from the early 1930s (discussed in a separate section below entitled "The New Deal Excise Taxes") were increased and new taxes were introduced. In particular, the tax on distilled spirits was increased from $2.00 per gallon to $9.00 per gallon, a hike of this magnitude apparently being feasible as a result of the demand for liquor greatly exceeding the supply (Leff 1984, 35).[9] By war's end, the list of new federal taxes included an admissions and dues tax, a manufacturers' excise tax, a retailers' excise tax, and excises on certain facilities and services (Anderson 1951, 409). A tax was also imposed on freight over the opposition of the Treasury (Due 1956, 207). Items subject to the federal excise tax ranged from automobiles and automobile tires to refrigerators, furs, and electrical energy.

As in all previous wars, revenue raising was the primary reason for imposing the World War II excise taxes. However, Anderson (1951, 409) contends that this was not the only reason. For the first time, excise taxes were justified for their supposed "anti-inflationary effects" and because they would "discourage the purchase" of "certain scarce items such as tires, tubes, and leather goods." Finally, Anderson states that the "intent was to place some additional burden on luxury goods such as furs, toilet preparations, jewelry, and luggage." Based on these considerations, "war" taxes were beginning to reincorporate elements of "sin" into the federal revenue system.

Keeping with the tradition of repealing wartime excise taxes after hostilities ended, Congress began work on a measure to reduce the taxes by up to 50 percent.[10] But just as a bill to accomplish this goal was passed by the House, the Korean War began. Thus, the World War II excise taxes remained in effect for a few more years.

*The Korean War*

The Revenue Act of 1950 originally contained provisions substantially reducing the excise taxes levied to help finance World War II. The outbreak of war on the Korean peninsula caused the tax reduction provisions to be removed and tax increases to be substituted in their place. These changes converted a potential $910 million reduction in excise taxes into a $55 million increase (Paul 1954, 557).

New items, such as television sets, deep freezers, and diesel fuel, were again added to the excise tax rolls (Anderson 1951, 410; Pechman 1987, 306). However, the bulk of the revenue continued to come from a relatively small number of excises. The lion's share of total federal excise tax receipts was generated by liquor and tobacco taxes (47 percent). The gasoline tax (11 percent) and the taxes on automobiles and related products (16 percent) were also important revenue contributors; all other taxed items accounted for the remaining 26 percent (Due 1956, 206).

By the Korean War, according to Due (1956, 206–7), excise taxes had become "so well grounded in tradition that consideration of elimination of them is not worthwhile." The taxes, largely justified by the money they raised, were also widely accepted by society. The dominant point of view was apparently that the "consumption of...particular commodities warranted the payment of a high tax penalty" (Due 1956, 207).

As in previous periods, the logical basis for some of the excises as taxes on "luxuries" or "sin" was elusive. Critics objected particularly to the excise tax on freight imposed as a war revenue measure in 1942. Due (1956, 207), for instance, argued that it provided an artificial incentive for the transport of goods by private rather than public carrier, thereby hindering the development of an efficient transport system. Congress and the Treasury Department seemingly were determined to maintain high revenue levels regardless of the cost. In the words of Due (1956, 207), Congress would have supported the "retention of an excise on bread and milk if one had been levied during the war."

As in the past, federal excise taxes were reduced after the Korean War ended. The majority of the tax rates were lowered to prewar levels in April 1956 (Committee for Economic Development 1955, 8). Over the next ten years, many of the excise taxes, including (in 1958) the freight tax, were repealed (Pechman 1987, 306). In 1965, Congress pared the Korean War excise taxes down to just a few major ones, including liquor, tobacco (cigarettes), and gasoline.

## The New Deal Excise Taxes

Prior to the Great Depression (1929–41), and for most of the time afterward, Congress enacted major excise tax increases only during wartime emergencies. Franklin D. Roosevelt's New Deal was an exception to this rule.

As in the earlier periods of heavy excise taxation, Roosevelt's primary justification for increasing taxes was to generate additional federal revenues. The Depression had devastated the economy, and tax receipts were consequently down. Just before the introduction of income taxes on the eve of the United States' entry into World War I, alcohol taxes had surpassed tariffs as the primary source of federal revenues. While the excise tax on distilled spirits technically remained on the law books, the passage of the Eighteenth Amendment, ratified on 29 January 1919, mandated Prohibition (Kirshon 1989, 613). Realizing the revenue-generating power of liquor taxes, Roosevelt pledged to repeal Prohibition in order "to provide therefrom a proper and needed revenue" (Johnson and Porter 1973, 332). The Democratic party's platform had a very un-Keynesian theme: "If only given a chance, Americans might drink themselves into a balanced budget" (Leff 1984, 31).

Roosevelt was elected president in 1932. The Twenty-first Amendment repealed the Eighteenth Amendment shortly thereafter, and in 1933 liquor was again legal (Kirshon 1989, 661). The House Committee on Ways and Means proposed a liquor tax schedule that was designed to generate the maximum possible revenue without at the same time perpetuating illegal liquor sales due to excessive rates (Leff 1984, 33). The pre-Prohibition federal alcohol tax of $1.10 per gallon was increased to $2.00.

Other New Deal taxes included a series of manufacturers' excises on automobiles, trucks, buses, appliances, and other consumer durables. Long-distance telephone calls were also added to the list. These federal excise taxes were extended at varying rates until 1965 (Pechman 1987, 305).

It was also during Franklin Roosevelt's administration that the federal gasoline tax was introduced. While all of the states levied a gasoline tax by that time, 1932 was the first year in which the federal government began tapping this source of revenue.[11] The tax, levied on gasoline refiners, was set at one cent per gallon (Crawford 1939, 9). Unlike other taxes included as part of the New Deal, the federal excise tax on gasoline was explicitly submitted to Congress as a temporary revenue measure and subsequently adopted for only one year.

At the time, the federal tax on gasoline was characterized as a "nuisance tax" (Crawford 1939, 13). It was to be a special tax enacted only because Congress needed emergency sources of revenue. In addition, it was sold as a "benefit tax" that helped defray the expenses of a related spending program—building and maintaining roads (Leff 1984, 18). The states were strongly opposed to a federal gasoline tax, on the grounds that it resulted in double taxation and placed too heavy a tax burden on a necessity. Ignoring these arguments, Congress continued to extend and to increase the "temporary" gasoline tax. At present, it is considered to be a permanent part of the federal tax system. Even the surcharge of 4.3 cents per gallon added by the Clinton administration in 1994 seems to have achieved a life of its own.

## The Role of the Excise Tax after 1913

Before the Income Tax Act of 1913, the federal government relied almost exclusively on customs duties for its daily bread. During the initial period of excise taxation (1791–1801), these levies accounted for a relatively small share (10 percent at its highest point) of the federal government's total tax receipts. In contrast with the trend in customs revenue, excise taxes for the most part continued to decline in importance until the Civil War.[12]

The first individual income tax, enacted to raise revenues during the Civil War, was in effect from 1862 through 1871. The tax had a flat $600.00 personal exemption, with marginal income tax rates rising to a top rate of 10 percent. It was collected at the source on wages, salaries, interest, and dividends. Income tax receipts accounted for almost 25 percent of total federal revenue at their peak in 1866 (Pechman 1987, 299). After the tax lapsed in 1872, customs duties again became the government's revenue mainstay.

Following the passage of a tax on corporate income in 1909, the 1913 Income Tax Act imposed a tax rate of 1 percent on the taxable net incomes of individuals, with an additional surtax ranging from 1 percent to 6 percent on persons with annual incomes exceeding $20,000.00. An exemption of $3,000.00 was granted to single taxpayers; married taxpayers were granted a $4,000.00 exemption (Ratner 1942, 333).

Because of the generous exemptions and low rates, for almost thirty years the personal income tax applied only to high-income individuals. In the prosperous late 1920s, however, the corporate and individual income tax contributed approximately two-thirds of all federal tax revenues (Leff 1984, 13). Excise tax receipts were declining in importance as a result. The Depression's onset caused a sharp decline in government income tax receipts, and, as discussed above, selective excise taxes (specifically, the alcohol tax) were called on to make up the difference.

In an effort to raise much-needed revenue during World War II, the individual income tax code was given a major overhaul. Personal exemptions were reduced (to $750.00 for single individuals and to $1,500.00 for married couples), and surtaxes on affluent taxpayers went as high as 77 percent (Paul 1954, 278–79). Congress thereby converted the personal income tax into a "mass" tax.

Prior to the changes made in the income tax during World War II, the New Deal excise taxes contributed between 30 percent and 45 percent of total federal tax collections. Between 1941 and 1945, excise taxes accounted for 20 percent of the federal government's total annual receipts, on average. The excise tax has continued to decline in importance as a revenue source since then. In fiscal year 1993, the most recent observation available, excise taxes accounted for only 4.2 percent of total federal tax receipts. (See tables 2.2 and 2.3.)

TABLE 2.2
Federal Internal Tax Collections and Excise Receipts
Fiscal Years 1791 through 1993, Thousands of Dollars

| Fiscal Year | Total Tax Collections | Total Excise Taxes | Excise Percent of Total | Fiscal Year | Total Tax Collections | Total Excise Taxes | Excise Percent of Total |
|---|---|---|---|---|---|---|---|
| 1791[1] | — | — | — | 1833 | 3 | 3 | 100.0 |
| 1792 | 209 | 209 | 100.0 | 1834 | 4 | 4 | 100.0 |
| 1793 | 338 | 338 | 100.0 | 1835 | 10 | 10 | 100.0 |
| 1794 | 274 | 274 | 100.0 | 1836 | a | a | 100.0 |
| 1795 | 338 | 338 | 100.0 | 1837 | 5 | 5 | 100.0 |
| 1796 | 475 | 475 | 100.0 | 1838 | 2 | 2 | 100.0 |
| 1797 | 575 | 575 | 100.0 | 1839 | 3 | 3 | 100.0 |
| 1798 | 644 | 644 | 100.0 | 1840 | 2 | 2 | 100.0 |
| 1799 | 779 | 779 | 100.0 | 1841 | 3 | 3 | 100.0 |
| 1800 | 809 | 809 | 100.0 | 1842 | a | a | 100.0 |
| 1801 | 1,048 | 1,048 | 100.0 | 1843 | a | a | 100.0 |
| 1802 | 622 | 622 | 100.0 | 1844 | 2 | 2 | 100.0 |
| 1803 | 215 | 215 | 100.0 | 1845 | 4 | 4 | 100.0 |
| 1804 | 51 | 51 | 100.0 | 1846 | 3 | 3 | 100.0 |
| 1805 | 22 | 22 | 100.0 | 1847 | a | a | 100.0 |
| 1806 | 20 | 20 | 100.0 | 1848 | a | a | 100.0 |
| 1807 | 13 | 13 | 100.0 | 1849 | — | — | — |
| 1808 | 8 | 8 | 100.0 | 1850 | — | — | — |
| 1809 | 4 | 4 | 100.0 | 1851 | — | — | — |
| 1810 | 7 | 7 | 100.0 | 1852 | — | — | — |
| 1811 | 2 | 2 | 100.0 | 1853 | — | — | — |
| 1812 | 5 | 5 | 100.0 | 1854 | — | — | — |
| 1813 | 5 | 5 | 100.0 | 1855 | — | — | — |
| 1814 | 1,663 | 1,663 | 100.0 | 1856 | — | — | — |
| 1815 | 4,678 | 4,678 | 100.0 | 1857 | — | — | — |
| 1816 | 5,125 | 5,125 | 100.0 | 1858 | — | — | — |
| 1817 | 2,678 | 2,678 | 100.0 | 1859 | — | — | — |
| 1818 | 955 | 955 | 100.0 | 1860 | — | — | — |
| 1819 | 230 | 230 | 100.0 | 1861 | — | — | — |
| 1820 | 106 | 106 | 100.0 | 1862 | — | — | — |
| 1821 | 69 | 69 | 100.0 | 1863 | 41,003 | 30,568 | 74.6 |
| 1822 | 68 | 68 | 100.0 | 1864 | 116,966 | 83,149 | 71.1 |
| 1823 | 34 | 34 | 100.0 | 1865 | 210,856 | 118,074 | 56.0 |
| 1824 | 35 | 35 | 100.0 | 1866 | 310,120 | 196,509 | 63.4 |
| 1825 | 26 | 26 | 100.0 | 1867 | 265,065 | 166,135 | 62.7 |
| 1826 | 22 | 22 | 100.0 | 1868 | 190,375 | 119,039 | 62.5 |
| 1827 | 20 | 20 | 100.0 | 1869 | 159,124 | 93,452 | 58.7 |
| 1828 | 17 | 17 | 100.0 | 1870 | 184,303 | 111,904 | 60.7 |

TABLE 2.2 (continued)
Federal Internal Tax Collections and Excise Receipts
Fiscal Years 1791 through 1993, Thousands of Dollars

| Fiscal Year | Total Tax Collections | Total Excise Taxes | Excise Percent of Total | Fiscal Year | Total Tax Collections | Total Excise Taxes | Excise Percent of Total |
|---|---|---|---|---|---|---|---|
| 1829 | 15 | 15 | 100.0 | 1871 | 143,198 | 105,538 | 73.7 |
| 1830 | 12 | 12 | 100.0 | 1872 | 130,890 | 111,382 | 85.1 |
| 1831 | 7 | 7 | 100.0 | 1873 | 113,504 | 104,208 | 91.8 |
| 1832 | 12 | 12 | 100.0 | 1874 | 102,191 | 98,300 | 96.2 |
| 1875 | 110,072 | 105,477 | 95.8 | 1918 | 3,698,956 | 669,322 | 18.1 |
| 1876 | 116,768 | 112,351 | 96.2 | 1919 | 3,850,150 | 837,276 | 21.7 |
| 1877 | 118,549 | 114,299 | 96.4 | 1920 | 5,407,580 | 808,047 | 14.9 |
| 1878 | 110,654 | 106,817 | 96.5 | 1921 | 4,595,357 | 685,413 | 14.9 |
| 1879 | 113,450 | 109,972 | 96.9 | 1922 | 3,197,451 | 593,386 | 18.6 |
| 1880 | 123,982 | 120,247 | 97.0 | 1923 | 2,621,745 | 625,046 | 23.8 |
| 1881 | 135,230 | 131,233 | 97.0 | 1924 | 2,796,179 | 666,522 | 23.8 |
| 1882 | 146,523 | 141,070 | 96.3 | 1925 | 2,584,140 | 542,937 | 21.0 |
| 1883 | 144,553 | 140,498 | 97.2 | 1926 | 2,836,000 | 571,319 | 20.1 |
| 1884 | 121,590 | 121,242 | 99.7 | 1927 | 2,865,683 | 482,157 | 16.8 |
| 1885 | 112,421 | 112,174 | 99.8 | 1928 | 2,790,536 | 481,435 | 17.3 |
| 1886 | 116,903 | 116,708 | 99.8 | 1929 | 2,939,054 | 459,017 | 15.6 |
| 1887 | 118,837 | 117,890 | 99.2 | 1930 | 3,040,146 | 468,930 | 15.4 |
| 1888 | 124,326 | 123,302 | 99.2 | 1931 | 2,428,229 | 457,626 | 18.8 |
| 1889 | 130,894 | 129,909 | 99.2 | 1932 | 1,557,729 | 409,229 | 26.3 |
| 1890 | 142,595 | 141,672 | 99.4 | 1933 | 1,619,839 | 719,599 | 44.4 |
| 1891 | 146,035 | 144,701 | 99.1 | 1934 | 2,672,239 | 1,354,000 | 50.7 |
| 1892 | 153,858 | 152,350 | 99.0 | 1935 | 3,299,436 | 1,439,000 | 43.6 |
| 1893 | 161,005 | 159,166 | 98.9 | 1936 | 3,520,208 | 1,631,000 | 46.3 |
| 1894 | 147,168 | 145,294 | 98.7 | 1937 | 4,653,195 | 1,876,000 | 40.3 |
| 1895 | 143,246 | 141,208 | 98.6 | 1938 | 5,658,765 | 1,863,000 | 32.9 |
| 1896 | 146,831 | 145,427 | 99.0 | 1939 | 5,181,574 | 1,871,000 | 36.1 |
| 1897 | 146,620 | 145,451 | 99.2 | 1940[2] | 6,217,000 | 1,977,000 | 31.8 |
| 1898 | 170,867 | 169,349 | 99.1 | 1941 | 8,347,000 | 2,552,000 | 30.6 |
| 1899 | 273,485 | 264,535 | 96.7 | 1942 | 14,265,000 | 3,399,000 | 23.8 |
| 1900 | 295,316 | 284,073 | 96.2 | 1943 | 23,693,000 | 4,096,000 | 17.3 |
| 1901 | 306,872 | 293,739 | 95.7 | 1944 | 43,330,000 | 4,759,000 | 11.0 |
| 1902 | 271,868 | 258,872 | 95.2 | 1945 | 44,818,000 | 6,265,000 | 14.0 |
| 1903 | 230,741 | 223,439 | 96.8 | 1946 | 38,872,000 | 6,998,000 | 18.0 |
| 1904 | 232,904 | 229,925 | 98.7 | 1947 | 38,037,000 | 7,211,000 | 19.0 |
| 1905 | 234,188 | 232,406 | 99.2 | 1948 | 41,157,000 | 7,356,000 | 17.9 |
| 1906 | 249,103 | 247,948 | 99.5 | 1949 | 39,048,000 | 7,502,000 | 19.2 |
| 1907 | 269,664 | 268,289 | 99.5 | 1950 | 39,036,000 | 7,550,000 | 19.3 |
| 1908 | 251,666 | 250,289 | 99.5 | 1951 | 51,007,000 | 8,648,000 | 17.0 |

TABLE 2.2 (continued)
Federal Internal Tax Collections and Excise Receipts
Fiscal Years 1791 through 1993, Thousands of Dollars

| Fiscal Year | Total Tax Collections | Total Excise Taxes | Excise Percent of Total | Fiscal Year | Total Tax Collections | Total Excise Taxes | Excise Percent of Total |
|---|---|---|---|---|---|---|---|
| 1909 | 246,213 | 244,713 | 99.4 | 1952 | 65,634,000 | 8,852,000 | 13.5 |
| 1910 | 289,957 | 267,286 | 92.2 | 1953 | 69,012,000 | 9,877,000 | 14.3 |
| 1911 | 322,526 | 287,236 | 89.1 | 1954 | 69,159,000 | 9,945,000 | 14.4 |
| 1912 | 321,616 | 290,866 | 90.4 | 1955 | 64,866,000 | 9,131,000 | 14.1 |
| 1913 | 344,424 | 307,590 | 89.3 | 1956 | 73,905,000 | 9,929,000 | 13.4 |
| 1914 | 380,009 | 306,881 | 80.8 | 1957 | 79,255,000 | 10,534,000 | 13.3 |
| 1915 | 415,681 | 328,036 | 78.9 | 1958 | 78,854,000 | 10,638,000 | 13.5 |
| 1916 | 512,723 | 339,737 | 66.3 | 1959 | 78,324,000 | 10,578,000 | 13.5 |
| 1917 | 809,394 | 387,986 | 47.9 | 1960 | 91,387,000 | 11,676,000 | 12.8 |
| 1961 | 93,406,000 | 11,860,000 | 12.7 | 1978 | 392,988,000 | 18,376,000 | 4.7 |
| 1962 | 98,534,000 | 12,534,000 | 12.7 | 1979 | 455,863,000 | 18,745,000 | 4.1 |
| 1963 | 105,355,000 | 13,194,000 | 12.5 | 1980 | 509,938,000 | 24,329,000 | 4.8 |
| 1964 | 111,361,000 | 13,731,000 | 12.3 | 1981 | 591,189,000 | 40,839,000 | 6.9 |
| 1965 | 115,375,000 | 14,570,000 | 12.6 | 1982 | 608,912,000 | 36,311,000 | 6.0 |
| 1966 | 129,068,000 | 13,062,000 | 10.1 | 1983 | 591,907,000 | 35,300,000 | 6.0 |
| 1967 | 146,921,000 | 13,719,000 | 9.3 | 1984 | 655,087,000 | 37,361,000 | 5.7 |
| 1968 | 150,935,000 | 14,079,000 | 9.3 | 1985 | 721,978,000 | 35,992,000 | 5.0 |
| 1969 | 184,563,000 | 15,222,000 | 8.2 | 1986 | 755,764,000 | 32,919,000 | 4.4 |
| 1970 | 190,377,000 | 15,705,000 | 8.2 | 1987 | 839,058,000 | 32,457,000 | 3.9 |
| 1971 | 184,548,000 | 16,614,000 | 9.0 | 1988 | 892,756,000 | 35,227,000 | 3.9 |
| 1972 | 204,022,000 | 15,477,000 | 7.6 | 1989 | 974,357,000 | 34,386,000 | 3.5 |
| 1973 | 227,611,000 | 16,260,000 | 7.1 | 1990 | 1,014,614,000 | 35,345,000 | 3.5 |
| 1974 | 259,890,000 | 16,844,000 | 6.5 | 1991 | 1,038,323,000 | 42,402,000 | 4.1 |
| 1975 | 275,414,000 | 16,551,000 | 6.0 | 1992 | 1,073,094,000 | 45,569,000 | 4.2 |
| 1976 | 293,986,000 | 16,963,000 | 5.8 | 1993 | 1,134,733,000 | 48,057,000 | 4.2 |
| 1977 | 350,409,000 | 17,548,000 | 5.0 | | | | |

Figures are rounded.
*Sources*: For the years 1940 through 1993, the information was obtained from *Office of Management and Budget* 1994. For the years 1863 through 1939, the amounts were obtained from *U.S. Bureau of the Census* 1975. Information for the period of 1791 through 1862 was obtained from *U.S. Bureau of the Census* 1960. This table includes in total tax collections federal receipts from internal taxes only. Amounts received from external sources (customs duties) are excluded from total tax collections. A detail of customs receipts is provided in table 2.3.
[1] For the period of 1791 through 1862, a breakdown of total excise taxes was not provided in the source information. The total "internal revenue collections" listed for this period in *Historical Statistics* was assumed to represent excise tax collections, since during this period no other internal taxes were in use.
[2] For the period of 1940 through 1993, total tax collections were computed by subtracting "customs duties and fees" from the "total federal receipts." See table 2.5 and table 2.1 in *Office of Management and Budget* 1994.
[a] Less than $500.00

**TABLE 2.3**
Total Federal Collections—Internal Tax and Customs Receipts
Fiscal Years 1791 through 1993, Thousands of Dollars

| Fiscal Year | Total Federal Receipts | Internal Tax Receipts | Percent of Total | Customs Receipts | Percent of Total |
|---|---|---|---|---|---|
| 1791 | 4,399 | 0 | .0 | 4,399 | 100.0 |
| 1792 | 3,652 | 209 | 5.7 | 3,443 | 94.3 |
| 1793 | 4,593 | 338 | 7.4 | 4,255 | 92.6 |
| 1794 | 5,075 | 274 | 5.4 | 4,801 | 94.6 |
| 1795 | 5,926 | 338 | 5.7 | 5,588 | 94.3 |
| 1796 | 7,043 | 475 | 6.7 | 6,568 | 93.3 |
| 1797 | 8,125 | 575 | 7.1 | 7,550 | 92.9 |
| 1798 | 7,750 | 644 | 8.3 | 7,106 | 91.7 |
| 1799 | 7,389 | 779 | 10.5 | 6,610 | 89.5 |
| 1800 | 9,890 | 809 | 8.2 | 9,081 | 91.8 |
| 1801 | 11,799 | 1,048 | 8.9 | 10,751 | 91.1 |
| 1802 | 13,060 | 622 | 4.8 | 12,438 | 95.2 |
| 1803 | 10,694 | 215 | 2.0 | 10,479 | 98.0 |
| 1804 | 11,150 | 51 | .5 | 11,099 | 99.5 |
| 1805 | 12,958 | 22 | .2 | 12,936 | 99.8 |
| 1806 | 14,688 | 20 | .1 | 14,668 | 99.9 |
| 1807 | 15,859 | 13 | .1 | 15,846 | 99.9 |
| 1808 | 16,372 | 8 | .0 | 16,364 | 100.0 |
| 1809 | 7,300 | 4 | .1 | 7,296 | 99.9 |
| 1810 | 8,590 | 7 | .1 | 8,583 | 99.9 |
| 1811 | 13,315 | 2 | .0 | 13,313 | 100.0 |
| 1812 | 8,964 | 5 | .1 | 8,959 | 99.9 |
| 1813 | 13,230 | 5 | .0 | 13,225 | 100.0 |
| 1814 | 7,662 | 1,663 | 21.7 | 5,999 | 78.3 |
| 1815 | 11,961 | 4,678 | 39.1 | 7,283 | 60.9 |
| 1816 | 41,432 | 5,125 | 12.4 | 36,307 | 87.6 |
| 1817 | 28,961 | 2,678 | 9.2 | 26,283 | 90.8 |
| 1818 | 18,131 | 955 | 5.3 | 17,176 | 94.7 |
| 1819 | 20,514 | 230 | 1.1 | 20,284 | 98.9 |
| 1820 | 15,112 | 106 | .7 | 15,006 | 99.3 |
| 1821 | 13,073 | 69 | .5 | 13,004 | 99.5 |
| 1822 | 17,658 | 68 | .4 | 17,590 | 99.6 |
| 1823 | 19,122 | 34 | .2 | 19,088 | 99.8 |
| 1824 | 17,913 | 35 | .2 | 17,878 | 99.8 |
| 1825 | 20,125 | 26 | .1 | 20,099 | 99.9 |
| 1826 | 23,363 | 22 | .1 | 23,341 | 99.9 |
| 1827 | 19,732 | 20 | .1 | 19,712 | 99.9 |
| 1828 | 23,223 | 17 | .1 | 23,206 | 99.9 |
| 1829 | 22,697 | 15 | .1 | 22,682 | 99.9 |
| 1830 | 21,934 | 12 | .1 | 21,922 | 99.9 |
| 1831 | 24,231 | 7 | .0 | 24,224 | 100.0 |
| 1832 | 28,477 | 12 | .0 | 28,465 | 100.0 |

TABLE 2.3 (continued)
Total Federal Collections—Internal Tax and Customs Receipts
Fiscal Years 1791 through 1993, Thousands of Dollars

| Fiscal Year | Total Federal Receipts | Internal Tax Receipts | Percent of Total | Customs Receipts | Percent of Total |
|---|---|---|---|---|---|
| 1833 | 29,036 | 3 | .0 | 29,033 | 100.0 |
| 1834 | 16,219 | 4 | .0 | 16,215 | 100.0 |
| 1835 | 19,401 | 10 | .1 | 19,391 | 99.9 |
| 1836 | 23,410 | a | .0 | 23,410 | 100.0 |
| 1837 | 11,174 | 5 | .0 | 11,169 | 100.0 |
| 1838 | 16,161 | 2 | .0 | 16,159 | 100.0 |
| 1839 | 23,141 | 3 | .0 | 23,138 | 100.0 |
| 1840 | 13,502 | 2 | .0 | 13,500 | 100.0 |
| 1841 | 14,490 | 3 | .0 | 14,487 | 100.0 |
| 1842 | 18,188 | a | .0 | 18,188 | 100.0 |
| 1843 | 7,047 | a | .0 | 7,047 | 100.0 |
| 1844 | 26,186 | 2 | .0 | 26,184 | 100.0 |
| 1845 | 27,532 | 4 | .0 | 27,528 | 100.0 |
| 1846 | 26,716 | 3 | .0 | 26,713 | 100.0 |
| 1847 | 23,748 | a | .0 | 23,748 | 100.0 |
| 1848 | 31,757 | a | .0 | 31,757 | 100.0 |
| 1849 | 28,347 | — | .0 | 28,347 | 100.0 |
| 1850 | 39,669 | — | .0 | 39,669 | 100.0 |
| 1851 | 49,018 | — | .0 | 49,018 | 100.0 |
| 1852 | 47,339 | — | .0 | 47,339 | 100.0 |
| 1853 | 58,932 | — | .0 | 58,932 | 100.0 |
| 1854 | 64,224 | — | .0 | 64,224 | 100.0 |
| 1855 | 53,026 | — | .0 | 53,026 | 100.0 |
| 1856 | 64,023 | — | .0 | 64,023 | 100.0 |
| 1857 | 63,876 | — | .0 | 63,876 | 100.0 |
| 1858 | 41,790 | — | .0 | 41,790 | 100.0 |
| 1859 | 49,566 | — | .0 | 49,566 | 100.0 |
| 1860 | 53,188 | — | .0 | 53,188 | 100.0 |
| 1861 | 39,582 | — | .0 | 39,582 | 100.0 |
| 1862 | 49,056 | — | .0 | 49,056 | 100.0 |
| 1863 | 110,063 | 41,003 | 37.3 | 69,060 | 62.7 |
| 1864 | 219,282 | 116,966 | 53.3 | 102,316 | 46.7 |
| 1865 | 295,784 | 210,856 | 71.3 | 84,928 | 28.7 |
| 1866 | 489,167 | 310,120 | 63.4 | 179,047 | 36.6 |
| 1867 | 441,483 | 265,065 | 60.0 | 176,418 | 40.0 |
| 1868 | 354,840 | 190,375 | 53.7 | 164,465 | 46.3 |
| 1869 | 339,172 | 159,124 | 46.9 | 180,048 | 53.1 |
| 1870 | 378,841 | 184,303 | 48.6 | 194,538 | 51.4 |
| 1871 | 349,468 | 143,198 | 41.0 | 206,270 | 59.0 |
| 1872 | 347,260 | 130,890 | 37.7 | 216,370 | 62.3 |
| 1873 | 301,594 | 113,504 | 37.6 | 188,090 | 62.4 |
| 1874 | 265,295 | 102,191 | 38.5 | 163,104 | 61.5 |

TABLE 2.3 (continued)
Total Federal Collections—Internal Tax and Customs Receipts
Fiscal Years 1791 through 1993, Thousands of Dollars

| Fiscal Year | Total Federal Receipts | Internal Tax Receipts | Percent of Total | Customs Receipts | Percent of Total |
|---|---|---|---|---|---|
| 1875 | 267,240 | 110,072 | 41.2 | 157,168 | 58.8 |
| 1876 | 264,840 | 116,768 | 44.1 | 148,072 | 55.9 |
| 1877 | 249,505 | 118,549 | 47.5 | 130,956 | 52.5 |
| 1878 | 240,825 | 110,654 | 45.9 | 130,171 | 54.1 |
| 1879 | 250,700 | 113,450 | 45.3 | 137,250 | 54.7 |
| 1880 | 310,504 | 123,982 | 39.9 | 186,522 | 60.1 |
| 1881 | 333,390 | 135,230 | 40.6 | 198,160 | 59.4 |
| 1882 | 366,934 | 146,523 | 39.9 | 220,411 | 60.1 |
| 1883 | 359,259 | 144,553 | 40.2 | 214,706 | 59.8 |
| 1884 | 316,657 | 121,590 | 38.4 | 195,067 | 61.6 |
| 1885 | 293,893 | 112,421 | 38.4 | 181,472 | 61.7 |
| 1886 | 309,808 | 116,903 | 37.7 | 192,905 | 62.3 |
| 1887 | 336,124 | 118,837 | 35.4 | 217,287 | 64.6 |
| 1888 | 343,417 | 124,326 | 36.2 | 219,091 | 63.8 |
| 1889 | 354,727 | 130,894 | 36.9 | 223,833 | 63.1 |
| 1890 | 372,264 | 142,595 | 38.3 | 229,669 | 61.7 |
| 1891 | 365,557 | 146,035 | 39.9 | 219,522 | 60.1 |
| 1892 | 331,311 | 153,858 | 46.4 | 177,453 | 53.6 |
| 1893 | 364,360 | 161,005 | 44.2 | 203,355 | 55.8 |
| 1894 | 278,987 | 147,168 | 52.8 | 131,819 | 47.2 |
| 1895 | 295,405 | 143,246 | 48.5 | 152,159 | 51.5 |
| 1896 | 306,853 | 146,831 | 47.9 | 160,022 | 52.1 |
| 1897 | 323,174 | 146,620 | 45.4 | 176,554 | 54.6 |
| 1898 | 320,442 | 170,867 | 53.3 | 149,575 | 46.7 |
| 1899 | 479,613 | 273,485 | 57.0 | 206,128 | 43.0 |
| 1900 | 528,481 | 295,316 | 55.9 | 233,165 | 44.1 |
| 1901 | 545,457 | 306,872 | 56.3 | 238,585 | 43.7 |
| 1902 | 526,313 | 271,868 | 51.7 | 254,445 | 48.3 |
| 1903 | 515,221 | 230,741 | 44.8 | 284,480 | 55.2 |
| 1904 | 494,179 | 232,904 | 47.1 | 261,275 | 52.9 |
| 1905 | 495,987 | 234,188 | 47.2 | 261,799 | 52.8 |
| 1906 | 549,355 | 249,103 | 45.3 | 300,252 | 54.7 |
| 1907 | 601,897 | 269,664 | 44.8 | 332,233 | 55.2 |
| 1908 | 537,779 | 251,666 | 46.8 | 286,113 | 53.2 |
| 1909 | 546,925 | 246,213 | 45.0 | 300,712 | 55.0 |
| 1910 | 623,640 | 289,957 | 46.5 | 333,683 | 53.5 |
| 1911 | 637,023 | 322,526 | 50.6 | 314,497 | 49.4 |
| 1912 | 632,938 | 321,616 | 50.8 | 311,322 | 49.2 |
| 1913 | 663,315 | 344,424 | 51.9 | 318,891 | 48.1 |
| 1914 | 672,329 | 380,009 | 56.5 | 292,320 | 43.5 |
| 1915 | 625,468 | 415,681 | 66.5 | 209,787 | 33.5 |
| 1916 | 725,909 | 512,723 | 70.6 | 213,186 | 29.4 |

## TABLE 2.3 (continued)
### Total Federal Collections—Internal Tax and Customs Receipts
### Fiscal Years 1791 through 1993, Thousands of Dollars

| Fiscal Year | Total Federal Receipts | Internal Tax Receipts | Percent of Total | Customs Receipts | Percent of Total |
|---|---|---|---|---|---|
| 1917 | 1,035,356 | 809,394 | 78.2 | 225,962 | 21.8 |
| 1918 | 3,878,954 | 3,698,956 | 95.4 | 179,998 | 4.6 |
| 1919 | 4,034,608 | 3,850,150 | 95.4 | 184,458 | 4.6 |
| 1920 | 5,730,483 | 5,407,580 | 94.4 | 322,903 | 5.6 |
| 1921 | 4,903,921 | 4,595,357 | 93.7 | 308,564 | 6.3 |
| 1922 | 3,553,894 | 3,197,451 | 90.0 | 356,443 | 10.0 |
| 1923 | 3,183,674 | 2,621,745 | 82.3 | 561,929 | 17.7 |
| 1924 | 3,341,817 | 2,796,179 | 83.7 | 545,638 | 16.3 |
| 1925 | 3,131,701 | 2,584,140 | 82.5 | 547,561 | 17.5 |
| 1926 | 3,415,430 | 2,836,000 | 83.0 | 579,430 | 17.0 |
| 1927 | 3,471,183 | 2,865,683 | 82.6 | 605,500 | 17.4 |
| 1928 | 3,359,522 | 2,790,536 | 83.1 | 568,986 | 16.9 |
| 1929 | 3,541,317 | 2,939,054 | 83.0 | 602,263 | 17.0 |
| 1930 | 3,627,147 | 3,040,146 | 83.8 | 587,001 | 16.2 |
| 1931 | 2,806,583 | 2,428,229 | 86.5 | 378,354 | 13.5 |
| 1932 | 1,885,484 | 1,557,729 | 82.6 | 327,755 | 17.4 |
| 1933 | 1,870,589 | 1,619,839 | 86.6 | 250,750 | 13.4 |
| 1934 | 2,985,673 | 2,672,239 | 89.5 | 313,434 | 10.5 |
| 1935 | 3,642,789 | 3,299,436 | 90.6 | 343,353 | 9.4 |
| 1936 | 3,907,020 | 3,520,208 | 90.1 | 386,812 | 9.9 |
| 1937 | 5,139,552 | 4,653,195 | 90.5 | 486,357 | 9.5 |
| 1938 | 6,017,952 | 5,658,765 | 94.0 | 359,187 | 6.0 |
| 1939 | 5,500,411 | 5,181,574 | 94.2 | 318,837 | 5.8 |
| 1940 | 6,548,000 | 6,217,000 | 94.9 | 331,000 | 5.1 |
| 1941 | 8,712,000 | 8,347,000 | 95.8 | 365,000 | 4.2 |
| 1942 | 14,634,000 | 14,265,000 | 97.5 | 369,000 | 2.5 |
| 1943 | 24,001,000 | 23,693,000 | 98.7 | 308,000 | 1.3 |
| 1944 | 43,747,000 | 43,330,000 | 99.0 | 417,000 | 1.0 |
| 1945 | 45,159,000 | 44,818,000 | 99.2 | 341,000 | .8 |
| 1946 | 39,296,000 | 38,872,000 | 98.9 | 424,000 | 1.1 |
| 1947 | 38,514,000 | 38,037,000 | 98.8 | 477,000 | 1.2 |
| 1948 | 41,560,000 | 41,157,000 | 99.0 | 403,000 | 1.0 |
| 1949 | 39,415,000 | 39,048,000 | 99.1 | 367,000 | .9 |
| 1950 | 39,443,000 | 39,036,000 | 99.0 | 407,000 | 1.0 |
| 1951 | 51,616,000 | 51,007,000 | 98.8 | 609,000 | 1.2 |
| 1952 | 66,167,000 | 65,634,000 | 99.2 | 533,000 | .8 |
| 1953 | 69,608,000 | 69,012,000 | 99.1 | 596,000 | .9 |
| 1954 | 69,701,000 | 69,159,000 | 99.2 | 542,000 | .8 |
| 1955 | 65,451,000 | 64,866,000 | 99.1 | 585,000 | .9 |
| 1956 | 74,587,000 | 73,905,000 | 99.1 | 682,000 | .9 |
| 1957 | 79,990,000 | 79,255,000 | 99.1 | 735,000 | .9 |

TABLE 2.3 (continued)
Total Federal Collections—Internal Tax and Customs Receipts
Fiscal Years 1791 through 1993, Thousands of Dollars

| Fiscal Year | Total Federal Receipts | Internal Tax Receipts | Percent of Total | Customs Receipts | Percent of Total |
|---|---|---|---|---|---|
| 1958 | 79,636,000 | 78,854,000 | 99.0 | 782,000 | 1.0 |
| 1959 | 79,249,000 | 78,324,000 | 98.8 | 925,000 | 1.2 |
| 1960 | 92,492,000 | 91,387,000 | 98.8 | 1,105,000 | 1.2 |
| 1961 | 94,388,000 | 93,406,000 | 99.0 | 982,000 | 1.0 |
| 1962 | 99,676,000 | 98,534,000 | 98.9 | 1,142,000 | 1.1 |
| 1963 | 106,560,000 | 105,355,000 | 98.9 | 1,205,000 | 1.1 |
| 1964 | 112,613,000 | 111,361,000 | 98.9 | 1,252,000 | 1.1 |
| 1965 | 116,817,000 | 115,375,000 | 98.8 | 1,442,000 | 1.2 |
| 1966 | 130,835,000 | 129,068,000 | 98.6 | 1,767,000 | 1.4 |
| 1967 | 148,822,000 | 146,921,000 | 98.7 | 1,901,000 | 1.3 |
| 1968 | 152,973,000 | 150,935,000 | 98.7 | 2,038,000 | 1.3 |
| 1969 | 186,882,000 | 184,563,000 | 98.8 | 2,319,000 | 1.2 |
| 1970 | 192,807,000 | 190,377,000 | 98.7 | 2,430,000 | 1.3 |
| 1971 | 187,139,000 | 184,548,000 | 98.6 | 2,591,000 | 1.4 |
| 1972 | 207,309,000 | 204,022,000 | 98.4 | 3,287,000 | 1.6 |
| 1973 | 230,799,000 | 227,611,000 | 98.6 | 3,188,000 | 1.4 |
| 1974 | 263,224,000 | 259,890,000 | 98.7 | 3,334,000 | 1.3 |
| 1975 | 279,090,000 | 275,414,000 | 98.7 | 3,676,000 | 1.3 |
| 1976 | 298,060,000 | 293,986,000 | 98.6 | 4,074,000 | 1.4 |
| 1977 | 355,559,000 | 350,409,000 | 98.6 | 5,150,000 | 1.4 |
| 1978 | 399,561,000 | 392,988,000 | 98.4 | 6,573,000 | 1.6 |
| 1979 | 463,302,000 | 455,863,000 | 98.4 | 7,439,000 | 1.6 |
| 1980 | 517,112,000 | 509,938,000 | 98.6 | 7,174,000 | 1.4 |
| 1981 | 599,272,000 | 591,189,000 | 98.7 | 8,083,000 | 1.3 |
| 1982 | 617,766,000 | 608,912,000 | 98.6 | 8,854,000 | 1.4 |
| 1983 | 600,562,000 | 591,907,000 | 98.6 | 8,655,000 | 1.4 |
| 1984 | 666,457,000 | 655,087,000 | 98.3 | 11,370,000 | 1.7 |
| 1985 | 734,057,000 | 721,978,000 | 98.4 | 12,079,000 | 1.6 |
| 1986 | 769,091,000 | 755,764,000 | 98.3 | 13,327,000 | 1.7 |
| 1987 | 854,143,000 | 839,058,000 | 98.2 | 15,085,000 | 1.8 |
| 1988 | 908,954,000 | 892,756,000 | 98.2 | 16,198,000 | 1.8 |
| 1989 | 990,691,000 | 974,357,000 | 98.4 | 16,334,000 | 1.6 |
| 1990 | 1,031,321,000 | 1,014,614,000 | 98.4 | 16,707,000 | 1.6 |
| 1991 | 1,054,272,000 | 1,038,323,000 | 98.5 | 15,949,000 | 1.5 |
| 1992 | 1,090,453,000 | 1,073,094,000 | 98.4 | 17,359,000 | 1.6 |
| 1993 | 1,153,535,000 | 1,134,733,000 | 98.4 | 18,802,000 | 1.6 |

Figures are rounded.

Sources: For the years 1940 through 1993, the information was obtained from Office of Management and Budget 1994. Information for the period of 1791 through 1939 was obtained from the U.S. Bureau of the Census 1960.

ª Less than $500.00

## Excise Taxes in the Postwar Environment

A major new development in federal excise taxation occurred in 1956. The revenue generated by a number of excise taxes was earmarked for the Highway Trust Fund, a special account established for the construction and maintenance of the federal highway system (Pechman 1987, 306). The dedicated revenue sources included the existing federal excise taxes on gasoline, diesel and other special motor fuels, trucks, and tires. New taxes were also imposed on tread rubber and on the operation of heavy trucks and buses on the highways.

A similar special-purpose program financed by earmarked excise tax receipts was created by Congress in 1970. The revenue generated by taxes on passenger tickets, air freight, general aviation fuels, and other aviation-related goods and services was set aside for the Airport and Airway Trust Fund. Another such account, the Hazardous Substances Superfund, was established in 1980 to pay the costs of cleaning up chemically polluted sites in cases where the source of the pollution cannot be identified. Superfund is financed with an excise tax on crude oil, an excise tax on various chemicals whose production creates hazardous waste, and a tax on corporate income as defined by the alternative minimum tax.

Possibly the most significant postwar selective tax took effect in 1980. In the Crude Oil Windfall Profit Tax Act of 1979, Congress imposed a 70 percent windfall-profits tax on revenues from domestic crude oil. The tax was assessed on the difference between the prevailing market price of oil and its price in May 1979. To fully understand the reasons for imposing the tax, it is necessary to briefly review federal oil price controls during the 1970s.

Crude-oil prices had remained remarkably stable until 1970. However, with inflationary fears on the loose, oil prices were frozen by President Nixon when he imposed general wage and price controls in 1971. Following the 1975 OPEC oil embargo and the sharp increase in world oil prices that ensued, oil price controls were extended until May 1979 (U.S. House 1979, 89).

In April 1979, President Carter announced his intention to phase out oil price controls between 1 June 1979 and 30 September 1981. Congress apparently believed that both the demand for and the supply of oil were inelastic in the short run (U.S. House 1979, 90). In other words, neither consumers nor producers were thought to be very responsive to changes in oil prices in the short run, and because of this, the worry was that relatively small shifts in either supply or demand might produce large swings in prices. Congress anticipated that decontrol of domestic oil prices (along with expected further increases in world oil prices) would result in substantial—and largely unjustified—increases in the revenues of U.S. oil producers and royalty owners.

The new windfall-profits tax was explained in the report of the House Committee on Ways and Means in the following terms:

The revenues resulting from these higher prices would provide income to oil producers far in excess of what most of them originally anticipated when they drilled their wells and in excess of what they might now be expected to invest in energy production. Indeed, some producers are now using their excess revenues to acquire unrelated businesses.

Thus, the committee believes that the additional revenues received by oil producers and royalty owners...are an appropriate object of taxation. (U.S. House 1979, 91)

Demonstrating a complete misunderstanding of the concept of opportunity costs, federal tax policy was thereby applied to a new sin—the making of too much money. The windfall-profits tax imposed on oil revenues in 1979 had much in common with the excess-profits taxes traditionally enacted by Congress during wartime emergencies.[13] In this case, revenue generated by governmental decontrol of oil prices was taxed away on the faulty theory that the profitability of investments in energy production was determined by historical costs rather than by current replacement costs.

The windfall-profits tax was repealed in 1988, but federal excise taxes on cigarettes and distilled spirits were raised in revenue measures enacted during the 1980s. The cigarette tax was increased to its current rate of $12.00 per thousand (or twenty-four cents a pack), and the tax on distilled spirits was increased to $13.50 per gallon.

Another significant development in excise taxation occurred in the Omnibus Budget Reconciliation Act of 1990. This act imposed a 10 percent luxury tax on the sale of passenger vehicles selling for more than $30,000.00, boats selling for more than $100,000.00, aircraft selling for more than $250,000.00, and furs and jewelry with prices exceeding $10,000.00. The Omnibus Budget Reconciliation Act of 1993 repealed the luxury excise taxes on jewelry, furs, boats, and aircraft. The tax on luxury automobiles remains in effect, but is now indexed to take account of inflation.

As of mid-1994, federal excise taxes applied to seven general product categories. These categories are (1) retail taxes on automobiles (with prices exceeding $30,000.00), trucks, trailers, and certain fuels; (2) manufacturers' excise taxes on gasoline, mined coal, sporting goods, firearms and shells, alcohol, and tobacco; (3) facilities and services taxes, including local telephone service and air transportation; (4) documentary stamp taxes on foreign insurance policies, including casualty insurance policies or indemnity bonds, and life, sickness, and accident insurance policies; (5) wagering taxes, which impose annual licensing fees on any person accepting wagers and taxes on wagers placed with bookmakers and lottery operators; (6) a highway vehicle use tax that applies to certain heavy motor vehicles, such as trucks, truck tractors, and buses with taxable gross weights of 55,000 pounds or more; and (7) environmental taxes on ozone-depleting chemicals and other chemicals and petroleum products, which apply to all taxpayers, including all levels of government and nonprofit educational organizations.

## The Clinton Administration's Excise Tax Proposals

In September 1993, President Bill Clinton announced health care reform proposals. Several funding measures, including increases in sin taxes, were suggested as ways of financing the administration's health care plan. The president indicated in his address to a joint session of Congress that tobacco would be one of the main sources of revenue. Specifically, the federal excise tax would be raised by between $0.75 and $1.00 per pack, thus placing the total federal cigarette tax in the range of $0.99 to $1.24 per pack.[14]

The president's proposal was only one of several financing plans put forward at the time. The cigarette tax would have been increased by only sixty cents per pack in an alternative financing plan advanced by the House Committee on Ways and Means (Rogers 1994). Under yet another plan, authored by Daniel Patrick Moynihan, chairman of the Senate Committee on Finance, the federal cigarette tax would have increased to $2.00 per pack and the levy on handgun ammunition sales would also have been raised (Rogers and Stout 1994).

The ultimate sizes of the tax increases contemplated are of less importance to this discussion than the reasoning used to justify the proposed tax hikes. Hillary Rodham Clinton, testifying before the Senate Committee on Finance about her husband's health care plan, asserted that "tobacco should be taxed as part of this package, largely for health reasons, and particularly to try to deter smoking among young people" (U.S. Senate 1993, 35). In her testimony before the House Committee on Ways and Means, Mrs. Clinton repeated these assertions, adding that "tobacco...if used as directed can have damaging health consequences" and is "particularly damaging to young people" (U.S. House 1993, 35).[15] Based on this reasoning, she said, the president believes "tobacco taxes are a fair way to support health care" (U.S. Senate 1993, 36).

## Conclusion

The selective excise tax has played roles of varying importance throughout U.S. tax history. The first excise tax—the whiskey tax enacted in 1791—gained the support of a majority in Congress on the basis of Alexander Hamilton's condemnation of whiskey as a luxury that corrupted the nation's morals and damaged its citizens' health. Made immortal by the rebellion it spawned, the whiskey tax was subsequently rescinded when Thomas Jefferson assumed the presidency, but the selective excise tax soon returned.

During the War of 1812, astute politicians reinvented excise taxation as a wartime emergency measure and thereby began a tradition of increasing existing excise taxes and imposing new ones during most of the major wars thereafter. The majority of these war taxes were temporary and were generally repealed at the conclusion of hostilities.

A break with the tradition of wartime excise taxes occurred during the New Deal. Campaigning on a promise to repeal Prohibition, President Roosevelt saw liquor taxes as a way of helping the U.S. economy recover from the Great Depression. While most politicians still thought that the consumption of liquor might be harmful to an individual's health, the purported benefits of the additional tax revenues to the health of the economy were apparently more important.

The relative contribution of excise taxes to total tax revenues was reduced substantially following passage of the 1913 Income Tax Act. Still, an elaborate system of excise taxes is in effect today, and lawmakers continue to find ways to justify new ones.

In 1980, a windfall-profits tax was enacted to slash the profits oil producers and royalty owners were expected to earn following the decontrol of domestic oil prices. In 1990, a new luxury tax was created to tax the sale of expensive cars, boats, aircraft, jewelry, and furs. At present, only the luxury tax on automobiles remains in effect, but the message it sends is clear: if individuals can afford expensive consumer items, then they should be made to pay for their affluence.

The argument for imposing new excise taxes (or increasing existing ones) has come full circle. President Clinton proposed to drastically increase the federal excise tax on cigarettes to help pay for his health care reforms. The justification for increasing the tax is that smoking can have damaging health consequences. This is essentially the same argument Alexander Hamilton used to gain enactment of the first sin tax on whiskey over 200 years ago.

## Notes

1. According to Charles Adams (1993), requisitions based on real-estate values supplied a common denominator that avoided the definitional problems posed by the differential treatment accorded to slaves in the North (population) as opposed to the South (personal property).
2. Forsythe (1977, 15–16) contends that the problems with the requisition system were complicated by the refusal of Congress to accept either supplies or the states' own currencies in payment. The fact that states were not credited for payments made directly to the troops created another complication. These problems were encouraged by individuals who supported giving Congress the power to tax and therefore wanted the state requisition system to prove inadequate.
3. The first tariff legislation was enacted on 4 July 1789. Between 1794 and 1816, twenty-five tariff bills were passed. Although the duties were protectionist in effect, they were enacted chiefly as revenue measures (Ratner 1942, 26–27).
4. It is not surprising that Adam Smith influenced early lawmakers. Henry Carter Adams (1884, 20–21) stated that Smith's *Wealth of Nations* was a "work well known" during this time and "quite generally endorsed." In fact, "the framers of the Constitution had in mind certain distinctions made by Adam Smith when they adopted into that document the words 'capitation, direct, and indirect tax.'"
5. Tax collections were administered by the Office of the Commissioner of the Revenue, established in 1792 (Paul 1954, 6). The country was divided into fourteen districts, each headed by a district director. Directors received 1 percent of

the taxes collected in their districts, and agents received 4 percent of the taxes they collected (C. Adams 1993, 317).

6. Note that the excise tax collections reported by Henry Carter Adams differ slightly from those reported in table 2.2, which were obtained from U.S. Bureau of the Census 1960.

7. The Internal Revenue Act of 1862 was the second income tax law signed by President Lincoln. The first such act was signed by him on 5 August 1861; it was not enforced, however. The 1862 act materially extended the original law's income tax provisions and was actually put into operation (Ratner 1942, 67–68).

8. Note that the excise taxes were reimposed in 1898 (during the Spanish-American War) and subsequently repealed in 1901 (Ratner 1942, 249–50).

9. The discrepancy between the demand for and the supply of liquor was due to the wartime conversion of many distilling facilities to the production of grain alcohol (Leff 1984, 35).

10. President Truman had indicated that he would support a measure to reduce excise taxes, but he wanted any resulting revenue reductions to be offset by measures aimed at closing loopholes in other taxes (Paul 1954, 539).

11. Oregon became the first state to enact a gasoline tax in 1919. The tax was one cent per gallon. Within ten years, every state had adopted a tax on motor fuel. By the time the federal excise tax on gasoline was passed in 1932, many states had increased their tax rates to between six and seven cents per gallon. State gasoline tax revenues were used primarily to finance highway construction and maintenance programs (Crawford 1939, 1–12).

12. One exception to the excise tax's dwindling importance as a revenue source occurred during the War of 1812. Due to the fall-off in international trade, excise tax receipts accounted for as much as 39 percent of total wartime federal revenues (see table 2.3).

13. Revenue collections during World War I, World War II, and the Korean War were supplemented by an excess-profits tax. The tax applied to the excess of a corporation's profits over a designated prewar base period or over a "normal" rate of return. The tax rates reached as high as 95 percent during World War II (Pechman 1987, 304).

14. The administration also floated a proposal to tax energy use by levying a tax on all fossil fuels based on their BTU content.

15. Mrs. Clinton's claims regarding the salutary effects of tobacco tax increases on the incidence of smoking among "young people" were based on empirical estimates suggesting that the demand for cigarettes on the part of teenagers is much more elastic than it is among older individuals. The implication is that a given tax-induced price increase will reduce cigarette consumption among young people to a greater extent than among other age groups and, moreover, that this response will generate particularly important social benefits by creating incentives for young people either to quit before they take up the habit or to refrain from starting smoking in the first place. Neither of these conclusions is warranted, however. The cigarette-demand elasticity estimates for young people are biased upward because they fail to take account of the fact that many teenagers try cigarettes as a way of rebelling against social taboos. They smoke without any intention of taking up lifelong habits. Hence, reductions in cigarette consumption that appear, on the surface, to represent responses to increases in price are largely noise introduced into the data by normal teenage experimentation.

# References

Adams, Charles. 1993. *For Good and Evil: The Impact of Taxes on the Course of Civilization*. London: Madison Books.

Adams, Henry Carter. 1884. "Taxation in the United States." In *Institutions and Economics*, edited by Herbert B. Adams. Johns Hopkins University Studies in Historical and Political Science. Baltimore: Johns Hopkins University.

Anderson, William H. 1951. *Taxation and the American Economy: An Economic, Legal, and Administrative Analysis*. New York: Prentice-Hall.

Becker, Robert A. 1980. *Revolution, Reform, and the Politics of American Taxation, 1763–1783*. Baton Rouge: Louisiana State University Press.

Bullion, John L. 1982. *A Great and Necessary Measure: George Grenville and the Genesis of the Stamp Act, 1763–1765*. Columbia: University of Missouri Press.

Commerce Clearing House Tax Law Editors. 1992. *Federal Excise Tax Reporter*. Chicago: Commerce Clearing House.

Committee for Economic Development. 1955. *Federal Tax Issues in 1955*. New York: Committee for Economic Development.

Committee on Postwar Tax Policy. 1945. *A Program for a Solvent America*. New York: Ronald Press.

———. 1947. *A Program for a Solvent America*. New York: Committee on Postwar Tax Policy.

Committee on Taxation of the Twentieth Century Fund. 1937. *Facing the Tax Problem*. New York: Twentieth Century Fund.

Comstock, Alzada. 1929. *Taxation in the Modern State*. Longmans' Economics Series. New York: Longmans, Green & Co.

Cooke, Jacob E., ed. 1964. *The Reports of Alexander Hamilton*. New York: Harper & Row.

Crawford, Finla Goff. 1939. *Motor Fuel Taxation in the United* States. Syracuse, N.Y.: Finla Goff Crawford.

Due, John F. 1956. "The Role of Sales and Excise Taxation in the Overall Tax Structure." *Journal of Finance* 11:205–20.

Forsythe, Dall W. 1977. *Taxation and Political Change in the Young Nation, 1781–1833*. New York: Columbia University Press.

Groves, Harold M. 1946. *Postwar Taxation and Economic Progress*. New York: McGraw-Hill.

Hansen, Susan B. 1983. *The Politics of Taxation*. New York: Praeger.

Hershey, Barry J. 1984. *The American Tax System: A Call for Reform*. New York: Philosophical Library.

Johnson, Donald B., and Kird H. Porter. 1973. *National Party Platforms, 1840–1972*. Urbana: University of Illinois Press.

Kirshon, John W., ed. 1989. *Chronicle of America*. New York: Chronicle Publications.

Leff, Mark H. 1984. *The Limits of Symbolic Reform: The New Deal and Taxation, 1933–1939*. New York: Cambridge University Press.

"Luxury Excise Tax." 1991. *National Public Accountant* 36 (March): 50.

Office of Management and Budget. 1994. *Historical Tables, Budget of the United States Government, Fiscal Year 1995*. Washington, D.C.: U.S. Government Printing Office.

*Omnibus Budget Reconciliation Act of 1990*. U.S. Public Law 508. 101st Cong., 2nd sess., 29 November 1990.

*Omnibus Budget Reconciliation Act of 1993*. U.S. Public Law 66. 103rd Cong., 1st sess., 10 August 1993.

*Omnibus Trade and Competitiveness Bill of 1988*. U.S. Public Law 418. 100th Cong., 2nd sess., 1988.

Paul, Randolph E. 1954. *Taxation in the United States*. Boston: Little, Brown & Co.

Pechman, Joseph A. 1987. *Federal Tax Policy*. 5th ed. Studies of Government Finance: Second Series. Washington, D.C.: Brookings Institution.

Ratner, Sidney. 1942. *American Taxation: Its History as a Social Force in Democracy*. New York: W. W. Norton & Co.

Rogers, David. 1994. "Panel Offers Tax Concessions on Health Bill." *Wall Street Journal*, 7 June A-3.

Rogers, David, and Hilary Stout. 1994. "Moynihan Lays Out Health Proposals, Including Big Increase in Cigarette Tax." *Wall Street Journal*, 10 June, A-3.

Simonson, Kenneth D. 1990. "The Dubious Virtue of Higher 'Sin' Taxes." *Tax Notes* 49 (1 October): 99–102.

Smith, Harry Edwin. 1914. *The United States Federal Internal Tax History from 1861 to 1871*. Boston: Houghton Mifflin.

Steuerle, Gene. 1992. "Postwar Changes in the Overall Tax System: Post–World War II." *Tax Notes* 54 (2 March): 1163–70.

U.S. Bureau of the Census. 1960. *Historical Statistics of the United States, Colonial Times to 1957*. Washington, D.C.: U.S. Government Printing Office.

U.S. Bureau of the Census. 1975. *Historical Statistics of the United States, Colonial Times to 1970*. Bicentennial ed. Part 2. Washington, D.C.: U.S. Government Printing Office.

U.S. House. 1979. Committee on Ways and Means. *Crude Oil Windfall Profit Tax of 1979: Report of the Committee on Ways and Means*. 96th Cong., 1st sess., H.R. Rept. 304. 22 June.

———. 1993. Committee on Ways and Means. *The President's Health Care Reform Proposals: Hearings before the Committee on Ways and Means*. 103rd Cong., 1st sess., 28 September.

U.S. Senate. 1993. Committee on Finance. *President's Health Care Plan: Hearings before the Committee on Finance*. 103rd Cong., 1st sess., 30 September.

"The Wages of Sin: Cigarette Taxes." 1993. *Economist* 326 (20 March): 28–29.

*Webster's New World Dictionary*. 1973. Nashville: The Southwestern Company.

Weisberger, Bernard A. 1991. "Seeking a Real Tax Revolt: Whiskey Rebellion of 1794." *American Heritage* 42 (May-June): 22–24.

# 3

# Whiskey, Margarine, and Newspapers: A Tale of Three Taxes

*Adam Gifford, Jr.*

A review of the history of selective excise taxes illustrates most, if not all, of the sources of conflict between the state and the taxpayer, problems not unique to sin taxes but rather found in taxes of all forms. These problems center around the state's use of its coercive powers against its own citizens. Today we tend to think of liberty arising from a private-property-based market system with a democratic form of government. Historically, liberty meant freedom from abusive taxation.

The Greeks, in fact, equated taxes with tyranny. Taxes destroy liberty not just as a result of the obvious taking of wealth, property, and income they entail, but also through the abusive administrative systems often set up to collect them. For example, the bureaucracy created by Rome to collect taxes in Asia Minor in the first century B.C. had the power to scourge and behead tax dodgers. Confronted with tax collectors imbued "with the arrogance of bureaucrats and the power of military executioners," it is not surprising that taxpayers soon lost the inclination to evade payment (Adams 1993, 86).

Historically, death has not been an uncommon penalty for nonpayment. Little wonder then that the belief that "a man is only free if his name does not appear on a tax roll" has been prevalent throughout history.[1] Indeed, this belief explains much of the difficulty in studying the history of taxes. Often when taxpayers have been successful—through either rebellion or peaceful means—in inducing the state to eliminate a tax, they have also eliminated the tax rolls. At the conclusion of the Napoleonic wars, when the British Parliament voted to eliminate the income tax used to help finance the war, it not only abolished the hated tax, but also voted to destroy all records pertaining to it.[2]

This chapter does not aim at being either chronological or comprehensive, but rather will focus on selected historical episodes that clearly illustrate the issues raised by the taxing of "sin." Sin taxes in modern economic terms are chiefly externality taxes, taxes designed to reduce behavior that is felt to be "harmful to society."

Percival S. Menken, writing in the late nineteenth century, summed up the traditional position: "Civilization rests upon the basis of restraint, whether self-imposed or enjoined by the state. It advances only when each individual so acts within the sphere of personal liberty as not to impede or injure his neighbor in the exercise of individual rights. It necessitates the subjection of individual liberty to the welfare of the whole" (Menken 1891, 25). Discussing the regulation of liquor consumption by taxation as well as by prohibition, Menken continues: "On this account, if it can be shown that the unrestricted sale of liquors tends to the disadvantage of the community, laws restricting such sale, even to the extent of destroying it, have their justification" (Menken 1891, 25).

Of the four possible reactions to the imposition of a tax, according to Charles Adams, "three of them are bad: rebellion, flight to avoid tax and evasion" (Adams 1993, 447). Another nineteenth-century commentator summed up the reaction side of the sin tax issue this way:

> The history to these taxes [on liquor] is connected with the habits, the morals and the health of the people; with smuggling and all the evil consequences to a nation that ensue from lawlessness, the idleness, the meanness and the ferocity which it engendered; with adulteration of so dire a kind as seriously to affect the health of the subjects; with our foreign and our domestic policy, as when...[taxes on drinks]...have, on occasion, proved the cause of serious disputes with foreign powers, have altered the course of trade, or have given rise to serious riots at home—in short, with very much that is interesting from other points of view than a mere fiscal point. (Dowell [1884] 1965, 47)

The quote identifies most of the common reactions to sin taxes: smuggling by middlemen or consumers, a very typical response that Canada, for example, is currently facing as a result of imposing extremely high taxes on cigarettes; adulteration of a product by producers in such a way that taxes are reduced or no longer applicable; substitution by consumers of a similar nontaxed product.

A good illustration of the substitution option is the response to high taxes on whiskey in the United States in the second half of the nineteenth century, when many people simply switched to beer, and others to opium and marijuana (Hu 1950, 40). One reason this is such a good example is that it shows how often the substitute product causes more problems than the original. As we will see, there are usually several margins for substitution or adjustment available to both consumers and producers when an excise tax is imposed, and these margins include legal as well as illegal options.

Finally, there is protest. Rebellion has been a historically important response to unpopular taxes, including excise taxes, and the Whiskey Rebellion is a classic example of this response.

Excise taxes, like all taxes and laws in general—even those passed with the best of intentions—can obviously have undesirable consequences. Furthermore, externality, like beauty, is in the eye of the beholder, and often what the beholder really wants is not control of externality but special protection and privilege. In other words, excise taxes are often the result of less than honorable intentions. Rent seeking has played a significant role in the excise tax story. In the nineteenth century, the dairy industry lobbied for taxes on margarine so as to protect the "wholesomeness" of the food people were consuming. And governments have used excise taxes to suppress activities they find threatening. In Britain and its American colonies, knowledge taxes, imposed on newspapers, books, pamphlets, and other sources of information, were used to stifle criticism of the government itself, as well as any other idea or opinion found objectionable.

The following history of three excise taxes will examine the various motives for imposing the taxes, the responses of consumers and producers to them, and the effects of excise taxes on the underlying political constitution.

## Taxes and Regulation of Alcoholic Beverages

When the consumption of alcoholic beverages began appears to be lost in prehistory, yet attempts to regulate the consumption of alcohol have been chronicled for thousands of years. The inventor of rice wine was banished by the Chinese Emperor Yute in the year 2200 B.C. to check public drunkenness, and in 1122 B.C. grape wine was prohibited in China and laws ordering the destruction of all vines were proclaimed, though these measures were apparently not very successful. In Egypt, the pharaohs enacted laws against the consumption of wine, and in ancient Greece and Rome, there were laws passed curtailing alcohol abuse, again apparently to little effect. Governments have a long and undistinguished history of trying to cope with alcohol use among their citizens.

The identity of the first person to use distillation to make strong spirits is also uncertain. The process was refined in Europe in the thirteenth century by Arnauld de Villeneuve, a Montpelierian alchemist, who called the result of his labor *aqua vita*, water of life. Whiskey was developed in Scotland, where they recently celebrated the 500th anniversary of its discovery. Its name is a Gaelic word that originated as an abridged version of *aqua vita* (Dowell [1884] 1965, 156).

During the English Civil War, the Long Parliament adopted the first excise taxes in that nation's history. Included were taxes on distilled spirits. Excise taxes were "the most hated of all European taxes. In England, liberty was equated with the absence of an excise tax" (Adams 1993, 254). The British antipathy toward excise taxes stemmed from the intrusive nature of the bureaucracy used to collect the taxes and from the observation that excises destroyed the economies of nations.

Later, in the 1720s, a cheap form of distilled spirits was introduced, made with materials that paid little or no tariffs. This beverage, made with jeneva, the juniper berry, was called geneva—gin. Soon cheap gin had increased spirit consumption among the lower classes to such an extent that tax legislation was proposed to halt the "increasing tide of drunkenness...'tending to the destruction of the health of the people, enervating them, and rendering them unfit for useful labor and service'...By intoxication the people were debauched in morals, and driven into all manner of vices and wickedness" (Dowell [1884] 1965, 167). This excise tax, called the Act Against Geneva of 1727, resulted in the introduction of a new spirit not covered by the act, termed "Parliament Brandy," which was unfortunately even more harmful than gin. The act was repealed in 1733, and gin drinking came roaring back.

In 1736, the British Parliament passed the Act Against Spiritous Liquors, covering all strong spirits. It imposed prohibitive taxes designed to curtail all consumption, but this law also failed, because it was impossible to enforce, was widely ignored, and was the cause of large-scale social disruption and protest that led to its replacement with moderate taxes in 1743. In 1778, the predominant purpose of taxes on spirits shifted to revenue raising—and high taxes to finance the fight against American independence led to widespread illicit distillation and smuggling (Dowell [1884] 1965, 180).

Britain's experiences with excise taxes presage the American experiences with both taxes and prohibition. The American colonies early on restricted the consumption of alcohol with a combination of taxes, licenses, and regulations. Massachusetts forbade the sale of "strong water" to Indians. Punishment for intoxication and other violations of the various liquor laws included confinement to the stocks, imprisonment, the lash, and fines.

An excise on distilled spirits was the first internal tax passed by the government of the new United States, on 1 March 1791. Americans inherited the British hatred for excise taxes, so it is no surprise that this one caused many problems and resulted in the infamous Whiskey Rebellion. Though this tax was not specifically a sin tax, since it was enacted to help refund the Revolutionary War debt, the problems caused by the consumption of spirits were felt to make the tax more palatable. Secretary of the Treasury Alexander Hamilton proposed the tax, arguing in part that it would have a desirable impact "from the standpoint of health and morals" (Hu 1950, 13).

It is worth spending some time reviewing this episode, because it illustrates not only the classic problems of excise taxes in general and sin taxes in particular, but also many of the problems we observe in modern confrontations between the coercive power of the state and the citizen, as well as some features unique to the birth of the nation. In this episode we will find the establishment of federal authority; a harsh system of enforcement and collection; rent seeking; big producers coming around to support the tax because they gain at the expense of small producers; differential impacts on the various states; evasion; and rebellion. This episode also confirms, more than 180 years before the proposition advanced by Barzel (1976), that a per unit excise tax discriminates in favor of higher-quality output—a fact that led to some of the problems with the tax.

When the whiskey tax bill was introduced in Congress in June 1790, opposition to it was heated. Southern representatives were especially antagonistic, arguing that while the "East" had beer and cider to fall back on, the South had no breweries or orchards. The bill was passed with the support of the middle-Atlantic and northeastern states (Hu 1950, 14). The tax hit the farmers on the Western frontier especially hard, as they—especially those in Pennsylvania, Virginia, and North Carolina—dealt with poor roads across the Alleghenies, and had found hauling grain to Eastern markets to be unprofitable. Whiskey, on the other hand, was of greater value and lesser bulk, and the farmers had been profitably transporting their grain in this form to markets in the East.

Compounding the problem, the Constitution required that taxes be uniform, and at the time this constitutional restriction was taken seriously. Because the tax per gallon on Western whiskey was the same as that on the higher-quality whiskey distilled in the East, which commanded twice the price,[3] the effect of the tax was to reduce the price of Eastern whiskey relative to that distilled in the West.

Yoram Barzel (1976) makes the point that per unit taxes cause a market substitution toward higher-quality goods. This point is essentially the same as that made by Alchian and Allen (1983, 39) regarding shipping costs: When it costs the same per pound to ship high-quality oranges to New York from California as it does to ship low-quality oranges, the percentage of high-quality oranges sold in New York will be greater than that sold in California. Similarly, the effect of a per unit tax is to lower the relative price of the high-quality commodity. This tax-induced change in relative prices inflamed the Western farmers, but, as might be expected, the large Eastern distillers began to support the tax when they realized that it gave them a competitive edge.

So far we see that the whiskey tax pitted the South and West against the middle-Atlantic and northeastern states, as well as big producer against small—divisiveness fairly typical of most legislation. And here remember that Congress was bound by the constitutional constraint that taxes be geographically and otherwise uniform. Uniformity on one margin—a fixed per unit tax, did not necessarily mean uniformity on other margins. The tax discriminated against the South and the West, which lacked readily available substitutes, and adversely affected small distillers, who tended to produce whiskey of lower quality than the larger producers in the East. Of course, an ad valorem tax assessed on the value of sales would be uniform per dollar of whiskey sold, but it would have tended to favor the Western producer relative to the Eastern. Moreover, any tax would still be biased against the consumers in the West and South, who had fewer untaxed substitutes to turn to.

This illustrates an important aspect of excise taxes as well as taxes in general. When there are several margins of adjustment available to the producers and consumers of a taxed commodity, and when the costs of adjustment are different for different producers and consumers, a tax that is uniform (i.e., imposes the same cost) on one margin will not usually be uniform on the others. Uniformity is virtually impossible in a complex world where there are several possible margins of adjustment.

Although the differential impact of the tax was galling, the administration of the tax was even more of a problem for farmers in western Pennsylvania. Those caught evading the tax were required to appear in court in Philadelphia. This meant absence from home for a considerable time, heavy expenses for witnesses and lawyers, and fines as high as $250.00, which "confronted the great majority of distillers with what seemed almost certain ruin, seeing that farms and stills were worth from $300 to $500 at most.... It was, moreover, regarded a clear contravention of Anglo-Saxon liberties to take men to a great distance from their vicinage [neighborhood] for trial" (Hu 1950, 20). These intrusions reinforced the usual complaints about the administration of excise taxes: revenue agents snooping around buildings and property, attempts to induce neighbor to spy on neighbor, and creation of a climate of fear, anger, and hostility among the citizens. A further aggravation was that currency was scarce in the region and whiskey was used as a local medium of exchange—but was not accepted as payment for taxes.

At a meeting in Pittsburgh, Albert Gallatin, later a U.S. senator and secretary of the Treasury under Thomas Jefferson, declared that "all taxes upon the articles of consumption, because of the power that must necessarily be vested in the officers who collect them, will in the end destroy the liberty of any people that permits them to be introduced" (Adams 1993, 317). The prevailing sentiment was that the whiskey tax was a betrayal of the Revolution.

During the Whiskey Rebellion, several revenue collectors were tarred and feathered, and others were threatened with physical violence and destruction of their property. Some distillers who complied with the law had their property destroyed and their stills shot full of holes by "Tom the tinker." At this point some attempt was made to ease the special burden of the law on those in the West by allowing cases to be tried in state courts, which eliminated the burden of traveling to Philadelphia. But this was too little, too late. The violence continued.

Alexander Hamilton felt that "[a] government can never be said to be established, until some signal display has manifested its power of military coercion" (Hu 1950, 29). He was confirming the proposition that the unique feature of government as an institution is that it claims the power to use force, and further, he felt that it was necessary to demonstrate that power to assert the authority of the new national government.

The Whiskey Rebellion gave Hamilton that opportunity. Troops were called out, and with President Washington initially at their head, started for western

Pennsylvania. Confronted with an approaching force of nearly 13,000 men, the "Whiskey Rebels" dispersed before the army reached its destination, and the rebellion was over (Nash and Jeffrey 1986, 247). The tax, however, remained unpopular, and evasion was widespread, so after all this, it was not much of a revenue producer.

Thomas Jefferson, though an Anglophobe, had the traditional Anglo-Saxon dislike of excise taxes, and when he was elected, he vowed to work toward their repeal. The tax on distilled spirits, along with other excise taxes, was in fact repealed by an act passed in April 1802 and effective 1 July 1802.

Jefferson felt so strongly about the relationship between taxes and liberty that he suggested that there should be a rebellion every twenty years to keep government in check. And he was not speaking in the abstract. As Charles Adams points out, there were nearly a dozen major rebellions during Jefferson's lifetime—six in the United States including the Revolution and the Whiskey Rebellion—all to a greater or lesser extent tax revolts. According to Adams (1993, 321), "Jefferson justified tolerance for civic disorder and rebellion by referring to a Latin maxim,...'*Malo periculosam libertatem quam quietam servitutem*' ('Rather a dangerous liberty than a peaceful servitude')." In this light, the Second Amendment to the Constitution could be thought of as providing for a rather drastic early form of term limits if taxes became abusive.

Internal taxes including, once again, a tax on distilled spirits were revived to finance the War of 1812. These taxes were repealed in 1817, and until the Civil War, the federal government imposed no excise taxes on whiskey. Nor were any other internal taxes levied during this period, the government relying entirely on tariffs for revenue.

Between 1817 and the Civil War, taxation and the regulation of alcoholic beverages were left to the states. During this period the temperance movement was founded and began gathering momentum. States used their taxing and licensing prerogatives to raise revenue and control the consumption of alcohol. Campaigns pushing local-option laws and laws banning the sale of liquor altogether began on a wide front—issues which will be taken up in the next section.

The outbreak of the Civil War brought the enactment of a variety of federal taxes, including a tax on income and an excise on distilled spirits, which was imposed in July 1862. Taxes on spirits were increased rapidly, and additional taxes were imposed at the manufacturing level as well as at the wholesale and retail levels.

At this time distilled alcohol had many uses other than as a beverage, including "burning fluid" (used for illumination), and in the manufacture of varnishes, patent medicines, and dyes, as well as for processing photographs. The manufacturers of these and other products were forced to switch to substitutes, and many went out of business. For example, as a result of the tax, the price of alcohol used as burning fluids went from $0.34 per gallon in 1861 to $4.25 in 1865, pricing the product out of the market (Hu 1950, 38). The effect on the use of distilled spirits as a beverage was not so dramatic. Apparently there was significant adulteration of whiskey with nontaxed substances, as well as a significant amount of whiskey produced that evaded the tax. The amount of whiskey that was taxed decreased to a much greater extent than did consumption.

In 1868, taxes were reduced from $2.00 per proof gallon to $0.50 per proof gallon and the use of spirits in manufacturing resumed,[4] with illegal distilling no longer being a problem. Taxes were increased from time to time between 1868 and World War I. The event of note during this period, aside from the march toward the Eighteenth Amendment, was the notorious Whiskey Ring, which was organized to evade taxes (Hu 1950, chap. 2).[5]

## The Prohibition Movement

This examination of the prohibition movement will focus on its relationship to excise taxes and the similarity of responses generated by prohibition to those generated by taxation. From 1873 to 1915, revenue from taxes on alcoholic beverages exceeded revenue from all other internal sources combined, and for nineteen of those years, these taxes provided more than three-fourths of the revenue from all internal sources (Manning 1949, 22). Giving up much of this revenue for the "Noble Experiment" would involve a hardship that in part reflects the intensity of feeling about the whole issue. Part of this revenue loss was made up by taxes from other sources, including, initially, a relatively small contribution from the income tax.

The temperance movement gained momentum in the early 1800s, with initial emphasis on moral suasion to discourage drinking, an effort that proved substantially unsuccessful. As the century progressed, various states adopted some form of alcohol prohibition, often including local-option laws. Because communities found that alcohol could easily be brought in from neighboring "wet" areas, there was a push for statewide prohibition. Eventually many states abandoned this effort when it became evident that statewide restrictions were no more successful than local option, and that nationwide prohibition was necessary to truly halt the abuse of alcohol (Hu 1950, 49–50).

Once again we find attempts to control the consumption of alcoholic beverages stymied by evasion involving smuggling from adjacent wet areas as well as illegal production. For example, in 1852 Massachusetts enacted statewide prohibition, which remained in force until 1875. Massachusetts was the only state that attempted to collect statistics on establishments known to sell liquor—they (the ones they knew about) increased in Boston from 1,500 in 1854 to 1,516 in 1866 (the last year reported). But because arrests for public drunkenness increased in Boston from 6,983 to 15,542 over the same period, there must have been a significant number of uncounted establishments (Menken 1891, 47).

Other states, such as Kansas, *reported* better success. However, the basic feeling at the time was that the system was not working very well. Dr. Dio Lewis, on a tour through several large cites in the Midwest where he was told that liquor was simply not available, saw drunken men lying in the street. In Iowa City, which was covered by prohibition, he saw "seventy-five to one hundred kegs of beer being delivered in a truck from a brewery...and concluded that prohibition was a wild theory" (Menken 1891, 51).

The perception in the nineteenth century was that alcohol consumption led to a great deal of crime. Reports at the time attributed over half of all criminal arrests to intoxication. In Suffolk County, where Boston is situated, "it was shown that sixty per cent. of all sentences for crime in the Commonwealth during the last twenty years [prior to 1881] were distinctly rum offenses" (Menken 1891, 26). In Cleveland, in 1887, 4,720 out of 8,588 arrests were attributed to intoxication (Menken 1891, 26). In Philadelphia, in a single year 40,000 out of 45,000 arrests were claimed to be alcohol related (Menken 1891, 27).

These figures are undoubtedly exaggerated; moreover, it is hard to say how many of those arrested were intoxicated but behaving harmlessly. The Suffolk County data, which are probably more accurate than most, reveal that 48 percent of those arrested for larceny or assault and battery were under the influence of liquor (Menken 1891, 27). It is impossible to say whether drink drove these individuals to crime or whether they would have been criminals in any case (but needed a shot or two of courage beforehand). The perception at the time, however, was that liquor was imposing an enormous cost on society. In today's jargon, alcohol consumption was generating negative externalities in the form of criminal behavior. It was this behavior that the Eighteenth Amendment was designed to eliminate. In this, as we know, it was only partially successful—at a cost of the significant rise in criminal activity associated with the evasion of Prohibition.

It is not the purpose here to delve deeply into the history of the Eighteenth Amendment or the prohibition movement.[6] Rather we want to look at those areas where the response to prohibition is similar to that of taxes. Specifically, we saw that in the 1700s the British imposed a prohibitory tax on spirits and, as might be expected, the results were similar to those under the Eighteenth Amendment. There was widespread evasion through smuggling and illegal production; even moderate taxes resulted in a significant amount of evasion.

Table 3.1 presents some of the results of a study of the economic impact of Prohibition (see Hu 1950, 52–54).[7] The table shows the average yearly per capita consumption of alcoholic beverages for the period of 1911–14 (before the abnormal World War I binge years and the Eighteenth Amendment), the early Prohibition years of 1921–22, and the later Prohibition years of 1927–30. Several things stand out: First, there was a lag between the onset of Pro-

## TABLE 3.1
### Average Yearly Consumption in Gallons per Capita

| Period | Spirits | Beer | Wine | Total Pure Alcohol |
|---|---|---|---|---|
| 1911–14 | 1.47 | 20.53 | 0.59 | 1.69 |
| 1921–22 | 0.92 | 1.49 | 0.51 | 0.73 |
| 1927–30 | 1.62 | 6.27 | 0.98 | 1.14 |

The data in this table are reproduced from Hu 1950, 53, table B. The data were originally collected by Clark Warburton 1932.

hibition and the extensive establishment of alternative sources of supply; second, after allowing for this adjustment, the total per capita consumption of alcohol (in terms of pure alcohol) dropped by a third, from 1.69 gallons in the 1911–14 period to 1.14 gallons in 1927–30; third, there was considerable substitution among the categories of alcoholic beverages.

That there is a considerable adjustment period between the imposition of a prohibition law and the full development of illegal economic markets is not surprising. Jeffrey A. Miron and Jeffrey Zwiebel (1991) report similar results using more extensive data. They look not only at alcohol consumption but also at the per capita incidence of cirrhosis, alcoholic deaths, and arrests for drunkenness and alcoholic psychosis. All of the time series show a steep initial decline at the onset of Prohibition and then a steady increase (Miron and Zwiebel 1991, 244–45).

They find further that the reduction in alcohol consumption associated with Prohibition reflects increased economic costs—specifically, the higher costs borne by suppliers associated with evading detection, as well as the higher search costs borne by consumers trying to find sources of illegal supply and the higher costs associated with increases in the probability of being cheated. Possible reductions in consumption resulting from moral suasion emanating from the belief that alcohol consumption was immoral, or reductions as a result of respect for the law, were not evident (Miron and Zwiebel 1991, 245). The reduced consumption of alcohol during Prohibition appears to be almost entirely the result of the increased economic costs associated with illegal production and consumption.

Prohibition, like taxes, induces substitutions along various margins. If the illegal supply is being smuggled from areas where the prohibited product is legal or where enforcement is lax, then prohibition should result in substitutions similar to those provoked by excise taxes or by shipping costs. The risks of capture are essentially the same whether 50 pounds of high-quality, pure heroin or 50 pounds of low-quality, impure heroin are smuggled into the United States. Because the penalties if one is caught (the costs) are essentially the same, prohibition should increase the purity or quality of the product smuggled into the country, as opposed to what would be supplied if consumption were legal (ignoring the effects of tariffs on legal imports). On the other hand, if the product is produced domestically and if quality is associated with large-scale production or, as in the case of distilled spirits, a long period of aging, then prohibition should cause a reduction in the quality since the bigger the scale of an operation or the longer the production period, the greater the likelihood of arrest.

Prohibition will also result in the sale of alcohol in more concentrated forms for a given market value since greater bulk, other things equal, increases the likelihood of arrest. One is obviously more likely to be noticed hauling beer barrels, for example, than the much smaller containers of whiskey containing the same quantity of pure alcohol. This observation in part explains the significant drop in beer consumption per capita shown in table 3.1, relative to the slight increase in the consumption of spirits and wine from the pre-Prohibition period to the 1927–30 period. Wine falls between beer and distilled spirits in terms of alcoholic content, but the direct application of the theory to wine consumption during Prohibition is complicated by the fact that sacramental wine and home-produced wine remained legal.

Outright prohibition, like prohibitive taxes and even more moderate taxation, leads to adjustments on several margins. Most obvious is a shift from legal to illegal consumption. Second is a reduction in overall consumption, which Miron and Zwiebel find in the case of the alcohol prohibition was almost entirely the result of the higher costs of consumption and production. Third, because prohibition has the same effect as a per unit tax or high transportation cost, there will be a shift toward products with less bulk and higher value. We would expect a shift away from bulky products like beer in favor of more concentrated distilled spirits.

Further, since the production of higher-quality whiskey takes longer and is more capital intensive, and since both factors increase the possibility of detection and arrest, we would expect in domestic production a shift toward lower-quality, more easily concealed products. Together, the last two effects result in a shift toward more expensive, higher-quality goods being smuggled into dry areas from regions where production is legal as well as a shift toward lower-quality production in the restricted areas.

Two provisos must be added to this last set of observations: First, if higher-valued illegal production is as easily concealed as lower-valued production, then due to the Alchian and Allen effect (see above), we expect production in areas covered by prohibition to shift toward higher-valued output. Second, because those selling illegal goods face higher costs establishing a brand name (among other reasons, they are less likely to deal with repeat customers and more likely to leave the business as a result of arrest), they are more likely to behave opportunistically and cheat their customers by misleading them about the quality of the merchandise. They are more likely to sell a lower-quality adulterated product that they represent as being of higher quality.

Consumers will be aware of this behavior, and it will be reflected in the prices they are willing to pay for illegal products. As predicted by the literature dealing with the market for "lemons," which emerge when there is an asymmetric distribution of information between buyers and sellers about the quality of the product, the reactions of consumers will have the effect of shifting sales toward lower-quality output. In other words, the sellers know the quality of the product they are selling, while the buyers, who cannot easily determine product quality at the point of sale, suspect the quality will be lower than represented by the seller and thus adjust the price they are willing to pay downward. Cheap whiskey drives out good.

## Post-Prohibition

A major problem facing government upon the repeal of the Eighteenth Amendment in 1933 was the vast illicit market in alcohol that was still in place. This illicit market, according to Hu, "was entrenched, organized, and efficient, with a smoothly operating system of production and distribution" (Hu 1950, 64). The underground market was necessarily of prime concern in the establishment of post-Prohibition tax rates on alcoholic beverages: if tax rates were set too high, the illegal market would continue uninterrupted.

In addition, state governments were experiencing budget problems and were looking at alcohol consumption as a source of revenue. These concerns dictated coordination between the states and the federal government so that combined tax rates would not be so high that the illicit market would continue to operate and adversely affect revenue collection. But because of the differential impact of the proposed tax-sharing schemes on the distribution of revenue among the states, no coordinated effort was worked out.[8]

Some argued that Congress had an obligation to use the excise for sumptuary purposes and to impose a "high" tax rate to discourage drinking, while others recognized the futility of this approach, which would simply maintain reliance on the illegal market and result in the collection of little revenue. Calculations were performed to estimate the maximum tax consistent with the elimination of bootlegging, based in part on the spread between the costs of the bootlegger and the costs of the legitimate producer.

The tax rate consistent with this objective was between $2.00 and $2.20 per gallon. The sumptuary camp argued for taxes up to $6.00 per gallon, which, by allowing the profitable operations of the bootleggers to continue, would not have achieved their purpose (Hu 1950, 78). A bill with a tax rate of $2.00 per gallon on distilled spirits was signed into law on 11 January 1934, a victory for those who recognized that taxpayers and markets adjust rationally to the taxes they confront.

## The Oleomargarine Tax

The federal tax on oleomargarine is of interest because it represents a case of Congress and the executive succumbing to pure rent seeking on the part of the dairy industry. Moreover, the acceptance of this tax by the Supreme Court represented a significant extension of the federal government's police powers.

The Constitution reserved police powers to the states and the individual citizens. The whole regulatory edifice built by the federal government beginning in the latter part of the nineteenth century had to overcome this constitutional constraint. The government breached this barrier by way of its constitutional powers to tax, regulate interstate commerce, and regulate the mail. The constitutional question raised by the oleomargarine tax was whether the federal government had the power to impose a tax that did not have the specific purpose of raising revenue (Lee 1973, chap. 1). The excise tax on distilled spirits did not face this constitutional hurdle, because its primary purpose was to raise revenue; officially the sumptuary aspects of the tax were of secondary importance.

Use of federal taxing authority to regulate rather than merely raise revenue would significantly expand the police powers of the federal government, based on the long-recognized principle, reiterated by Justice Marshall,[9] that the power to tax is the power to destroy. This power to destroy is constrained when the primary reason for a tax is raising revenue, since destruction of a taxed activity eliminates all tax revenue. As the deliberation over tax rates following the repeal of Prohibition shows, a revenue-maximizing tax authority has an incentive to assure the long-run survival of the activity that produces revenue. This objective requires tax rates that are moderate enough not to go beyond the peak of the so-called Laffer curve.[10]

> The Industrial Revolution and modern chemistry wrought fundamental changes in the production of food. Increasing technological expertise in the latter part of the nineteenth century made possible the manufacture of table foods from ingredients hitherto unused for such purposes, such as cottonseed oil or animal fats, that closely resembled the genuine farm commodity. The manufacture of oleomargarine was an outstanding example of this trend. (Lee 1973, 12)

Oleomargarine, developed in France and introduced into the United States in 1874, was first manufactured by mixing skimmed milk with processed animal fat. With the addition of yellow dye, oleomargarine resembled butter in appearance as well as food value, but was cheaper to manufacture. Coincidentally, technological progress in the dairy industry was increasing the supply of butter and driving down its price (Lee 1973, 13).

Caught in this vise of falling butter prices and rising competition from a new product, the dairy industry's response was predictable: they appealed to government for protection from "unfair" competition from the upstart oleomargarine manufacturers. The dairy industry's early rent-seeking success came with action by the states, especially the dairy states. In the 1880s, most states passed legislation regulating the manufacture and sale of oleomargarine, levied taxes on it, or both, while several states banned its sale altogether. Other states passed laws prohibiting manufacturers from adding yellow dye to the product, thereby making margarine less attractive. New Hampshire required the addition of an unappealing pink color (Lee 1973, 15).

As with the control of alcohol, the dairy industry asserted that federal legislation was necessary to truly regulate the abuse and fraud perpetrated by the production and sale of margarine. Arguments used by the industry were that oleomargarine was unwholesome, that consumers were being defrauded because margarine was often mislabeled as butter, and that the use of yellow coloring was fraudulent and should be prohibited—or that at least, the manufacture and sale of margarine should be restricted in some way.

Oleomargarine properly made was a "wholesome nutritious food," and occasional fraud in labeling or in the use of substandard ingredients could be dealt with without driving the product off the market (Lee 1973, 13–14). Furthermore, the dairy industry was not above adulterating butter with cheap ingredients and coloring their own product to make it more appealing (Lee 1973, 17). The real issue was the competition the dairy industry faced from the cheaper substitute, and the industry went to great lengths to eliminate this competition. Finally, in 1886, the industry was successful in getting a law passed by Congress and signed by the president requiring the licensing of manufacturers, wholesalers, and retailers of oleomargarine (with annual fees of $600.00, $480.00, and $48.00, respectively) and imposing an excise tax of two cents per pound. As a result of this legislation, the number of oleomargarine manufacturers dropped by more than a third (Lee 1973, 22–23).

The federal law and several state laws were challenged in the courts. Since the tax was designed solely to inhibit an industry and not to raise revenue, it was argued that it entailed an unconstitutional usurping of police powers that were reserved to the states. In a series of landmark decisions, the Supreme Court accepted this federal encroachment of the powers originally reserved for the states; some of the state laws that seemed to violate the due-process clause (by, for example, completely banning the industry) were also upheld (Lee 1973, 23–27).

Rent seeking is, in effect, the hiring of the coercive power of the state by some private citizens to gain an advantage over others. This is one of the abuses the Constitution was designed to prevent. As in many other cases, politicians and justices found ways around these constraints to allow the central government to grow ever more powerful.

With the door opened by the oleomargarine tax, over the next few years other industries demanded that the federal government provide them with protection from "unfair competition." Attempts were made by various producer groups to limit competition from such products as lard diluted with processed cottonseed oil, filled cheese, phosphorous matches, and various drugs. Not all of these and other attempts were successful. For example, a tax on adulterated lard failed not because of some higher principle but because two powerful special interests were on opposite sides of the issue—the cottonseed oil industry lobbied against the tax, while the cattle industry was in favor of it. Taxes were, however, successfully used to eliminate from the market filled cheese, phosphorous matches,[11] artificially colored oleomargarine, opium, and a number of other drugs.

As a result of shortages of dairy products caused by a combination of World War II and price controls, considerable consumer dissatisfaction with the laws regulating margarine (which by now was made with vegetable oil) developed.[12] Because of pressure by various consumer groups, margarine manufacturers, and the League of Women Voters—and to help gain the support of organized labor—the Democrats promised to repeal the taxes on oleomargarine during the 1948 election campaign. This promise was fulfilled, and the national tax on margarine was ended by a bill signed by President Truman in March 1950 (Lee 1973, 58). As in the case of adulterated lard, the tax on margarine was not repealed because the federal government suddenly came to its senses and decided it had overstepped its constitutional authority. Rather, the shortages of the war years helped alter the balance of political power, and as a result, competing interests and "public opinion" could no longer be ignored. In the next section, we will see an example of the use of a tax to constrain the formation of public opinion.

## Knowledge Taxes

Censorship is probably as old as human speech. As every schoolboy knows, Socrates was condemned to death in ancient Greece for "blasphemy against the gods and because his teaching was impious" (Piñon-Tiana 1960, 10). The invention of moveable type in the mid-fifteenth century brought increased demands on the censors from both the church and the crown. Knowledge taxes, in the form of stamp taxes on paper, pamphlets, books, and newspapers, represent a considerable refinement in the censors' tools. These taxes allowed the censors to focus with precision on offending material and tax it out of existence. Gone were the difficult-to-enforce lists of banned books, executions for sedition or treason, and many other forms of punishment.

Censorship is a way for the church—when it enjoys a monopoly, as did the Catholic church in the West prior to the Reformation—and the state to maintain their positions of authority. In the case of the state, censorship creates a barrier to entry by prohibiting the dissemination of competing ideas and criticism. The state uses censorship to protect the rents that accrue to it by virtue of its control of the levers of power—"the state" here meaning the individuals who are actually making decisions to protect their access to rents. These individuals include kings, majority parties in parliaments, presidents, prime ministers, and bureaucrats.

Taxes on knowledge were first implemented in England during Queen Anne's reign. The stated purpose of these taxes was to "check 'false and scandalous libels' against Government and 'the most horrid blasphemies against God and religion.'" However, according to Collet's history of the knowledge tax, the actual reason for this initial tax—as well as the duties placed on linen and soap—was to help finance the War of Spanish Succession. The government placed a tax on legal documents and "on papers, pamphlets and advertisements, and required a stamp to be placed on every paper that [Parliament] chose to call a newspaper" (Collet 1899, 8). Special dispensations were allowed for uses by the universities and the church and for certain other scholarly books. When first imposed in "1712 the tax was a halfpenney on half-a-sheet or less, and one penney on publications of more than half-a-sheet" (Piñon-Tiana 1960, 24). The press recognized the danger the knowledge tax represented to it and fought the tax from the very beginning.

During the reign of George III, hostility between government and the press grew. Rapid economic growth and technological progress created conflicts by disrupting the established order between employers and employees and between social classes. Political corruption, in part resulting from the existence of rotten boroughs and the whole issue of electoral reform, also generated conflict between government and the press. In the 1760s, John Wilkes engaged in a heated print campaign against the government for freedom of the press and electoral rights. Wilkes' attacks led to demonstrations in the streets and provoked the resignation of the prime minister, Lord Brute. His successor, George Grenville, had Wilkes sentenced to the Tower and his papers confiscated. This sentence was overturned by the chief justice (Piñon-Tiana 1960, 21–22).

Another failure to suppress the press by force eventually turned Parliament to a more subtle means of censorship. Ancient privilege prevented the reporting of speeches made in Parliament. However, a Parliamentary speech delivered in 1770 by Lord Chatham, which took to task government officials for engaging in a system of "bribes and corruption...allowing them to wax fat at the expense of the State and of the Empire," was memorized and subsequently reported by Sir Philip Frances, writing under the name Junius. The resulting uproar led George III to order that "a stop once and for all [be put] to the pretensions of the press" (Piñon-Tiana 1960, 23).

Hostilities continued to increase as Parliament attempted to use force to impose its will on the press. Once again demonstrations broke out. Members of Parliament were struck by stones and potatoes thrown by an angry crowd; the prime minister's carriage was destroyed (Piñon-Tiana 1960, 23). The crown and Parliament were forced to back down.

These setbacks led to a change in tactics. When force failed to halt the growing threat to the rents controlled by the crown and Parliament, they substituted the knowledge tax. Just as consumers of alcoholic beverages will substitute when confronted with a tax or prohibition, those in control of government will find (or attempt to find) other means to maintain control of rents associated with the coercive power of the state when the costs of using the current means increase.

Exacerbating the government's problem was the emerging symbiotic relationship between the press and public opinion. Beginning in the latter part of the eighteenth century, technical progress and innovation were dramatically lowering the cost of printing. Simultaneously—and not coincidentally—public opinion was becoming important as a political force (Johnson 1991, chap. 6). Crucial to this formation of public opinion were the newspapers; thus, the knowledge tax was used in an attempt to tame this growing monster when other means had failed.

Antonio Piñon-Tiana summarizes the government's attack on the press as follows:

> In 1756 the tax was increased by another halfpenney. In 1789 it went up to 2d. In 1792 it rose to two and a half pence. In 1804 to 3d., and in 1815 to 4d. less 20 per cent. As a consequence of this increase in taxes the London papers, *The Times* among them, were compelled to raise their prices to 7d. which necessarily reduced circulation to a few thousands, with the result that the press simply existed for the governing classes. (Piñon-Tiana 1960, 24)

There was not only a stamp duty on newspapers, but also a levy on paper and advertising, and laws requiring the registration of printers and printing presses were also enacted.

In 1815, an act ensured for the first time that various provisions of the knowledge tax covered pamphlets and printed papers containing "observations on the news"; it also required the posting of a bond before publishing a newspaper, pamphlet, or printed paper. Many of the modifications in the law were designed to extend coverage to forms of printed material that had been created to escape coverage of earlier provisions of the tax, or to extend coverage to new areas the government found troublesome, such as editorial "comments on the news" (Collet 1899, 17).

These actions indicate a fairly widespread legitimate attempt to avoid the tax by altering the format of printed material so that it would escape coverage or be taxed at a reduced rate. Outright tax evasion was also widespread. One provision adopted in 1815 specified substantial fines for street hawkers caught selling unstamped papers. The law also encouraged citizens' arrests by offering a reward of twenty shillings to anyone who apprehended such a tax evader (Collet 1899, 13).

Taxing newspapers, however, was like stirring up a hornet's nest—with the predictable result that the press continuously campaigned against the taxes and argued for their repeal. There were also committees and societies organized to fight for the repeal of the taxes on knowledge. These efforts were finally successful. The tax on advertising revenue was repealed in 1853, the stamp duty in 1855, the paper duty in 1861, and the remaining provisions in 1865.

## Colonial Censorship

Early censorship in the American colonies followed the initial English model of suppression by brute force and was abandoned in the colonies between 1725 and 1730 (Piñon-Tiana 1960, 31). In 1765, Parliament extended the stamp duties that were already in place in England to the American colonies. The stated purpose of these taxes was to help defray Britain's cost of defending the colonies. Ironically, the "[tax] money was to be spent entirely in the colonies for their benefit and protection" (Adams 1993, 293). The Stamp Act of 1765 required stamps on every colonial newspaper, pamphlet, legal document, pack of playing cards, and pair of dice.

Colonial newspapers declared war on the British.[13] There were riots in Boston directed against those associated with the stamp duty. Violent protests broke out in New York and Rhode Island. By late 1765, crowds were burning revenue collectors in effigy throughout the colonies and "convincing" them to resign their commissions (Nash and Jeffrey 1986, 145). Here again, Parliament, by antagonizing newspapers, stirred a hornet's nest, which this time helped lead to the loss of the American colonies.

## Conclusion

We have examined three different excise taxes: the whiskey tax, the oleomargarine tax, and the tax on knowledge. These taxes are not only of historical significance; they illustrate the different reasons that can motivate government to impose a tax aside from the search for additional revenue. Examination of these tax episodes also reveals the various responses to taxes on the part of those who bear the tax burden. Finally, each of these taxes played an important role in either the founding or the early formation of the United States.

The whiskey tax and the knowledge tax also illustrate the tendency of a tax to evolve from one primarily designed to raise revenue (though in both cases the sumptuary aspects of these taxes were used as selling points) to one designed to discourage consumption and production. Anticonsumption fervor can lead to an increase in the tax to prohibitive levels and, finally, in the case of the whiskey tax, to outright prohibition. The oleomargarine tax was always a nonstarter as a generator of funds, never raising much more than 1 percent of total internal revenue and in most years significantly less than that; it was a tax designed solely to discourage the production and consumption of margarine.

Aside from revenue, the motives of the British, Colonial, and U.S. governments in imposing taxes on whiskey and other alcoholic beverages have been to reduce the perceived harmful effects of their consumption. In the cases we have examined of both prohibitive taxes and outright prohibition at the national level, the combined political, economic, and social costs of prohibition led to their repeal and replacement by more moderate taxes.

In the nineteenth century, the federal government instigated a regime of regulatory taxation with rent seeking as its sole motivation. The oleomargarine tax best illustrates this governmental tax motive. The dairy industry, through its manipulation of the political process, was able to secure legislation that severely constrained the ability of the rival manufacturers of margarine to compete. Interestingly, this tax was repealed only when wartime shortages changed the political balance. Among other forces, consumer anger over shortages of dairy products convinced the Democrats to favor repeal of the margarine tax to help the party during the 1948 election.

Another tax motive, illustrated by the knowledge taxes, is found in the attempt by government to strengthen its own grip on governmental rents by handicapping the competition in the market for political ideas. These taxes were also eventually repealed, in part because they inflamed the very sources of communication that carried the political competition. From the beginning, newspapers fiercely opposed the knowledge taxes and were finally successful in obtaining their repeal.

Tax evasion is another major feature of the history of excise taxes. High taxes always lead to evasion. Selective excise taxes are evaded by substitution to the production and consumption of legal but nontaxed—or less heavily taxed—alternatives, and by substitution to illegal underground transactions that avoid taxation entirely. As a result, attempts to reduce crime and other social problems caused, for example, by the consumption of whiskey, led to a whole new set of criminal and social problems associated with illegal tax evasion. We also saw examples of how supposedly "uniform" taxes have nonuniform results.

This is because products are multidimensional, resulting in substitution along one or more of several possible margins. In the case of the whiskey tax of 1791, each proof gallon of whiskey bore the same per unit tax, but the tax per dollar of sales was much higher on the lower-quality Western whiskey than on the higher-quality whiskey produced by the large distillers. This was one of the grievances that led to the Whiskey Rebellion.

Finally, these episodes illustrate the important role taxes have played historically in shaping and, in fact, leading to the overthrow of the existing government. The whiskey tax and the suppression of the subsequent rebellion were used by Alexander Hamilton to assert the power and authority of the central government. He felt that a show of force was necessary to demonstrate that the national government was a major player as a wielder of power.

The constitutional issues raised by the oleomargarine tax triggered a series of Supreme Court decisions that significantly enhanced the police power of the federal government. And perhaps most dramatically, resistance to the colonial extension of the knowledge tax helped to set in motion the American Revolution. This resistance, as well as the Whiskey Rebellion, illustrates a very common historical response to taxes: open rebellion. Though this response has been seen less frequently in recent years, especially in the developed world, it remains to be seen whether rebellion as a response to taxes perceived to be unjust has passed forever into history.

## Notes

1. This is quoted by Charles Adams (1993, 140). The original quote is from a chronicler in the mid-1700s by the name of Grapperhaus.
2. Charles Adams (on page 347 of his 1993 book and elsewhere) presents many examples of the burning of tax records. Burning records was in fact very common historically. These records usually represented the only detailed account of the population, so their elimination made it more difficult to reinstate the tax at some future date.
3. Hu (1950, chap. 1) describes the relative impact of the whiskey tax on the various geographic and economic interests. He also presents an account of the events associated with the Whiskey Rebellion, from which much of the sequence of events presented here is taken.
4. A proof gallon is a gallon of spirits that contains 50 percent alcohol. The tax is adjusted proportionally for spirits containing more or less than 50 percent alcohol.
5. The Whiskey Ring affair was one of the numerous scandals that rocked U.S. Grant's two terms as president. The scandal involved distillers bribing federal tax officials to avoid paying the excise tax. Grant's private secretary became involved in the scandal (Gruver 1981, 429).
6. See chapters 7 and 8 for more details.
7. The statistics presented in this section relating to alcohol consumption during Prohibition are "subject to considerable margin of error" (Hu 1950, 54). However, the errors should not be so large as to affect the overall changes in the consumption patterns caused by Prohibition.
8. The states had problems reaching an agreement over a unified state-federal tax policy because of problems in determining how to distribute the revenue among themselves. Some states, such as New York, were primarily consumers, and some, such as Kentucky (which was dry), were primarily producers. The suggested distribution formulas were based on either consumption or production, and no single formula could satisfy all the states (Hu 1950, 66–68).
9. *McCulloch v. Maryland*, 4 Wheat. 316 (1819).
10. The Laffer curve, named after the economist Arthur Laffer, illustrates the simple point that as the tax rate increases from zero, tax revenue will increase up to a point and then begin to decrease. To see why revenue eventually decreases, consider what would happen if income was taxed at a rate of 100 percent. No one would work (or at least report any income) and tax revenue would be zero. As the rate decreased from 100 percent, people would begin to earn income and tax revenue would increase. Revenue is maximized at some rate between zero and 100 percent.

11. There was a considerable health hazard involved in the manufacture of phosphorous matches, causing many workers in the industry to die grisly deaths. However, under proper conditions these matches could be manufactured safely.
12. As a result of a tax on artificially colored margarine, if consumers wanted yellow margarine for purely aesthetic reasons, they were forced to mix in the yellow dye at home. This obvious inconvenience annoyed consumers.
13. See Schlesinger (1957) for a detailed account of this interesting episode.

## References

Adams, Charles. 1993. *For Good and Evil: The Impact of Taxes on the Course of Civilization*. London: Madison Books.

Alchian, Armen A., and William R. Allen. 1983. *Exchange and Production: Competition, Coordination, and Control*. 3rd ed. Belmont, Calif.: Wadsworth.

Barzel, Yoram. 1976. "An Alternative Approach to the Analysis of Taxation." *Journal of Political Economy* 84 (December): 1177–97.

Collet, Collet Dobson. 1899. *History of Taxes on Knowledge*. 2 vols. London: Unwin.

Dowell, Stephen. [1884] 1965. *A History of Taxation and Taxes in England*. Vol. 4. Reprint, New York: Augustus M. Kelley.

Gruver, Rebecca B. 1981. *An American History*. Vol. 2. 3rd ed. Reading, Mass.: Addison-Wesley.

Hu, Tun Y. 1950. *The Liquor Tax in the United States*. New York: Columbia University Press.

Johnson, Paul. 1991. *The Birth of the Modern: World Society 1815–1830*. New York: Harper Collins.

Lee, R. Alton. 1973. *A History of Regulatory Taxation*. Lexington: University Press of Kentucky.

Manning, Raymond E. 1949. *Federal Excise Taxes*. Public Affairs Bulletin No. 72. Washington, D.C. July.

Menken, Percival S. 1891. *Regulation of the Liquor Traffic*. New York: Columbia College.

Miron, Jeffrey A., and Jeffrey Zwiebel. 1991. "Alcohol Consumption During Prohibition." *American Economic Review* 81 (May): 242–47.

Nash, Gary B., and Julie Roy Jeffrey. 1986. *The American People*. Cambridge, Mass.: Harper & Row.

Piñon-Tiana, Antonio. 1960. *The Freedom of the Press*. Manila, Philippines: University of Santo Tomas Press.

Schlesinger, Arthur M. 1957. *Prelude to Independence: The Newspaper War on Britain, 1764–1776*. New York: Knopf.

U.S. Bureau of the Census. 1946. *Historical Statistics of the United States, 1789–1949*. Washington, D.C.: U.S. Government Printing Office.

# Part II

# The Politics of Excise Taxation

# 4

# Selective Excise Taxation from an Interest-Group Perspective

*Randall G. Holcombe*

Economic theory provides three clear rationales for selective excise taxation: (1) Excise taxes can be part of an efficient tax structure if they are placed on goods with inelastic demands, following the Ramsey rule for allocating taxes among markets. (2) An excise tax can be applied as a substitute for a user charge, as, for example, a gasoline tax earmarked for financing highway expenditures, or the federal excise tax on airline tickets earmarked for the Airport and Airway Trust Fund. (3) An excise tax can be placed on goods whose consumption is considered to be undesirable; in this case, the tax can be viewed as either a penalty for consuming the good, a tax on a negative externality associated with the good's consumption, or both. These justifications for excise taxes can provide an omniscient and benevolent government with the guidance it needs to set taxes optimally.

In reality, of course, taxes are not set by benevolent despots, but are created through the political process. Interest groups, not social-welfare criteria, determine the structure of excise taxes. When one recognizes that the political pressures of interest groups, rather than the public's interest, determine the tax structure, the distinctions among justifications for excise taxes have only minor significance. From the standpoint of a political economist, the important features of selective excise taxes can be analyzed by abstracting from the motivations behind the taxes and focusing on the politics and economics of creating such taxes.

Within the public-policy arena, all taxes are justified based on their furtherance of someone's conception of the public interest. Protective tariffs that have the obvious goal of enhancing domestic producers' incomes at the expense of foreign producers and domestic exporters and consumers are justi-

The author gratefully acknowledges the helpful comments and assistance of Russell Sobel. Any shortcomings remain the responsibility of the author.

fied by arguments that they save jobs, help the economy, prevent unemployment, or level the playing field in international trade. Proponents never bring up the fact that they increase the incomes of some individuals or groups at the expense of others.[1] Similarly, traditional selective taxes are justified based on public-interest arguments, such as discouraging undesirable behavior or internalizing the negative externalities associated with the consumption of some goods. But arguments on both sides of tax issues are almost always made by individuals who personally have something to gain from winning the argument.[2] People choose to favor or oppose taxes based on the costs and benefits of the taxes *to them,* and the nature of the tax simply determines which arguments will be most effective in public debates regarding the desirability of the tax.

Whether a proposed tax can be classified as a sin tax, or whether it might be proposed to save domestic jobs or to finance some specific public program, may affect the tenor of the public debate on the tax, and may even sway the opinions of those who have little personally at stake in the outcome. People become politically active, however, when they have a lot personally at stake, and in that case, the nature of the tax does little to influence their support for (or opposition to) it. Taxes are created through the political system; hence, special interests supply the driving force behind them.

This chapter begins by examining several examples of goods and services that face selective excise taxes. Soft-drink excise taxes are used in several states and have been considered in nearly every state, so they provide a good starting point. The economic rationale for such a tax might be that soft drinks have a relatively inelastic demand, so can be taxed more heavily than other goods. This follows rationale (1) in the first paragraph, which implies that tax rates on different goods can be fine-tuned to minimize the excess burden associated with raising a given amount of revenue. Next, the chapter examines the user charge justification of excise taxation by looking at the Airport and Airway Trust Fund financed by the recently reenacted excise tax on airline tickets. This excise tax, which follows rationale (2) listed earlier, is shown to operate more like a general-revenue source than an earmarked user fee. The chapter then looks at the justification of using excise taxes as sin taxes, which is rationale (3), by examining the structure of cigarette taxes across the states. There it is shown that political interests are more relevant to explaining the structure of the tax than the justification that the tax is a tax on sin. The rationales both for and against these taxes are evaluated, along with the welfare losses that result from political activity surrounding the taxes.

After discussing these particular cases of selective excise taxation, the chapter analyzes selective excise taxation both from the standpoint of traditional public finance and from a public-choice perspective that takes account of the resources consumed in the political process. It develops a basic model of selective excise taxation and shows the relationship between the breadth of the tax base and the welfare losses that result from the imposition of a tax. The chapter then examines the argument of Brennan and Buchanan (1980) that narrow-based taxes are preferable to broad-based taxes as protections against the intrusions of a revenue-maximizing government. The Brennan and Buchanan argument is shown to be less relevant when governments employ a mix of broad-based and narrow-based taxes. Furthermore, the Brennan and Buchanan argument does not take account of the political costs associated with determining what narrow tax bases will be used.[3] The chapter concludes that on efficiency grounds, selective excise taxes impose high costs on an economy relative to broad-based taxes.

### Political Costs of Excise Taxation: The Case of Soft-Drink Taxes

Often excise taxes are applied to goods when popular opinion judges their consumption to be of questionable value. Taxes on cigarettes and alcohol fall into this category, as do taxes levied on luxury goods, and even those on gasoline when energy conservation is seen as a desirable goal. Thus, it is instructive to begin an examination of selective excise taxes by looking at the taxation of a widely consumed good that, while it does not have any strong arguments favoring its consumption, also does not have any strong arguments against it. This section examines excise taxes placed on the soft drink industry to see how the possibility of selective excise taxation creates inefficiencies and political costs.[4]

The tax treatment of soft drinks is not uniform among the states. From a political standpoint, states view selective excise taxes on soft drinks as a potential source of revenue, while the sellers of soft drinks view such taxes as an added cost of doing business they want to avoid. The soft drink industry, like other industries, has a national trade association that monitors pending legislation and engages in lobbying on behalf of its members. The National Soft Drink Association and associated state organizations actively oppose selective excise taxes on soft drinks, as one might expect, and the costs of this opposition are a part of the political cost associated with selective excise taxation.

While there is no national excise tax on soft drinks today, this was not always the case. A federal soft drink tax was established during World War I to help finance the war, and was repealed in 1924. In 1932, a federal excise tax on soft drinks was again established, but was repealed in 1934. During World War II, Congress again considered an excise tax on soft drinks, but the tax legislation was not passed. Many states have considered soft drink taxes and rejected them. Still others have imposed a tax and later repealed it. As table 4.1 shows, the trend is clearly away from special soft drink taxes. By 1997, only seven states had excise taxes on soft drinks, and two of those, North Carolina and South Carolina, have passed legislation phasing out the tax. Only twenty-two states applied their general sales tax to soft drinks. One

## TABLE 4.1
### Soft Drink Tax Trends

| State | Year Enacted | Action |
|---|---|---|
| Arkansas | 1992 | On July 15, 1996, Governor Jim Guy Tucker, an ardent soft drink tax supporter, resigned after his conviction on numerous fraud charges. New Governor Mike Huckabee is a vocal opponent of the Arkansas soft drink tax. |
| Louisiana | 1938 | In 1994, soft drink tax reduced by one half; repealed in 1997 (retroactively to 1 February 1996). |
| Mississippi | 1985 | In 1992, soft drink tax eliminated. |
| North Carolina | 1969 | In 1996, legislation passed completely phasing out soft drink tax. |
| Ohio | 1992 | In 1994, voters overwhelmingly supported ballot initiative which eliminated the discriminatory tax on soft drinks imposed by Governor Voinovich and the legislature only two years earlier. |
| South Carolina | 1925 | In 1996, legislation passed completely phasing out special soft drink tax. |
| Tennessee | 1937 | |
| Virginia | 1977 | |
| Washington | 1989 | In 1994, state legislature repealed the large tax on canned and bottled soft drinks and slightly increased the syrup tax—action ratified by voters in November, 1994. |
| West Virginia | 1951 | |

can see the possibilities for substantial political costs in this situation. Soft-drink producers prefer that soft drinks be treated like food products and not taxed when other food products are exempt. Other beverages, such as coffee, tea, and fruit juice, are typically treated like food. There is sound justification for that as soft drinks are defined as food in the federal drug and food laws. In the Food and Drugs Act of 1906, food was defined to include "all articles used for food, drink, confectionery, or condiment by man or other animals, whether simple, mixed, or compound." In the Federal Food, Drug and Cosmetic Act of 1938, food continues to be similarly defined: "The term 'food' means (1) articles used for food or drink for man or other animals, (2) chewing gum, and (3) articles used for components of any such article." More recently, in 1993, in connection with the soft drink industry's challange to the Ohio soft drink tax (later repealed by the voters), Judge John A. Connor, Court of Common Pleas, Franklin County, found that soft drinks are food. State legislatures, despite all the evidence, always interested in finding new sources of revenue, often consider applying the sales tax to soft drinks and imposing a selective excise tax on them.

Selective excise taxes can also be placed on the containers in which soft drinks are sold, or can be imposed on vending-machine sales. Container taxes are often viewed as a tax on a negative externality, because the container will be discarded, but soft drink associations see little difference between soft drink containers and other types of waste. Thus, they lobby against container taxes and taxes that treat vending-machine sales differently from other sales. The merits of the arguments on either side are not really the issue here. What is relevant are the political costs involved in opponents of selective excise taxes trying to keep them from being imposed or trying to remove them once they are imposed, and the political costs of proponents who are trying to see that they are imposed or increased.

## How Large Are the Political Costs?

Data on the political costs associated with selective excise taxation are hard to come by, because lobbyists do not like to publicize the amounts they are spending. All states have some regulatory reporting requirements for lobbyists, but the rules vary considerably from state to state. Some states require substantial disclosure and have heavy penalties for violating lobbying regulations, while others have relatively few rules and minor penalties for reported violations.[5] However, one can get some idea of the magnitude of the political costs by looking at out-of-pocket spending on a few recent campaigns seeking to prevent selective excise taxes from being levied on soft drinks.

Political costs will be incurred when the tax legislation is proposed, to try to keep it from passing, and the fact that these taxes have been repealed or phased out is evidence that once enacted, the political costs continue to mount as those taxed work to get the taxes reduced or eliminated. Two recent campaigns serve as good examples. In late 1992, Arkansas and Ohio passed soft drink excise taxes which took effect in 1993. In 1994, opponents of the tax in each state waged ballot initiative referendums to repeal the tax. Ohio voters repealed their tax as a part of a 1994 ballot measure to prohibit hidden taxes on food, while Arkansas voters chose to keep theirs. The out-of-pocket expenses incurred by the soft-drink associations and allied opponents in trying to repeal those taxes were in the neighborhood of $4 million in Arkansas and $10 million in Ohio. The Ohio tax raised revenues of about $70 million a year, so the political costs were well over 10 percent of the annual tax revenues. Undoubtedly these lobbying expenditures understate the total political costs, because the trade associations have other routine expenses not included in that figure, groups are campaigning on the other side, and the legislature itself incurs costs in the process of passing legislation. It is noteworthy that former Arkansas Governer Jim Guy Tucker, who resigned in July 1996 after conviction on several fraud charges, was a strong advocate of the soft drink tax, originally enacted to help cover a deficit in the state budget left by his predecessor, Bill Clinton. His successor, former Lieutenant Governor Mike Huckabee, has always been a vocal opponent of the tax. Further substantial political costs can be predicted for Arkansas.

To take another example, Chicago established a municipal tax on soft drinks of one cent per 12 ounces. The Illinois Soft Drink Association has been unable to get this tax repealed, but did get a bill passed through the state legislature to prevent other Illinois municipalities from placing excise taxes on soft drinks, and capping the excise tax rate in Chicago at its current rate. The cost of that campaign was about $1 million, in response to a municipal tax that was projected to raise about $10 million per year. Again, the direct cost to the group on only one side of the issue was about 10 percent of the projected annual revenue from the tax, and the political costs are likely to continue to be borne as the taxed group attempts to repeal the tax and groups in favor of the tax try to keep the tax in place or to increase the rate. Obviously, the law that caps the rate in Chicago can be undone by future legislation, which creates an ongoing interest-group issue that will continue to generate political costs.[6]

Putting a dollar figure on the political costs of selective excise taxation would be difficult, but some casual evidence suggests that the costs are substantial. A model developed later in the chapter suggests that interests on both sides of an issue roughly balance. If one side spends resources amounting to at least 10 percent of the projected annual tax revenues, and if interests on the other side match that, then factoring in legislative costs and other political costs that have not been measured, a not unreasonable estimate of the total political costs of selective excise taxation would be in the neighborhood of 25 percent of the revenue raised from the tax. These costs are borne whenever there is the possibility of imposing a selective excise tax, the possibility that one could be repealed, the possibility of a rate change, or the possibility that the tax could be avoided in some way.

In 1993, Florida established a tax on containers that have low recycling rates. Among the containers subject to the tax are the cardboard milk containers used in school lunch programs. Schools lobbied to be exempt from the tax because of the potentially large expense, but their efforts were unsuccessful. Meanwhile, E. I. du Pont de Nemours and Company put a proposal before the legislature to allow school milk to be served in plastic pouches that would be exempt from the tax. The plastic pouches are very thin, and according to du Pont, would take up less landfill space if none of the pouches were recycled than the cardboard containers would take up if half of them were. Du Pont's lobbying efforts to avoid the tax then prompted the paperboard industry to lobby against granting the exemption to du Pont. In the end, du Pont was unable to avoid the tax, so the status quo prevailed, despite significant lobbying costs that were borne on both sides. The issue has now been temporarily settled because the tax expired in 1995. The case is interesting in its own right, but it also illustrates the larger point that selective excise taxes are sure to generate substantial political costs.

## Earmarked Taxes and the Airport and Airway Trust Fund

One justification for selective excise taxation is to dedicate the revenues to financing expenditures that benefit those who are taxed. Thus, the benefit principle of taxation can be applied directly through selective excise taxation. One example of an earmarked selective excise tax of this type is the excise tax on airline tickets used to finance the Airport and Airway Trust Fund.[7] Taxes are paid into the fund by airline passengers, and money disbursed from the fund is used to improve air traffic control facilities, runways, and terminal areas.

There is general agreement among aviation experts that the money could be productively spent, particularly in updating the air traffic control system, and the establishment of the Airport and Airway Trust Fund with its ear-

**TABLE 4.2**
**Airport and Airway Trust Fund (totals in billions of dollars)**

| Year | Receipts | Outlays | Balance |
|------|----------|---------|---------|
| 1975 | 1.1 | 0.6 | 2.0 |
| 1980 | 2.3 | 1.2 | 5.4 |
| 1981 | 0.6 | 1.3 | 4.7 |
| 1982 | 0.7 | 1.5 | 3.9 |
| 1983 | 2.7 | 1.8 | 4.8 |
| 1984 | 3.0 | 1.4 | 6.4 |
| 1985 | 3.6 | 2.6 | 7.4 |
| 1986 | 3.6 | 2.4 | 8.6 |
| 1987 | 3.9 | 2.6 | 9.9 |
| 1988 | 4.1 | 2.9 | 11.1 |
| 1989 | 4.7 | 2.8 | 13.0 |
| 1990 | 5.1 | 4.0 | 14.2 |
| 1991 | 6.2 | 5.3 | 15.3 |
| 1992 | 5.9 | 6.0 | 15.2 |
| 1993 | 4.0 | 7.0 | 13.0 |
| 1994 | 6.0 | 7.0 | 12.0 |
| 1995 | 7.0 | 7.0 | 12.0 |

*Source*: U.S. Bureau of the Census, various years.

marked source of revenues was welcomed by the aviation industry. As the benefit principle of taxation suggests, the airlines viewed the fund as an opportunity for them to pool their resources in order to undertake expenditures for the collective benefit of the taxpaying group. Since it was established, though, the trust fund has not worked out as well as those in the industry had hoped. The fund has built up a huge surplus of unspent revenues. Table 4.2 summarizes some of the Airport and Airway Trust Fund's history.

As table 4.2 shows, the Airport and Airway Trust Fund's receipts have usually exceeded its outlays by a wide margin. In 1980, the fund had receipts approximately double its outlays, and a balance of more than twice its 1980 receipts. Receipts dropped substantially in 1981 and 1982, which were recession years (and the only two years during the 1980s when outlays exceeded receipts), but the trust fund continued to grow throughout the decade. From a beginning balance of $5.4 billion in 1980, the fund's balance grew to $13 billion by decade's end, and continued to grow through the early 1990s. The trust fund's growth has apparently slowed in the mid-1990s, in part due to industry lobbying, to the point where receipts and outlays are roughly equal. Still, a substantial surplus remains despite the well-publicized problems plaguing the federal infrastructure that serves the industry.

In this case, the industry being taxed favors the earmarked tax to finance projects supported by the fund. The problem is that expenditures have not been made after revenues have been collected. The reason is that the fund's receipts and outlays are on-budget items. Thus, receipts into the fund lower the federal budget deficit and outlays from the fund raise it. Because red ink is politically unpopular, the fund has remained largely unspent in order to help reduce the federal deficit.

The stated purpose of the selective excise tax earmarked for the Airport and Airway Trust Fund was to create a surrogate for a user charge, but as the history of the fund shows, political expediency can thwart the original intent of a tax. From a political standpoint, the problem with excise tax receipts going into the trust fund is that the taxpayers and intended beneficiaries are a minority of the population, and in a majority-rule system, it is easy for the peripherally related goals of the majority (in this case, the goal of deficit reduction) to derail a program intended to benefit a minority. In theory, having airline passengers pay for aviation improvements through an excise tax on airfares is a sound idea. In reality, once the tax money is collected, it can be held hostage by a majority in the political process rather than being used as it was originally intended.

If the result of this process were merely a transfer from excise taxpayers to the general public, the economic implications would be relatively minor. Apparently, the taxed industry believes that the improvements to aviation facilities that could be purchased with the tax dollars are worth the cost, so there could be a welfare loss as a result of too little government production in

this area. However, once the program was established and the aviation industry was being taxed to pay for the improvements, the industry wanted the
revenues to be spent for that purpose. When the expenditures were not made,
the industry engaged in lobbying in order to try to persuade Congress to spend
money that had already been collected. This is the classic rent-seeking situation, where the rent-seeking costs must be added to the social-welfare losses
resulting from inefficiently allocated resources.

The Airport and Airway Trust Fund provides an example of a selective
excise tax that was enacted in order to approximate a user charge in a manner
consistent with standard public-finance theory. However, once the program
was established, political pressures resulted in the revenues not being used
for the purpose for which they were intended. Even when selective excise
taxes are established for sound purposes that are favored by the taxpayers,
political incentives are still able to work against the efficient allocation of
resources, and political costs are still incurred by those who have an interest
in the disposition of the tax revenues.[8]

## Special Interests and Cigarette Taxes

Tobacco provides a good example of a selectively taxed product whose
consumption is politically unpopular. Cigarette taxes are the prototypical sin
tax. This section looks at the way state tobacco taxes are imposed in the United
States to see if they are levied in a manner consistent with the idea that consumption of the good is undesirable, or if the interest-group explanation for
tobacco taxes is more persuasive. A regression model is used to explain variations in the tax per pack of cigarettes, $TTAX$, in forty-nine of the fifty United
States.[9]

If the standard explanations for excise taxes are valid and excise taxes are
in fact applied mainly to raise revenue or to internalize externalities, then one
would expect to find substantial similarity in excise tax structures among the
states. States that rely relatively heavily on one excise tax would be expected
to rely heavily on others as well. Thus, one would expect to find a positive
correlation between tobacco taxes in a state and the gasoline tax per gallon,
$GTAX$. If interest-group politics explains more of the cross-state variation in
tax structures, on the other hand, one would expect to find less of a correlation between $TTAX$ and $GTAX$.

Undoubtedly those with the strongest interests in opposing tobacco taxes
are the tobacco growers. If they are able to influence the political process, one
would expect tobacco taxes to be lower in those states with a substantial amount
of tobacco farming. The variable $TA/POP$ measures tobacco acres per capita
in a state, and is expected to be negatively correlated with $TTAX$.

Other pressure groups are also involved in attempting to influence tobacco
taxes. If tobacco taxes really are viewed as sin taxes, then the strength of

organized religious interests in a state should also be influential. The variable *%CHRIST* represents the percentage of a state's population belonging to an organized Christian religion, and is expected to have a positive influence on *TTAX*. As people become more conscious of health hazards associated with exposure to secondhand smoke, political opposition to smoking in public places has strengthened. People in metropolitan areas are more likely to oppose smoking for this reason; *%METRO* measures the percentage of a state's population living in metropolitan areas, and is expected to have a positive effect on a state's tobacco tax. While *TA/POP* and *%CHRIST* are clearly special-interest variables, *%METRO* might be interpreted in two ways. It proxies the interests of those who might be bothered by secondhand smoke, but it also might represent the external cost smokers potentially impose on nonsmokers. In either case, its expected sign is positive, and in either case it represents the interests of nonsmokers.

The regression model was estimated for two years, 1985 and 1991, both to see that the results are robust and to see what changes might have occurred over time.[10] The results for 1985 are (absolute values of *t*-statistics in parentheses):

$$TTAX = 3.26 + .21GTAX - .35TA/POP + .15\%CHRIST + .05\%METRO + e.$$
$$\quad\ (0.28)\quad (0.89)\qquad (4.81)\qquad\quad (2.57)\qquad\qquad (1.76)$$

$R^2 = .45$

These results lend support to the special-interest theory of selective excise taxation. The coefficient on *GTAX* is not statistically significant, indicating that there is no consistent relationship between these two excise taxes among the states.[11] If excise taxes are used primarily as a tool of efficient public finance, this variable should be positive and significant; the fact that it is not calls into question the standard public-finance justifications for excise taxes. The special-interest variables *TA/POP* and *%CHRIST* have the expected algebraic signs and are statistically significant, showing that states with stronger tobacco interests have significantly lower tobacco taxes while those with stronger religious interests have significantly higher tobacco taxes, ceteris paribus. The estimated coefficient on *%METRO* is significant at the 10 percent level, and positive as expected, providing some evidence that tobacco taxes are higher in states where residents live in closer proximity to their neighbors.

The same regression was run with 1991 data, yielding the following coefficient estimates (absolute values of *t*-statistics again in parentheses):

$$TTAX = 4.75 + .14GTAX - .43TA/POP + .03\%CHRIST + .24\%METRO + e.$$
$$\quad\ (0.51)\quad (0.51)\qquad (3.48)\qquad\quad (0.32)\qquad\qquad (2.70)$$

$R^2 = .37$

The results for 1991 are qualitatively similar to those for the earlier year. All of the coefficient signs are the same, but some changes in significance of the variables did occur. *GTAX* is again not significant, while *TA/POP* is negative and significant. The coefficient on *TA/POP* is slightly larger in 1991 than in 1985. The coefficient on *%CHRIST* falls from .15 to .03, with the result that in 1991 it is no longer significantly different from zero. The magnitude and significance level of the estimated coefficient on *%METRO* increased between 1985 and 1991.

These results lend additional support to the interest-group theory of selective excise taxation. To reiterate, if revenue were the main motivation for excise taxes, *GTAX* and *TTAX* should be positively correlated, but there was not a statistically significant relationship in either regression. A model developed later in the chapter suggests that an important difference between tobacco taxes and gas taxes is the proportion of the population that pays each tax. The gas tax is a very broadly based excise tax, so it is expected to be less subject to special-interest pressures, whereas tobacco taxes, as more narrowly based taxes, are expected to be more influenced by special interests.[12] Meanwhile, the most significant variable in both regressions is *TA/POP*, indicating that there is a stronger relationship between tobacco interests and tobacco taxes than any of the other variables in the model. There was a surprising decline in the significance of *%CHRIST*, measuring religious interests within a state.[13] *%METRO* becomes more important as an explanatory variable in 1991, having both a larger coefficient and a smaller standard error.

The increase in the significance of *%METRO* suggests that those who are affected by the proximity of smokers through secondhand smoke or other factors have lately had more of an influence on tobacco taxes. This variable has a straightforward public-finance interpretation in that tobacco taxes can be looked at as a way of correcting a negative externality. It also is an interest-group variable because the people affected by the externality comprise an interest group that wants action taken to reduce the external costs they bear. Thus, even while thinking of selective excise taxes as determined through the political pressures of interest groups, it must be recognized that interest groups can be motivated by economic costs and benefits as much as by incentives to capture transfers. Becker (1983) models a relatively efficient political market in which costs and benefits are weighed rationally, but interest groups are not likely to discriminate sharply between the various types of benefits (real economic gains versus pure transfers) available through rent-seeking processes.

### Welfare Losses from Selective Excise Taxation

When the political environment within which selective excise taxes are enacted is taken into account, the welfare losses from selective excise taxes are significantly higher than those from broad-based taxes. The reason is that with selective excise taxes, a subset of the population is being taxed to provide revenues that can be used for the benefit of the majority.[14] Thus, interest groups have more at stake with selective excise taxes. With broad-based taxes, the population at large will be put in a position of evaluating whether the value of the expenditures to be undertaken with the tax revenues will be more than the cost imposed by the broad-based tax. With selective excise taxes, the majority has an opportunity to get something for nothing by establishing a selective tax that imposes costs on others. However, an attempt to impose selective excise taxes will meet resistance from those who are called upon to pay them. Those who will be taxed will incur costs to try to prevent the taxes from being approved (and will try to repeal them if they are approved), while those who want the taxes to be approved will incur costs to push their agenda. These costs, which are the result of pitting one interest group against another, will not be incurred for general broad-based taxes for which everyone has the same interest.

The source of the welfare losses associated with selective excise taxation is relatively easy to understand, and was illustrated clearly in the preceding examples. With broad-based taxes, taxpayers have common interests and do not enter the political process and use resources against each other. While it is true that some interest groups do try to narrow the bases of broad-based taxes to exempt themselves from taxation, and that some taxpayers pay more than others with broad-based taxes, taxpayers' interests are much more congruent the more broadly based a tax is. With selective excise taxation, groups with opposing interests are created, and have incentives to use resources within the political process to further their own agendas. Thus, selective excise taxes create economic costs that are not associated with general broad-based taxes.

If selective excise taxes impose greater costs on the economy than broad-based taxes, why would they be used? First, those who will not pay the taxes have an incentive to try to get others to foot the bill for government expenditures. Second, politicians who want to increase revenues may encounter general opposition to broad-based taxes, but if they can restrict their tax-raising efforts to a small segment of the population, they may find a majority who would favor the tax despite its costs—because the bulk of those costs will be borne by a minority of voters. The next section of the chapter looks at how these political costs will vary depending upon the breadth of a proposed selective excise tax base.

## The Political Costs

In order to see the political pressures behind selective excise taxation, this section develops a simple model of the tax process. The typical excise tax, such as a tax on beer, will be borne by a large cross-section of the population, but some people will be hit harder than others. Furthermore, suppliers in a taxed industry can always expect to suffer from an excise tax, regardless of the breadth of its incidence on consumers. Other excise taxes, such as a tax on cigarettes, are targeted at a minority of the population, with most people left untaxed. For modeling simplicity, this section starts with the assumption that the population can be divided into two groups: those who pay the tax and those who do not. The political marketplace is then used as the forum to decide how broad the excise tax base will be.[15]

The first step in examining the political costs of selective excise taxation is to consider the strength of the political opposition of those who will bear the tax. Just as rent seekers will become involved in the political process to attempt to capture politically generated rents, so will those who are the target of politically imposed costs become involved in the political process to try to avoid those costs.[16] Following Tullock (1967), those who are threatened with the prospect of being taxed will be willing to expend as much as the expected increase in the tax in order to avoid having to pay it. Expenditures made to avoid taxation, while productive for the individual, are a net loss from a social standpoint, and this is one component of the political costs of selective excise taxation.

From an analytical standpoint, the total costs of rent seeking into the tax code can be broken down into two components. First, one can examine the amount that each individual in the group to be taxed would be willing to spend to avoid the tax. Second, one can look at the number of individuals in the group. Multiplying the political costs incurred by each member times the number in the group yields the total political costs incurred by the group on which the burden of the tax will fall. Consider the strength of an individual taxpayer's opposition to a selective excise tax of magnitude T. For simplicity, assume that the tax revenue will be redistributed and shared equally among all members of society, and that N percent of the population will find themselves in the taxpaying group. If we assume further that there are no costs of collecting taxes, the analysis is greatly simplified, because each tax dollar returns a dollar of benefits to some citizen. In this case, the cost of the tax imposed on an individual taxpayer is the amount of the tax minus the share that the individual will get back when the revenues are redistributed, or T − (N*T/100). When 1 percent of the population pays the tax, N = 1, and a cost of .99T is imposed on the taxpayer. As N increases, the burden declines linearly until, when N = 100, everybody is taxed and the net burden, including the distribution of tax revenues, equals zero.

A number of factors might affect this specific relationship, making the cost imposed on the taxpayer something other than T − (N*T/100). The excess burden of taxation should be included, along with the recognition that there will be administrative costs, and that the benefits a particular taxpayer receives may be greater (or lower) than those given to the population as a whole. While these factors might affect the specific relationship, the cost to the taxpayer will still decline linearly with an increase in the number of taxpayers. So more generally, substituting constant a for T and a constant b for T/100, the cost imposed on the individual taxpayer can be represented by

$$S = a - b*N. \tag{1}$$

The left-hand variable S is the strength of the taxpayer's opposition, assuming that it varies with the individual's share of the tax. However, following Olson (1965), small groups may be able to organize more effectively than large groups, so it is possible that there will be more rapid decay in the strength of the taxpayer's opposition as the taxpaying group grows. Thus, an alternative assumption, which represents what can be called the Olson effect, implies an exponential decay in support, so

$$S = a/N. \tag{1a}$$

These two alternative assumptions determine the strength of an individual taxpayer's opposition to the selective excise tax. In order to determine the total political cost, the cost the individual is willing to incur must be multiplied by the number of affected individuals, which will be directly proportional to N. People might over- or underinvest in rent-seeking activities, so allowing for either possibility, and representing the size of the opposing group as P,

$$P = f*N, \tag{2}$$

where f is a constant. This seemingly simple relationship is worth at least one additional remark, since Wittman (1989) has argued that, in contrast to most of the interest-group literature, large groups have an advantage due to their greater size and greater voting power.[17] Thus, equation (2) directly captures what might be called the Wittman effect.

The total rent-seeking losses from those who oppose the selective excise tax can be represented by R, and will be the strength of the opposition from each potential taxpayer times the size of the group, represented by the Wittman effect, which is S*P, or equation (1) times equation (2). If equation (1) is represented as in (1a) to incorporate the Olson effect, rent-seeking losses as a function of the breadth of coverage of the tax will be given by

$$R = a/N * (b*N). \tag{3}$$

N can be divided out in equation (3), and because a and b are constants, they can be represented as c = a*b, another constant, yielding

$$R = c. \tag{4}$$

If we make the assumptions implied by the Wittman and Olson effects, the rent-seeking losses will not vary regardless of how comprehensive the proposed excise tax is. The greater number of individuals involved in rent-seeking activity, which is the Wittman effect, is just offset by the exponential reduction in rent-seeking activity on the part of each individual. This result is worth noting because it shows a set of assumptions under which any tax, no matter how broad or narrow, has the same political costs associated with it as any other tax.

The Olson effect embodied in equation (4) implies a decay in individuals' oppositional activity that is more rapid than the decay in individuals' tax burdens. If the linear decay from equation (1) is used instead, which means that individuals take full account of their economic interests and that there are not any organizational problems associated with larger groups,[18]

$$R = (a - b*N) * (f*N). \tag{5}$$

Consider the case where the strength of the opposition decays linearly to zero as N approaches 100 percent of the group. Then equation (1) can be rewritten as $S = 100b - b*N$, and equation (5) becomes $R = (100b - b*N)*(f*N)$, which simplifies to

$$R = bf*(100N - N^2). \tag{6}$$

Taking the first derivative of equation (6) and setting it equal to zero yields $N = 50$ as the opposition-maximizing group size. In other words, rent-seeking costs of those opposing the tax will be maximized when 50 percent of the population will be required to pay it. Substituting zero and 100 for N in equation (6) shows that under these assumptions, rent-seeking costs will be zero at either extreme.

This simple model suggests that the political costs of selective excise taxes will be minimized either when nobody is taxed ($N = 0$) or when everybody is taxed ($N = 100$).[19] The political costs of rent seeking by those who will be liable for the tax are maximized at $N = 50$, or when the burden of the proposed selective excise tax would fall on exactly half the population. If the strength of opposition decays exponentially, as with the Olson effect shown in equation (1a), then the political costs do not vary with the size of the taxed group. But even if the outcome is somewhere between the two extremes represented by equations (1) and (1a), the conclusion is still that taxes covering about half the population exact the highest political costs.

Interpreting equation (6), the political costs associated with general broad-based taxes that apply to 100 percent of the population are zero, because all taxpayers have a common interest. As the tax base declines from 100 percent of the population, the political costs rise as a political opposition group is created, and the political costs are at a maximum when the selective tax covers half the population. Beyond that point the political costs begin to fall, reaching zero when the tax covers zero percent of the population. The key conclusion from equation (6) is that the political costs associated with lobbying to avoid selective excise taxation are maximized when the selective excise tax covers half the population.

## Rent Seeking on the Revenue Side

Some individuals will be beneficiaries of tax revenues but, with selective excise taxation, will not have to pay the tax cost. This causes rent seeking on the revenue side of the issue, as potential beneficiaries lobby to have selective excise taxes imposed on others. For a given tax rate, the revenue raised will increase linearly with the number of taxpayers. Representing the revenue raised as G and the individual's tax liability as X, $G = X*N$. Revenue is maximized when everyone pays the tax, but when everyone is taxed, there is no interest group that favors the tax because of its redistributive effects. As the proportion of the population that pays the tax goes down, the interest group of nontaxpayers who favor the tax will rise linearly, approaching 100 percent as the taxpaying population goes to zero. The effect of the size of the benefiting interest group, T, can be represented by $T = (100y - y*N)$, where y is a constant. The rent-seeking incentive is the size effect times the revenue raised, or $G*T$. G is the same functional form as in equation (2), while T is the same form as equation (1), so the product, represented as H, follows the form of equation (6) and is

$$H = xy*(100N - N^2).  \tag{7}$$

The similarity between equations (6) and (7) should not be surprising, because equation (6) shows the rent-seeking incentives of those who will be taxed, while equation (7) shows the rent-seeking incentives of the untaxed beneficiaries of the resulting expenditures. Because the excise tax is modeled as a transfer, the benefits to the gainers will equal the costs to the losers. In a transfer like this, the gains of the gainers are the highest when the losses of the losers are the highest. As in equation (6), taking the first derivative of equation (7) shows that rent-seeking costs are at their maximum when $N = 50$, or when the excise tax is imposed on 50 percent of the population.

## Political Equilibrium

The legislature acts as a political market, following Becker (1983), where opposing interests are weighed against each other in order to produce a political equilibrium outcome. This section compares the political demands of those opposing a selective excise tax with the demands of those in favor of it to find the politically optimal size of a selective excise tax base—optimal in terms of maximizing the political support for the tax. Subtracting the demand of those opposed in equation (6) from those in favor in equation (7) and calling the result M yields

$$M = xy*(100N - N^2) - bf*(100N - N^2).  \tag{8}$$

Simplifying and taking the first derivative,

$$dM/dN = (xy - bf)*(100 - 2N),  \tag{9}$$

and setting $dM/dN = 0$ shows that M has an extremum at $N = 50$. If $xy > bf$, M is maximized at $N = 50$, and the politically optimal excise tax covers half the population. This also maximizes the rent-seeking losses from the selective excise tax. If $xy < bf$, M is minimized at $N = 50$, and the maxima occur at $N = 0$ and $N = 100$.

Constants bf and xy from equations (5) and (7), respectively, show the relative strengths of the rent-seeking incentives of the groups to be taxed and left untaxed. When xy > bf, those in favor of selective excise taxation engage in more rent seeking and have a higher political demand for the tax. When supporters are stronger than opponents, the politically optimal selective excise tax covers half the population and maximizes the rent-seeking losses from selective excise taxation. When those opposed engage in more rent seeking (or, more accurately, rent-avoiding) activity than those in favor, xy < bf, and the politically optimal tax is either zero or a completely general broad-based tax, covering 100 percent of the population.

Practical considerations might modify this result somewhat, because excise taxes must be levied on some tax base, and it may be difficult to find tax bases such that taxes cover exactly half the population. Nevertheless, there is some intuition to these results, in that those in favor of imposing an excise tax on someone else will derive more benefits from the revenues the broader is the tax base. However, if the tax applies to more than 50 percent of the population, the political support for it will decline because more than a majority of the population will be taxed. As the breadth of the tax base increases, then assuming that the expenditures are equally distributed throughout the population, the tax becomes less and less redistributive because people are paying more of the tax cost of financing the benefits they will receive.

An excise tax covering exactly 50 percent of the population maximizes the rent-seeking expenditures both for and against the tax, but also maximizes the political support for the excise tax. In this model, when taxes are established they either are completely general, covering 100 percent of the population and entailing relatively small welfare losses, or cover about half the population and entail large welfare losses from rent-seeking and rent-avoiding activities. The politically optimal selective excise tax is also the one that maximizes the social cost of selective excise taxation.[20]

## Selective versus General Taxation

The standard theory of public finance opposes narrowly based taxes such as selective excise taxes in most cases. The excess burden of taxation is minimized when taxes are broadly based so that the marginal tax rate is minimized for the amount of revenue that is raised.[21] Still, selective excise taxes have been promoted using a number of economic efficiency arguments, as previously noted. These include minimization of excess burden when goods have different demand elasticities (following the Ramsey rule) as well as correcting an externality, discouraging consumption of undesirable goods, and implementing the benefit principle. One of the more intriguing rationales for the narrow tax bases implied by selective excise taxation was given by Brennan and Buchanan (1980), who argued that if government is a revenue-maximizing Leviathan, then narrowing the tax base available to the government can act as a constraint on the government's revenue-raising powers. Is this an argument for selective excise taxation rather than broad-based general taxes?

The Brennan and Buchanan argument assumes government to be a revenue-maximizing Leviathan unhindered by political constraints in its pursuit of tax revenue. In the real world, some political constraints exist. However, Holcombe and Mills (1994) extend the Brennan and Buchanan model by incorporating political constraints and show that even within an explicitly political environment, the Brennan and Buchanan conclusions hold, and broader tax bases increase government revenue. Holcombe and Mills present empirical evidence from 1986 U.S. income tax reform legislation, as well as from the European Community's introduction of the value-added tax, suggesting that while nations adopting base-broadening taxes explicitly stated an intention that reform be revenue-neutral, they actually ended up increasing tax collections by substantial amounts. Thus, an argument can be made for a narrow tax base rather than a broad one.

This argument does not imply the desirability of selective excise taxation, however, especially when a selective excise tax is added to an existing set of taxes rather than used as a replacement for a broader-based tax. Because the imposition of a new selective excise tax does not repeal any other taxes, a selective excise tax always either broadens the tax base or (if the good is already taxed) creates a differential tax rate for the taxed good. Thus, the Brennan and Buchanan argument would always weigh against selective excise taxes unless the proposed selective tax were designed to replace an existing broad-based tax.

The Brennan and Buchanan argument deals with how broad a tax base should be. For example, what items should be excluded from taxable income? Should a retail sales tax be applied to food? To services? Political determination of those issues is prone to the same type of political costs discussed in this chapter, and those political costs were not incorporated into the Brennan and Buchanan model. Still, the issue of how broad a tax base should be is different from deciding whether specific goods or services should be singled out for a selective excise tax. Buchanan (1993) recognizes that when the issue is broad-based general taxes versus selective excise taxes, the broad-based taxes are preferable.

## Conclusion

Selective excise taxes can be justified on a number of theoretical grounds. They might be applied as a corrective tax on an externality. They might be used as a surrogate for a user charge, with the revenues dedicated to financing expenditures that benefit the taxed group. They might be used as an optimal revenue-generating device when some goods have more elastic demands than others. These justifications all look at excise taxes as applied by a government guided by the single goal of economic efficiency. In reality, excise taxes are the outcome of a political process in which opposing interests express their demands in the legislative arena. The legislature acts as a broker of these demands, balancing the political forces on both sides of an issue to produce a political equilibrium outcome. When one recognizes that excise taxes are the product of political pressures rather than the rote application of standard welfare economics, the standard justifications for selective excise taxation are on shaky ground.

The problem is that selective excise taxes always place more of a burden on some groups than on others. Those who bear the burden have an incentive to expend resources to enter the political process to try to prevent the taxes from being enacted, or to repeal them if they already have been enacted. Those who benefit from the revenue, or who might bear higher taxes if the particular tax in question is not implemented, have an incentive to incur costs to try to see that the tax is enacted. These political costs impose the same types of rent-seeking welfare losses on society that Gordon Tullock (1967) described decades ago. Because of these political costs, selective excise taxation imposes a larger excess burden on an economy than would a general tax raising the same amount of revenue. With a general tax, citizens can weigh the costs of the tax against the benefits of the expenditure. With a selective tax, some people will bear heavy costs while others bear almost none. From a political standpoint, general taxation will be evaluated more from an efficiency standpoint, while selective excise taxation will be more of a distributive issue.

In theory, selective excise taxation might be justified as a corrective tax on an externality or as an earmarked tax to provide benefits to those in the taxed group. For example, Barthold (1994) discusses environmental excise taxes in an economic framework, ignoring the political process that produces those taxes. In reality, it is politics, not the prescriptions of public-finance economists, that determines the tax structure. An examination of state cigarette taxes in the United States showed that interest-group variables were better able to explain the levels of those taxes than economic variables. Even when an excise tax is earmarked to benefit the taxpayers, the revenues may be diverted toward other purposes once they are collected, as the example of the federal Airport and Airway Trust Fund showed. An analysis of selective excise taxation is not complete unless it accounts for the political environment in which those taxes are created, and when the political environment is considered, selective excise taxes have political costs associated with them far exceeding those of general, economy-wide taxes. This chapter examined some evidence on the political costs associated with selective excise taxation of soft drinks, and while the data were sketchy, it was clear that the political costs associated with selective excise taxes are substantial.

Given the political environment in which selective excise taxes are created, a simple model was developed to look at the political costs as a function of the breadth of the tax base. The model assumed the tax was levied on a subset of the population, that all taxpayers paid the same amount, and that the benefits of the tax were spread equally across the population. The model then looked at the political opposition and support that would be produced by broadening or narrowing the tax base, and assumed that the tax base that received the greatest net political support would be chosen. There were three possible outcomes that could maximize political support under the model: no tax, a completely general tax covering the entire population, or an excise tax covering half the population. It turned out that the excise tax attracting the greatest political support was also the excise tax that maximized the political cost of excise taxation.

This result has some intuitive appeal, because if excise taxes are viewed as transfers from the taxpayers, the transfer that confers the greatest net benefit to the beneficiaries is also the one that imposes the greatest net cost on the taxpayers. Because the political costs incurred by both supporters and opponents of an excise tax will be in proportion to the costs and benefits they expect to bear or receive, the tax that creates the greatest benefit to some shifts the greatest cost to others, and induces both groups to expend the greatest amount of resources to promote their interests. Thus, the excise tax chosen in the political market will be the one with the greatest political cost.

The conclusion of this chapter is straightforward. General economy-wide taxes minimize the political costs and associated welfare losses from taxation. Selective excise taxes create large political costs and associated welfare losses, and the most politically popular excise taxes will be the ones with the largest political costs. Thus, the tax policy that would minimize the resources expended in the political arena to determine the tax structure is one that relies on broad-based taxes rather than selective excise taxes. Fortunately, this conclusion, based on an analysis of the political costs of selective excise taxation, also corresponds closely to the conclusion that would be arrived at to design an economically efficient tax structure.

Arguments in favor of selective excise taxes essentially are arguments about tinkering with the fringes of tax policy. They assume that within an efficient revenue-generating structure that relies mainly on broad-based taxes, a benevolent government with no political pressures could adjust the tax rate on this good or that to squeeze out a bit more economic efficiency or generate a bit more revenue. When the political costs associated with selective excise taxation are considered, it is apparent that the use of selective excise taxes is, in general, not good tax policy.

## Notes

1. Of course, such rent-seeking activity may create welfare losses in the economy, as described by Tullock (1967) and Krueger (1974). Tullock (1975) shows that the gains to the gainers are likely to be transitory as well. Many people have

observed that the government is inefficient as a producer of goods and services. Tullock's model (1975) shows that the government may not even be very successful in attempts to give things away.

2. People might favor a tax on their own activities as an incentive to reduce behavior they might view as undesirable. See Crain et al. 1977 for a discussion of this possibility.

3. Buchanan (1993), arguing in favor of broad-based taxes, draws similar conclusions with regard to his 1980 book with Brennan.

4. Much of the information in this section on soft-drink taxes is found in National Soft Drink Association 1992.

5. Brinig, Holcombe, and Schwartzstein (1993) view lobbying regulations as a way for legislators to discover the lobbying organizations' willingness to pay for legislation, so that legislators can price discriminate among demanders of legislation and favor high-demand legislation over low-demand legislation. Brinig, Holcombe, and Schwartzstein discuss details of differences among states in lobbying regulations.

6. As Landes and Posner (1975) point out, transfers that are vulnerable to repeal are worth less than more durable transfers, suggesting the benefits of constitutional mandates or prohibitions on taxes rather than legislation. The sugar industry in Florida has started an attempt to shelter itself from some of the costs of Everglades cleanup through a constitutional amendment, for example.

7. Money for the trust fund comes primarily from an excise tax on airline tickets, but other revenue sources have contributed to the fund in some years. The tax expired temporarily on 1 January 1996; it was reimposed in March 1997.

8. The Clinton administration is examining the possibility of separating air traffic control from the Federal Aviation Administration and making air traffic control the responsibility of an independent government-owned corporation, much like the U.S. Postal Service. This would insulate air traffic control to a degree from political pressures, and perhaps might make air traffic control as efficient as mail delivery.

9. Hawaii is excluded because Hawaii taxes cigarettes as a percentage of the wholesale price rather than using a per pack tax like all other states.

10. All data are from U.S. Bureau of the Census, various years. *TTAX* excludes municipal taxes on tobacco.

11. One might be concerned that the low level of significance of *GTAX* is due to correlation between *GTAX* and *%METRO*, but when *%METRO* is dropped from the regression, *GTAX* does not become more significant.

12. While the gas tax is broadly based when looking at consumers of gasoline, it is narrowly based in terms of sellers, so should generate more special-interest activity than a general sales tax.

13. One explanation is that moral considerations have less to do with excise taxes nowadays. In examining the data, there is also a surprising amount of change in the *%CHRIST* variable. Many states report large declines in the fraction of the population who are church members, but a few states report increases.

14. The taxpayers may also receive benefits, but as a rule the value of these benefits will be less than their tax price.

15. Hettich and Winer (1988) develop a model of political influences in the design of an income tax structure. The present model is in the same spirit, but examines selective excise taxation, where some people are exempt from the tax, rather than income taxation, where peoples' burdens depend on their incomes and the degree of progressivity in tax rates. With regard to the income tax, the pretax distribution of income may shift to counteract progressive taxation, as explained

by Holcombe and Caudill (1989). No similar effect is likely for selective excise taxation, so resources expended in the political process may be even greater with excise taxation than with income taxation.

16. McChesney (1987) discusses the rent-seeking implications of a legislature that can impose costs on groups as well as distribute benefits. In this situation, rent-seeking losses can far exceed the losses implied by the model in which rent seekers compete only for positive benefits.
17. For examples of interest-group literature that Wittman believes does not take adequate note of this size effect, see Weingast, Shepsle, and Johnsen 1981 and Holcombe (1985).
18. Wittman (1989) suggests that there are not. While people may free ride, as Olson (1965) suggests, when groups get larger, there may also be economies of scale in organizing large political groups.
19. See Buchanan (1993) for a similar conclusion that general taxation is more efficient than selective taxation. Buchanan recognizes that his conclusions are at odds with those in Brennan and Buchanan (1980).
20. Kaempfer and Lowenberg (1988) develop a model in which the supply and demand for political support is a function of the ability of groups to organize. Differential organizational costs allow for a result other than 50 percent in their model.
21. This was the theoretical rationale for the 1986 income tax reform in the United States. See Hall and Rabushka (1985) for a theoretical defense of broad-based taxes.

## References

Barthold, Thomas A. 1994. "Issues in the Design of Environmental Excise Taxes." *Journal of Economic Perspectives* 8 (Winter): pp. 133–51.

Becker, Gary S. 1983. "A Theory of Competition Among Pressure Groups for Political Influence." *Quarterly Journal of Economics* 98 (August): 371–400.

Brennan, Geoffrey, and James M. Buchanan. 1980. *The Power to Tax.* Cambridge: Cambridge University Press.

Brinig, Margaret F., Randall G. Holcombe, and Linda Schwartzstein. 1993. "The Regulation of Lobbyists." *Public Choice* 77 (October): 377–84.

Buchanan, James M. 1993. "The Political Efficiency of General Taxation." *National Tax Journal* 46 (December): 401–10.

Crain, Mark, Thomas Deaton, Randall Holcombe, and Robert Tollison. 1977. "Rational Choice and the Taxation of Sin." *Journal of Public Economics* 8:239–45.

Hall, Robert E., and Alvin Rabushka. 1985. *The Flat Tax.* Stanford, Calif.: Hoover Institution Press.

Hettich, Walter, and Stanley L. Winer. 1988. "Economic and Political Foundations of Tax Structure." *American Economic Review* 78 (September): 701–12.

Holcombe, Randall G. 1985. *An Economic Analysis of Democracy.* Carbondale: Southern Illinois University Press.

Holcombe, Randall G., and Steven B. Caudill. 1989. "Taxation and the Redistribution of Income." *Atlantic Economic Journal* 17 (September): 39–42.

Holcombe, Randall G., and Jeffrey A. Mills. 1994. "Is Revenue-Neutral Tax Reform Revenue Neutral?" *Public Finance Quarterly* 22 (January): 65–85.

Kaempfer, William H., and Anton D. Lowenberg. 1988. "The Theory of International Economic Sanctions: A Public Choice Approach." *American Economic Review* 78 (September): 786–93.

Krueger, Anne O. 1974. "The Political Economy of the Rent-Seeking Society." *American Economic Review* 64 (June): 291–303.

Landes, William M., and Richard A. Posner. 1975. "The Independent Judiciary in an Interest-Group Perspective." *Journal of Law and Economics* 18 (December): 875–901.

McChesney, Fred S. 1987. "Rent Extraction and Rent Creation in the Economic Theory of Regulation." *Journal of Legal Studies* 16 (January): 101–18.

National Soft Drink Association. 1992. *Soft Drinks, Hard Taxes*. Washington, D.C.: National Soft Drink Association.

Olson, Mancur. 1965. *The Logic of Collective Action: Public Goods and the Theory of Groups*. Cambridge: Harvard University Press.

Tullock, Gordon. 1967. "The Welfare Cost of Tariffs, Monopolies, and Theft." *Western Economic Journal* 5 (June): 224–32.

———. 1975. "The Transitional Gains Trap." *Bell Journal of Economics* 6 (Autumn): 671–78.

U.S. Bureau of the Census. Various years. *Statistical Abstract of the United States*. Washington, D.C.: U.S. Government Printing Office.

Weingast, Barry R., Kenneth A. Shepsle, and Christopher Johnsen. 1981. "The Political Economy of Benefits and Costs: A Neoclassical Approach to Distributive Politics." *Journal of Political Economy* 89 (August): 642–64.

Wittman, Donald. 1989. "Why Democracies Produce Efficient Results." *Journal of Political Economy* 97 (December): 1395–1424.

# 5

# Overcoming Taxpayer Resistance by Taxing Choice and Earmarking Revenues

*Dwight R. Lee*

An aging Muhammad Ali was once asked if he was continuing to fight because he needed the money. His response was, and I am paraphrasing here, that of course he needed more money, but so does everyone, even the government. The only way Ali could have improved on his response would have been by saying, "especially the government."

No matter how much of our money is captured through taxes, there seems to be no lessening in the desire of politicians, and their special-interest clients, for yet more. The desire for more is, of course, everywhere insatiable, but this insatiability is particularly acute among those whose interests are served by an ever-expanding public sector. For most of us, the desire for more is disciplined by the fact that we have to pay the entire cost of satisfying that desire. By exercising political influence, however, organized interests can secure benefits that are concentrated on them while the costs are imposed primarily on others. Politicians are particularly sensitive to the exaggerated demands for government spending that result, since satisfying them is the source of their most effective political support. Costs are, of course, associated with satisfying special-interest demands, but because these costs are diffused over the general taxpaying public, there is little organized opposition to them. So the political benefit-cost ratio from government spending programs invariably exceeds the social benefit-cost ratio from that spending.

Government spending has reached the point, however, where public opposition to taxation is roughly in balance with special-interest demands for more spending. Taxpayers do not have to organize overtly to communicate to their political representatives that there are limits to the tax burdens they will bear. This communication becomes loud and clear as those limits are approached.

Increased public resistance to additional taxation has done nothing, of course, to reduce the desire of special interests for more government spending. So as taxpayer opposition to more taxation has intensified, so has political ingenuity in finding ways to circumvent that opposition and reduce the political costs of securing more tax revenue. One manifestation of this ingenuity is seen in the increase in the number of proposals put forth to impose new, or to increase old, taxes on "sin" and then earmark the additional revenues to programs that are popular because they generate easily recognized benefits or seem to promote virtuous objectives, or both. By advancing tax proposals in the name of discouraging "sin" and encouraging "virtue," politicians are able to exploit the free-rider problems associated with "rational ignorance" and "expressive voting" to push back the limits of taxpayer resistance to further tax increases.

Ideally, politicians would prefer more latitude than selective taxes and tax earmarking seem to allow. But a tax increase on "sin" is better from the politician's perspective than no tax increase at all, and, as we shall see, tax earmarking actually does little to limit the ability of politicians to allocate tax revenues over different spending alternatives in ways that maximize their political support.

## The Fungibility of Tax Revenue

There is little doubt that taxpayers are more tolerant of a tax increase if the stated objective is to reduce activities that are widely frowned upon and to increase funding for projects or programs that are widely believed to promote worthy objectives. For example, a significant majority of the population indicates support for dramatically increasing taxes on cigarettes to support health care reform, with this majority even including many who smoke.[1] And even in the face of general taxpayer hostility to tax increases during the Reagan administration, public-opinion polls found large majorities willing to go along with tax increases if the revenues were to be used for such purposes as cleaning up toxic-waste dumps, improving public education, making loans to deserving students, funding scientific research, and paying for health care programs for women and children.[2] In 1990, for example, voters in California approved an increase in the state gasoline tax with the revenues earmarked for more freeway construction.[3]

At first glance, the increased willingness of the public to support so-called sin taxes to generate revenues for particular expenditures may seem understandable. Most people have a paternalistic urge, and support for a tax penalty on objectionable behavior is a good way of giving this urge expression. And the more control members of the public feel they have over how the revenues from a tax are spent, the more favorably they can be expected to view the tax. I shall consider the importance of expressive urges in the political process in some detail later in the chapter, but in this section I concentrate on the control taxpayers appear to have over expenditures under tax earmarking.

The view that tax earmarking lowers public resistance to tax increases because it gives the public more control over expenditures faces a serious problem. In actual fact, the public has little, if any, more control over how tax revenues are spent when those revenues are earmarked than it does when they go into the general fund. Money is the most fungible of all the things we value. Indeed, the primary reason that money is valuable at all derives from its fungibility; it is immediately and easily exchanged for anything else of value. The fact that additional tax revenue from an increase in a tax is earmarked for a particular program does not mean that spending on that program will be increased by anything close to the amount of the additional revenue raised by the tax. The earmarked revenue may simply be substituted for the revenue from other sources that was being, or would have been, spent on the designated program.

A classic example is the Arkansas soft drink tax passed in 1992. In 1994 there was an attempt to repeal the measure by initiative. Then Governor Jim Guy Tucker led the opposition claiming the proceeds of the tax were used to fund the state's Medicaid program. Prior to the repeal initiative, soft drink tax revenue went into the general fund, commingled with other general revenues. Only in August 1994, in the heat of the repeal campaign, did the embattled Legislature and the Governor create the "Medicaid Trust" dedicated to receiving the proceeds of the soft drink tax for Medicaid purposes only. The result is the same. The earmarked revenues are substituted for the revenue sources used prior to 1993 to fund Medicaid and those "freed up" tax dollars are then spent by the politicians and bureaucrats on programs of their choosing.

A candid sanction for this kind of government sleight of hand appeared in the Salem, Oregon, *Statesman Journal* on 24 July 1996 in a commentary by an advocate of another proposed "earmarked" soft drink tax, this one supposedly to fund Oregon's parks system. Mr. Blankenbaker, a writer for the *Statesman Journal*, in making his case for a tax, states:

> Also, to this day there's an aversion among the State's decision makers against dedicated taxes. Historically, they want the freedom to spend the tax monies where they see fit. The point missed is that a dedicated tax can often free up the state's general fund money, money that isn't dedicated to specific uses, to bankroll more pressing needs.

So much for "earmarking"!

Substituting earmarked tax revenues for, rather than adding earmarked revenues to, general-fund spending on a particular program is not only possible, but exactly what the economic theory of politics would predict. Politicians tend to expand spending up to the point where the additional political benefits from doing so equal the additional political costs. And in the process, politicians are constantly alert to the advantages of allocating spending across different programs in ways that maximize the total political benefit derived from available revenues. This requires that the political return from spending an additional dollar be roughly the same for all programs. When such a political equilibrium is disturbed, strong incentives to restore it come into play. If, beginning from a political equilibrium, additional revenues from a tax are earmarked, and actually spent, for education, for example, the additional expenditure would drive the marginal political return from educational spending below the marginal political return from spending on alternative government programs. The political advantage would then be in substituting the earmarked revenue for much of the general revenue that would otherwise have funded educational spending. The predicted result of a large increase in government revenue from a tax earmarked to education is a small spending increase in a number of government programs (including education) rather than a large spending increase for education alone.

The tendency to circumvent the stated intention of an earmarked tax in order to maintain the political equilibrium just described is supported by more than theoretical speculation. Borg and Mason (1990), for example, examined empirically the effect of earmarking state lottery revenues to education in Florida, and found that such earmarking did not increase the share of spending going to education.

## Voting and the Free-Rider Problem

If earmarking tax revenues does not give taxpayers more control over how those revenues are spent, then why is taxpayer resistance to higher taxes weakened by tax earmarking? Having justified a tax as a sin tax, why do politicians bother to take the next step, which they so often do, and claim to earmark the revenue for some popular program? An answer to this puzzle comes from considering limitations inherent in the primary means by which the general public attempts to control political decisions, namely, voting. And by understanding how the limitations of voting make tax earmarking an effective political ploy for securing tax increases, we can also understand why sin taxes are even more effective than at first glance we might think they should be in overcoming taxpayer resistance.

A fundamental justification for coercive government action is that it has the potential for improving the general well-being by overcoming free-rider problems that often arise with private voluntary action. For example, certain public goods can be provided at costs that are less than the resulting benefits. When this is the case, the costs can be divided up in such a way that everyone is better off if the public good is provided. Unfortunately, since no one in the relevant community can be excluded from the benefits of the public good, once it is provided, everyone is tempted to claim that he or she receives little or no benefit from the public good in an attempt to free ride on the contributions of others. The result is that valuable public goods will not be provided if left to voluntary action. Government action can overcome this problem by providing the public good and forcing everyone to pay for it. But since the power to make people pay for governmentally provided goods, public or otherwise, invites abuse, the public should have some means of communicating accurately its demand for public goods. Political democracies offer the best opportunity for such communication to occur by allowing citizens to vote, either directly or indirectly, for or against government spending proposals and the taxes necessary to finance them.

It is often thought that voting motivates the honest communication of preferences by eliminating the possibility of free riding. When voting for the taxes that are required to finance public expenditures, each individual recognizes that if a majority favors a tax expenditure package, it will be implemented regardless of how he or she votes. Nothing is therefore to be gained by voting against a proposal he or she favors, since there is no hope of avoiding his or her share of the taxes if it receives a majority vote. Similarly, there is no fear that others can exploit his or her favorable vote as free riders, since neither will they be able to avoid their share of the taxes if it passes. Of course, those who feel that the public good is worth less to them than the taxes they will have to pay for it will have a strong reason to express themselves honestly at the polls by voting against the proposal. So regardless of a citizen's preferences, it would seem that voting is a way of motivating an honest expression of those preferences.

The ability of voting to overcome one of the free-rider problems associated with the expression of political preferences is a real advantage, but not an untarnished one. To overcome one free-rider problem, voting establishes incentives that create additional free-rider problems. These new free-rider problems seriously hamper the motivation of citizens to acquire information on the issues under consideration and to utilize the information they do acquire in ways that make their preferences known honestly and effectively through their voting decisions. As I will explain, politicians can, and do, exploit these free-rider problems with selective taxes and tax earmarking to help satisfy their craving for more revenue.

## The Simple Arithmetic of Voting

To understand how voting creates new free-rider problems that make voters vulnerable to political manipulation, consider the simple arithmetic of voting.

In almost all elections, the number of voters is at least in the thousands, and it is commonly the case that millions of voters are making the decision on what passes and what fails. The unavoidable implication of these large numbers is that any one vote is extremely unlikely to be decisive in determining the outcome. Even in elections with only a few hundred votes, the probability that the vote of any one individual will be decisive is quite small. For example, if an individual is one of 501 voters, his or her vote will be decisive only if the other 500 voters are evenly divided. Obviously, the probability of such an even split is small, and the larger the number of voters, the smaller it becomes.[4] In a statewide election, the probability that a voter will be killed in an auto accident on the way to the polls is quite likely larger than the probability that his vote will affect the outcome of the election.

While few people consciously consider the probability that their vote will not be decisive, at some level they are surely aware of that simple fact. There is no doubt that voters behave as if they are aware of their individual impotence as voters.

Consider the free-riding opportunity that each voter is given by virtue of the fact that his or her vote is highly unlikely to decide the outcome of an election. Each voter stands to benefit from public policy that is guided by well-informed citizens. For most people, however, significant costs are associated with becoming informed on the candidates and proposals at issue in an election. Each individual would find these costs worth incurring if doing so were the only way he or she could receive the benefits from well-informed public policy (i.e., if his or her vote were decisive). But because any one vote is so unlikely to make a difference, the payoff in terms of better policy from being an informed voter can safely be ignored by individual voters. Each voter knows that he or she will benefit from good public policy, regardless of whether or not he or she becomes informed, if enough other voters make informed choices at the polls. So unless an individual simply enjoys being informed for the sake of being informed, the sensible thing to do from his or her perspective is to attempt to free ride on the informed voting of others.

Of course, when most people attempt to free ride on the informed voting of others, there will not be much of a ride, because less information is brought to bear on public policy decisions than everyone would like to see. Yet this fact does not reduce the free-rider temptation, since each individual recognizes that if he or she became well informed, it would have no effect on public policy. Certainly the evidence suggests that voters do attempt, though rather unsuccessfully, to free ride on the information others bring to the polls. Survey after survey finds that voters have very little information on the candidates and the proposals on which they are voting. This "rational ignorance" results directly from the free-riding motivation prompted by the fact that voters are individually impotent.

Because of rational ignorance, voters are easily swayed by superficial considerations. It has long been recognized that charisma rather than competence, style rather than substance, and rhetoric rather than reality are the most important factors in swaying the choices of voters. Arguments that are superficially plausible and easy to understand are more effective at influencing voters than substantive, but subtle, arguments based on often complicated analysis.

Not surprisingly, voters are easily persuaded that earmarking tax revenues to a particular public program limits the increased expenditures to that program without increasing government spending in general. Certainly it is superficially plausible that earmarking the revenues from a particular tax to education, for example, is an effective way of favoring educational expenditures over other government expenditures. How many voters are willing to go to the trouble and expense of examining the actual impact of tax earmarking on the pattern of government expenditures?

If voters were well informed on the effect of tax earmarking, they would recognize that it does little, if anything, to favor spending on the earmarked program over government spending in general. Well-informed voters would make it difficult, if not impossible, for politicians to overcome voter opposition to general tax increases by masquerading such an increase under the guise of tax earmarking. But because the simple arithmetic of voting ensures that the individual voter has almost no impact on the outcome of an election, voters have little motivation to become informed.

Furthermore, because individual voters lack decisiveness in determining electoral outcomes, they are likely to vote for noble-sounding proposals, such as sin taxes earmarked to worthy objectives, even if they are fully informed and even if the proposals are detrimental to their personal interests. In the next section I consider why this is so.

## Expressive Voting and the Importance of Political Packaging

To obtain further insight into the reason why selective taxes and tax earmarking reduce voter opposition to tax increases, I now consider a question that arises from the discussion in the previous section. If individual voters have an insignificant effect on the outcome of elections, why aren't voter turnouts even lower than they are? If each voter recognizes that his or her vote is unlikely to be decisive, people must not go to the polls individually expecting to effectively promote their personal interests by voting. Clearly the cost of voting in terms of time alone is greater than the benefit an individual can expect to realize from casting one vote. Surely something else provides the primary motivation for voting.

The urge to express oneself in favor of things of which one approves and against things of which one disapproves is strong. People vote for much the same reason that they send get-well cards to friends, or cheer for the home team and jeer the opposing team in athletic contests. People don't send get-well cards to friends because they believe that their cards will determine whether or not their friends get well. Neither do people cheer for the home team because they believe that their cheer will make the difference between victory and defeat. Sending get-well cards and cheering for the home team provide the senders and cheerers with the good feeling that comes from expressing support for people and activities they feel are important. Voting provides people the same opportunity to feel good about themselves for express-ing support for things they feel are worthy.

Once we recognize that individual votes are not likely to affect election outcomes and that people vote primarily because of the satisfaction they re-ceive from expressing themselves, the importance of packaging over sub-stance in political proposals becomes clear. If a political proposal is packaged in a way that makes people feel even moderately good about supporting it, they will tend to do so even though the substance of the proposal is against their best interests. Indeed, a cleverly packaged political proposal may easily receive majority support at the polls even though everyone recognizes that it is against his or her best interest. The rational ignorance discussed in the previous section makes the seductiveness of clever political packaging worse, but this seductiveness is powerful even when voters are fully informed. The problem, as we are about to see, is another variation of the general free-rider problem, the problem that voting is often given credit for overcoming.

To illustrate the problem as clearly as possible, consider a rational voter's response to a proposal justified as necessary for helping the poor. Assume that the voter has been brought up to feel that she should be sympathetic to the plight of the poor, and therefore she will feel good about herself if she votes for the proposal. On the other hand, assume that the voter is fully aware that if the proposal passes, it will impose a cost on her as a taxpayer, say $1,000.00, that is far greater than the value she is willing to pay for the feeling of righteousness realized from voting in favor of the proposal, say ten cents.[5] The question is: Will the individual vote for or against the proposal?

At first the answer may seem obvious. Certainly the individual would not make a private charitable contribution of $1,000.00 when the satisfaction realized from making the contribution is worth only ten cents. But there is an important difference between making a private charitable contribution and voting in favor of an equally costly public charitable donation. And because of this difference, the individual, who would donate only a small amount privately, may vote to donate a large amount publicly. The decision to make a private donation is completely decisive. The individual who "votes" to donate $1,000.00 privately incurs an unequivocal cost of $1,000.00. On the other hand, the decision to favor a public donation at the polls is not at all decisive, since an individual vote is not likely to affect the outcome of the election. The cost to the individual of voting at the ballot box for a proposal that will cost her $1,000.00 if it passes is equal to $1,000.00 times the probability that the votes of everyone else will be evenly split. For reasons already discussed, this probability is extremely low.

For the purpose of illustration, assume the probability that the individual's vote will be decisive is equal to 1/20,000 (which, for elections on federal and state issues, is far larger than the probability that the outcome will in fact be decided by one vote). With this probability it follows that the expected cost to the individual of voting in favor of the proposal is equal to only $1,000.00/ 20,000, or five cents. Since it is assumed that the voter values the feeling of virtue she will receive from casting a favorable vote at ten cents, it makes sense from her perspective to vote yes. Voting in this case, and in many other cases, allows people to express their superior virtue, and therefore feel good about themselves, at low cost.[6]

While the individual voter incurs little or no cost as a consequence of his or her vote for an expensive proposal, when a majority of the voters respond to the opportunity to feel good on the cheap by expressing their generosity at the polls, the result is heavy costs imposed on everyone. Indeed, expanding on our example, if each voter realizes ten cents' worth of satisfaction from voting in favor of the poverty proposal, and yields to the temptation to do so, the proposal will pass unanimously and everyone will end up paying $1,000.00 for a benefit that no one values at more than a few cents. In other words, everyone would be better off if everyone passed up the opportunity to realize a cheap feeling of virtue at the polls by voting against the poverty proposal.[7] This small sacrifice would constitute a contribution that each individual could make to the general well-being. The obstacle here is the same one we have encountered before, namely the free-rider problem. From the perspective of each individual, the best situation finds him or her not sacrificing the satisfaction of voting in favor of the proposal, but a majority of the other voters sacrificing it. Each individual would like to free ride on the sacrifice (contribution) of others. Of course, with everyone attempting to free ride, there is no ride provided (or, in this example, the voters are indeed taken for a ride—a very expensive ride), and everyone is worse off. But this fact provides no motivation for an individual to make the sacrifice of voting against the proposal, since his or her contribution is unlikely to make any difference to the final outcome.

So the outcome of an election can be, and often is, extremely sensitive to the way the proposal at issue is packaged. If the proposal is packaged so that people receive even a mildly virtuous feeling from identifying with it, then that proposal will likely receive strong support at the polls quite independently of its substance or consequences. As indicated by our example, repackaging a proposal to shift the public perception of it just slightly in its favor can greatly increase the support it receives at the polls.

## Back to Taxing Choice and Earmarking Revenues

Bringing the discussion back to tax policy, we now have a better understanding of why the public is more likely to support a selective tax with the revenue earmarked to some approved public purpose than to support a general tax increase, even though the fiscal effects (at least on the expenditure side) are the same in either case.

With most people of the opinion that government spending in general is excessive, voters who realize a feeling of moral virtue, or some other form of psychic satisfaction, from expressing themselves in favor of a general tax increase (or in favor of a candidate proposing such an increase) are surely in the minority. The expressive satisfaction most voters would receive from favoring a general tax increase is no doubt negative. So although the cost of a favorable vote on a general tax increase is extremely low for all voters, the payoff for most of them in terms of feeling that they have done the right thing comes from a negative vote on such a tax increase.

The situation is altered significantly when a tax increase proposal is repackaged as one taxing a good that most people (including many of those who enjoy the good) feel is disreputable and earmarking the revenue to finance some good that most people (including many of those who do not consume the good) feel we should consume more of. There is no surprise in the growing political tendency to recommend increasing taxes on "sinful" products or activities (such as cigarettes, smokeless tobacco products, alcoholic beverages, gasoline, bullets, the production of chemicals, and getting rich in the greedy 1980s) and to claim that the revenues are to be earmarked for things that most people think deserve more support. Public programs for improving education, reducing traffic congestion, cleaning up toxic wastes, assisting the elderly, providing more opportunities for preschool educational, and reforming health care have been, or are likely to be, candidates for earmarked tax revenue. Do not expect to see politicians putting forth proposals to impose special taxes on Bibles, small family farms, and shelters for battered women, with the revenue earmarked to augment the governor's discretionary slush fund, bail out defense contractors, or compensate oil companies for losses due to oil spills.

When a tax increase is packaged as a penalty on the unworthy and more public support for the worthy, it is likely to receive a favorable vote from an electorate that would vote overwhelmingly against a general tax increase. The fact that imposing or increasing an earmarked selective tax is practically equivalent to a general tax increase will be without significance to rationally ignorant voters who find satisfaction in expressing support for what they believe is good, true, and beautiful, especially when the personal cost of doing so is low.

## Conclusion

Governments tax and spend more than they would if politicians considered all the costs, as well as all the benefits, of their taxing and spending decisions. Unfortunately, much of the costs of taxing and spending are ignored by politicians since taxpayers, who bear these costs, are less effective at communicating their concerns politically than are organized interest groups, which receive much of the benefits. The free-rider problem explains the relative ineffectiveness of taxpayers at communicating politically. Each taxpayer will benefit from lower taxes achieved by organized opposition to tax increases, whether or not he or she contributes to that opposition. The ideal, then, from the perspective of each taxpayer, is to avoid contributing to tax resistance efforts while free riding on the contributions of others. Of course, with almost everyone attempting to free ride on the contributions of others, the opposition to tax increases is insufficiently communicated through the political process.

Opposition to tax increases does get communicated, even if insufficiently, since taxpayers can, without having to formally organize, express that opposition through their voting behavior. Voting is a means of moderating the free-rider problem faced by taxpayers, and imposes limits on how much politicians can exploit the lack of organization on the part of those paying the bills. But voting comes with free-rider problems of its own, and politicians can be expected to take advantage of them to push back the limits of taxpayer resistance even more. When politicians begin reaching the limits of the revenues they can raise through general taxation, they will respond by moving more toward earmarked selective taxes, which allow them to take advantage of new variations of the free-rider problem. Because of the free-rider problems of rational ignorance and expressive voting, taxpayers/voters are more favorably disposed toward cleverly packaged earmarked selective taxes than toward increases in general taxes, although there is little important difference between the two.

## Notes

1. In the 28 March 1994 issue of *Newsweek*, it was reported on page 27 that "a recent Cancer Society poll suggests that 66 percent of all voters, including a third of those who smoke, support a tax hike of $2 a pack." The tax hike was being proposed as a means of paying for health care reform.
2. See Harris (1987, 363). A related phenomenon is the tendency of public-opinion polls to find that while majorities believe that government spending is too large in the aggregate, they oppose reducing spending on specific programs.
3. Commenting on this election result, *Newsweek* states:

   > Voters are likely to resist general tax increases to fund government across the board.... But polls show that voters are willing to pay higher taxes for specific purposes like building schools or cleaning rivers. ("Saying Yes to Taxes" 1990, 15)

   While a tax on gasoline is not the best example of a sin tax, there can be no doubt that the environmental lobby has attempted to depict the use of gasoline and other fossil fuels as an assault on, if not exactly a sin against, the environment. For example, a 1993 editorial in the *New York Times* stated in support of a large increase in the federal gasoline tax that "lower gas consumption slows the growth of pollution in the cities, where most driving takes place, easing the disproportionate pollution burden on the urban poor" (Schipper 1993).

4. The likelihood of an even split is very sensitive to the probability that any one voter will vote yes or no (or for candidate A or candidate B), with the likelihood of an even split being maximized when the probability that any one voter will vote yes (or no) is 0.5. The likelihood of an even split falls quickly as the probability of a yes vote from a particular voter falls below (or rises above) 0.5. For a detailed discussion of the likelihood of decisive voting, see chapter 4 of Brennan and Lomasky (1993).

5. The choice of ten cents is not to suggest that people place such a small value on the sense of virtue that comes from efforts to help the unfortunate. The value is chosen to emphasize the point that people will often vote for proposals that provide them with a sense of virtue even when the cost of the program is high and the value of the sense of virtue is low.

6. For a detailed discussion of the broad political implications of the tendency of people to attach little weight to the consequences of the propositions they favor at the polls, see Brennan and Lomasky (1993).

7. We abstract from the interests of the poor in making this statement, or, not unrealistically, assume that even if the poverty program passes, it will be subjected to so many special-interest claims and inefficiencies that the poor will realize little if any benefit from it.

## References

Borg, Mary O., and Paul M. Mason. 1990. "Earmarked Lottery Revenue: Positive Windfalls or Concealed Redistribution Mechanism?" *Journal of Education Finance* 15 (Winter): 289–301.

Brennan, Geoffrey, and James M. Buchanan. 1984. "Voter Choice: Evaluating Political Alternatives." *American Behavioral Scientist,* 185–201.

Brennan, Geoffrey, and Loren Lomasky. 1993. *Democracy and Decision: The Pure Theory of Electoral Preference.* Cambridge: Cambridge University Press.

Harris, Louis. 1987. *Inside America.* New York: Vintage Books.

"Saying Yes to Taxes." 1990. *Newsweek,* 18 June, 14–15.

Schipper, Lee. 1993. "A Tax That Does Double, Triple Duty." *New York Times,* 31 January, F-11.

# 6

# Taxing Choice to Fund Politically Correct Propaganda

*Thomas J. DiLorenzo*

*We will never know how many smokers' lives we prolong...when we force them to do the right thing for themselves.*
—Glenn Barr, Americans for Nonsmokers' Rights

*Paternalism toward others has long been camouflage for power for oneself.*
—Thomas Sowell, *The Vision of the Annointed*

Would it be fair to tax the Democratic party and give the money to the Republican National Committee? Or to impose a special surtax on Planned Parenthood in order to finance the political activities of the anti-abortion movement? Would it be just to tax labor unions and use the proceeds for anti-union corporate lobbying? Apparently, a number of state legislatures (particularly California's) and a large and growing lobbying force believes so. Special taxes on "sin" are being imposed by state and local governments to finance propaganda campaigns for certain (government-approved) lifestyles. Led by the likes of Senator Ted Kennedy (D-Mass.), political activists who might best be labeled neo-Puritans are trying to force Americans to adopt their own version of "clean living."

These activists strongly believe that most citizens are inherently incapable of making decisions for themselves regarding what to eat and drink, whether or not to smoke, and so on, and that they should be forced by government into politically correct consumption behavior. The antismoking crusade, which seems to have intensified over the past few years, is especially fanatical with its moral denunciations of smokers.

117

Nobel laureate economist James Buchanan captures the essence of neo-Puritanism with the phrase "meddlesome preferences." He points to

> an implicit recognition by all parties...that, although each may have preferences over the others' behavior, any attempt to impose one person's preferences on the behavior of another must be predicted to set off reciprocal attempts to have one's own behavior constrained in a like fashion. An attitude of "live and let live," or mutual tolerance and mutual respect, may be better for all of us, despite the occasional deviance from ordinary standards of common decency.

> Such an attitude would seem to be that of anyone who claimed to hold to democratic and individualistic values, in which each person's preferences are held to count equally with those of others. By contrast, the genuine elitist, who somehow thinks that his or her own preferences are "superior to," "better than," or "more correct" than those of others, will, of course, try to control the behavior of everyone else, while holding fast to his or her own liberty to do as he or she pleases. (Buchanan 1988)

Many of the neo-Puritans are especially offended by the concept of individual freedom, frequently mocking and ridiculing such concepts as consumer choice and individual rights within the rule of law. The danger of such attitudes, economist Ludwig von Mises once wrote, is that

> once the principle is admitted that it is the duty of government to protect the individual from his own foolishness, no serious objections can be raised against further encroachments. A good case could be made out in favor of the prohibition of alcohol and nicotine. And why limit the government's benevolent providence to the protection of the individual's body only? Is not the harm a man can inflict on his mind and soul even more disastrous than any bodily evils? Why not prevent him from reading bad books and seeing bad plays, from looking at bad paintings and statues and from hearing bad music? The mischief done by bad ideologies surely is much more pernicious, both for the individual and for the whole society, than that done by narcotic drugs.

> These fears are not merely imaginary specters terrifying secluded doctrinaires. It is a fact that no paternal government, whether ancient or modern, ever shrank from regimenting its subjects' minds, beliefs, and opinions. If one abolishes man's freedom to determine his own consumption, one takes all freedoms away. The naive advocates of government interference with consumption delude themselves when they neglect what they disdainfully call the philosophical aspect of the problem. They unwittingly support the cause of censorship, inquisition, intolerance, and the persecution of dissenters. (von Mises 1966, 733–34)

Once it becomes "legitimate" for government to protect individuals from their own follies, there is no way to establish limits to governmental power. Anything can be banned, for virtually everything can be harmful to health if consumed in excess. Should red meat, beer, and potato chips be banned? Should obesity be treated with mandatory treadmill sessions? Should there be fines or jail sentences for excessive exercise that is known to cause damage to joints or lead to arthritis? Do we really need the government to dictate what kind of oil we can use to pop popcorn (as Ralph Nader's Public Interest Research Group recently argued)?

The remainder of this chapter will explore the use of sin taxes to finance politically correct propaganda in the context of recently imposed taxes on tobacco products that are earmarked for funding antitobacco political activism. The purpose is not to defend smoking (which the author believes is unhealthful) or the tobacco industry, but to highlight the threat to freedom such taxes entail, how they have been used to create large, meddlesome government bureaucracies, and how they are very unlikely to accomplish their ostensible purpose: the improvement of public health.

## California's New Puritanism

> *puritan... 1 cap: a member of a 16th and 17th century Protestant group in England and New England opposing as unscriptural the ceremonial worship and the prelacy of the Church of England 2: one who paractices or preaches a more rigorous or professedly purer moral code than that which prevails.*
> —*Webster's Ninth New Collegiate Dictionary*

In 1987, the American Cancer Society (ACS), American Lung Association (ALA), American Heart Association (AHA), and California Medical Association (CMA) combined to lobby to more than triple the state's cigarette tax (from ten cents to thirty-five cents a pack). The tax was expected to raise over $500 million annually, much of which would go to those very organizations, ostensibly for research, indigent medical care, and antismoking "education" campaigns.

Clearly, these organizations had a major stake in the revenue that would result from the tax, although, being "nonprofit" organizations, they denied it. A lobbyist for the CMA, Jay D. Michael, proclaimed: "The principal reason [for the tax] is not to raise money. The principal reason is to stop smoking.... If a tax were imposed and it raised nothing, we would be delighted—that would mean nobody would be buying cigarettes."[1]

The facts, however, present a very different picture. The proposed cigarette tax increase could have been approved by the California legislature if the coalition's only objective was to reduce the incidence of smoking by raising the price of cigarettes—a straightforward application of the economic law of demand. There was a problem, however, in that in 1979 California voters had passed Proposition 4, a constitutional amendment that limited state spending. If the state were to reach its spending limit, then tax revenues from cigarette taxes would have to be refunded to smokers in particular and to the public in general. The ACS, ALA, AHA, and CMA would get nothing, even though the tax's supposedly salutary effects on cigarette consumption, which the coalition claimed were its *principal* concern, would still prevail.

The coalition simply could not countenance such an outcome, so it pushed for a statewide referendum, Proposition 99, that would add another constitutional amendment. This strategy was necessary, according to state assemblyman Lloyd Connelly (D-Sacramento), the coalition's legislative "connection," because of "the so-called Gann spending limit passed by voters in 1979." He said "without a constitutional amendment, the legislature could be forced to refund the tax if the state reaches its spending limit."[2]

Hence, rhetoric aside, the main objective of the coalition was not to discourage smoking, but to capture the revenue from the cigarette tax. Expecting a windfall of hundreds of millions of dollars, the coalition reportedly spent over $400,000.00 lobbying for the initiative. "It's the biggest project the American Cancer Society has ever undertaken in terms of staff commitment," said a spokesperson for the society (Carson 1988).

Proposition 99 passed in November 1988 by a 58 percent to 42 percent margin and increased the state's cigarette tax from ten cents to thirty-five cents per pack. A new 42 percent ad valorem tax was also imposed on tobacco products other than cigarettes, and the proposition required that six accounts be established to disburse the revenues. The revenues were to be allocated as follows:

20% for antitobacco education in schools and communities
35% for treatment of indigent hospital patients
10% for treatment by individual physicians for indigent patients
 5% for research on tobacco-related disease
 5% for "environmental concerns"
25% left unallocated, theoretically to be applied as needed to the previous categories

Even though the California Medical Association claimed that money was not "the principal reason" for its support of Proposition 99, it has been battling its other coalition partners over its "share" of the funds almost from the day the tax receipts first became available. The CMA initially became worried that cigarette tax receipts targeted for financing the provision of health care to the indigent might be substituted for the general revenues appropriated for Medi-Cal, the state-funded program that paid the medical bills of the uninsured. If this were to occur, the medical profession would not experience any net financial gains (Bennett 1990). The CMA immediately began lobbying for a greater share of the tobacco tax revenues, much to the consternation of the health charities, who accused the CMA of attempting to "undermine Proposition 99." The president of the CMA admitted to legislators that his organization and the health charities were "fighting for this money like jackals over a carcass."[3]

Subsidized health insurance increases the demand for medical care and therefore increases physicians' incomes. But if such subsidies come at the expense of money earmarked for antismoking "education," which is conducted by the health charities, then their allocation is diminished and the incomes of health charity managers and employees decline. This is the source of the ongoing battle over Proposition 99 revenues, which, curiously, seems to make virtually no mention of public-health issues.

More recently, a coalition of California nonprofit antismoking organizations, directed by the umbrella group Americans for Nonsmokers' Rights, sued Governor Pete Wilson for "illegally diverting" more than $165 million that supposedly should have been spent on "education" programs and instead was "improperly used for health screening and immunizations of poor children and for prenatal care for poor women who are pregnant" (Lucas 1994). This is an amazingly bold charge. Who but the neo-Puritans would have the audacity to launch a political attack against programs that benefit poor women and children who are in need of medical care? When it comes to the choice between the health of low-income Americans and the budgets and salaries of nonprofit political activist organizations like Americans for Nonsmokers' Rights, the latter is always the top priority with the neo-Puritans. It is instructive that the president of Americans for Nonsmokers' Rights is Stanton Glantz, a professor at the University of California, San Francisco, who has been one of the largest recipients of research grants funded by Proposition 99 revenues.

## How Much Bureaucracy?

*When the Prop 99 money came in, there were*
*more schemes than I could begin to count on*
*how to spend that money.*
—American Lung Association spokesman, 1992

That Proposition 99 is being held up as a model for other states (Massachusetts recently enacted a similar law) should be of concern to all who think government is already too big, bloated, and bureaucratic. California's cigarette tax revenues have fueled an enormous bureaucracy of state health "officials," university researchers, and nonprofit political activists, all of whom have created a formidable coalition lobbying for the continuation and expansion of the program.

Proposition 99 funds have been used to establish "regional coalitions," dividing the state into ten geographic areas within which a government-funded organization coordinates antitobacco propaganda activities. These regional coalitions attempt to influence newspaper editors, radio and television stations, public-school teachers, and other public-opinion leaders.

The regional coalitions administer grant programs and funnel hundreds of millions of dollars to "subcontractors," mostly nonprofit organizations. Each of California's fifty-eight counties, along with its major cities, now has a "Local Lead Agency" whose purpose is to make sure that all the governmental largesse is distributed by seeking out and soliciting grant recipients. Thus, although the antismoking crusade in California is often labeled a "grass roots" effort, in reality it has been instigated by the state government and orchestrated by various grant-receiving nonprofit organizations.

Many of the local nonprofit organizations that have received Proposition 99 funding never had anything to do with smoking or health issues. For example, a "public service" advertisement that appeared in a number of California newspapers asked, "Are you involved in a nonprofit program looking for money? If your work can incorporate tobacco prevention, there may be funding available." Nonprofits were then urged to contact their local Health Department Tobacco Control Program to apply for funding. Among previously funded programs listed in the ad were a "teen theater program" with an antismoking message and a "Bingo game in Spanish."[4]

Proposition 99 even provides funding to "protect, restore, enhance, or maintain fish, waterfowl, and other wildlife habitat areas" and to "improve state and local park and recreation sources." This has nothing to do with smoking or disease prevention, but it provides a reason for local environmental groups to supply lobbying efforts in support of the continuation and expansion of the program.

## Expanding the Public-School Bureaucracy

For decades, American public schools have been spending more and more per student while student performance, by virtually every measure, has declined steadily. That the public schools are failing miserably is universally acknowledged by commentators of all political persuasions. Nevertheless, Proposition 99 showers California's state educational bureaucracy with money through the state department of education's "Healthy Kids, Healthy California" program. Over $250 million has been allocated to this account annually, ostensibly to educate children to be nonsmokers. In light of all the failures of the public schools to teach even the basics of reading, writing, and arithmetic, however, one has to be skeptical about how much "health education" is occurring in these Proposition 99-funded programs.

The state's antitobacco educational programs seem of dubious value, at best, if one assumes that the objective is to educate children about the hazards of tobacco use. If, on the other hand, the objective is to increase taxpayer funding for the state educational bureaucracy, the program must be judged a success.

The basis of these programs is to give students (and their parents) small gifts if they promise not to smoke. For example, according to the *Stanislaus County Tobacco Control Education Incentive Plan,* "incentives such as a back pack, stroller or gift certificate of comparable value will be awarded to quitters who stay quit 3 months from the end of the cessation class. Their word will be taken as validity of quit status."[5]

Since little, if any, attempt is made to verify that students have actually stopped smoking, the program is simply a giant giveaway of taxpayers' money. Among the gifts given to students and their parents are diapers, baby clothes, movie tickets, T-shirts, record albums, compact discs, AM/FM radio cassette players, tickets to theme/amusement parks, sports equipment, cameras, watches and clocks, bathroom scales, Sizzler steak house gift certificates, cash for baby showers, and even lottery tickets. In Stanislaus County, "half of the people joining said that the lottery was an important reason for joining the program."[6]

This particular program, which is not atypical in California, recently began *unannounced* visits by "project group leaders who verified students' reported non-use of tobacco with a breath ecolyzer exam. Students who passed the breath test were immediately given a small prize as a reinforcement for their tobacco-free status."[7] These project leaders were paid $24.00 per hour for their services, or nearly $50,000.00 annually, for giving away toys, trinkets, and other gifts. The American Civil Liberties Union, which has fought so strenuously against random drug testing in schools and workplaces, seems to have been inactive in the case of random cigarette smoke testing in California's schools.

Sometimes Proposition 99 funds are simply used to throw a party. The Hanford, California, school system sponsored "a pool party for 13- to 19-year-olds.... Free food, drinks, and deejay music [were] provided by the Kings County Health Department, which used Proposition 99 money to sponsor the six-day event. The beach balls, Frisbees, buttons and magnets that were given to children this week were also paid for using Proposition 99 money" (Hele 1992). At other, similar festivals, there are "outrageous stunt" contests, which pay prize money to whoever promises to perform the most outrageous stunt to shock a loved one into quitting smoking. Among the past winners is a young girl who consumed an entire can of Mighty Dog dog food.

There is always some discussion of tobacco use at the festivals, but in some cases the students seem to have been misinformed rather than educated. According to one thirteen-year-old interviewed by a local reporter, "if you're around someone who is smoking, and you smell it, it's just like smoking yourself"(Hele 1992). So-called secondhand smoke is not, in fact, "just like smoking yourself," and there is no sound evidence that it poses a health hazard. It may someday be determined that it does, but at the time the thirteen-year-old made the statement, in August 1992, no such evidence existed.

The Martinez, California, school district used Proposition 99 funds to pay for a trip to Yosemite National Park. "Spring is in the air, flowers are blooming and the days are getting longer. It's time to pack up the baby, put on your walking shoes, and get ready for a great day strolling around Yosemite National Park," read an advertisement for the "Breathe Easy, Smoke Free Walk" sponsored by the local schools. Anyone participating—including both smokers and those who claim to have quit smoking—had their park entrance fee paid for and were given "a free Alpenlite belted pouch with water bottle and a box lunch."[8]

In some cases California students are used as political pawns by the local government bureaucrats seeking to enlarge their budgets and by professional political activists seeking to justify their Proposition 99 grants. Calaveras County parents were "infuriated" in 1993 by "a survey of teens' views on family, school, drugs and sex" administered by a county government "Teen Health Care Task Force." The Proposition 99-funded task force was comprised of the local chapter of the American Association of University Women, the Calaveras County Probation and Sheriff's departments, and Planned Parenthood of San Joaquin County.[9] Only one-third of the county's parents gave their children permission to participate in the survey, and many of them denounced it as "inappropriate" and "demeaning and invasive of family privacy" because it included "26 direct and specific questions on the subject of sexual activity, promiscuity, abuse, contraceptive use, etc. and at least 24 probes into personal and private family relationships."[10]

The purpose of the survey was apparently to secure more state funds: "Before the state could be persuaded to provide money for teen services, a survey of teens was necessary to prove a need and identify what is lacking," said a member of the task force.[11]

Apparently, any "problems" that existed were so minor that they were not visible to the naked eye. A politically contrived survey was necessary to "justify" more state funding for the local school bureaucracy, and Proposition 99 funds were used to conduct it. There was not even any pretense that the state funds would be used for antismoking education. The objecting parents were convinced that "future grants would fund free condoms or school-based health clinics that would provide contraceptives or abortions."[12]

Despite spending hundreds of millions of dollars on its public-school antismoking education campaign, evidence gathered by the California Department of Health Services "did not indicate a decline in adolescent smoking between 1990 and 1992" (California Department of Health Services 1992). A wealth of anecdotal evidence supports the findings of the department's survey. "With smoldering cigarettes balanced between their fingers, groups of teen-agers...scoffed at the state's recent move to pump up anti-smoking campaigns. They say ads, pro or con, don't influence their behavior at all—they're going to smoke no matter what." "I've been smoking since I was fourteen," said one teen, and "I don't even look at the ads" (Hill 1993).

In fact, common sense suggests that an antismoking campaign in the schools will actually *increase* the incidence of smoking among at least some teens. According to Sharon Lee, a smoking-prevention educator at ValleyCare Health Systems in Livermore, California, "I smoked when I was a kid, and it wasn't because of ads. It was just [that] I thought I was doing something taboo that I could get away with" (Hill 1993). What better way to encourage teenagers to smoke than to tell them it's taboo?

Proposition 99 grantees are also apparently teaching school children that they are sometimes justified in breaking the law. The *San Francisco Chronicle* reported how the Novato, California, "Police Department has denounced a 'vigilante' sting operation by an anti-smoking group that used a 16-year-old girl to buy cigarets at stores in Novato" in order to "spotlight the widespread illegal sale of cigarets to minors." "A group financed through Proposition 99 tobacco-tax funds has conducted more than 100 such operations in the North Bay since 1988." The local police chief complained that these taxpayer-supported teenagers and anti-smoking activists are "out breaking the law to prove a point, and that's vigilantism." "What are they going to do next, put drunk drivers out on the road to see if they're caught?" (Taylor 1994)

Proposition 99's grantee, the nonprofit group STAMP (for Stop Tobacco Access for Minors), defended this "merchant education" campaign by saying that "this was technically illegal, but there are a lot of people out there who support what we're doing" (Taylor 1994). What a lesson to be teaching children: As long as "a lot" of people (i.e., other Proposition 99 grantees) agree with the ends, any means of achieving them can be justified.

There is something odious about the government paying a small group of citizens to spy on their neighbors and to conduct private "sting" operations. If the police trample on civil liberties in the course of their law enforcement activities, the police department and local governmental authorities will be held accountable, and are often sued for such transgressions. But who will be held accountable if civil liberties are trampled by extragovernmental nonprofit organizations? Are these tax-financed groups to be viewed as arms of the government, or simply as private citizens?

One also has to wonder why the STAMP activists did not recruit their own children to act as vigilantes. Paying *other peoples'* children to participate in these "sting" operations, especially if they are conducted without the knowledge or permission of the children's parents, is insidious.

## Wealth, Not Health

Many of the programs funded by Proposition 99 may not deter smoking among teenagers, and may even encourage it by creating a taboo and thereby providing an opportunity to rebel. Nevertheless, antismoking activism can be extremely lucrative for California's neo-Puritans. According to the California Department of Health Services, Proposition 99 funds have been used to pay the very handsome salary of $167,113 to a public-health nurse (California Department of Health Services 1994), and a public-relations firm employed to lobby for more restrictive antismoking ordinances was paid the following hourly rates:[13]

| | |
|---|---|
| Project Director | $265/hr. |
| Political Director | 145/hr. |
| Legislative Manager | 345/hr. |
| Communications Director | 150/hr. |
| Research Manager | 160/hr. |
| Media Manager | 110/hr. |

The lowest salary was for the Assistant Project Manager, who was paid $65 per hour, or more than $130,000.00 annually, assuming a 40-hour work week. If the highest-paid grantee, the Legislative Manager, worked full time on the project, his annual salary would amount to over $700,000.00.

Many of the nonprofit organizations and local government agencies that receive Proposition 99 funds apparently use the funds simply to pay the salaries of their employees, who are not necessarily working on tobacco-related issues. The treasurer of the Sacramento NAACP admitted that a $159,000.00 grant from the state health department was not used for tobacco education, as it was supposed to be, but "had been spent instead on salaries for other branch employees and other expenses" (Davila 1993). One can only speculate how widespread this practice is.

Proposition 99 funds are also apparently used throughout California to pay or partially pay the salaries of local government employees. In Butte County, Proposition 99 funds were used to pay a portion of the county code enforcement officer's salary as well as the entire salaries of three full-time county government employees. School districts throughout the state have used Proposition 99 funds to pay the salaries of school counselors and psychologists (Meilink 1992).

### Tax-Funded Politics

By law, the tax revenues raised by Proposition 99 are to be used only for health research and education, hospital subsidies, and natural resources and public parks. This was the understanding the voters had when they passed the initiative. But as soon as the initiative was passed and revenues amounting to some $600 million annually became available, the professional political activists who had orchestrated the campaign in support of the initiative began spending a large portion of the funds—perhaps the majority—on political organizing and lobbying for laws restricting smoking. The voters, in other words, were misled. If the purpose of Proposition 99 was to create a political war chest for the neo-Puritans, then that is what should have been voted on.

Such a subterfuge seems entirely in keeping with the patronizing attitude of the neo-Puritans. "What the voters don't know won't hurt them" seems to have been the philosophy of the Proposition 99 campaign. California's neo-Puritans have even gone so far as to claim that there is a need for *them* to educate *doctors* on the hazards of smoking ("We're trying to teach doctors about tobacco smoke," said Molly Cage, a state health department official [Meilink 1992]). According to the neo-Puritans, physicians who have spent eight, twelve, or more years of their lives studying medicine need to be "educated" by nonmedical political activists whose careers are devoted to political rabble-rousing such as sponsoring (human) dog food-eating contests.

It is illegal to use Proposition 99 funds "to promote partisan politics or candidates" or "to promote the passage of any law, including public ordinances and regulations,"[14] but Proposition 99 grantors and grantees routinely flout the law. For example, the Tobacco Control Coalition of Contra Costa County published the minutes of a public meeting in which it announced: "It is the intention of the State that community tobacco coalitions become involved in the implementation of policy change at the local level. *The Contra Costa Coalition will play a crucial role in mobilizing community support for the...model ordinance developed by the City/County Relations Committee*" (emphasis added).[15]

The media have apparently caught on that funds that have been earmarked for education, research, and patient care are being massively diverted to political activism. As one newspaper reported:

> When voters approved Proposition 99, many people didn't realize the funds would be used to pass laws restricting smoking. According to the proposition, the funds are earmarked for health research and education, to offset medical costs relating to tobacco users, and to contribute to natural resources.... But employees from the Butte County Tobacco Education Project have lobbied heavily for more restrictive smoking laws throughout the county. (Meilink 1992)

This has occurred despite the fact that the Butte County general counsel had ruled that a public agency may not use public funds to promote a partisan position in an election campaign.

The neo-Puritans disingenuously argue that their lobbying activities are really "education," not politics. For example, the Sacramento County Environmental Management Department spent over $3,000.00 to mail out with utility bills a flyer declaring that "local smoking laws are helping you. Choose a smoke-free Sacramento" to push Measure G, an antismoking ordinance. When criticized by a county supervisor candidate, the department baldly claimed the flyers were not an attempt to influence voters, but were "an educational service" (Sebelius 1992).

A September 1992 "Revolt Against Tobacco" conference in Los Angeles featured many of the key political activists funded by Proposition 99 as well as political luminaries in the national neo-Puritanical movement. An examination of the transcripts of that conference leaves no doubt that Proposition 99 was always a subversive means of financing a political crusade to compel Californians to engage in politically correct behavior. Tobacco is only the starting point. As Julia Carol, co-director of Americans for Nonsmokers' Rights, recently told the *Washington Post*, if tobacco "magically disappeared" she would "simply move on to other causes" (Schwartz 1994). A good bet is that among her next "causes" would be attacks on the beer and beef industries, which the neo-Puritans also don't seem to approve of.

Not a single speaker at the three-day "Revolt Against Tobacco" conference discussed anything but political strategy.[16] Health education did not play a part in the conference. Barbara Wells, formerly director of communications and government affairs (i.e., lobbyist) for the American Lung Association of Los Angeles County and currently director of the Proposition 99-funded tobacco control program for the San Luis Obispo County Health Department, discussed in great detail the politics of lobbying for local anti-smoking ordinances. She boasted of how a coalition including the ACS, ALA, AHA, "and of course, Americans for Non-smoker's Rights" passed a "100% no-smoking in Beverly Hills" ordinance. As is typical of the neo-Puritans, she spoke disrespectfully of ordinary citizens who opposed her political agenda, referring to "a motley crew of restaurant owners" who she claimed were "puppets" of the tobacco industry. Ever so typical of the neo-Puritan movement, she chose not to debate her opponents on the merits of the proposed legislation, but simply to smear them with innuendo concerning alleged ties to the tobacco industry.

Also typical of neo-Puritanism, she spoke disdainfully of freedom of choice, claiming that the restaurant owners fabricated a brand new idea—"choice, a new word, choice being attached to one's behavior"—and warned her audience that this "new word" could be used as a weapon to defeat their prohibitionist agenda. Freedom of choice is obviously anathema to the neo-Puritans, for their whole reason for being is to use the coercive powers of the state to deny others *their* freedom of choice.

Ms. Wells also explained how in Butte County she and her political allies denied the claim by their political opponents that they were illegally using Proposition 99 funds for politics. Their response, she told the audience, was to insist that they were involved in "education," not politics. Then, in the next sentence, she inadvertently admitted it was all a lie by explaining that "some of the strengths we had up there were we had a very strong grass roots committee working for the ordinance. We also had a politically active community."

Another speaker, Paul Neprath of the American Lung Association, advised the local political activists at the conference to try to get hospitals to fund their activities if Proposition 99 funds are not available, "'cause they [hospitals] bring in a lot of dollars, even in a recession the hospitals are doing great, and they're a good source of funds." Among the advice the expert from the ALA gave was to "build coalitions.... Get your [city] council people before you go to a vote. Count your noses before you walk into any council meeting.... Know exactly where your votes are gonna come from." Also, associate yourself with the ACS, ALA, and AHA "whenever you go before the cameras, because the public trusts them."

Mr. Neprath didn't seem particularly concerned about frugality in spending the taxpayers' money to underwrite his political activism. When asked by an incredulous citizen how he managed to spend $65,000.00 in just a few weeks, he explained: "We spent it on campaign expenses, law firms, blah, blah, blah, a lot of different stuff." When pressed by the audience to be more specific, he simply changed the subject.

Another speaker, Julia Carol, co-director of Americans for Nonsmokers' Rights, described her organization as being comprised of "sort of an anti-preemption rah, rah, local ordinance mantra people." She seemed singularly possessed by a hatred of corporations in general and tobacco companies in particular, demonstrating that many of the neo-Puritans are motivated more by an anticapitalist ideology than by concern for the public's health. "Is there anyone worse than cigarette companies?" Ms. Carol asked. "Well, the oil companies," she answered, "or the airlines, or insurance companies."

Like the previous speaker, she had nothing at all to say about public health, but spent her time instructing the audience on tactics to pressure institutions to divest their tobacco company stock holdings. This seems to be a particularly quixotic use of Proposition 99 funds, however, because divesting tobacco company stock simply transfers ownership to the buyer without influencing tobacco company policy or harming the company financially. In describing her own politically correct investment portfolio, she boasted of investing only in "socially responsible" funds that are "Rah Rah environmental and Rah Rah South Africa and Rah Rah anti-nuclear," but complained that there are not yet many investment funds that are "Rah Rah anti-tobacco."

Another speaker was Joan Twist, director of the California Healthy Cities Project, who explained how "when Prop. 99 monies came through...we had our own tobacco control coalition within the city of Long Beach" and the "coalition had at the very top of their list to revise our current city ordinance" in such a way that would totally ban smoking in all restaurants and workplaces. Because of this experience, "our coalition members all increased their skills in advocacy."

Most speakers at the three-day conference simply recited "war stories" about their lobbying efforts and shared political strategies. A few "big guns" from the national neo-Puritan network were flown in from Washington, D.C., to contribute their political perspective. Some insights into the philosophy of neo-Puritanism were presented by one such expert, Debra McClellan, the antitobacco "coordinator" for the American Public Health Association in

Washington, D.C. She was introduced as one who "from her office in Washington, D.C., and other places around the country and the world...manages the Association's scientific and policy activities concerning tobacco control." This entails "designing advocacy efforts" on myriad antismoking political initiatives. She "helps to build local, state, national and international coalitions." In this capacity, she is closely associated with the Washington-based Advocacy Institute, whose phone number she announced to the audience.

Ms. McClellan's presentation is of interest not so much for her political war stories as for the political philosophy she espoused. Coming from a top spokesperson for the American Public Health Association and a key ally of the Advocacy Institute, a national political clearinghouse for neo-Puritanical politics, one would think that her views must be somewhat representative of the general philosophy that informs neo-Puritanism.

Her views can perhaps best be described as 1960s-era third-world Marxism. "The multinational tobacco companies," she argues, "have had free rein to scamper around the world killing millions...and profiting billions from it all." She talked of "the rape of the citizens of the world by the multinational tobacco companies," as though they were somehow able to force people to submit to purchasing their product, and expressed deep indignation that "Marlboro signs were erected in Thailand."

She seems to believe that women, gays, and African Americans are especially gullible and incapable of judging for themselves the well-known health hazards of smoking, for much of her political efforts are directed at opposing "the targeting of women" and "other oppressed groups in the U.S." Women are supposedly inherently incapable of resisting the advertising claims of the tobacco companies because they are "of a lower socioeconomic status, encountering sexism, and not being socially able to express their negative emotions such as anger, having low self-esteem, holding strict body image requirements, and experiencing multiple role conflicts.... All of these lead women to start and keep smoking."

She was not asked, nor did she explain, how she, as a woman, was able to escape such oppression and enjoy a well-paying job that included considerable national and international travel on what must be a very generous expense account.

The international marketing of tobacco products, she claimed, "is imperialism and racism of the most insidious kind and it must be stopped." "United we must fight the oppression which many of us experience," she declared, and she advised the audience to "become political" and "never forget that the multinational tobacco companies are cold and calculating in their drive for profits. They will buy governments and kill millions. It is time for tobacco control to truly become political."

The view that most people, and especially women, African Americans, and gays, are easily bamboozled by tobacco advertising is completely at odds

with the statistics on the educational attainment of the American public offered by the neo-Puritans themselves. The 1990 edition of *Tobacco Use in
California,* published by the California Department of Health Services and
the University of California, San Diego, proclaimed on page 1 that "the hazard of smoking is widely acknowledged; 84% of California smokers agree
that smoking harms their own health. This acknowledgment is, if anything,
somewhat stronger among black and Hispanic smokers" (California Department of Health Services 1990).

This admission raises a more fundamental question: If virtually everyone
already knows that smoking is bad for their health, why is there a need for the
taxpayers of California—or of any state, for that matter—to contribute hundreds of millions of dollars annually to employ literally thousands of antismoking "activists" as "educators"? What can they possibly teach the public
that the public doesn't already know? And why are blacks and Hispanics
being "targeted" if survey data reveal that they are even more cognizant of the
health hazards of smoking than the population in general? The obvious answer to these questions is that, despite the rhetoric to the contrary, Proposition 99 really has very little to do with "education," but is a means of acquiring
tax revenues to force citizens to engage in politically correct behavior and,
more important, to provide employment and income for the neo-Puritan movement. California's neo-Puritans have constructed many smoke screens to disguise this fact. Perhaps the largest smoke screen is the use of Proposition 99
funds to finance politically correct "research."

## Politically Correct Research

Five percent of Proposition 99 funds are earmarked for research performed
by researchers in the California university system and at nonprofit research
institutions within the state. "In 1992 [the state] awarded 92 new research
grants for a total of $24,626,594 to investigators at 26 public and private
nonprofit research institutions" (University of California 1993).

According to the widely accepted canons of the scientific method, researchers first employ theory or logic to deduce falsifiable hypotheses. Statistical
methods are then brought to bear in testing the hypotheses, which are rejected
or not, based on the evidence. In most disciplines, a theory or explanation
does not gain wide acceptance until it has been tested by many different researchers, with different data sets, over different periods of time. Only if the
same results are repeatedly reproduced do scientists incorporate the new theory
into their accepted body of knowledge.

This is *not* the approach taken by the Proposition 99 research program.
Like many government-funded research programs, the state's Tobacco-Related Disease Research Program is explicitly designed to fish for "research"
that supports preconceived conclusions. On page 1 of the program's 1993

annual report, the purpose of the program is defined as "providing data and technical assistance pertinent to the establishment of State and local policies that restrict smoking" (University of California 1993). No mention is made of the possibility that some research results may not support such policies, and it is highly unlikely that any such research would ever be funded. No Proposition 99 research grant recipient would ever be likely to report the results of a study, for example, that found smoking bans to reduce the revenues of California restaurants, for if he did, he could be assured of never receiving additional state funding for his research.

In fact, Stanton Glantz, a researcher at the University of California, San Francisco, published a questionable study claiming that such bans may actually *increase* restaurant revenues, implausibly arguing that thousands of California businesses may have been forgoing millions of dollars of profits that they now have gratefully discovered right under their noses, thanks to the efforts of the neo-Puritans (University of California 1993, 9).

Because Proposition 99-funded research is so politicized, many of the research results are of questionable use. Did California taxpayers really need to fund the research of USC Professor Karen M. Hennigan, for example, to "discover" that teenage "trouble makers" tend to smoke? "Early-smoking boys report high levels of antisocial behaviors such as stealing, shoplifting, and fighting," the professor soberly reported (University of California 1993, 7). Other Proposition 99-funded "research" has revealed that smoking may cause one's face to wrinkle prematurely and one's teeth to become yellowed.

During the 1990–92 period, the state awarded almost $117 million in Proposition 99 research grants. The grants were allocated to medical researchers in the areas of cancer, epidemiology, engineering, biomedicine, and cardiovascular and pulmonary disease, and to the nonmedical categories of "intervention" and public policy. The largest single grant, $4,559,102.00, went to the University of California, San Francisco, for public-policy research overseen by Stanton Glantz, director of the university's Institute for Health Policy Studies and president of Americans for Nonsmokers' Rights. His institution was also the largest single grantee, receiving $20,043,926.00 during the three-year period (University of California 1993, 6).

The research results funded by Proposition 99 are always announced with great certainty and confidence, when in reality considerable uncertainty exists. Take, for example, the assertion in the 1993 report that "one in five deaths in California is attributable to smoking" (University of California 1993, ii). Such an assertion bolsters the case for the prohibitionist policies promoted by the neo-Puritans, but cannot stand up to even cursory scrutiny.

Smoking may aggravate various diseases, but that is very different from being "the" cause.[17] Lung cancer is the most dreaded disease associated with smoking, yet the American Lung Association claims that significant numbers of lung cancer cases are attributable to air pollution, especially radon gas. Many other factors are contributing causes as well, according to the ALA, such as the radiation from X rays, diet, heredity, genetic defects, stress, and even personality (American Lung Association 1987, 8; Kamiya 1989, 92–93). Moreover, more than 50 million Americans who smoke never contract lung cancer. "Even cigarette smoking, the most heavily studied of all carcinogenic risks, still remains much of a mystery. For example, two-thirds of all cigarette smokers do not get lung cancer and 25 percent of the people who do get lung cancer do not get it from smoking. No one knows why" (Stroup and Goodman 1991, 21).

In light of these well-known uncertainties, the assertion by the Proposition 99-funded researchers that they know with certainty how many Californians died in recent years because of tobacco use is unfounded.

Another questionable statement that is made with great confidence is that "the total economic burden of smoking in California is $7.6 billion annually, or $256 per Californian per year" (University of California 1993, ii). This number is arrived at by first *assuming* that it is possible to determine with complete certainty how many deaths are directly attributable to smoking, and then adding up the estimated health care costs borne by those afflicted with various smoking-related diseases. Stanton Glantz has even gone so far as to state that since Proposition 99 passed, exactly $1.5 billion in health care costs have been saved (Schwartz 1994).

But a 1991 Rand Corporation study showed that because cigarettes are already so heavily taxed, smokers pay *more* in taxes than the additional costs of health care they are estimated to cause. Smokers were found to generate a "net external cost of smoking of 33 cents per pack. [But] since current federal, state and local taxes are 50 cents per pack or more...smokers are already paying their way" (Gravelle and Zimmerman 1994). In other words, *there are no net costs to society of smoking.* As explained by Jane Gravelle and Dennis Zimmerman (1994), economists at the Congressional Research Service of the Library of Congress:

> The Rand study identifies all of the costs and benefits that smokers impose on others—and excludes the costs smokers pay for themselves. Thus, the study includes as external costs only that portion of smokers' excess medical expenditures (49 cents per pack) and sick leave costs (1 cent per pack) not paid by smokers, the higher life and fire insurance premiums due to smoking (7 and 3 cents per pack respectively) and the lost tax revenue smokers would have paid to retirement and health programs had they not died prematurely (12 cents per pack).

> Additionally, the authors of the Rand study include the offsetting savings that smokers' premature deaths provide to nonsmokers—an obvious but often overlooked factor. After all, the alternative to death from a smoking-related illness is not immortality and perfect health—it is later death, and perhaps from a more costly illness or larger nursing home costs. Nonsmokers may not realize it, but they also benefit from the pension and social security payments that are not paid to smokers who die prematurely (33 cents per pack).

This is not to suggest that smokers should be subsidized (although that is what economic theory would suggest), but rather that the alarming statement that smoking costs Californians billions of dollars a year is baseless. It is typical, however, of how the neo-Puritans are constantly attempting to shock the public into embracing their political agenda. Despite these uncertainties and contradictions, Proposition 99 provided for a $28 million media campaign to broadcast the above-cited research results as gospel.

Perhaps the most blatant example of tax-funded politics under the guise of "research" is the $4,559,102.00 grant to Stanton Glantz, president of Americans for Nonsmokers' Rights, a 501(c)(4) organization. As a 501(c)(4) organization, Americans for Nonsmokers' Rights is explicitly a political, as opposed to an educational or charitable, organization and is permitted to spend much more of its resources on politics than a 501(c)(3) organization can. Glantz's research, moreover, is of the type one would expect to see produced by the research arm of one of the political parties, not a university "scientist." Specifically, his research is devoted to "tracking tobacco industry activities in California" (University of California 1993, 120) and advising the neo-Puritans on how they should respond to the industry's political arguments. He is involved, in other words, in political intelligence gathering for use in future political campaigns. This is "what we in politics do to each other when we're running for reelection," said former California House Speaker (now San Francisco mayor) Willie Brown, who believes it "doesn't deserve to be classified as research" (Jacobs 1994).

Glantz is also co-author of *Legislative Approaches to a Smoke Free Society*, a how-to-lobby handbook (Hanauer, Barr, and Glantz 1986). There is nothing inherently "wrong" with publishing such a handbook or with Glantz's political intelligence-gathering activities in general; the point is that *taxpayers' funds are being used* to promote a political agenda of which many taxpayers disapprove.

Some of the Proposition 99 research funding does go to legitimate medical researchers, but one also has to wonder about the propriety of such subsidies to high-income medical professionals in light of the fact that the lion's share of medical research funding comes from the federal government. The annual budget of the National Cancer Institute alone exceeds $2 billion, 4 times more than the American Cancer Society has spent on research in its entire seventy-five-year history (Bennett and DiLorenzo 1994). Proposition 99 funding of research at California medical schools, in other words, is a mere drop in the bucket and is not likely to significantly improve the chances of discovering cures for disease. Its primary impact is to enhance the bank accounts of already highly paid medical researchers and of their respective institutions. Virtually every university charges its researchers "overhead" fees that sometimes exceed 50 percent of the amount of the research grant. The University of California, San Francisco, being the largest recipient of Proposition 99 funds (about $20 million in 1990–92), has undoubtedly profited handsomely.

## Politically Correct "Addictions"

Even though millions of Americans have quit smoking, the neo-Puritans continue to claim that tobacco is addictive. Proposition 99-funded researchers argue that "nicotine addiction appears to be the result of the reduction of activity of neurons in the nucleus accumbens region of the brain" (University of California 1993, ii). The head of the Food and Drug Administration, Dr. David Kessler, convinced President Clinton to declare tobacco an addictive drug so that it can eventually be banned, just like cocaine and heroin.

If this is all true, then the neo-Puritans have stumbled upon one of the most remarkable medical discoveries in human history: human addictions can be cured with excise taxes. The implications are mind boggling. Drug addiction can be eliminated by legalizing heroin, cocaine, and other illicit drugs and simply imposing an excise tax on them. The same service can be performed for those who are addicted to chocolate, alcohol, coffee, tea, exercise, work, gambling, and myriad other products and activities.

## Conclusions

The neo-Puritans are prohibitionists whose often-stated objective is to achieve a "smoke-free society." Smoking is unhealthy, and virtually everyone knows it. The same can be said for other drugs that have been the target of prohibitionists, including alcohol (in excessive amounts), cocaine, heroin, and other illicit drugs. But governmental attempts to drive these from the legal marketplace have always resulted in the development of large underground markets controlled by organized crime. In Canada, where excise taxes on cigarettes exceed $4.00 per pack, it has been reported that one-third of all cigarettes sold are sold illegally on the black market.

Prohibition did not significantly curtail the consumption of alcohol in the 1920s, and the "war on drugs" certainly has not curtailed drug use; instead, it has created a level of crime unimaginable by Al Capone and his contemporaries and has spawned a governmental assault on civil liberties. Prohibitionists of the 1920s thought they could rid the country of alcohol; the objective of the federal government's "war on drugs" is to create a "drug-free society"; and now the neo-Puritans want us to be "smoke free" as well, and are sure to move on to beer, beef, and myriad other "harmful" and politically incorrect products. Just during the time in which this chapter was being prepared, neo-Puritans have held press conferences and published reports alleging the dangers of hot dogs, golf courses, steak, Mexican food, and popcorn!

If California's Proposition 99 establishes a trend, then Americans can expect to be perpetually harassed by an army of government-funded nonprofit busybodies who have discovered careers for themselves lecturing other people on what to consume. Telling others how to behave and what to think are the next logical steps, for in California, Proposition 99 has funded literally thousands of public-health bureaucrats, nonprofit political activists, public-school teachers, university researchers, and others who, because they benefit financially from the antismoking campaign, constitute a formidable lobbying force behind its expansion. And they can't be antismoking activists forever; either the public will get tired of it and pressure the legislature to end the program, or they will "succeed" and tobacco will be driven entirely into the underground economy. At that point, as Julia Carol of Americans for Nonsmokers' Rights has stated, they will all "move on to other causes."

Imposing a tax on an industry's product—any industry's—in order to finance a political propaganda campaign against the industry is a dire threat to free speech. Business people are already deprived of free speech to a large degree because government regulation is so pervasive; speaking up against government intervention into one's industry runs the risk of regulatory retribution or a dreaded tax audit. But the use of excise taxes to finance politically correct propaganda carries the governmental assault on commercial speech to an entirely new level. It is tyrannical to use general tax revenues to wage a propaganda campaign against a legal product, but it is an abomination to tax that very industry to fund such a campaign. Once such a precedent is established, where will it end? How many industries will be attacked in this way? If the government has so little respect for commercial speech, then it cannot hold noncommercial speech in very high regard either.

## Notes

1. Richard Paddock, "Health Care Groups Join to Push Cigarette Tax Hike," *Los Angeles Times,* 2 February 1987. Cited in Bennett 1990.
2. Sandra N. Michioku, "Health Coalition Urges 35-Cent Cigarette Tax," *United Press International,* 23 February 1987. Cited in Bennett 1990.
3. Ken Hoover, "Health Groups Squabble for Tobacco Tax Funds," *United Press International,* 31 July 1989. Cited in Bennett 1990.
4. "Tobacco Prevention," *Mammoth Lakes (Calif.) Weekly,* 18 February 1993, p. 53.
5. *Stanislaus County Tobacco Control Education Incentive Plan, 1990–92,* Stanislaus County, California.
6. Ibid.
7. Ibid.
8. "Breathing Easy, Smoke Free Theme to Be Celebrated With Free Walk-in-the-Park," *Martinez* (Calif.) *News Gazette,* 5 June 1992, p. 1.
9. "Parents Want Sex Survey Kept Off Calaveras County Campuses," Gannett News Service, 8 January 1993.
10. Ibid.
11. Ibid.
12. Ibid.
13. *Grant Proposal to City and County of San Francisco Tobacco Control Project by the GCA Group,* 13 January 1992. Obtained through state Freedom of Information Act request.

14. Santa Clara County, Calif., Tobacco Control Plan grant announcement, 1993. This is stated in the law, and is promulgated in local governments' written announcements of grants that are available.
15. Tobacco Control Coalition of Contra Costa County, minutes of public meeting, 10 October 1991, 75 Santa Barbara Road, Pleasant Hill, CA 94523.
16. The following discussion is based on a written transcript of the three-day conference "Revolt Against Tobacco," held in Los Angeles in September 1992. The text is available from the author.
17. No one claims that smoking is healthful, and most Americans are convinced that it is indeed a health hazard. Nevertheless, it is still impossible to establish a precise scientific link between mortality and smoking. Based on an exhaustive survey of the hundreds of studies of the relationship between smoking and various diseases, Dr. Hans J. Eysenck (1986, 70), author of forty books and more than 800 articles in academic journals, has concluded that

> the received view—that smoking causes lung cancer and coronary heart disease and is responsible for the major portion of the deaths that occur from these two causes—has not been proven correct by existing research, but has encountered so many anomalies and difficulties, and is based on such insecure foundations (largely due to the lack of reliability of the data, and the incautious use of statistics based on these data) the only possible conclusion is a verdict of "not proven."

## References

American Lung Association. 1987. *Annual Report*. New York.

Bennett, James T. 1990. *Health Research Charities: Image and Reality*. Washington, D.C.: Capital Research Center.

Bennett, James T., and Thomas J. DiLorenzo. 1994. *Unhealthy Charities: Hazardous to Your Health and Wealth*. New York: Basic Books.

Buchanan, James M. 1988. "Politics and Meddlesome Preferences." In *Clearing the Air: Perspectives on Tobacco Smoke*, edited by Robert Tollison. Lexington, Mass.: D.C. Heath.

California Department of Health Services. 1990. *Tobacco Use in California, 1990*. San Diego: University of California.

———. 1992. *Tobacco Use in California, 1992*. San Diego: University of California.

———. 1994. Tobacco Control Section. *Local Lead Agency Quarterly Cost Report*, 1 January–30 June.

Carson, Daniel. 1988. "Campaign Laws Clouded by Taxpayer Subsidies for Prop. 99 Cigarette Tax Initiative." *San Diego Union*, 17 October.

Davila, Robert D. 1993. "NAACP Hit by Financial Allegations." *Sacramento Bee*, 4 February, B-1.

Eysenck, Hans J. 1986. "Smoking and Health." In *Smoking and Society: Toward a More Balanced Assessment*, edited by Robert D. Tollison. Lexington, Mass.: D.C. Heath.

Gravelle, Jane, and Dennis Zimmerman. 1994. "The Marlboro Math." *Washington Post*, 5 June, C-1.

Hanauer, Peter, Glenn Barr, and Stanton Glantz. 1986. *Legislative Approaches to a Smoke Free Society*. Berkeley, Calif.: American Nonsmokers' Rights Foundation.

Hele, T.S. 1992. "Pool Program Quenching Smoking Finishes Tonight." *Hanford Sentinel*, 22 August, 1.

Hill, Angela. 1993. "Teen Smokers Say Ad Blitz Won't Make Any Difference." *Danville (Calif.) Tri-Valley Herald,* 24 February, 1.

Jacobs, Paul. 1994. "State Test on Tobacco Funds Sparks Fires." *Los Angeles Times,* 27 June, A-1.

Kamiya, Gary. 1989. "The Cancer Personality." *Hippocrates,* November-December.

Lucas, Greg. 1994. "Suit Questions Use of State Fund." *San Francisco Chronicle,* 24 March, A-19.

Meilink, Linda. 1992. "Is It Education or Lobbying?" *Paradise (Calif.) Post,* 17 March.

Schwartz, John. 1994. "California Activists' Success Ignites a Not-So-Slow Burn." *Washington Post,* 30 May, 1.

Sebelius, Steve. 1992. "Costa Says County Using Public Funds in Campaign." *Sacramento Union,* 22 May.

Sowell, Thomas. 1995. *The Vision of the Annointed: Self-Congratulation as a Basis for Social Policy.* New York: Basic Books.

Stroup, Richard, and John Goodman. 1991. "Making the World Less Safe: The Unhealthy Trend in Health, Safety and Environmental Regulation." *Journal of Regulation and Social Costs,* January.

Taylor, Kate. 1994. "Use of Teenager in Cigarette-Buying Sting Upsets Novato Police." *San Francisco Chronicle,* 11 January, A-18.

University of California. 1993. *Tobacco-Related Disease Research Program.* Sacramento: University of California, February.

von Mises, Ludwig. 1966. *Human Action: A Treatise on Economics.* 3rd ed. Chicago: Henry Regnery.

# 7

# Bureaucratic Incentives and the Transition from Taxes to Prohibition

*Gary M. Anderson*

Governments have taxed certain activities deemed by someone to be "sinful" throughout recorded history. For at least as long, those same governments have sometimes gone so far as to prohibit those "sinful" activities outright.

The common pattern observed throughout history can be simply stylized: the "sin" is first subjected to a tax; sometime later this tax is increased to prohibitive levels; and finally, the same government institutes an outright prohibition directed against the activity in question. Prohibitions typically find their origins in fairly moderate levels of taxation of the same goods and services.

Tax rates are "moderate" if they are consistent with the raising of significant revenues. In theory there is a unique tax rate that maximizes the potential revenue available to the government in that case. Depending on the elasticity of demand in that particular market, revenue-maximizing tax rates will sometimes be high and sometimes be low. If a particular tax is set at a rate that is consistent with the collection of a significant amount of revenue by the taxing authority, then it is reasonable to describe the rate as "moderate." Note that "moderate" in this context does not presuppose "optimal." A moderate tax rate might be set too high, or too low, from the perspective of revenue maximization.

Consider government as a decision maker. Obviously, governments have many competing goals. But a rational government will consistently act to maximize income, subject to relevant constraints.

Thus the historical record presents a seeming paradox: governments have frequently sacrificed substantial revenue by transforming revenue-generating taxes into explicit prohibitions—which, by definition, eliminate any possibility of earning revenue by taxing the prohibited good or service.

Of course, it is logically possible that the government in question might act to prohibit some activity, thereby sacrificing whatever revenue might have

139

been generated by a tax, because it has concluded that prohibition is an effi-cient mechanism for minimizing costs to society generally. For example, imag-ine that prohibiting the consumption of narcotic drugs were a significantly more effective way of reducing the quantities consumed of these substances than a moderate tax on the drugs. If a benevolent government felt that reduc-ing drug consumption were in society's best interest, then that government might reasonably sacrifice revenue to achieve this goal.

The problem is that outright prohibition does not seem to reduce the level of the activity prohibited more than the imposition of a moderate tax on that form of behavior. The "war on drugs" has not resulted in reduced drug con-sumption, but appears to have coincided with a significant increase in the market for illegal narcotics. Thus, the government appears to have sacrificed a significant amount of potential tax revenue for no purpose.

The present chapter explores this apparent paradox. We will argue that, like most apparent paradoxes, there is a rational explanation for this peculiar pattern of public policy. Governments are not monolithic entities with single-minded goals, but are organizations composed of rational, self-interested ac-tors. The politicians, bureaucrats, and officials often face economic incentives to pursue agendas at variance with the officially proclaimed purposes of the governments to which they belong. This agency problem helps to explain the from curious progression of moderate taxation to outright prohibition, at least in certain cases.

The chapter is divided into four sections. The following section outlines the basic puzzle of the progression from tax to prohibition, and explains how this transition results from the characteristic structure of incentives confront-ing those charged with enforcing public policy. The next section applies this model to explaining actual instances of the progression from tax to prohibi-tion in U.S. history. We consider the cases of drugs, alcoholic beverages, fire-arms, and cigarettes. The conclusion addresses the relevance of the model to understanding current controversies concerning actual and proposed selec-tive taxes, bans, and other restrictions.

## The Perverse Incentive to Prohibit

Common sense might lead us to presume that government always maxi-mizes net revenue. Whatever government's goals may be, they all require that government first secure resources to implement them, and unless government is simply irrational, it will consistently try to acquire as much money as it can from the citizens it administers, subject to whatever constitutional, legal, and political constraints are relevant. Therefore, we would expect to see a ten-dency for tax rates to gravitate toward revenue-maximizing levels. But the actual practice of real-world governments seems inconsistent with this com-monsense expectation. Real governments often violate this presumption by seeming to deliberately sacrifice tax revenue by prohibiting an activity instead of imposing a levy on it. This section discusses this phenomenon.

Our starting point is elementary: Legal prohibitions by their very nature sacrifice potential revenue available from the imposition of a moderate tax on the sale and use of the prohibited good or service. Prohibitions also require resources to enforce, therefore making this policy choice doubly costly from the standpoint of a prohibitionist government. The fact that governments throughout history have frequently resorted to prohibitions in place of taxation in their attempts to regulate certain consumption choices consequently merits serious investigation.

One possible solution to this puzzle involves some reference to the public interest. Government, according to this view, is a mechanism through which society expresses its rational decisions pertinent to the maximization of social welfare. When we observe a government undertaking to prohibit a seemingly voluntary act between consenting adults, that government could be thought of as engaged in an effort to reduce or eliminate externalities and thereby to improve the welfare of society. This explanation conveniently disposes of the apparent problem: we sometimes see a government acting in ways that sacrifice potential tax revenue because that government has judged the costs to society of permitting legal exchange of commodity X, subject to a moderate tax, to exceed the benefits.

Even granting the contention that government prohibitions on peaceful behaviors actually internalize external costs and raise efficiency—about which there is much controversy in the economics literature[1]—the public-interest model is subject to a more basic objection: it is unmotivated. The model is inconsistent with the most basic assumption of neoclassical economic theory— that all decisions are undertaken by self-interested individuals seeking to maximize their own well-being. Government is not a single organism capable of making independent decisions, but merely an organization of individuals. Human beings make decisions, designed to maximize their utility. The public-interest model is not really an explanation at all, but merely a circular argument: good X was prohibited because the individual decision makers composing the government decided to prohibit it.

*Government as Leviathan*

These difficulties suggest that a search for alternative models is in order. A plausible alternative to the public-interest model involves the assumption that government, as an organization, is at all times a simple revenue maximizer. Following Brennan and Buchanan (1981), we can conveniently refer to this as the "Leviathan model." Others, however, have long offered related arguments. For example, Adam Smith presented the essential elements of a similar model in his *Wealth of Nations*.[2] And, of course, Brennan and Buchanan adopted the term "Leviathan" from Thomas Hobbes, who used it as the title of his famous seventeenth-century treatise developing a different, but related, theme.

Government is assumed to have a simple goal in this view, that of raising the largest net revenue possible subject to relevant constraints. At all times government undertakes to maximize the value of its tax base.

This Leviathan model is capable of handily disposing of some obvious objections. Government may on occasion accept a reduction in tax revenue in the short run in exchange for maximizing the long-run value of its income stream (the Leviathan model does not imply any specific discount rate applicable to Leviathan's decision making). Government may take certain actions that raise no revenue directly, but which represent measures designed to maximize the size of the wealth base available for future taxation. Therefore, activities such as regulation of externalities, protection of private-property rights, and wars, in addition to other policies that fail to raise any revenue for government directly, can be modeled as devices for increasing future revenue opportunities.

In the context of this Leviathan model, the deliberate sacrifice of tax revenue in cases where specific voluntary activities between consenting adults are prohibited, rather than taxed, can also be explained. Say, for example, that government is observed to substitute a regime of revenue-raising taxation with the outright prohibition of some intoxicating substance. The Leviathan model would imply that this policy is actually consistent with maximizing long-run government revenue. Perhaps, for example, the prohibition can be expected to significantly reduce the actual consumption of this substance below the level a simple tax would, and that as a by-product, external costs associated with the consumption of this particular commodity would be reduced enough to cause a net expansion of the overall economy over time (i.e., increase the value of the tax base). Granted, this sort of argument sounds much like the public-interest model applied to the same problem, but there is an important difference: the Leviathan model assumes that government is motivated by the pursuit of tangible wealth (net revenue), and its predictions are therefore potentially testable in a way that those of the public-interest model are not. In the latter case, government's goal—maximizing social welfare—involves claims relating to intangible, and nonmeasurable, objectives.

Unfortunately, the Leviathan model is not completely satisfactory either. It is subject to problems similar to those that afflict the public-interest alternative. Most important, the Leviathan model implicitly assumes that government is a kind of giant individual that pursues its own interests independent of the utility functions of the persons who staff its offices and are actually in charge of day-to-day decision making. While Leviathan resembles *Homo economicus* more closely than the public-interest-maximizing government does (Leviathan is at least clearly portrayed as self-interested), in its pure form, it is not an organization of separate and distinct individuals pursuing their own self-interested agendas, but a kind of self-motivated machine.[3]

Therefore, the apparently persuasive Leviathan explanation of government prohibitions that sacrifice significant potential tax revenue is fundamentally flawed as well. If the model fails to satisfactorily describe public policy in general, we are at a loss to explain why government sometimes enacts prohibitions of otherwise peaceful, voluntary exchange.

We need to address another problem related to the decision of government to prohibit rather than merely tax. This is the apparent ineffectiveness of governmental prohibitions directed at consensual activities. Actual prohibitions undertaken in American history have tended to be miserable failures, in that they have failed to effectively prohibit.

Time and time again, government has banned a good or service, only to find that the prohibition fails to eliminate the market in question. The current war on drugs is a good example. Draconian penalties for drug possession and sale, combined with tremendous resources allocated to drug law enforcement, has failed to prevent the (illegal) drug market from thriving.

Worse, imposing a legal prohibition on the sale and use of a particular commodity might backfire under some circumstances. Demand might actually increase because of the ban. There are several reasons why we would expect this to be the case.

The returns available to sellers of the prohibited good or service are significantly increased by the legal restriction. Under prohibition, the potential profits available to a successful evader of the law are likely to be huge. These potential supranormal returns attract new users to the pool of existing consumers, because entry into the ranks of successful producers presupposes familiarity with the prohibited good or service; if a person hopes to get rich selling cocaine, it is first necessary to become a user and acquaint himself with the characteristics of the product he wishes to ultimately deal in. Thus, the rents available to successful (illegal) sellers indirectly encourage prospective future competitors to become demanders of the illicit good or service. This may actually tend to increase demand, and use, other things held equal.

Another contributing factor involves promotion and advertising. Government often invests heavily in promoting forms of consumption that it bans. Consider the problem facing a perfectly competitive market, say the market for marijuana. The optimal scale of plant in the case of marijuana production is tiny—anyone with a backyard, in practically any climate, can enter the business—and consequently the many millions of competing producers will all earn normal profits in the long run. Any investment designed to promote the consumption of marijuana would be in the interest of all producers—but this means that any investment made by any producer will create benefits that are available to rival suppliers as well. Free riding will drastically reduce the willingness of any producer of marijuana to bear advertising costs. Worse, millions of competing producers will be virtually impossible to organize in a manner that might restrict free riding. Therefore, marijuana will go largely unadvertised and will receive little or no promotion by producers in the marketplace.

But assume that government implements a ban on marijuana. The prohibiting government then invests heavily in marijuana education—it runs advertisements in magazines, on TV, on radio, on billboards—ostensibly designed to educate the public on the hazards of marijuana use. This "educational effort" solves the free-riding problem faced by the marijuana industry. Marijuana education increases the general public's awareness of the drug, and in the long run, this may increase demand for the substance.

One key to reconciling this apparent paradox (i.e., government willingly sacrificing tax revenue by banning "sinful" commodities) is the recognition of the principal-agent relation involved in government decision making. Government does not and cannot make decisions "itself," because it is an organizational structure, not a conscious individual. "Government decisions" are necessarily the decisions of individual government employees, who are the agents selected to represent that government.

Whenever the roles of agent and principal are separable in practice, the possibility arises of an agency problem: the goals of the agent(s) may not perfectly coincide with the goals of the principal. This is relevant even if we assume—contrary to the objections outlined above—that the principal in this case (government) is a separate individual with its own peculiar agenda. In other words, even Leviathan must hire agents to conduct its business, and therefore needs to confront the agency problem.

*The Interest-Group Model*

Fortunately, there is a viable alternative to the public-interest and Leviathan models of government decision making that both avoids the problems of the failure of these approaches to provide a satisfactory explanation of economic motivation and is consistent with the agency problem. This is the interest-group model of government regulation.

The essential elements of this alternative approach can be simply stated: government regulation produces wealth transfers by its very nature, and organized groups representing the interests of the potential beneficiaries of a particular measure will have a strong incentive to undertake investments (in terms of money, time, or other resources) designed to influence political outcomes in their members' favor.

This approach has proven to be extremely fruitful in recent years, and has generated a large volume of empirical research. As a framework it offers a far superior motivational model compared to the alternative views. The alternative models of government policy determination all rely on the assumption that government acts in pursuit of objectives that do not resemble the motivations we normally attribute to rationally self-interested individual economic actors. The interest-group model is not based on arbitrary assumptions about governmental irrationality or altruism, or of some quasi-mystical pursuit of the public interest. The interest-group model merely assumes that government is an organization (albeit with specific institutional characteristics) composed of rational self-interested individuals, and that governmental coercion imposes costs and benefits on other rational self-interested individuals who can be expected to lobby to promote their own personal agendas.

The interest-group model has been applied to federal environmental regulations, restrictions on the use of high-sulfur coal, the minimum wage, and many other examples of government regulation.[4] In these and many other episodes, the interest group benefiting from the implementation of the specific government regulation is relatively easy to identify clearly.

These examples showcase the advantages of the interest-group model. However, government regulation is often seemingly less amenable to the interest-group type of explanation. Some activities and behaviors restricted by government do not seem to produce obvious tangible benefits to readily identifiable private interest groups. Examples include issues such as government regulation of abortion, restrictions on "hate speech," and motorcycle helmet laws. Other examples include laws prohibiting the consumption and sale of narcotics and restrictions on the ownership of firearms. It is difficult to identify powerful private economic interests—at least those in a position to effectively lobby government—who can expect to obtain economic benefits from such regulations.

Of course, there is one major potential beneficiary of a governmental prohibition aimed at punishing otherwise peaceful capitalist acts between consenting adults. We refer to the economic interests of organized crime.

Prohibitions tend to produce powerful incentives for the emergence of black markets in the prohibited good or service. Some individuals and firms who are willing to bear the costs associated with the resulting risk of operating underground may enjoy extraordinary profits as a consequence. We naturally expect that individuals who have a comparative advantage in a particular undertaking will tend to occupy that niche in the economy. The people with a comparative advantage in operating black-market enterprises are professional criminals.

The profits of crime are the equivalent of restriction rents due to artificial barriers to entry. The only difference between the restriction rents available to the organized criminal suppliers of, say, illegal heroin, and the restriction rents available to the providers of a legal product who are protected against competition by government entry barriers (e.g., licensing laws) is that the latter represent benefits of legal monopoly power. In the latter case, government has granted specific firms official sanction. In the former case, the suppliers enjoying the advantages of government-provided barriers to entry are de facto beneficiaries. But regardless of the precise legal status of the beneficiaries who receive restriction rents, those individuals and firms have the incentive to lobby in favor of the entry barriers that provide their benefits, at least up to the point where the cost of those lobbying activities equals the expected benefit at the margin.

This would seem, then, to provide a plausible answer to the problem of identifying the winners in cases of government regulations that seem of no especial tangible benefit to law-abiding, nongovernmental interest groups. The gangs of organized criminals who capture control of the now-illegal industry, and who receive the resulting restriction rents, have a strong incentive to lobby in favor of the maintenance of the prohibition in question.

The difficulty with this approach is fairly obvious. Organized crime will normally face very high transaction costs associated with political lobbying aimed at furthering their peculiar economic interests. After all, the very business they operate is illegal, and open admission of their activities is tantamount to volunteering for jail time. Of course, lobbying may take the form of cash bribes, and given the comparative advantage of criminal entrepreneurs, this will probably be the preferred form of political influence. But here, too, the transaction costs are very high; in modern America laws against outright bribery are tightly enforced and the penalties are severe. Therefore, organized crime might be expected to have the will but lack the way. Black-market suppliers are not a very plausible candidate for the dominant interest group behind most government prohibitions, although they may sometimes play some significant role at the margin.[5] In most cases, then, we must look elsewhere.

There is another group of beneficiaries from government prohibitions who do not share these lobbying disadvantages, however. These are the bureaucrats and officials charged with the implementation and enforcement of the prohibition.

Consider the incentives of the bureaucracy in relation to a legal prohibition it is charged with enforcing. The more severe and inclusive the prohibition, the larger the size of the enforcement bureaucracy the government will require to make the prohibition effective. This implies that tighter restrictions on a commodity lead to bigger budgets and more employees for the agencies assigned to enforce them. Both outcomes tend to be associated with higher incomes for enforcement bureaucrats, in both pecuniary and nonpecuniary terms.

Those same bureaucratic enforcement agencies have a minimal (or nonexistent) incentive to act in ways designed to protect the flow of government revenue in general. For example, the Drug Enforcement Administration (DEA) might conceivably be able to lobby Congress to relax the existing drug laws in a particular way, say making medicinal use of marijuana legal and subject to federal tax, that would lead to increased tax revenue for the Treasury. Even if we imagined a situation in which such a move would make no dent in the DEA's budget allocation, that agency would have no incentive to advocate such a reform unless a sufficient share of the resulting increase in federal revenue were earmarked for its own use.

We still need to explain a peculiar aspect of the political history of prohibitions in America, however: why these bans seem to begin in the form of moderate taxes imposed on "sinful" goods. This, too, is understandable in terms of bureaucratic incentives. Opportunism by bureaucrats charged with enforcing specific taxes tends to lead to higher and higher tax rates, and finally, to outright prohibition. This is a pattern we see repeatedly in recent U.S. history.

To a rent-seeking bureaucracy, a prohibition is a more effective device for generating bureaucratic rents than a mere tax. After all, tax revenue collected from a legal trade typically must be shared with other agencies; but a given agency's budget is all its own. A general legal prohibition placed on some good or activity represents a golden opportunity for the bureaucracy charged with its enforcement. A legal prohibition maximizes the political demand for enforcement services. A moderate tax, by contrast, will tend to produce some law violations, but is likely to leave most of the production and sale of the taxed commodity in the legal sector of the economy.[6] The enforcement bureaucracy will be limited to tracking down and sanctioning violators of the tax law, only a subset of the total population of producers and consumers. In contrast, an actual prohibition criminalizes all demanders and suppliers of the prohibited good. Unless the prohibited good is subject to highly elastic demand conditions, and the willingness of potential customers and potential producers to participate in the now-illegal activity falls drastically, the political demand for enforcement activity will almost by definition be maximized. Prohibitions in U.S. history have in fact tended to focus on goods the demand for which is highly *in*elastic.

This outcome, while predictable, is ironic. Prohibitions render entire ranges of behavior illegal, and therefore beyond the tax code, while at the same time those same goods and services, if subject to tax instead of prohibition, would be exactly the targets of revenue-maximizing taxes if the government consistently pursued this goal.

*Bans and Bribes*

William Niskanen (1971) deserves credit for developing the modern theory of the budget-maximizing bureaucracy. He argues that rational, self-interested individual bureaucrats seek to expand their agency's domain because by so doing they can expect to obtain higher wages, more employees, better amenities, and more power (i.e., increased personal wealth). Niskanen's important contribution to our understanding of the agency problems associated with public bureaucracies is incomplete in at least one important respect, however. Niskanen stops short of exploring the rent-seeking opportunities available to public bureaucrats that take the form of actual corruption.

Most of the large literature devoted to the problem of bribery in human history fails to make a simple, basic point: bribery is made possible only by governmental barriers to entry. In the absence of laws or other regulations that prevent the free flow of resources through voluntary transactions, the basic motivation for bribery disappears.

There is an important analogue to this problem in the literature devoted to the analysis of comparative economic systems. Sovietologists and other experts on socialist economies have long recognized that the level of corruption among officials administering these systems is extremely high. Some economists have gone so far as to suggest that these centrally planned systems depend for their very viability on the informal systems of bribes and graft payable to their officials, which admit at least a minimal degree of flexibility into these generally very rigid economies.[7]

The high level of graft in such economies is easy to explain. Socialist states are dedicated to the prohibition of capitalist transactions between consenting (private) adults. Therefore, virtually all prospective voluntary exchanges that would benefit both willing participants are impossible without the payment of appropriate bribes. Bribery, quite simply, becomes a way of life in a socialist state—life without the opportunity of "paying off" public officials standing in the way of simple transactions would be nearly impossible (as P. T. Bauer once observed, the corruption endemic in Marxist economic systems makes life under such regimes bearable). Individuals fortunate enough to occupy strategic positions in a socialist state have access to tremendous power. Consequently, they have the opportunity to translate this power—through the taking of bribes—into tremendous wealth. This relationship, in the form of naked venality, may explain much about how socialist regimes operate.

The same principle applies to situations involving prohibitions of voluntary acts between consenting adults in otherwise free-market economies. Here, too, the taking of bribes represents an important factor in explaining the motivation of public enforcement bureaucracies to lobby in favor of more and stricter prohibition policies.

The corruption associated with alcohol prohibition was notorious. The frequency with which Bureau of Prohibition agents solicited and actually received bribes from black-market liquor suppliers was evidently a serious problem.[8] Similarly, bribery of police and drug enforcement agents in the current war on drugs is apparently widespread. Some drug enforcement officials have demonstrated a willingness to turn a blind eye to certain illegal drug activities, for a price.[9]

Any law prohibiting a voluntary act between consenting adults is a microcosm of the socialist state. Socialism can be viewed as a kind of giant machine through which those in charge systematically exploit government's monopoly power over the lives of ordinary people. Analogously, in the U.S. economy government agencies charged with the enforcement of particular prohibitions against capitalist acts between consenting adults are mechanisms through which corrupt bureaucrats and public officials can seek rents in the form of bribes from violators of the prohibition. Prohibitions are thus islands of socialism— and the rent seeking that socialism entails—in the market economy.

## When Bureaucrats Ban Revenue: The Model in American History

Examination of U.S. history reveals a recurring pattern in public policy. Time and time again, a moderate tax on some form of consumption behavior has been gradually increased to a prohibitive level, and then supplanted with an out-and-out prohibition on the possession and sale of the good or service in question. This transition has repeatedly occurred in a manner consistent with the perverse incentives of the law enforcement bureaucracy. For example, drug prohibition started out as drug taxation, but powerful bureaucracies emerged and sought to extend their bureaucratic domains—leading to the war on drugs, which directly costs many billions of dollars and indirectly sacrifices many billions of dollars in potential government revenue. The waging of the war on drugs in a manner seemingly designed to *maximize* financial losses to the government is only one illustration of the predictable effects of bureaucratic rent seeking in practice. This section considers several important cases showing how this process works.

### The War on Drugs

The war on drugs is today a monumental bureaucratic enterprise. The federal government spends about $10 billion a year on drug control efforts.[10] A sizable portion of the nonfederal law enforcement establishment in the United States is also devoted to the prosecution of drug offenders. These state and local enforcement costs may add as much as $10.1 billion each year to the total direct costs.[11] Total spending by all levels of government in the United States expressly devoted to enforcing drug laws probably exceeds $20 billion per year.

But these are only the direct costs of drug law enforcement. The indirect costs include potential tax revenue sacrificed by the drug war. The governments of the United States refuse to collect billions of dollars in potential tax revenue each year as a result of drug prohibition. The value of illicit drugs purchased by consumers in the black market has been estimated as worth up to $140 billion a year.[12] As such, a moderate tax rate would be capable of raising tens of billions of dollars in revenue annually.

One irony is that drugs are, in theory, an ideal commodity for government to tax in terms of potential revenue productivity. Narcotic drugs are the classic textbook example of a good with inelastic demand. The quantity demanded of such a good is relatively unresponsive to changes in the price per unit.

Basic economic theory teaches that imposing a tax on a good with this characteristic is potentially most productive in terms of raising revenue, for a simple reason: consumers will tend to accept the higher price due to the tax, rather than shift their purchases into other, nontaxed alternatives. Indeed, many standard economics textbooks use the demand for addictive drugs as an example of perfectly inelastic demand (i.e., a complete lack of responsiveness among consumers to an increase in price).

The war on drugs is defended primarily as an effort designed to reduce the extent of drug abuse in society. If this is taken to be the real goal of the drug war, that effort has not merely been a miserable failure, but seems to have made the problem much, much worse than it was previously.

Due to the severe limitations in the available data, it is very difficult to accurately track rates of drug use through U.S. history before the past two decades. But there is widespread agreement that the drug user population of the country has grown enormously in recent times. According to one authority, "the Second World War ended with relatively few opiate addicts and very little use of cocaine or marijuana in the United States" (Musto 1987, 67). At that time, combined government resources devoted to prosecuting drug-related crimes were puny. By comparison, in 1991 the usage of illegal drugs was clearly higher than it was fifty years before, despite the fact that the war on drugs has been intense and enormously expensive.

Consider the relationship between drug prohibition and crime. The war on drugs enjoys widespread support from the general public, but not because of some deep and abiding Puritanical spirit in the American psyche. Rather, Americans see drug use as causing crime, and the war on drugs as an anti-crime measure.

This is ironic, because crime rates have risen as the war on drugs has been consuming ever greater amounts of government resources. Take one example: the number of prisoners received into all prisons—federal, state, and local—was falling from 1961 to 1969. The war on drugs, a child of the Nixon administration, began about the end of that period. From 1970 to 1987, the number of prisoners per 100,000 population rose dramatically, about two and a half times (Friedman 1991, 56). According to one recent estimate, the discounted costs of drug prohibition in the United States are over $20.6 billion per year, *not* counting the direct enforcement costs associated with the drug war mentioned above (Ostrowski 1989, 20). These costs represent a pure deadweight loss to society—resources unavailable for productive purposes.

Therefore, the war on drugs seems a paradox. Drug prohibition not only imposes huge direct costs on government, but also entails the sacrifice of many more billions in potential tax revenue. Moreover, the various social problems that the war on drugs is ostensibly designed to combat seem to be worse after this prohibition than they were before. We turn now to a short review of the history of this prohibition, which began as an effort to raise tax revenue.

Before 1914, the possession and use of narcotic substances in the United States were not subject to any federal restrictions. Regulation of domestic consumption of narcotic drugs basically began in 1914 with the passage of the Harrison Narcotics Act, which imposed a tax on the production, sale, and use of opium. In 1937, Congress enacted another tax act, this time imposing a levy on the production, sale, and use of marijuana. Although drug laws proliferated later (particularly during the 1960s) these two measures provided the basis for all subsequent legislative policy making.

The federal government began to collect revenue from taxes imposed on narcotic drugs early in the nineteenth century. Beginning in 1842, imports of crude opium (a substance that could not be produced domestically) were subject to a tariff. During the next few decades, the duty on opium fluctuated, reaching a high of $12.00 per pound in 1890. The intention clearly was to raise revenue, not to reduce drug use. The Treasury Department attempted to seize smuggled opium, and then turned around and sold it to the highest bidder (Lee 1973, 108)!

Imported opium was a significant source of revenue for the federal government. For example, between 1891 and 1896 an average annual total of 76,348 pounds of smoking opium were legally imported into the United States. At a duty rate of $12.00 per pound, this translated into an average annual revenue to the U.S. Treasury of over $916,000 (see Courtwright 1982, 23).

Thus, well before 1914, the federal government was collecting substantial revenue from opium imports. Then, in 1909, Congress enacted a law that prohibited importation of opium for nonmedicinal purposes (thereby requiring that opium be purchased through a physician). The Harrison Act had the potential to expand this revenue base by generating tax receipts from domestic sellers and users of opium. The act required that anyone who dealt in any way with opium or coca leaves, or their derivatives, must register and pay a yearly $1.00 license fee. One writer has described this provision as an "awkward revenue mechanism," which is probably true, but nevertheless it *was* a revenue mechanism.[13]

Similarly, the 1937 Marijuana Tax Act had the potential to raise still more revenue from the sale and use of this drug. All importers, manufacturers, dealers, and "practitioners" (i.e., growers) were required to pay an occupational tax. The law required that all persons buying or selling marijuana register with the Federal Bureau of Narcotics, and pay a transfer tax of $1.00 per ounce. Unregistered individuals were required to pay $100.00 per ounce (Bonnie and Whitebread 1974, 124).

However, neither law's revenue potential was to be realized. In practice, the bureaucracy charged with the enforcement of both of these statutes interpreted the legislation so strictly as to practically foreclose any federal revenue potential. Federal revenue from the taxes consequently proved insignificant. In the case of the Harrison Act, the enforcement bureaucracy simply refused to allow physicians to prescribe narcotics to addicts.[14] Similarly, the 1937 act required that marijuana users register with the Bureau of Narcotics before making a legal—taxed—purchase of the substance. The Bureau of Narcotics just stopped accepting registration requests.

Clearly, then, both marijuana and opiates were subject to tax, set at rates capable of generating some revenue, long before outright prohibition was seriously proposed. Granted, the levels of revenue were probably not as high as they might have been; the tax rates were almost certainly set too high to maximize the flow of tax revenue. But the revenue that was actually collected was substantial. This revenue flow did not persist for very long, though: taxation for revenue from drugs rapidly degenerated into taxation for prohibition of drugs, which in turn was soon transformed into the explicit prohibition on the possession, sale, and use of narcotics. We now turn to a consideration of how and why this peculiar result came about.

The government drug enforcement bureaucracy spends many billions of dollars on lobbying activity designed to support and expand the war on drugs. We use the term "lobby" to refer to all investments made for this purpose; it is illegal for government agencies to actually lobby Congress directly. However, spending that influences public support for the drug war among voters—who elect Congress—clearly serves the same basic purpose as spending devoted to jawboning members of Congress on Capitol Hill. For example, the federal government budgeted over $1.2 billion for "drug education" in fiscal year 1991 (White House 1990, 100). This figure, of course, does not include the enormous efforts at the state and local levels devoted to the same basic purpose.

Historians have tended to take the rhetoric of drug tax advocates at face value. These proponents placed strong emphasis on the purported ill effects of these substances on society, and claimed that the proposed taxes on these drugs were actually intended exclusively to reduce drug use.

But the historians fail to explain why the governmental rhetoric should simply be assumed to perfectly match the reality of tax policy. Governments misrepresent the real goal of public policy all the time. Rent control ordinances are proclaimed to protect the rights of tenants, while in practice they render some tenants homeless. Minimum-wage laws are advocated to help entry-level workers, while in reality these laws create unemployment among those with low skills. Similarly, the antidrug rhetoric was, in part, a smoke screen to justify the new taxes. We know that this must be true because the tax rates implemented by the government in these cases were, at least at first, sufficiently low enough to generate substantial revenue.

## The War on Alcohol

The premier example of a sin tax transformed into a prohibition is, of course, the Prohibition era. Between 1920 and 1933, the manufacture, distribution, possession, and consumption of alcoholic beverages were crimes in the United States.

Alcoholic beverages are currently legal and subject to tax. Nowadays, proponents of increased alcohol taxes often utilize rhetoric designed to disparage this good; higher levies are proclaimed to be a device for reducing the consumption of alcohol, thereby purportedly improving public health, public morals, or both. The sincerity of those making such claims is perhaps open to question. But there is no doubt that taxes on alcoholic beverages raise huge amounts of revenue for various levels of government. For example, in 1991 U.S. governments at all levels collected over $10 billion from this source.[15] Although alcohol taxes were a relatively minor contributor to the combined total revenue collected by all governments from all sources,[16] they generated almost enough to cover the total direct government spending on fire protection in that year.[17]

The basic facts of this peculiar episode are easy to relate. In 1917, the U.S. Congress passed the proposed Eighteenth Amendment to the U.S. Constitution, banning the manufacture and sale of alcoholic beverages, and sent it to the states for ratification. Ratification by the thirty-sixth state was achieved in 1919. Prohibition actually began in 1920, with the passage of the implementing legislation, the National Prohibition (Volstead) Act. Prohibition ended in December 1933, with repeal of the Eighteenth Amendment by vote of two-thirds of the states (utilizing the mechanism of state constitutional conventions).[18]

In the case of alcohol prohibition, we again see the perverse tendency of a ban on a substance actually leading to a worsening of the social problems related to abuse of the substance. For example, Clark Warburton (1932), in his classic economic analysis of the effects of Prohibition, noted that the Volstead Act actually interrupted the downward progression of domestic alcohol consumption per capita. Moreover, there is some evidence that alcohol usage rates actually went up during Prohibition. Compared with a figure of 1.69 gallons in the 1911–14 period, the amount of pure alcohol ingested per capita was 0.73 gallons per annum in the period 1921–22 (Prohibition took effect in 1920); per capita consumption then rose to 1.14 gallons per annum in the period 1927–30 (see table 3.1). Other scholars have come to the conclusion that Prohibition may have reduced alcohol consumption slightly—for example, another recent study argues that alcohol consumption first declined sharply but by 1927 had returned to levels comparable to those found in the United States prior to Prohibition (Miron and Zwiebel 1991)—but agree that the "total ban" had relatively little effect on the total amount of alcohol consumed.

Warburton (1932) cites data showing that death rates from cirrhosis of the liver, a disease associated with the abuse of alcohol, rose consistently from a level of 1.0 per 100,000 population in 1920 to 3.7 in 1929 (the rate actually peaked in 1927–28 at 4.0 per 100,000 population). One recent writer concludes that "prohibition was a policy satisfying moral precepts which had nothing to do with diminishing alcohol hazards that it actually enhanced" (Morgan 1991, 417). While the degree of satisfaction of alleged moral precepts is inherently problematical, there seems little doubt that Prohibition made the alcohol "problem" in the United States no better and perhaps worse.

This is another similarity between the impact of Prohibition and the impact of the war on drugs: both efforts to ban "sinful" substances from being peacefully exchanged between consenting adults seem to have drastically increased the rate of violent crime in the United States. Consider murder and assault rates. In 1920, the first year of Prohibition, there were about 11.7 murders and assaults per 100,000 population. This figure had risen to 16 per 100,000 by the last year of Prohibition, 1933. And the rate fell dramatically with repeal; by 1940, the rate was about 9.8 per 100,000, and continued to fall thereafter (U.S. Bureau of the Census 1975, part 1, 441).

This, then, is the paradox. Alcohol prohibition not only sacrificed a windfall of tax revenue that would otherwise have been available to government for public purposes, but actually seems to have made alcohol-related social problems worse. One is tempted, as in the case of the war on drugs, to simply conclude that sometimes government is guilty of flagrant irrationality. However, there is an explanation for these events that does not require resorting to an ad hoc claim of governmental myopia. Alcohol prohibition served the interests of a well-defined enforcement bureaucracy, which actively lobbied for Prohibition and for its continuation. The fact that the ban on alcohol was not kept in place very long can also be explained by reference to this factor.

Prior to Prohibition, the taxation of alcoholic beverages was a major source of government revenue. In 1915, for example, combined federal, state, and local government income from the taxation of alcohol amounted to about $245 million. Between 1900 and 1919, the U.S. Treasury alone collected a total of over $4.7 billion in alcohol tax receipts. This revenue was reduced drastically with the onset of Prohibition.[19]

Following the repeal of Prohibition, the tax revenue collected by state and local governments from alcoholic beverage sales snapped right back. In 1935, alcohol tax revenue amounted to $143 million; in 1937, $221 million; and in 1945, $368 million. In 1991, federal alcohol tax revenue amounted to a staggering $7.2 billion (U.S. Bureau of the Census 1946, 302, 317; U.S. Bureau of the Census 1993, table 468).

Granted, Prohibition was a complex phenomenon, and several important factors no doubt contributed to both its origin and its (short) existence.[20] Notwithstanding this complexity, once Prohibition got started there quickly emerged a significant new concentrated interest group with a powerful incentive to lobby in support of the antiliquor measure: the bureaucracy charged with enforcing Prohibition.

A comparison of the bureaucracy tasked with the enforcement of Prohibition and the later generation of bureaucrats charged with enforcing the war on drugs is instructive in this regard. Prohibition was essentially the bureaucratic domain of the relatively small Bureau of Prohibition (although some other agencies, such as the U.S. Coast Guard, were also significantly involved). Not only was federal government participation in enforcement relatively minor, but during Prohibition state and local police forces were essentially uninvolved. Prohibition violations were federal cases, and despite the fact that almost all states passed their own laws making the possession and sale of alcoholic beverages a crime, these laws were very poorly enforced.

Compared to the massive government investment in the war on drugs, the resources made available to enforce Prohibition were minuscule.[21] The budget of the Bureau of Prohibition, charged with the implementation of the Volstead Act, never exceeded $1.7 million per annum (U.S. Bureau of the Census 1946).

Prohibition (with a capital "P") was eventually repealed, in part because the size—and subsequently, clout—of the public bureaucracy that benefited from the existence of Prohibition was relatively tiny. Prohibition was repealed in 1933, fourteen years after it was first instituted. Drug prohibition is now decades old, and directly benefits a huge public bureaucracy with tentacles throughout the various levels of government in our federal system. This suggests that the war on drugs is much more stable and secure than Prohibition was earlier in this century. Prohibition simply did not directly benefit enough public bureaucrats to protect it from the efforts of opponents.[22]

*Gun Control*

Americans are, and have always been, free to buy, sell, own, and operate firearms, albeit subject to gradually accelerating restrictions. Many of these laws and regulations have traditionally been aimed at limiting access by professional criminals to firearms. Such restrictions lead to a minimal sacrifice in potential tax revenue to the government. There is a large and powerful lobby in the United States, however, favoring what amounts to gun prohibition, and these special-interest groups seem to be making inroads at the federal and state levels. This prohibitionist effort seems to be rapidly gathering political strength, and if effective, it would lead to a quite significant loss in government revenue—not even counting the resources that would be required in order to enforce the ban.

Nowadays there are about 212 million privately owned firearms in the United States.[23] In 1990, U.S. consumers spent approximately $2.3 billion on firearms (U.S. Bureau of the Census 1993, 242, table 397). These sales are a source of tax revenue to the forty-five state governments that impose a general sales tax (and the local governments in the twenty-six states where local sales taxes are added onto the state government levy), in addition to the revenue collected by the federal government from an 11 percent excise tax on guns and ammunition and license fees paid by gun dealers.[24] A revenue-maximizing government might be expected to at least consider undertaking efforts designed to increase gun purchases and ammunition usage, given that this form of consumption raises significant amounts of revenue for government. Instead, governments in the United States have persistently acted to increase the severity of restrictions on gun ownership and use, and these efforts seem to be accelerating in the direction of outright prohibition of at least certain kinds of firearms.

One possible explanation of this trend is that gun use generates significant negative externalities for society, and that government therefore has a legitimate interest in attempting to reduce these costs to society by regulating guns. The problem, as we will see below, is that the evidence for a causal relationship between gun ownership rates and crime rates (the primary alleged negative externality associated with the possession and use of private firearms) is extremely dubious.

It is obvious that gun prohibition would require sacrificing a large amount of tax revenue. Therefore, in order to justify the prohibition of private gun ownership, we would have to assume that such a ban would produce benefits that outweigh this disadvantage. Unfortunately, this does not seem to be the case.

Obviously, gun control regulations are supposed to reduce gun ownership. Ironically, available evidence suggests that they actually tend to have the opposite impact, at least in the United States. For example, in a major empirical analysis of the impact of the 1968 Gun Control Act (a landmark in the history of federal gun control in the United States), Magaddino and Medoff (1984) find that after controlling for other significant factors in explaining handgun ownership, such as income, population, age distribution, and the level of crime, the act's passage seems to have significantly *increased* handgun ownership. They attribute this surprising result to the role of adaptive expectations on the part of the handgun-owning public: in other words, the passage of the 1968 act was widely interpreted by potential handgun purchasers as an indication of even more restrictive gun controls in the future, and this expectation led to an increase in current handgun demand (Magaddino and Medoff 1984, 247).

Beginning in the late 1870s, state and local governments began to restrict the private ownership of firearms. These postbellum measures were aimed mainly at preventing blacks and immigrants from arming themselves.[25] Firearms bought and sold for private use were a lucrative source of excise tax revenue at the state and local levels.

The first federal gun control measure was the National Firearms Act of 1934. It was a revenue-raising measure that imposed annual taxes on the sale and purchase of a subset of firearms.[26] This legislation was followed by the federal Firearms Act of 1938, which required manufacturers and dealers in firearms to be licensed.[27]

Gun controls at the federal level began with the 1934 law. Even a casual inspection of the relevant statistics suggests that gun ownership has grown under this regime of legal restriction. Not only the absolute number of firearms, but also the number per capita, has increased steadily since at least 1947. In that year, the estimated total stock of all firearms in the United States was 50,543,473, or 350.8 firearms per 1,000 population (91.3 handguns per 1,000 population). By 1968, there were 102,302,251 firearms of all types, or 513.1 per 1,000 population (139.7 handguns per 1,000 population). And since 1968—the date of passage of the most comprehensive gun restrictions prior to that date, the Gun Control Act of 1968—the stock of firearms has grown to about 212 million, which works out to about 818.5 guns per 1,000 population (Kleck 1984, 119).

Despite the seemingly widespread presumption that gun ownership somehow increases crime, a rather large empirical literature has failed to establish a consistent, statistically significant link (Kleck 1984; Kleck and McElrath 1991). Some studies have even reported a negative relationship (i.e., that gun ownership deters crime).[28] The consensus finding—no statistically significant link—seems consistent with ordinary common sense. Criminals can use guns to prey on law-abiding citizens. But if guns are legal, law-abiding citizens can also use guns to defend themselves from criminals.

Gun control laws affect only the possession and use of guns by law-abiding citizens. Professional criminals, who have already rejected legal job opportunities in favor of a life outside the law, are unlikely to give up their firearms in response to a legal gun ban. Some gun laws have been intended to reduce firearm availability to convicted felons and other so-called high-risk groups. Such measures may indeed work selectively to reduce gun access by the criminal element in society. But many actual and proposed gun control measures are aimed at restricting everyone's access to firearms, criminals and the law-abiding alike. Such measures seem almost certain to reduce gun possession among the law-abiding to a relatively greater extent.[29]

This is the paradox of gun control. While the ownership of guns by private citizens is currently legal in the United States, that ownership is increasingly subject to nontax restrictions of a variety of kinds. These regulations by their very nature sacrifice potential tax revenue, while at the same time having no particular impact on crime rates. Why would a rational government act in this peculiar manner, seemingly giving something (revenue) in exchange for nothing?

Gun control is a relatively recent development in the United States. Before the 1920s, there were essentially no restrictions imposed by U.S. governments on the right of citizens to keep and bear arms. In other words, there were no restrictions on the ownership of any gun, ammunition, or, for that matter, other weapons; no restrictions on the carrying of concealed weapons, under any circumstances; and no regulation of the manufacture or sale of firearms.

The key to resolving this apparent paradox involves recognizing the bureaucratic incentives confronting the relevant group of governmental agents.

It is indeed rational for those agents to pursue public policies that sacrifice potential government revenue.

The prohibition of handguns has received considerable active support from public law enforcement officials. The International Association of Chiefs of Police, in conjunction with the Fraternal Order of Police, has aligned itself with the gun control movement.[30] Numerous big-city police chiefs have gone on record as favoring strict gun control. Not all public police officers favor strict gun control, but there seems abundant evidence that many of them do, and this fact is consistent with their economic interests.

Firearms represent an important input in the production of personal defense. Guns allow private citizens to provide more effectively for their own protection. Not all firearms are purchased solely for the purpose of providing personal defense, of course. Obviously, there are a host of alternative uses available for firearms in general: hunting, target shooting, and so on (not to mention the small, but nonetheless significant, demand for guns by collectors). But personal defense is a by-product of virtually all firearms ownership, and a large proportion of the actual market demand for guns is motivated by the desire of individuals to improve their ability to defend themselves.

Therefore, privately owned firearms and public police forces are substitute inputs in the provision of defense of citizens.[31] Any legal restriction on the ability of private citizens to provide for their own defense will tend to increase the demand of the public for government police services.[32]

Prior to about 1920, most citizens of the United States did not live in jurisdictions that provided public police services. In 1902, all levels of government in the United States spent a combined (and tiny) total of only $114 million on all aspects of the criminal justice system—including public police protection, courts, and prisons. By 1975, this spending had multiplied over 75 times, to $8.5 billion (U.S. Bureau of the Census 1975, 416).

This is not to suggest that the only substitute available to citizens who did not have access to public police forces was the home production of defense. Those individuals living in jurisdictions that failed to provide public police services were not relegated to providing personally for their own defense. Private, for-profit firms abounded from the early days of the Republic, providing citizens with protective services for a market-determined price.[33]

Superficially, private defense firms would appear to have an incentive similar to that of monopoly public police forces to advocate and lobby for restrictions on the ability of citizens to home-produce defense for themselves. After all, the greater the ease with which a homeowner can defend himself, the lesser that person's willingness to contract with a private firm to provide a similar service, other things held equal. This did not, however, happen, and there are several reasons why.

One, the market for private defense was largely unregulated, and highly competitive. Producers tended to be relatively small and politically unorganized. It was relatively difficult for private defense firms to coordinate their activities, and even if they had succeeded in this endeavor, the gains (say, from an outright ban on the ownership of firearms by private citizens) would accrue to defense firms generally, eliminating the potential returns available to any particular firm from so acting. Two, private defense firms, being nongovernmental, competitive organizations, had relatively poor access to the halls of public policy making, making it relatively more difficult for them to achieve political results. And three, these private firms were direct competitors with the emerging public police organizations, and the latter were beginning to focus their efforts on the legal restriction of these private firms. [34]

## The Crusade Against Cigarette Revenue

The United States is edging closer and closer to the point where cigarette smoking will be entirely banned. Several states and numerous localities across the country already ban smoking in public places. The U.S. Congress has likewise considered a law that would prohibit smoking in public places, albeit with a few exceptions.[35]

This prohibitionist trend on the part of U.S. governments might seem hard to reconcile with the interest-group model of regulation. After all, there are no close substitutes for cigarettes, and it is therefore difficult to identify a well-defined industry interest group that would tangibly benefit from a tobacco ban. There are, of course, other potential beneficiaries of smoking bans who have the incentive to lobby for such measures. For example, prohibiting smoking in the workplace serves to transfer wealth from smokers to nonsmokers, as the latter benefit from the entry barrier facing the former.[36] But the tangible gains to private interest groups from the prohibition of smoking still do not seem very substantial. Meanwhile, as long as tobacco is legal, the substance is a veritable "cash cow" for U.S. governments. In 1991, all levels of government in the United States collected almost $11 billion in revenue from taxes on tobacco products.[37]

There is, however, a major additional potential beneficiary of antismoking laws and regulations: the enormous government public-health bureaucracy. Nationally, all levels of government employed about 1.8 million health workers, bureaucrats, and officials in 1991. These employees were paid about $2.25 billion (U.S. Bureau of the Census 1993, table 500). This group constitutes a large, concentrated, and potentially powerful lobby in favor of prohibiting cigarettes.

Consider cigarette prohibition from the standpoint of the potential enforcement bureaucracy. About 25 percent of U.S. adults smoke, spending an estimated $45 billion each year for the privilege. Enforcing a total ban on smoking would be a Herculean task, requiring armies of bureaucrats and billions of dollars in government resources. Moreover, cigarette smokers tend to exhibit highly inelastic demands for this good, so the potential for bribes and other illicit payoffs to enforcers is therefore likely to be huge as well.

Thus, the bureaucracy that constitutes the relevant interest group standing to benefit from a cigarette prohibition is not limited to the relatively small "antismoking bureaucracy"—the governmental and nongovernmental agencies (such as the Office on Smoking and Health, on the first side, and the American Cancer Society, on the second) that tend to dominate the public discussion of antismoking measures (see Berger 1986). Much of the rest of the huge public-health bureaucracy in the United States has a strong incentive to support the prohibition of smoking, and hence to back the antismoking activists.

In addition, the same public bureaucrats who currently benefit from the prohibition of drugs would also stand to gain from tobacco prohibition. The DEA would have another source of bigger budgets, and state and local police departments could expect the demand for their services to significantly increase. As we saw above, many other federal agencies have significant involvement in the drug war, and presumably would also obtain budgetary benefits from participation in a war on smoking.

## Conclusion

Taxes on choice are often defended by their proponents as devices intended to raise revenue. For example, in the recent debate over reform of the U.S. health care system, the Clinton administration suggested that cigarette taxes be raised in order to generate some of the revenue necessary to undertake its proposed new program. Granted, these proponents often admit that reducing the level of consumption of "sinful" goods is a desirable side effect of such taxes. But the primary argument offered in support of new sin taxes highlights the revenue such levies might earn for the government.

This chapter has not challenged the intentions of these advocates of selective. It may in fact be that these activists sincerely believe their own arguments claiming that selective excise taxes can be expected to raise useful public revenue. Instead, we have argued that in reality, sumptuary taxes tend to evolve naturally into out-and-out prohibitions.[38] This evolution tends to play out as the public bureaucracy charged with collecting the tax grows. Larger bureaucracies can more effectively lobby for their own interests, meaning bigger budgets and more employees. This lobbying takes the form of consistent pressure for higher tax rates, which lead to expanded black-market provision of the good and cheating on the tax law, which increase the demand for the services of the enforcement bureaucrats, in a vicious cycle. Eventually, tax rates become prohibitively high and, frequently, segue into outright prohibitions. Prohibition maximizes the demand for the services of enforcement bureaucrats, and permits these organizations to in turn maximize appropriable rents in the form of agency budgets, number of employees, graft opportunities, and so on.

Government is not a monolithic entity intent on maximizing net tax revenue; rather, government is an organization that tends to be overtaken by opportunism on the part of its individual agents. The tendency of revenue-raising taxes to slide into outright prohibition, driven by the predictable incentives confronting public bureaucracies, has an ominous public-policy implication. Although specific excise taxes imposed on "sinful" goods are superficially attractive devices for the raising of significant revenue, such taxes may represent the leading edge of a massively expensive, revenue-losing prohibition on the substance initially only subject to taxation. What start out as minor net contributors to government revenue transform into budgetary black holes, which drain larger and larger amounts of public resources over time.

## Notes

1. See, for example, Cheung (1978), Dahlman (1978), and Taubman (1991).
2. There were, of course, numerous inconsistencies in Adam Smith's discussion of the revenue maximization objective of government. Furthermore, Brennan and Buchanan deserve credit for developing and presenting a technically superior version of the basic argument, in testable form.
3. Note that this criticism is directed at Leviathan in its simplest manifestation. The argument of Brennan and Buchanan (1981), for example, is not subject to these objections, despite the fact that they have "recoined" the term Leviathan in connection with the behavior of government as an economic entity.
4. See, for example, the articles by Bartel and Thomas (1987), Gollop and Roberts (1985), Hughes, Magat, and Ricks (1986), Pashigian (1985), and Silberman and Durden (1976).
5. Note should be taken, however, of Yandle's "bootleggers and Baptists" model (see Yandle 1983). Basically, he argues that the interests of those seeking monopoly rents are often intertwined with the interests of those seeking utility gains associated with a society changed to their personal liking. The bootleggers expect to receive monopoly rents from a liquor ban, while the Baptists desire a liquor law to promote their preferred moral values. If the bootleggers can form a coalition with the Baptists, the former can supply the financial resources with which the latter do the actual politicking—in other words, the "crooks" launder their lobbying money through the "preachers." Organized crime might also work through other forms of "front" organizations (such as labor unions) to lobby for laws favorable to their economic interests. For a more detailed discussion of intertwined interests and rent seeking, see Yandle (1984).
6. Naturally, as long as there is any positive level of tax, there will be some incentive for bootlegging or smuggling of the substance in order to evade the tax. But if tax rates are kept moderate, the relative returns to smuggling will be low.
7. See Dallago 1991 for a good introduction to this literature.
8. The Bureau of Prohibition was a branch of the U.S. Treasury Department, which explains why Prohibition agents were sometimes referred to as "T-men."
9. On corruption in the war on drugs, see Johns (1992, 19–24).
10. According to the U.S. Department of Justice (1992, 128), the total federal drug control budget in (1991) was $10.8 billion.
11. Total state and local spending for police protection and corrections in 1988 was $56.4 billion (U.S. Bureau of the Census 1993, 191). The $10.1 billion figure

reflects the estimate by the U.S. Customs Service that 18 percent of all law enforcement at the state level in 1986 was for drug control (U.S. Department of Justice 1992, 131). Official Bureau of Justice Statistics (BJS) estimates for total state and local spending on drug control range from a low of $5.2 billion to a high of $9.2 billion per year. However, the BJS argues that the higher estimate is more realistic, and further that even this figure probably underestimates the state and local effort (U.S. Department of Justice 1992, 128).

12. This is the figure claimed by the Select Committee on Narcotics Abuse and Control for 1987. See U.S. Department of Justice 1992, 36.

13. See Lee (1973, 119). And it would seem that Congress passed the law with the understanding that the measure was intended to raise revenue and regulate the drug trade, not prohibit opium use. According to Trebach (1982, 49), the act "on its face was merely a law for the orderly marketing of opium, morphine, heroin, and other drugs—in small quantities over the counter, and in larger quantities on a physician's prescription.... It is unlikely that a single legislator realized in 1914 that the law Congress was passing would later be deemed [by the courts] a prohibition law."

14. For a detailed account of this development, see Hamowy (1987, 14).

15. Actually, the precise figure was $10,910 million, with $7,227 million going to the federal government, $3,400 million going to the states, and $283 million flowing to local governments (see U.S. Bureau of the Census 1993, table 468).

16. In 1991, the total revenue collected from all sources by the various levels of government in the U.S. was $2,124,206 million, of which taxes on alcoholic beverages equaled only .0047 percent (U.S. Bureau of the Census 1993, table 468).

17. In 1991, all governments in the U.S. spent a combined total of $13 billion on fire protection services (U.S. Bureau of the Census 1993, table 468).

18. For a brief summary of the pertinent events, see Foner and Garraty (1991, 871–74).

19. See U.S. Bureau of the Census (1946, 302, 317). Actually, the federal government continued to collect a minor amount of revenue from alcohol used in manufacturing, which was not made illegal by Prohibition.

20. For instance, a large, well-organized quasi-religious movement (in which many evangelical churches participated) fought long and hard for prohibition. Racist sentiments favored it as a barrier to immigration from southern Europe. Organized crime, anticipating future rents from prohibition, may have contributed to the cause (although its role was probably minor). And the Eighteenth Amendment was passed, ratified, and implemented (in the form of the Volstead Act) during a time when a large fraction of the young adult male population—the principal group of voters who could be expected to oppose prohibition—was otherwise occupied in recovering from their experiences in the mud of France.

21. Another crucial difference between Prohibition and the drug war is that the former ban failed to enlist the active involvement of federal agencies beyond the small Bureau of Prohibition and the U.S. Coast Guard. The drug war, by contrast, engages the attention of a panoply of federal bureaucracies. The Department of Justice, the parent agency of the Drug Enforcement Administration (DEA), devoted 50 percent of its total budget to antidrug programs in 1991; the DEA was responsible for only 18 percent of the $3.8 billion the department spent in the drug war. In addition, the Department of Health and Human Services, the Department of Defense, the Department of the Treasury, the Department of Transportation, and even the Department of State are major players in the antidrug

campaign. Naturally, these antidrug programs tend to be concentrated within these agencies; for example, 70 percent of the U.S. Marshals' budget (under Justice) is considered drug-related, as is 46.4 percent of the U.S. Customs Service budget (under Treasury), 42 percent of the Bureau of Alcohol, Tobacco, and Firearms budget (also under Treasury), and 16 percent of the Immigration and Naturalization Service budget (under Interior). Even the Secret Service (Treasury) and the IRS (also Treasury) get in on the act, at 16 percent and 2.1 percent, respectively. See U.S. Department of Justice (1992, 128–29). The drug war benefits the budgets of practically all the major federal bureaucracies. One consequence is that drug prohibition is supported by a huge array of federal bureaucrats whose jobs depend on continuing prohibition.

22. Leff (1984) suggests that the Depression, and the resulting expansion in the federal deficit, may have been a contributing factor behind the Roosevelt administration's strong support for repeal. A wag at the time suggested that Roosevelt wanted America to drink itself to a balanced budget. This motivation behind repeal may have been important, but the weakness of the small bureaucracy that benefited from continuing Prohibition presented the relevant opportunity.

23. See "Guns in America: Home on the Range," *Economist* 330 (26 March 1994): 23.

24. For state and local sales taxes, see U.S. Bureau of the Census (1993, 290, table 463). There are currently an estimated 284,000 licensed gun dealers in the United States, and the price of a federal license is $66.00 per year; multiplication yields a figure of $18.7 million in federal revenue from this source. See "Guns in America: Home on the Range," *Economist* 330 (26 March 1994): 23.

25. See Kates 1979 for a detailed discussion.

26. Importers and manufacturers were to pay an annual tax of $500.00, dealers $300.00, and pawnbrokers $200.00. Each transfer of these firearms required a $200.00 tax payment to the Internal Revenue Service. The law defined firearms as rifles or shotguns with short barrels, or automatic weapons and associated paraphernalia. See Lee (1973, 169).

27. The annual fee was $25.00 (Lee 1973, 169).

28. Kleck (1988) reports that victim resistance with guns is associated with lower rates of both victim injury and crime completion for robbery and assault compared with other victim action, including nonresistance (i.e., doing nothing). Kleck notes (p. 1) that in 1980 guns were used defensively about 1 million times in the United States.

29. There are other perverse effects of gun control laws. For example, legal restrictions that raise the cost of purchasing a gun tend to lower the relative price of extremely powerful guns if the restriction has the same impact regardless of firepower. Thus, following the predictions of the Alchian and Allen theorem (see ch. 1), restrictions such as mandatory waiting periods for gun purchases make high-firepower weapons (such as assault rifles) relatively more attractive to gun consumers. In fact, in many states current gun laws impose lower restrictions on the purchase of high-firepower, high-lethality rifles than on less-powerful, less-lethal handguns.

30. For example, this organization took out an ad promoting gun control in the *Washington Post,* 7 September 1988.

31. As Benson (1990, 240) notes, privately owned firearms complement the efforts of public police in deterring crime, to some extent. But, as Benson concludes, privately owned firearms are not substitutes for public police.

32. And, of course, government can more easily confiscate private property if it first disarms its citizens. Given that asset forfeiture/seizure has become a major tool of law enforcement (particularly, but not only, in the war on drugs) and that the seizing law enforcement agencies receive a major portion of these proceeds—totaling $560 million in 1990—making such seizure easier may well represent a relevant motivation behind the support for gun control by elements of law enforcement. For a brief review of asset forfeiture in the modern United States, see U.S. Department of Justice (1992, 156–57).
33. See Benson (1990) and Kopel (1993) for excellent summary discussions of this important historical record.
34. For a discussion of the interest-group dynamics that led to the replacememt of private fire-protection services by public fire departments, see McChesney (1986).
35. For details of these various measures, see "Smoked Out," *Economist* 330 (26 March 1994): 29–30.
36. See Shughart and Tollison (1986) for a discussion of these wealth transfers.
37. The precise figure was $10,952 million, of which $4,782 million went to the federal government, $5,980 million to the states, and $190 million to local governments (see U.S. Bureau of the Census 1993, table 468).
38. Actually, some proponents of higher sin taxes are quite frank in their admission that their real motive is to dry up consumption rather than maximize revenue. For example, the Bureau of Alcohol, Tobacco, and Firearms of the U.S. Treasury has vigorously lobbied for drastic increases in the license fees charged to gun dealers, for the express purpose of reducing the number of dealers, irrespective of likely government revenue losses. See "Guns in America: Home on the Range," *Economist* 330 (26 March 1994): 23–28, and *Los Angeles Times,* 7 January 1994, A-22:1.

# References

Bartel, Ann P., and Lacy G. Thomas. 1987. "Predation Through Regulation: The Wage and Profit Effects of the Occupational Safety and Health Administration and the Environmental Protection Agency." *Journal of Law and Economics* 30 (October): 239–64.

Benenson, Mark, and Don B. Kates, Jr. 1979. "Handgun Prohibition and Homicide: A Plausible Theory Meets the Intractable Facts." In *Restricting Handguns: The Liberal Skeptics Speak Out,* edited by Don B. Kates, Jr., pp. 91–138. Croton-on-Hudson, N.Y.: North River Press.

Benson, Bruce L. 1990. *The Enterprise of Law: Justice without the State.* San Francisco: Pacific Research Institute for Public Policy.

Berger, Peter. 1986. "A Sociological View of the Antismoking Phenomenon." In *Smoking and Society: Toward a More Balanced Assessment,* edited by Robert D. Tollison. Lexington, Mass.: Lexington Books.

Blais, Andre, and Stephane Dion, eds. 1991. *The Budget-Maximizing Bureaucrat: Appraisals and Evidence.* Pittsburgh: University of Pittsburgh Press.

Bonnie, Richard J., and Charles H. Whitebread II. 1974. *The Marihuana Conviction: A History of Marihuana Prohibition in the United States.* Charlottesville: University Press of Virginia.

Brennan, Geoffrey, and James M. Buchanan. 1981. *The Power to Tax.* New York: Cambridge University Press.

Cashman, Sean D. 1981. *Prohibition: The Lie of the Land.* New York: Free Press.

Cheung, Steven N. S. 1978. *The Myth of Social Cost.* San Francisco: Cato Institute.

Courtwright, David T. 1982. *Dark Paradise: Opiate Addiction in America before 1940.* Cambridge: Harvard University Press.

Dahlman, Carl, Jr. 1978. "The Problem of Externality." *Journal of Law and Economics* 22 (April): 141–62.

Dallago, Bruno. 1991. "The 'Second Economy': A Mechanism for the Functioning of Society in Eastern Europe." *In Depth* 1 (Spring): 76–113.

Foner, Eric, and John A. Garraty, eds. 1991. *The Reader's Companion to American History.* Boston: Houghton Mifflin Co.

Friedman, Milton. 1991. "The War We Are Losing." In *Searching for Alternatives: Drug Control Policy in the United States,* edited by Melvyn B. Krauss and Edward P Lazear, pp. 53–67. Stanford, Calif.: Hoover Institution Press.

Glaser, Ira. 1991. "Drug Prohibition: An Engine for Crime." In *Searching for Alternatives: Drug Control Policy in the United States,* edited by Melvyn B. Krauss and Edward P Lazear, pp. 271–82. Stanford, Calif.: Hoover Institution Press.

Gollop, Frank M., and Mark J. Roberts. 1985. "Cost-Minimizing Regulation of Sulfur Emissions: Regional Gains in Electric Power." *Review of Economics and Statistics* 43 (February): 81–90.

Hamowy, Ronald, ed. 1987. *Dealing with Drugs: Consequences of Government Control.* Lexington, Mass.: Lexingtoon Books.

Hughes, John S., Wesley A. Magat, and William E. Ricks. 1986. "The Economic Consequences of the OSHA Cotton Dust Standards: An Analysis of Stock Price Behavior." *Journal of Law and Economics* 29 (April): 29–59.

Johns, Christina Jacqueline. 1992. *Power, Ideology, and the War on Drugs.* New York: Praeger.

Kates, Don B., Jr. 1979. "Toward a History of Handgun Prohibition in the United States." In *Restricting Handguns: The Liberal Skeptics Speak Out,* edited by Don B. Kates, Jr., pp. 7–30. Croton-on-Hudson, N.Y.: North River Press.

———. 1984. "Handgun Banning in Light of the Prohibition Experience." In *Firearms and Violence: Issues of Public Policy,* edited by Don B. Kates, Jr., pp. 139–66. Cambridge, Mass.: Ballinger.

Kleck, Gary. 1984. "The Relationship Between Gun Ownership Levels and Rates of Violence in the United States." In *Firearms and Violence: Issues of Public Policy,* edited by Don B. Kates, Jr., pp. 99–132. Cambridge, Mass.: Ballinger.

———. 1988. "Crime Control Through the Private Use of Armed Force." *Social Problems* 35 (February): 1–21.

———. 1991. *Point Blank: Guns and Violence in America.* New York: Aldine de Gruyter.

Kleck, Gary, and Karen McElrath. 1991. "The Effects of Weaponry on Human Violence." *Social Forces* 69 (March): 669–92.

Kobler, John. 1973. *Ardent Spirits: The Rise and Fall of Prohibition.* New York: G. P. Putnam's Sons.

Kopel, David B. 1993. *The Samurai, the Mountie, and the Cowboy.* Buffalo, N.Y.: Prometheus Books.

Lee, R. Alton. 1973. *A History of Regulatory Taxation.* Lexington: University Press of Kentucky.

Leff, Mark. 1984. *The Limits of Symbolic Reform: The New Deal and Taxation, 1933–1939.* New York: Cambridge University Press.

Magaddino, Joseph P., and Marshall H. Medoff. 1984. "An Empirical Analysis of Federal and State Firearm Control Laws." In *Firearms and Violence: Issues of Public Policy,* edited by Don B. Kates, Jr., pp. 225–58. Cambridge, Mass.: Ballinger.

McChesney, Fred S. 1986. "Government Prohibitions on Volunteer Fire Fighting in

Nineteenth-Century America: A Property Rights Perspective." *Journal of Legal Studies* 15 (January): 69–92.

McWilliams, John C. 1990. *The Protectors: Harry J. Anslinger and the Federal Bureau of Narcotics, 1930–1962.* Newark: University of Delaware Press.

Michaels, Robert J. 1987. "The Market for Heroin Before and After Legalization." In *Dealing with Drugs: Consequences of Government Control,* edited by Ronald Hamowy, pp. 289–326. Lexington, Mass.: Lexington Books.

Miron, Jeffrey A., and Jeffrey Zwiebel. 1991. "Alcohol Consumption during Prohibition." *American Economic Review* 81 (May): 242–47.

Morgan, H. Wayne. 1981. *Drugs in America: A Social History, 1800–1980.* Syracuse, N.Y.: Syracuse University Press.

Morgan, John P. 1991. "Prohibition Is Perverse Policy: What Was True in 1933 is True Now." In *Searching for Alternatives: Drug Control Policy in the United States,* edited by Melvyn B. Krauss and Edward P. Lazear, pp. 405–23. Stanford, Calif.: Hoover Institution Press.

Musto, David F. 1973. *The American Disease: Origins of Narcotic Control.* New Haven: Yale University Press.

———. 1987. "The History of Legislative Control Over Opium, Cocaine, and Their Derivatives." In *Dealing with Drugs: Consequences of Government Control,* edited by Ronald Hamowy, pp. 37–72. Lexington, Mass.: Lexington Books.

Niskanen, William A. 1971. *Bureaucracy and Representative Government.* Chicago: Aldine Atherton.

Ostrowski, James. 1989. "Thinking About Drug Legalization." *Cato Policy Analysis* 121 (May).

Pashigian, B. Peter. 1985. "Environmental Regulation: Whose Self Interests Are Being Protected?" *Economic Inquiry* 23 (October): 551–84.

Schaffer, Ronald. 1991. *America in the Great War: The Rise of the War Welfare State.* New York: Oxford University Press.

Schaller, Michael. 1970. "The Federal Prohibition of Marijuana." *Journal of Social History* 4 (Fall): 61–74.

Schmeckebier, Laurence F. 1929. *The Bureau of Prohibition: Its History, Activities, and Organization.* Washington, D.C.: Brookings Institution.

Shughart, William F. II, and Robert D. Tollison. 1986. "Smokers versus Nonsmokers." In *Smoking and Society: Toward a More Balanced Assessment,* edited by Robert D. Tollison, pp. 217–24. Lexington, Mass.: Lexington Books.

Silberman, Jonathan I., and Gary C. Durden. 1976. "Determining Legislative Preferences on the Minimum Wage: An Economic Approach." *Journal of Political Economy* 84 (April): 317–29.

Taubman, Paul. 1991. "Externalities and Decriminalization of Drugs." In *Searching for Alternatives: Drug Control Policy in the United States,* edited by Melvyn B. Krauss and Edward P. Lazear, pp. 90–111. Stanford, Calif.: Hoover Institution Press.

Trebach, Arnold S. 1982. *The Heroin Solution.* New Haven: Yale Universtity Press.

U.S. Bureau of the Census. 1946. *Historical Statistics of the United States, 1789–1945.* Washington, D.C.: U.S. Government Printing Office.

———. 1975. *Historical Statistics of the United States, 1789–1970.* Washington, D.C.: U.S. Government Printing Office.

———. 1993. *Statistical Abstract of the United States, 1993.* Washington, D.C.: U.S. Government Printing Office.

U.S. Department of Justice. 1992. *Drugs, Crime, and the Justice System: A National Report from the Bureau of Justice Statistics.* Washington, D.C.: National Center for Justice/U.S. Government Printing Office.

Warburton, Clark. 1932. *The Economic Results of Prohibition*. New York: Columbia University Press.

White House. 1990. *National Drug Control Strategy*. Washington, D.C.: U.S. Government Printing Office.

Woodiwiss, Michael. 1988. *Crime, Crusades, and Corruption: Prohibitions in the United States, 1900–1987*. London: Pinter.

Yandle, Bruce. 1983. "Bootleggers and Baptists: The Education of a Regulatory Economist." *Regulation* 7 (May/June): 12–16.

———. 1984. "Intertwined Interests, Rent Seeking, and Regulation." *Social Science Quarterly* 65 (December): 1002–12.

# Part III

# Alcohol, Tobacco, and Drugs

# 8

# Prohibition: The Ultimate Tax

## Mark Thornton

*Prohibition, I venture to say, was the last thing in the
world the American people expected to have come upon
them.... "It can never happen" might be our national
slogan.... Let us wake up, and face conditions as they are.*
—Charles Hanson Towne, *The Rise and Fall of Prohibition*

The United States' "noble experiment" with the prohibition of alcohol is
widely thought to have been a policy blunder of constitutional proportions.
Many Americans see it as the one, the only, and the last American attempt to
enforce temperance and police morality. From this perspective, Prohibition
was the result of the peculiar spirit of the Progressive era and the democratic
instability that occurred in the wake of World War I and the women's suffrage
movement. Prohibition, in other words, was the product of a misguided public spirit.

It is not the purpose of this chapter to prove that prohibition is a public-
policy failure. Numerous studies of prohibition episodes have amply demonstrated that prohibitions consistently fail to achieve their stated public-interest
goals.[1] Rather, this chapter explores the shared ideology and important causal
link between selective excise taxes and prohibitions. While enforced total
abstinence is the goal, prohibitionists support other control measures, such as
regulations and excise taxes, as intermediate or coalition-building measures.
Such policies will not achieve the prohibitionists' objectives and will in fact
exacerbate the conditions the prohibitionists seek to address. The result is a
public-policy cycle that results in increased social degeneration and government control over time.[2]

Like the generation of the Roaring 'Twenties, Americans today seem unaware of their long history of experimenting with prohibition. From the
sumptuary legislation of the Puritans, through the Whiskey Rebellion and the
Progressive era, to the current "war on drugs," America has continued to

experiment with—and continued to experience—the cycle of reform, prohibition, and repeal. Rather than being a historical accident, alcohol prohibition was at the core of a puritan crusade that seeks to eliminate all types of "sin" through government coercion and to shore up individual free will by eliminating difficult choices.[3]

The national consensus about the future is similarly narrow and inexact. Most Americans feel that a new prohibition against alcohol, tobacco, or some other good is highly unlikely.[4] "It can never happen" may still be our national slogan, but this optimism is misguided from the perspective of both history and current policy trends. The neo-Puritan agenda is rapidly moving forward on all fronts, and this course, with all of its negative consequences, can be reversed only if the ideological foundations and economic effects of puritanical policies are properly understood.

The history of American prohibitionism teaches several key lessons. First, the prohibitionist ideology in America dates to the colonial period and is based on "heretical" religious doctrines and unorthodox scientific views. Second, a moving force behind this ideology is an elitist desire to secure a means of social control over the lower classes and immigrant groups. Third, in national politics, prohibitionists must form alliances and adopt coalition-building policies, such as selective excise taxes. Fourth, these policies do not achieve their public-interest goals, and actually aggravate the applicable social problems. Fifth, these failures contribute to the success of prohibitionist propaganda, the primary means of spreading and sustaining the crusade against "sin." Although American history supports a model that predicts future prohibitions, it also furnishes an alternative to prohibitionism from which rational policies can be derived.[5]

### A Model of Sumptuary Laws: From Excise Taxes to Prohibitions

The twin public policies of prohibition and sin taxes are enacted, implemented, and enforced to reduce the consumption of goods perceived to be potentially harmful (spiritually, physically, or economically) for both the individual and society. The goods are therefore declared to be immoral in a public-policy sense, so both policies, prohibition and sin taxes, share a common ideology.[6] This is so even though some radical prohibitionists oppose selective excise taxation on the grounds that it represents an alliance between their government and the "forces of evil." More pragmatic prohibitionists accept sin taxes as ways of penalizing consumers of "immoral" goods, recognizing that taxes are usually the only viable legislative alternative.

In addition to a common ideological source, sin taxes and prohibitions have similar economic effects. Both policies increase the price of the targeted good and reduce the quantity bought and sold below that which would be exchanged without the policy.[7] As a result, both policies produce incentives for a black market to emerge and create conditions that result in higher crime rates.[8] Black-market production tends to be inferior to legal-market production, and consumers have fewer remedies for low-quality and dangerous products. Consumer sovereignty ("the consumer is king") and caveat emptor ("let the buyer beware"), the great regulators of market activity, lose their force. In a black-market environment, buyers and sellers are often more attuned to avoiding arrest than to product quality.[9]

Sin taxes and prohibition also create similar changes in consumption patterns. Both policies encourage some consumers to reduce the quantity they consume, and others to switch to lower-quality or more-potent substitutes. Ultimately, the modification of consumption patterns will depend on a variety of factors, including the level and type of selective tax, the enforcement of the prohibition, and the penalties imposed on violators.[10]

Politically, the most significant difference between selective taxes and prohibitions relates to public finance. Contentious and inefficient as they may be, selective taxes do increase government revenues. Prohibition, conversely, increases public and private expenditures while generally adding nothing to the treasury's coffers.[11] Another important political difference is that prohibition, in effect, outlaws its opponents, while selective taxes tend to create interest-group opposition to higher tax rates.

The most striking similarity of these two policies has been the almost universal judgment, both over time and over a number of goods, that such policies rarely if ever make substantive progress toward achieving either the ancillary goal of reducing consumption or the primary goal of reducing "sinful" behavior. This failure is cited by opponents, impartial observers, and, importantly, proponents of prohibition themselves.[12]

## The History of "Sin" in America

America was colonized by Europeans seeking economic and religious liberty, with many of the colonies founded explicitly along theocratic lines. The most notorious of the religious groups, the Puritans, founded the Massachusetts Bay Colony. The Puritans adopted wide-ranging sumptuary legislation, including severe restrictions on alcohol and tobacco. However, these measures proved to be unenforceable and were replaced by strictures to maintain moderation instead (North 1988). It is this cycle of regulation and repeal that characterizes the American experience with social legislation. Over time these social-reform movements have been expanded in scope, become secularized, and achieved a degree of institutional permanence within the government bureaucracy.

### The American Rebellion

The American Revolution was a war fought for political and economic independence, primarily precipitated by the British domination of colonial trade and taxes. Specifically, Americans did not want to pay British excise taxes on the products they consumed. But equally important was the desire to eliminate British control of international trade that enriched the British at American expense. This was particularly true of tobacco farmers, who were forced to export their produce to Britain at extremely unfavorable terms (Bassett 1932, 143).

The success of the American Revolution ushered in a multitude of reforms honoring individualism at the expense of traditional hegemony. Slavery was abolished in several northern states, and freedom to manumit slaves was established in several southern states. After writing the Declaration of Independence, Thomas Jefferson set about abolishing entailment, eliminating primogeniture, and establishing religious freedom in Virginia; this was the first time such actions had ever been taken in so complete a form. Freedom of religion was established in several other states, and many established churches lost their state monopoly status.

The late eighteenth century produced not only the American Revolution but also the Industrial Revolution. This second revolution saw the new republic grow in territory and population. Manufacturing, agriculture, and trade thrived in the northeast. The plantation economy of the South prospered and expanded. And the Northwest Territory was explored and settled and became prosperous (North 1966, 64–89).

The freedom from British dominion, and the consequent economic growth, resulted in fundamental changes in the production and consumption of alcohol. New England lost its comparative advantage in the production of rum, while western grain farmers developed an advantage in the production of whiskey. The introduction of whiskey allowed the long-term trend of lower prices for spirits to continue. Lower prices combined with the new prosperity and freedom to generate increased consumption of alcohol.

Consumption of spirits continued to increase after the Revolution, peaking during the 1820s. Despite the fact that consumption was greater than ever before or since, the United States was not a nation of drunkards, and public drunkenness was not common. In fact, alcohol consumption in the United States was comparable to European patterns.[13]

Not all Americans felt the same way about the progress and freedom generated by these revolutionary spirits. Many of these grumblers had benefited from British colonial rule as administrators, tax collectors, and bureaucrats. Others had benefited from playing key roles in the system of triangular trade, which saw New Englanders sell their rum and other products in Africa for slaves who would then be transported on the "middle passage" to the West Indian sugar islands, where the slaves were sold in order to purchase molasses, the necessary ingredient for the burgeoning New England rum industry.[14]

The Revolution thus posed a threat to some members of the ruling upper classes of colonial society. A primary symbol of this threat to their hegemony was alcohol consumption. In colonial America, politicians controlled the issuance of licenses to sell spirits, the wealthy owned the taverns, and the clergy monitored consumption. Spirits were expensive enough that only the wealthy could regularly afford to consume them in large quantities. Public intoxication was viewed as a kind of status symbol.[15]

The elite's first line of defense against alcohol consumption by the lower classes had been the licensing of taverns. However, this measure had already lost much of its clout in 1764 when Benjamin Franklin's *Pennsylvania Gazette* labeled the tavern a "Pest to Society." John Adams had even led a crusade in 1760 to restrict or reduce the number of tavern licenses in Massachusetts, but was ridiculed by the public and defeated in his effort. Victory over Britain greatly strengthened owners of taverns (the "seedbed of the Revolution") in their fight against the elitists who sought to control alcohol consumption with policies of regulation and taxation.

The first anti-alcohol movement in the Republic turned to the British example of imposing excise taxes on spirits. After various anti-alcohol measures failed at the state level, temperance advocates began calling for federal intervention, but no action was forthcoming until the Articles of Confederation had been discarded. Alexander Hamilton had advocated the use of high excise taxes on spirits in the *Federalist Papers*, and he lobbied hard for such a tax as the secretary of the Treasury.[16]

The excise tax eventually passed Congress under the pressure of a budgetary shortfall, but was angrily opposed by citizens of the West and South. By 1794, hostilities had erupted into open warfare known as the Whiskey Rebellion. President Washington was persuaded by Hamilton to raise an army to crush this tax revolt. However, this demonstration of force solidified opposition to the federal tax. In 1802, the antifederalists, led by President Thomas Jefferson, repealed the tax on alcohol. The tax was briefly reinstated to pay for the War of 1812, but the Revolutionary spirit carried the day and it was soon repealed. The alcohol tax was not reinstated until the Civil War, when a new receptacle of federalist ideas, the Republican party, came to power under President Lincoln.

## The Puritanical Counterrevolution

The seeds of the puritanical counterrevolution can be found in the emerging temperance movement of the late eighteenth century. Quakers were the first religious group to declare their anti-alcohol beliefs. The Methodists also joined the temperance movement early. They felt that alcohol hindered their ability to reorganize and purify society in their image.

Possibly the greatest champion of the early temperance movement was Benjamin Rush, physician and signer of the Declaration of Independence. Rush published pamphlets condemning the use of alcohol as both unhealthy for the individual and destructive to society. His views, while of questionable scientific validity, were correctly seen by the temperance movement's leaders as one of the most powerful weapons in the anti-alcohol crusade. Rush's position as doctor and patriot rendered his message highly effective among the intellectual classes, culminating in the conversion of Jeremy Belknap, a minister from Boston who later become president of Harvard College. Rush also promoted his anti-alcohol message by requiring that his doctrines be taught at his medical school.[17]

Churches, however, were the principal players in the puritanical counterrevolution (Dow 1898). Traditional Christian churches held that sin was a voluntary act even when temptation was involved. In early-nineteenth-century America, "reformed," or "heretical," Christians began a mass movement to make a preemptive strike at sin. These Christians believed that sinful objects were in fact the causes of sin. It followed that sources of temptation had to be removed from society if sinners were to be saved.[18]

This new religious perspective can be characterized as postmillennial evangelical pietistic Protestantism. The heretical Christians were evangelical in that they were militantly zealous and emphasized preaching from the Bible. They were pietistic because they stressed Bible study, personal religious experience, and devotion like the seventeenth-century German religious movement that opposed formalism and intellectualism. Most important to this counterrevolution was the doctrine of millenialism, a prophecy or belief in an ideal society that would be created by revolutionary action.

Orthodox Christians, such as Catholics, Calvinists, Lutherans, and mainstream Protestants are typically amillennial in that they do not believe in a literal 1,000-year Kingdom of God on Earth. Premillenialists hold that Jesus will come again, defeat the forces of evil, and establish a Kingdom of God on Earth. (They are noted for predicting the date of the end of the world.) Postmillenialists hold the "reformed," or "heretical," view that man himself must purge the world of sin and imperfection and establish the Kingdom of God on Earth to prepare the way for the Second Coming of Christ. Obviously, postmillenial belief provides a wide, almost limitless latitude for the purger in terms of policy prescriptions. It was postmillenialism that would become the driving force behind the drive for prohibition.[19]

Geographically, postmillenial evangelical pietism emanated from New England, where the Puritans first settled.[20] The Puritans (who had already experimented with theocracy, witch hunts, and prohibitionism) and the Separatists evolved into the state-established Congregational and Unitarian churches, respectively, of New England. This Yankee influence spread into western New York, the Midwest, the Great Lakes region, and, eventually, the South and West as New Englanders, including clergy and educators, migrated along with the nation's expansion.[21]

The first anti-alcohol organization was the Massachusetts Society for the Suppression of Intemperance, which was formed in response to perceived heavy drinking during the War of 1812. The American Temperance Society was organized in 1826. By 1833 the temperance movement had over 1 million members, largely comprised of New England evangelicals from the Baptist, Congregational, Methodist, and Presbyterian churches.[22]

This surge in prohibitionist sentiment seems to be related both to an increase in alcohol consumption and to the religious revivalism of the Second Great Awakening.[23]

Alcohol consumption was estimated by Rorabaugh (1979, 9) to have increased from 3.5 pure gallons per capita in 1770 to almost 4 gallons in 1830. This increased consumption was the result of lower production costs, lower taxes, and higher incomes. Drinking was part of virtually every aspect of life for many in the Republic's early years. The notion that alcohol itself *causes* sin is a highly debatable matter, but "sinful" behavior is clearly *associated* with alcohol use. It is not surprising that reformers would base their efforts on this association.

More important, religious revivalism remained very strong in the 1820s and 1830s throughout New England. Revivalism had always meant reform of the individual and society, but Americans saw themselves as a special case. Americans had defeated the "savage" Indians, nature, and the British. America was the proverbial city on the hill, a shining example to the world.

An added push for religious revivalism was provided by church privatization in New England. The Congregational church was disestablished in 1818 in Connecticut and in 1824–33 in Massachusetts. This period of church privatization and religious revivalism is described by Olds (1994, 291):

> During the first half of the nineteenth century, religion in New England was changing in dramatic fashion. On the one hand, the number of preachers demanded in Connecticut and Massachusetts with respect to the population increased by more than half even as real preaching salaries almost tripled. The increase in total pastors reflected a fivefold increase in dissenting preachers. From 1800 to 1840, the proportion of dissenting preachers in these two states increased from under 20 percent to over 50 percent.

This separation of church and state involved not only the disestablishment of churches but also a movement from tax–funded churches to the voluntary funding of churches. According to Olds (1994, 291), 90 percent of churches in Massachusetts and Connecticut were supported by taxes in 1800, but by 1840, only 30 percent received such support in Connecticut (1850 in Massachusetts).

Despite the timing of privatization and religious revivalism, it is not possible to say definitively that privatization *caused* revivalism.[24] However, economic theory does provide some insights that suggest a causal connection. According to economic theory, a monopoly church with taxing power would be expected to reduce output below competitive levels and charge monopoly prices for its "services." We would therefore expect an increase in output after the privatization/demonopolization. Theory also predicts that new firms would enter the industry and supply competing products.[25]

As temperance groups formed and grew in the antebellum period, several important changes took place. Temperance efforts were initially attempts to promote voluntary moderation in alcohol consumption. Members of the temperance groups were expected to lead by example and provide education and assistance to others. Over time, however, alternative groups were established that advocated abstinence from spirits, but tolerated moderate consumption of beer, wine, and cider. Eventually, even these groups were replaced with more-intolerant societies whose members were required to sign an abstinence pledge. As the work of reform became more difficult over time, reform leaders became frustrated and dissatisfied with voluntary efforts and began to advocate government intervention to enforce temperance throughout society (Thornton 1991a, 43–45).

Temperance forces began to organize coalitions to pass restrictive legislation. The first reform measure typically sought was to replace the state tavern-licensing system with more-restrictive local-option laws that gave communities the right to prohibit liquor sales. Another restrictive policy was the minimum-quantity purchase law, which required individuals to buy large quantities (such as 15 or 28 gallons) of spirits at a time. Local prohibitions were also adopted. These policies were difficult to enforce and had few, if any, beneficial effects. The failure of these policies to satisfy prohibitionists ultimately led to calls for statewide prohibition.

Prohibitions were adopted in many northern states and territories between 1851 and 1855. These policies were based on a Maine law that was authored by the zealous prohibitionist Neal Dow. The "Maine Laws" allowed for search and seizure, reduced the requirements for conviction, increased fines, created mandatory prison sentences, and called for the destruction of contraband liquor.

The success of the Maine Laws was short-lived, however, as rapidly growing immigrant populations opposed such laws. The Maine Laws also suffered several important setbacks in court. Enforcement was difficult because professional police forces existed in only a few large cities, where the laws were least popular. Prohibition was considered a divisive issue by the emerging Republican party and was not enthusiastically embraced at the national level.

One event seemed to seal the fate of the Maine Laws. Neal Dow, who was at one time the mayor of Portland, Maine, was accused in 1855 of personally profiting from the government-controlled sale of alcohol. As described by Tyrrell (1979, 295–99):

> An angry mob assembled at the liquor agency on the night of June 2, 1855, after the existence of the liquor had become common knowledge. The mob demanded destruction of the liquor and threatened to break into the agency if the demands were not met and Neal Dow arrested for violation of his own law. Dow, who was

always quick to look to force in defense of morality, assembled the local Rifle Guards. In the confrontation which followed with the stone-throwing mob, Dow ordered his troops to fire when several rioters broke into the liquor agency.

Dow was condemned as a murderer and a fanatic, and the prohibition movement that he was instrumental in crafting quickly diminished in political significance (Byrne 1969, 60–69).

*Preparing for Prohibition*

The rise of the Republican party was the result of a long series of attempts to form a coalition strong enough to challenge the dominant position of the Democratic party. Forged from the Whig and Know-Nothing parties, the Republicans naturally captured the prohibitionist and abolitionist radicals and thereby dominated "Yankeedom." This coalition party did not completely satisfy the prohibitionist faction, but they were able to institute taxes on alcohol and tobacco that helped appease the reformers and allowed the Republican party to dominate American politics for decades.

After the Civil War, prohibitionists become increasingly political and better organized at the national level. Their progress was marked by the formation of the Prohibition party, the Women's Christian Temperance Union, and the Anti-Saloon League.

It was also during the period between the Civil War and the Progressive era that the prohibitionist movement became increasingly secular. According to Barkun (1986, 2), the "slow nineteenth-century separation of a secular from a religious vision of the perfect society" accelerated after (and possibly because of) the Civil War. By "the end of the nineteenth century, millennialism was dominated by secularizing tendencies," so "by the very time that it succumbed in religious circles its secular version triumphed in the society at large" (Barkun 1986, 151, 29).

The politicization and secularization of the movement stimulated the adoption of a more pragmatic strategy to promote temperance. In terms of public policy, the post–Civil War period is best classified as one of "modified" prohibition. While national temperance organizations thrived, state prohibition waned to such an extent that by 1875 only three states remained "dry." Although there was a resurgence in state prohibitions in the 1880s, there were still only three dry states in 1904. Modified prohibition, with its scientific and pragmatic veneer, consisted of local-option laws, high license fees, and restrictive regulations. These coalition-building and seemingly moderate policies ironically helped to establish the conditions under which national prohibition would be promoted and enacted.

The scientific veneer of modified prohibition was provided in part by political economist Richard T. Ely, founder of the American Economic Association. In a report to the Maryland legislature, Ely argued for a modified prohibition that consisted of local option laws and an annual auction of licenses granting large exclusive territories (retail monopolies) for the sale of alcoholic beverages. This policy, he argued, would greatly reduce the number of establishments selling alcohol and at the same time maximize public revenue. He argued further that retail liquor businesses would be easier to tax and to regulate because of the greatly reduced number of establishments operating under the threat of losing expensive liquor licenses for violating regulations. According to Ely (1888, 280–82), raising the level of concentration of the liquor business with modified prohibition "drags it before the public where all its evils must be conspicuous."

Modified prohibition was promoted as the pragmatic alternative to absolute prohibition. Champions of modified prohibition claimed that it resulted in fewer saloons, higher government revenues, and reduced public drunkenness. According to *The Nation,* it was "the same story that has been told of every State in which high-license or tax laws have gone into effect. That is, they provide 'corroborative evidence of the practical wisdom of this method of fighting the liquor evil.'"

*The Nation* also opposed the policy of absolute prohibition, finding that it was not "a proper or practical method of liquor regulation," and that "no amount of amendment or addition can make the Prohibitory Law a success." In its opposition to prohibition and support for repeal of such policies, *The Nation* concluded that "the lesson which has been taught over and over again [is] that prohibition laws cannot be enforced except where public sentiment in their favor predominates." In other words, when in the majority, use local option, but when in the minority, use high taxation to control drinking and make drinkers pay for their sins.[26]

Despite testimonials of modified prohibition's success, measures such as local option, high taxes, and high license fees cause a plethora of problems. These problems include black-market production, smuggling, monopoly pricing, reduced quality, possibly anticompetitive business practices, graft, and political corruption. While these problems are not as visible as the closing of a saloon, the dark side of modified prohibition was already apparent when Pennsylvania enacted a regulation prohibiting brewers from financing saloon operators' high license fees, in an attempt to limit some of the vertical restraints of trade brought on by modified prohibition elsewhere.[27]

Indeed, the political success of modified prohibition might suggest that true prohibitionist sentiment had all but died out in the late nineteenth century. The federal excise tax on distilled spirits had been increased by 120 percent between 1868 and 1894, most nonprohibition states had enacted local-option laws by 1900, and most states and local jurisdictions had enacted high license fees.[28] However, rather than dying out, the prohibition movement was growing, organizing necessary institutions and building coalitions, experimenting with political techniques, and training itself for the achievement of its ultimate goal.

Women were an important source of support for prohibition. The leaders of the women's suffrage movement were prohibitionists and encouraged their members to swell the ranks of prohibition organizations. The political alliance was clear: women would support prohibition (and vote for it when and where they could) while prohibitionists would support the women's suffrage movement. Women would get the vote and sober husbands, while prohibitionists would reestablish social control by drying up the nation. In 1873, the Women's Christian Temperance Union was formed to institutionalize this alliance.

In 1869, as the women's suffrage movement reemerged from the Civil War, the Prohibition party was formed. This party is often characterized as ineffective, but it played a key role in the ultimate success of national prohibition. While its electoral success was indeed limited, the Prohibition party was the first party to introduce ideas such as child labor laws, direct election of senators, the income tax, women's suffrage, and national alcohol prohibition—ideas that were subsequently absorbed into major-party platforms and enacted into law. In addition to providing prohibitionists with a valuable training ground, the Prohibition party contributed to the major political realignment that occurred during the 1890s, in which the Democratic party embraced prohibition.

The period between the Civil War and 1900 was seemingly stable with respect to alcohol policy. A general consensus emerged that modified prohibition (high excise taxes, local option, and high license fees) was the best form of alcohol control. But these policies created conditions that stimulated anti-alcohol forces to rise in anger against the most prominent institution of vice—the saloon. As the "evils" of drink emerged in new forms, prohibitionist forces began to organize for their final assault.

*Progressive Prohibitionism*

The Anti-Saloon League was formed in 1895 as a political arm of the postmillennial evangelical Protestant churches. By 1904, the league had organizations in forty-two states or territories. When Prohibition was enacted after World War I, the Anti-Saloon League could claim affiliations with over 30,000 churches and 60,000 agencies. It is important to note that the league, which was the prime mover behind national prohibition, explicitly labeled the licensed (and heavily taxed) saloon as the source of evil.[29]

Acting as a shield for the evangelical Protestant churches, the league completely split with the voluntary and educational efforts of past temperance movements. Coercion, propaganda, and candidate intimidation were the new tools. Professional reformers were paid to propagandize (often from the pulpit), frequently making outrageous claims about Negroes and Catholics. At its height, the league published over 40 tons of propaganda literature each month. To underwrite these efforts, the league concentrated its efforts on fundraising. It was able to shield its big contributors from public exposure by refusing to comply with the disclosure requirements of the Corrupt Practices Act. As a result, Clark Warburton (1932) was unable to determine the extent of commercial rent seeking against alcohol.[30]

The passage of the Eighteenth (Prohibition) Amendment to the Constitution and the National Prohibition (Volstead) Act should give pause to those who say "It can't happen again." As Towne (1923, 1) explained, Prohibition itself was unthinkable:

> The strange phenomenon of Prohibition, after an appearance amongst us of over three years, is still non-understandable to the majority of a great, and so-called free, people. It is one of the most astonishing manifestations the world has ever witnessed.

What was unthinkable to Towne and most Americans should now be obvious: American ideology and government policy had been heavily influenced by prohibitionists at least since the rise of the Republican party during the 1850s. The only questions since that time had been the type of coalitions prohibitionists would form and the kind of alcohol control policy they would choose.

In retrospect, the explanation for the transition from modified prohibition at the state level to absolute prohibition at the national level seems relatively obvious: the only important issue to be resolved was revenue. The selective excise tax on alcohol products was the second-largest source of revenue for the federal government prior to Prohibition. As Boudreaux and Pritchard (1994, 2) argue:

> The income tax proved a viable alternative to liquor taxation for raising revenue, thus making prohibition possible. To be sure, the ideology of voters and politicians mattered, but Congress could not afford the cost in foregone tax revenue (hence, foregone wealth redistribution) that an ideological vote for prohibition entailed until the income tax demonstrated its revenue-raising potential.

Boudreaux and Pritchard also argue that the shortfall of income tax revenue during the early years of the Great Depression stimulated Congress's interest in repealing Prohibition and restoring the federal excise tax on alcohol.

In support of this tax substitution thesis, it should be recalled that it was the Prohibition party that first called for an income tax and that prohibitionists widely supported the proposal. It is also noteworthy that a tax revolt was gathering momentum in the early years of the Great Depression. The revolts began as movements against property taxes in urban areas such as Chicago. Prior to Prohibition, local governments raised a great deal of revenue from high tavern license fees, revenue that was lost with Prohibition. The repeal of Prohibition would not only lower alcohol prices, but also reestablish revenue from license fees, thus lessening cities' reliance on property taxes. As Bieto (1989, 140) notes, "by the end of 1933, the effectiveness of the tax-resistance movement had started to wane."[31]

In addition to the economic issues connecting taxes and prohibition, "the ideology of voters and politicians mattered," as Boudreaux and Pritchard maintain. The antisaloon sentiment that emerged in the Progressive era was forged from the experience of "modified prohibition" and was symbolized in the very name of the Anti-Saloon League. As Timberlake (1963, 110) described, the saloon became the object of national opprobrium under modified prohibition in part because

> the liquor industry became thoroughly involved in political corruption through its connection with the saloon. The root of the trouble here was that the ordinary saloonkeeper, confronted by overcompetition, was practically forced to disobey the liquor laws and to ally himself with vice and crime in order to survive. Unable to make a living honestly, he did so dishonestly.

In response to modified prohibition, many saloons offered breweries exclusive selling rights in exchange for payment of their annual license fees.[32] With profits reduced, some saloons would also disobey "blue laws," serve low-quality and watered-down liquor, and employ prostitutes, professional gamblers, and pickpockets in order to generate sufficient revenues under modified prohibition. Of course, all of these practices often necessitated the bribery of police and other public officials.

The success of Prohibition depended vitally on defining its goal as ridding America of the crime- and vice-ridden saloon that was corrupting both the political leadership and the poor immigrants who relied on the saloon as a center of entertainment, politics, and much more. Indeed, destroying the saloon would achieve an underlying goal of prohibitionists—providing the old-line Protestants with a method of social control over the "drinking class," a group largely composed of recent Catholic immigrants from countries such as Ireland, Italy, and Germany.

### The Bureaucratic War on Drugs

The Progressive era also saw the prohibitionists launch their "wars" against narcotics, tobacco, and marijuana. In each of these wars, prohibitionists and progressives sought to stamp out "vice," control the behavior of recent immigrant groups, and discourage further immigration. The most prominent academic supporter of prohibition, the progressive economist Irving Fisher, drew the Fabian-socialist line in the American sand:

> Our society will always remain an unstable and explosive compound as long as political power is vested in the masses and economic power in the classes. In the end one of these powers will rule. Either the plutocracy will buy up the democracy or the democracy will vote away the plutocracy. (Fisher 1919, 16)[33]

The Progressive era completed the secularization of the prohibitionist movement, and with it, the theme of social control became more explicit than ever.

## Tobacco

The prohibitionist attack on tobacco paralleled the crusade against alcohol. The Puritans of Massachusetts and Connecticut placed prohibitions on tobacco use, only to later repeal them. The Federalists imposed excise taxes on manufactured tobacco products along with the infamous whiskey tax. The anti-alcohol doctor Benjamin Rush also published a pamphlet entitled "Observations upon the Influence of the Habitual use of Tobacco upon Health, Morals and Property." The federal tobacco tax was repealed under Jefferson but was restored and increased under Lincoln. As the Progressive era began, a movement to tax and restrict tobacco was in full swing. As with alcohol, many quasi-scientific arguments were employed on behalf of the tobacco tax, but social control remained the true purpose. As Randolph Paul (1954, 646) noted:

> In recent years alcohol taxes have brought in very substantial revenue, but the social desirability of the taxes is frequently advanced as a reason for increased rates. The same is true to a less pronounced percent of tobacco taxes, which have been regarded to some extent in the light of a measure of social control. (Paul 1954, 646)

Antitobacco—and, in particular, anticigarette—sentiment began to crystallize in the late nineteenth century in conjunction with the anti-alcohol movement. Beginning in the 1890s, the anticigarette campaign "attracted a number of organizations and individuals, particularly the Women's Christian Temperance Union." By the turn of the century, several hundred anticigarette leagues had formed with over 300,000 members; three states had banned the sale of cigarettes and cigarette papers. By 1909, a dozen states had enacted bans on cigarettes and many cities had passed anticigarette ordinances. However, by 1921 most cigarette prohibitions had been repealed as ineffective and unworkable. Kansas was the last state in the Progressive era to wipe out cigarette prohibition, in 1927 (Dillow 1981).

## Narcotics

The antinarcotics crusade began in the late nineteenth century as a movement against Oriental immigrants. In fact, most states had enacted prohibitive legislation against cocaine, opium, morphine, and heroin before the Harrison Narcotics Act was passed in 1914. The leading antinarcotic legislatures were in western states such as Arizona (1899), Colorado (1897), Montana (1889), Nevada (1877), North Dakota (1885), and Wyoming (1903); traditional prohibitionist states such as Connecticut (1905), Illinois (1897), Maine (1899), Massachusetts (1906), and Ohio (1902) joined in as well (Hamowy 1987, 10–11).

Although the federal antinarcotics crusade has often been considered "accidental" or the product of foreign policy, it is justifiably seen as a component of the progressive-prohibitionist campaign that originated with the religious precepts of the Puritan colonists. According to David F. Musto (1987, 46–47), the leading historian, of narcotics control,

in many ways, of course, the anti-alcohol movement was part of the Progressive Era; its startling success and later dramatic repeal have given the alcohol issue a somewhat *separate development in our minds*, but the interrelation between the battles against alcohol and against narcotics is an important one. The anti–alcohol crusade helped establish the attitude that there could be *no compromise with the forces of evil*, that "moderation" was a false concept when applied to alcohol: Prohibition was the only logical or moral policy when dealing with this great national problem.[34]

Prohibition might have been the only logical solution in the minds of anti-drug reformers, but it was also an unconstitutional one. In order to avoid the constitutional challenge, politicians crafted the antinarcotics legislation on the basis of the federal government's power to tax. In other words, the Harrison Narcotics Act was *designed* to regulate drug consumption by restricting the nonmedical uses of drugs and regulating the medical uses. However, the bureaucrats in charge of enforcing the act *implemented* the legislation as a prohibitive measure.

They achieved this by interpreting the writing of prescriptions for the maintenance of addictions as medical malpractice. Perhaps surprisingly, the Supreme Court agreed, deciding that a prescription for narcotics meant to maintain a drug addiction was improper and therefore not a legitimate prescription.[35] If the prescription was not legitimate, then the doctor in question would be found in violation of the law. The Harrison Narcotics Act was thereby turned from a regulatory measure based on the power to tax into the first major salvo in the war on drugs.

## Marijuana

The war against marijuana was initiated during the period of national alcohol prohibition and state cigarette prohibition . Twenty-four states adopted marijuana prohibitions between 1913 and 1927, with the mean date of adoption being 1920 (Hamowy 1987, 10–11). When Congress passed the Marijuana Tax Act in 1937, it did so with little fanfare. Modern students of the legislation look back with bewilderment to its origins, but marijuana prohibition is the prime example of mature prohibitionism in action.

Two major hypotheses have emerged to explain the origins of marijuana prohibition. The "Anslinger hypothesis" argues that Harry Anslinger, the director of the Federal Bureau of Narcotics, played a major entrepreneurial role in the legislative process by developing and effectively spreading the "killer weed" propaganda. The "Mexican hypothesis" contends that bigotry against Mexican immigrants and blacks combined with protectionist economic interests to create political conditions favorable for marijuana prohibition. Both of these hypotheses make valid points that are consistent with the sin model: the use of propaganda and bureaucracy to achieve social control.

However, the sin model goes beyond these two hypotheses to provide a comprehensive explanation for marijuana prohibition. First, the Anslinger model can be expanded to include his experience as commissioner of (alcohol) prohibition, where he took to heart the lessons that prohibition leaders had learned in the past: (1) there is never enough money to effectively enforce a prohibition, (2) prohibitions must punish the consumers as well as the producers in order to limit dissent, (3) propaganda is crucial in molding and maintaining public support, and, most important, (4) prohibitions must pit a substantial majority of the population against an unpopular, mistrusted, and powerless minority. Anslinger further saw the value in having the federal government control and direct policy, while leaving implementation and enforcement to the state and local levels of government. This would ensure that all levels of government could effectively deflect unfavorable public opinion.

Another important aspect of the sin model is how previous government interventions create conditions that promote additional interventions. Prohibitions of alcohol and narcotics created conditions that help to explain the development of marijuana prohibition. Prohibitions reduced the supplies and increased the prices of alcohol and narcotics. These higher prices were felt most acutely among lower-income immigrant groups, who were typically less able to pay black-market prices (Warburton 1932, 228–44). These groups were therefore the most likely to experiment with marijuana as a low-cost substitute for alcohol and narcotics. Without this additional consumption it is doubtful that marijuana could ever have become a matter of public concern or national legislation in 1937.

The Harrison Narcotics Act also served as the model of the Marijuana Tax Act, which placed a prohibitive excise tax on marijuana use. Given the favorable decisions by the Supreme Court and the expanding congressional power over interstate commerce, this policy of regulation through sin taxes evolved bureaucratically into a full-fledged prohibition.

## Summary

This chapter has presented a model of public policy toward politically incorrect behavior and examined American history in order to draw its findings. Its contribution derives from the comprehensive nature of the historical examination and the consistency of its findings. The major findings are as follows:

1. The religious view of postmillennial evangelical pietists, which incorporates the notions of objective sin and the divine directive that man must

perfect America, removing temptations for the weaker willed to pave the way for the Kingdom of God on Earth, is the genesis of prohibitionism.

2. Prohibitionists support selective excise taxes and prohibitions as alternative political policies to compel virtue, enforce morality, and suppress and control minority groups.

3. Prohibitions and excise taxes create conditions under which they must be substituted for one another. Prohibitions have been consistently found to be counterproductive and to create public-finance problems. Excise taxes, or modified prohibition, while appearing effective and pragmatic, corrupt the market process, aggravate social problems, and ultimately lead to calls for absolute prohibition.

4. Prohibitionists and government bureaucrats utilize extensive pseudo-scientific propaganda in order to achieve, maintain, and extend the prohibitionist agenda.

5. The prohibitionist agenda includes the elimination of alcohol, tobacco, gambling, amusements, luxury items, and extravagance. This agenda, religious in origin, has gradually been secularized over time.

6. Through precedent and bureaucratic growth, the prohibitionist agenda has evolved from emergency and war-time measures into a far-reaching social agenda that pervades all levels of government.

It is truly ironic that the colonists who originally embarked for the New World because of the suppression of dissent by the established churches and the burden of the despised excise tax would leave such a legacy. Even more ironic is that street gangs, drive-by shootings, bootleggers, and moonshiners are results of this religious fervor and its secular counterpart, progressive ideology.

## Conclusion

This chapter has sought to paint a truer picture of "conditions as they actually are." The cycle of reform initiated by the New England Puritans remains an important feature of American social-reform policy. Bruce Yandle's (1983) "Baptists and bootleggers" thesis explains how an interest group like the Baptists can pass a law, such as closing saloons on Sundays, that calls into being a new interest group, the bootleggers, with a financial stake in the policy's continuation. These two minority groups with seemingly divergent interests can in turn marshal support for even more restrictive legislation. If the coalition succeeds in achieving prohibition, however, conflicts are created with groups who oppose such policies based on concerns over government revenue, organized crime, political corruption, or public safety.

In addition to Baptists and bootleggers, interest groups of growing importance are the bureaucrats who administer the policies against smoking, drinking, and other kinds of politically incorrect behavior. Bureaucrats now play an active role in expanding the domain of predatory politics and preventing any retrenchment of their powers. Bureaucracies have also largely usurped and expanded the propaganda functions of private interest groups. The net effect of this bureaucratization has been to increase the scope and severity of the prohibition–sin tax cycle.

Yandle's thesis is discouraging with respect to the prospects for genuine reform, and current events do indicate little or no potential for improvement until after this millennium. Prohibitions against drugs have been strengthened and extended. The modified prohibitions on alcohol and tobacco have also been reinforced and expanded. Indeed, government policies that point toward absolute prohibition of smoking and drinking are now in place. New items have been added to the prohibitionist agenda, most notably under the environmental banner.

The war on drugs, which includes narcotics, cocaine, marijuana, peyote, and other products, expanded dramatically during the 1980s. Drug prohibition has become international in scope. In the United States, prohibition budgets and bureaucracies continue to increase, penalties continue to become more severe, and enforcement powers continue to expand. However, there also seems to be a growing awareness among the general public of the costs of prohibition and the many social problems prohibitions cause. Legalization and decriminalization are being openly discussed as alternatives to prohibition, and public-opinion polls seem to confirm a growing opposition to prohibition.

But while support for prohibition may have already peaked as it applies to cocaine, marijuana, and narcotics, policies toward alcohol and tobacco may be in the preliminary stages of a return to prohibition. The excise taxes on both products have been raised substantially in recent years, and new even more massive increases have been proposed. Although local-option laws have not resurfaced, the use of tobacco has been restricted in airplanes, public buildings, and private businesses and workplaces. Alcohol use has been curtailed by more-restrictive drunk-driving laws, higher legal-age requirements, and tougher licensing regulations. Manufacturers have been required to place government warning labels on their products and have been forbidden to market new brands that "target" the young, minority groups, or women. In fact, President Bush further expanded the scope of the war on drugs to alcohol and tobacco by declaring in 1989 that such products are of the same nature as illegal drugs.

Alcohol, narcotic drugs, marijuana, and tobacco are being vilified with a propaganda war of gigantic proportions. The "Just Say No" campaign was the most visible, but certainly not the most important, facet of this effort. The federal government alone spends billions of dollars and employs thousands of bureaucrats to wage the drug war. This effort includes "information" campaigns, "scientific" research, and indirect funding techniques to finance a plethora of state and local community groups that promote the war at the grassroots level. At the supreme, most visible level is the Partnership for a Drug-Free America, which has produced numerous "public service" announcements for the propaganda war.

Richard Karp (1992, 26–27) provides an insightful image of this behind-the-scenes bureaucratic network:

> Imagine the old Anti-Saloon League as a vast Government–sponsored, Government-financed national cottage industry. Imagine the 19th-century Women's Christian Temperance Union as a quasi-official organization, similar to a Great Society poverty program, operating in every state, county, and town social agency, clamoring for ever tougher crackdowns on alcohol abuse. Imagine 10,000 Carry Nations armed not with hatchets but with Federal matching funds and foundation grants; preaching not spiritual perfection but highway safety, child-abuse prevention, economic productivity, fetus health, physical fitness, feminism, minority rights; not smashing whiskey bottles but disseminating Government anti- alcohol pamphlets, lobbying for more police action against drunkenness, scaring pregnant mothers with visions of birth defects, frightening small children in schools with prospects of alcohol addiction, pressuring the liquor industry to pay for "responsible drinking" ads and the broadcast industry to air gratis their own more strident messages, threatening everyone, but especially young adults, with certain pain and imprisonment if they dare let liquor touch their lips.

Interestingly, not only has government become the primary purveyor of prohibitionism, but the religious origins of prohibitionism have been adopted by the secular leadership of the prohibitionist crusade. Philip Jenkins (1994), reflecting on recent public policy toward personal behavior and our now "thoroughly secularized puritanism," speculates that:

> future historians will certainly regard Neo-Puritanism as a hallmark of the times in which we are presently living. However, they will also be struck by the paradox of this particular outbreak in public righteousness, which differs from its predecessors in its conspicuous lack of *overtly* moral or religious foundation—which is not to say that the underlying agendas may not reflect religious assumptions.

Indeed, he draws an explicit connection between recent public-policy trends and puritanical religious beliefs, stating that

> the recent wave of Puritanism can more plausibly be seen as a revival of deeply entrenched attitudes within American culture, ideas that are ultimately religious in their origins but that survive vigorously after the decay of the overtly religious and moral contexts that would earlier have been used to justify them.

The neo-Puritans have already been highly successful. All of the necessary conditions for new prohibitions on alcohol and tobacco are in place. Restrictive legislation has been enacted (including age, sex, and location prohibitions) that has reduced the number of consumers and producers of these products while creating numerous unintended negative consequences in these markets. Propaganda, posing as the results of scientific research, has been disseminated and accepted by the general public. Finally, the federal government has already established an agenda to outlaw alcohol and tobacco in the near future.

That agenda consists of three primary parts. First, the "Healthy People 2000" program was established to accomplish, among other things, abstinence from alcohol consumption by the year 2000. Second, the policy of a "Smoke-Free America 2000" was also recently established in order to ensure the end of tobacco smoking by the year 2000. Finally, President Clinton's failed health care reform plan made a priority of eliminating health risks in the population, proposed establishing bureaucracies to assess those risks, and went a long way toward nationalizing the health care system so that taxpayers would be even less tolerant of the risky behavior and bad habits of their fellow citizens.

One need not concoct grand conspiracies or read between the lines in order to understand "conditions as they are." If current trends persist, the United States will be moving toward more prohibitions. The alternative policy to prohibitionism is an unrestricted free market where individuals are punished only for criminal acts and where goods are not discriminated for or against in terms of public policy. This would involve the elimination of all prohibitions, excises, and discriminatory restrictions on the use of products. This would prevent future harm from public policy, and although it is unclear when the natural conditions in these markets could be restored, it is clear that free markets provide the necessary ingredients for a cure for certain social problems: consumer sovereignty, economic growth, economic stability, and peace. Claims that reverting to a free-market policy might kill the patient are just as untrue as the notion that "going cold turkey" will kill someone who is addicted to heroin.

The chances of genuine reform seem remote as government is poised to make a grand puritanical leap into the twenty-first century. But as Yandle (1983) suggests, people can and do make a public-policy difference. Though rare, opportunities for shaping the direction of reform do exist. And while it is difficult for the average citizen to discern the true effects of prohibition policies, there is a growing recognition of prohibition's long history of failure. The rising opposition to the war on drugs and the declining state of public finance also provide some hope for stopping the neo-Puritan juggernaut. Ironically, it may be the passing of the millennium that provides the best chance for the nation to beat its addiction to predatory politics.

### Notes

1. Recent studies of prohibitions include Benjamin and Miller (1991), Hamowy (1987), Krauss and Lazear (1991), Meier (1994), Miller (1991), Rasmussen and

Benson (1994), and Staley (1992), all of which find prohibition generally lacking in any capability of fulfilling its policy goals or ability to pass a cost-benefit test. Thornton (1991a) found that prohibition cannot even pass a more lenient subjective cost-benefit test. Even advocates of prohibition such as Kleiman (1992) concede that the potential for a successful prohibition is tenuous and that the policy should be strictly reserved for limited cases.

2. See Thornton (1991a, especially chapter 4) for an explanation of this process as an example of the Misean, or Austrian, theory of interventionism (regulation). Also see McKie (1970) for a discussion of progressive interventionism as applied to the regulation of public utilities, a phenomenon labeled the "tar baby effect." Not only does policy failure stimulate the demand for stricter control measures, but it also provides the evidence that prohibitionists employ in their propaganda and policy advocacy.

3. H. L. Mencken simplified the puritan-prohibitionist ideology as the haunting fear that someone, somewhere might be having a good time. Earlier, C. F. Browne noted that "Puritans nobly fled from a land of despotism to a land of freedim, where they could not only enjoy their own religion but prevent everybody else from enjoyin his" (Mencken 1991, 996).

4. This attitude is supported by the recent legalization of gambling in many states and extensive public discussion of the relegalization of drugs. For an optimistic assessment of the prospects for relegalizing drugs, see Thornton (1991b).

5. This last point is more significant than it might appear. The major obstacle to eliminating sin policies is the absence, in many peoples' minds, of a viable alternative for the revenues from sin taxes and the social control of prohibition. The alternative can be derived either via economic theory or through investigation of periods when such policies were not in effect.

6. An important ideological distinction exists between excise taxes that are assessed as user fees (e.g., the gasoline tax, which is used to pay for road construction and maintenance) and excise taxes that are levied to discourage "sin" (e.g., the fluorocarbon tax).

7. The exception to this result is the possibility that a policy, such as prohibition, might increase the demand for a good due to the additional attention and information available about the good. For example, restricting the sale of glue to prevent people from using it as an intoxicant could inadvertently increase the demand for glue if there were limited information about the intoxicating effects of glue prior to the prohibition. There is also the often discussed "forbidden fruit" syndrome, where alienated and risk-loving individuals (such as teenage males) will demand anything that they are prohibited from consuming. As Michel de Montaigne wrote in 1580, "To forbid us anything is to make us have a mind for it" (Mencken 1991, 979). Of course, the increase in demand would have to more than offset the decrease in (legal) supply in order to increase total consumption.

8. Black marketeers do not have access to the legal system and must therefore resort to violence, or the threat thereof, to enforce contracts and defend sales territories. They also may resort to bribery of public officials in order to reduce the risk of black-market business in a cost-effective manner. Beil and Thornton (1993) show that by destroying jobs in the private sector, these policies increase the relative wage rates of criminals, the number of criminals, and the crime rate. For a more detailed overview of the impact of prohibition on crime rates see Thornton (1991a), chapter 5.

9. Both prohibition and excise taxes distort the production, characteristics, and overall quality of the product. Both policies produce a general tendency towards higher-potency, lower-quality, and therefore more dangerous products than would

be produced under free-market conditions (see Thornton 1993, and chapter 4, of Thornton 1991a).

10. See Barzel (1976) and chapter 4 of Thornton (1991a) for descriptions of some of these effects. In a static sense, excise taxes are superior to prohibitions in terms of both unintended consequences and impact on public finance.

11. An important exception to this is the case of legalizing the confiscation of property of suspected prohibition violators. See chapters 9 and 15 in this book.

12. See, especially, Fisher (1927 and 1929) and pages 15–23 of Thornton (1991a). Also see note 2.

13. Rorabaugh (1979, 5–21). He suggests that problem drinking was rare. The two types of drinking most prominent were dietary drinking, which involved numerous small servings throughout the day as a substitute for food and water, and communal binge drinking, in which the entire town might get intoxicated in celebration of Independence Day, harvests, weddings, and public events such as elections (generally less than once per month).

14. According to Bassett (1932, 140–45), many of the smaller towns of New England, but especially Boston and the Rhode Island ports, benefited materially from the production of rum and the slave trade.

15. According to Rorabaugh (1979, 23), even Increase Mather, a temperance clergyman, considered alcoholic beverages to be a good "creature of God."

16. For strategic reasons Hamilton emphasized that the federal government would rely on import duties, but he did qualify his arguments (in *Federalist Papers* 30 and 34) to allow for other sources of revenue. In addition to wanting to raise revenue, Hamilton felt that taxing the "pernicious luxury" contributed to nationalism by familiarizing the people directly with the ways of their government.

17. Prominent among Rush's medical teachings were purification techniques such as bleeding, blistering, and mercury cures.

18. This perspective on sin is analogous to an objective theory of value in economics. From the objective viewpoint, value and sin are innate aspects of the good, while from the subjective point of view, economic value and sin are a matter of individual choice.

19. An earlier example of a postmillenialist was Joachim of Fiore, a twelfth-century Calabrian monk who attempted to establish a heretical communist society and almost converted three popes to his beliefs. Postmillenialism continued to spring up in medieval Europe, especially in Germany and amongst the Anabaptists. This history is described by Cohn (1961). According to Rothbard (1990), postmillenialism is also an important component of secular movements such as Karl Marx's communism. Adolph Hitler's Nazism and Third (1,000-year) Reich could also be interpreted as a secular derivation of Joachim's millenialism and original thesis that history would be divided into three, rather than the two, periods of traditional Christian doctrine.

20. North (1988) finds that the original Puritans were actually less radical than latter-day neo-Puritans in terms of alcohol policy.

21. Much of this migration was concentrated in areas claimed by Massachusetts and Connecticut in the Treaty of 1783. See Cross (1950) and Odegard ([1928] 1966) on the dispersion of prohibitionists.

22. Ironically, both the anti-alcohol movement and the antislavery movement were centered in Boston, which dominated the early colonial triangular trade in rum and slaves.

23. The Second Great Awakening refers to a period of Protestant religious revivalism in antebellum America that peaked between the late 1820s and the early 1840s. The most concentrated and fervent revivalist activity took place in west-

ern New York and northern Ohio, where many New Englanders had settled. The First Great Awakening occurred during the 1740s.

24. In fact, many social and economic factors contributed to revivalism and the Second Great Awakening. Barkun (1986, chaps. 6 and 7), for example, explains that natural factors and natural disasters also contributed to revivalism.

25. Again, see Olds (1994) for evidence that the established churches did practice price discrimination, that output did increase after disestablishment (privatization), and that alternative churches expanded faster than the established churches after privatization.

26. *The Nation* 46 (12 January 1888): 24–26; 46 (16 February 1888): 127; 48 (31 January 1889): 83; 48 (14 March 1889): 214–15; 48 (25 April 1889): 336; and 48 (27 June 1889): 515.

27. *The Nation* 46 (16 February 1888): 127. Also with respect to high taxes, the *National Municipal Review* (January 1935, 63) noted that "high taxation thus becomes the chief foundation of the illegitimate trade," a trade that Hu (1950, 86) notes is "deeply disturbing" and can be "driven out" by reducing taxes.

28. Hu (1950, 3, app. 2) shows that the federal excise tax on distilled spirits was fifty cents per tax gallon in 1868 and one dollar and ten cents in 1894. He notes (p. 49) that thirty-seven states had local-option laws by 1900. *The Nation* (vol. 46, 12 January 1888, 25) describes the high license fees in several states. Ely (1888, 203–5) notes that in Savannah, Georgia, a liquor dealer would pay a federal license fee of $25.00, a state license fee of $50.00, a county license fee of $100.00, and a city license fee of $200.00. The barkeepers' license in Charlotte, North Carolina, was $1,000.00.

29. Blocker (1976, 157); Odegard ([1928] 1966, 20–21). The Congregational, Quaker, Methodist, Baptist, and Presbyterian churches were at the center of the prohibition movement. These churches and their ministers and flocks had radiated out from New England into western New York, the Midwest, and, by the turn of the century, most of the western and southern states. It is this geographic and demographic dissemination that enhanced the potential for national alcohol prohibition.

30. Odegard ([1928] 1966, 74, 181, 210); Warburton (1932, 263). The absence of data should not be taken to infer a lack of commercial interest in promoting prohibition.

31. See Bieto (1989) for an excellent history of tax revolts during the Great Depression. He finds that the tax revolts ultimately failed because of a failure to develop a coherent antitax ideology and an overreliance on a strategy that stressed "good government."

32. When adopted freely by wholesaler and retailer, such vertical contracts are now generally seen as promoting economic efficiency by reducing transaction costs. In this case, however, exclusive dealing contracts were directly related to government intervention and could therefore be expected to have unintended negative consequences.

33. This passage is from Fisher's presidential address to the American Economic Association and is unique because Fisher was simultaneously president of the American Statistical Association. Fisher was a socialist (Thornton 1991a, 15–29, especially p. 17). He was a most ardent supporter of prohibition, writing three books in its support and one book on the evils of drinking.

34. Emphasis added. Musto (1987, 57) notes how World War I patriotism combined with progressive and prohibitionist sentiments to create "an intense desire to purify the nation as it girded itself to fight for democracy...and the desire to be sure that the United States remained pure and strong."

35. *Webb et al. v. United States*, 249 US 96 (1919).

# References

Barkun, Michael. 1986. *Crucible of the Millennium: The Burned-Over District of New York in the 1840s*. Syracuse, N.Y.: Syracuse University Press.

Barzel, Yoram. 1976. "An Alternative Approach to the Analysis of Taxation." *Journal of Political Economy* 84 (December): 1177–97.

Bassett, John S. 1932. *A Short History of the United States: 1492–1929*. New York: Macmillan.

Beil, Richard O., and Mark Thornton. 1993. "Experimenting with Prohibition: The Economics of Prohibition, Crime, and Respect for the Law." Working paper, Auburn University.

Benjamin, Daniel K., and Roger Leroy Miller. 1991. *Undoing Drugs: Beyond Legalization*. New York: Basic Books.

Bieto, David T. 1989. *Taxpayers in Revolt: Tax Resistance During the Great Depression*. Chapel Hill: University of North Carolina Press.

Blocker, Jack S. 1976. *Retreat from Reform: The Prohibition Movement in the United States, 1890–1913*. Westport, Conn.: Greenwood Press.

Boudreaux, Donald J., and A. C. Pritchard. 1994. "The Price of Prohibition." *Arizona Law Review* 36(1): 1–10.

Byrne, Frank L. 1969. *Prophet of Prohibition: Neal Dow and His Crusade*. Gloucester, Mass.: Peter Smith.

Cohn, Norman R. C. 1961. *The Pursuit of Millennium: Revolutionary Messianism in Medieval and Reformation Europe and its Bearing on Modern Totalitarian Movements*. London: Harper & Row.

Cross, Whitney R. 1950. *The Burned-Over District: The Social and Intellectual History of Enthusiastic Religion in Western New York, 1800–1850*. Ithaca, N.Y.: Cornell University Press.

Dillow, Gordon L. 1981. "The Hundred-Year War Against the Cigarette." Reprint from *American Heritage* (February/March).

Dow, Neal. 1898. *The Reminiscences of Neal Dow, Recollections of Eighty Years*. Portland, Maine: Evening Express.

Ely, Richard T. 1888. *Taxation in American States and Cities*. New York: Thomas Y. Crowell & Co.

Fisher, Irving. 1919. "Economists and Public Service." *American Economic Review* 9 (March): 16.

———. 1927. *Prohibition at Its Worst*. Rev. ed. New York: Alcohol Information Committee.

———. 1929. *Prohibition Still at Its Worst*. New York: Alcohol Information Committee.

Hamowy, Ronald, ed. 1987. *Dealing with Drugs: Consequences of Government Control*. Lexington, Mass.: Lexington Books.

Hu, Tun Yuan. 1950. *The Liquor Tax in the United States, 1791–1947: A History of the Internal Revenue Taxes Imposed on Distilled Spirits by the Federal Government*. New York: Columbia University Graduate School of Business.

Jenkins, Philip. 1994. "The Puritanism That Dare Not Speak Its Name." *Chronicles* 18 (July): 20–23.

Karp, Richard. 1992. "Prohibition Redux? The Way the Government Spends Money on 'The Alcohol Problem,' You Just Might Think It's Got a Hidden Agenda." *Across the Board* (July/August): 26–32.

Kleiman, Mark A. R. 1992. *Against Excess: Drug Policy for Results*. New York: Basic Books.

Krauss, Melvyn B., and Edward P. Lazear, eds. 1991. *Searching for Alternatives: Drug-Control Policy in the United States*. Stanford, Calif.: Hoover Institution Press.

McKie, James W. 1970. "Regulation and the Free Market: The Problem of Boundaries," *Bell Journal of Economics and Management Science* 1 (Spring): 6–26.

Meier, Kenneth J. 1994. *The Politics of Sin: Drugs, Alcohol, and Public Policy*. New York: M. E. Sharpe.

Mencken, H. L. 1991. *A New Dictionary of Quotations on Historical Principles from Ancient and Modern Sources*. New York: Knopf.

Miller, Richard Lawrence. 1991. *The Case for Legalizing Drugs*. New York: Praeger.

Musto, David F. 1987. "The History of Legislative Control Over Opium, Cocaine, and Their Derivatives." In *Dealing with Drugs: Consequences of Government Control*, edited by Ronald Hamowy, pp. 37–72. Lexington, Mass.: Lexington Books.

North, Douglass C. 1966. *Growth and Welfare in the American Past*. Englewood Cliffs, N.J.: Prentice-Hall.

North, Gary. 1988. *Puritan Economic Experiments*. Fort Worth, Tex.: Institute for Christian Economics.

Odegard, Peter H. [1928] 1966. *Pressure Politics: The Story of the Anti-Saloon League*. Reprint, New York: Octagon Books.

Olds, Kelly. 1994. "Privatizing the Church: Disestablishment in Connecticut and Massachusetts." *Journal of Political Economy* 102 (April): 277–97.

Paul, Randolph E. 1954. *Taxation in the United States*. Boston: Little, Brown.

Rasmussen, David W., and Bruce L. Benson. 1994. *The Economic Anatomy of A Drug War: Criminal Justice in the Commons*. Lanham, Md.: Rowman & Littlefield.

Rorabaugh, W. J. 1979. *The Alcoholic Republic, an American Tradition*. New York: Oxford University Press.

Rothbard, Murray N. 1990. "Karl Marx: Communist as Religious Eschatologist." *Review of Austrian Economics* 4: 123–79.

Staley, Sam. 1992. *Drug Policy and the Decline of American Cities*. New Brunswick, N.J.: Transaction Publishers.

Thornton, Mark. 1991a. *The Economics of Prohibition*. Salt Lake City: University of Utah Press.

———. 1991b. "The Public Choice of Drug Relegalization." In *New Frontiers in Drug Policy*, edited by Arnold Trebach and Keven Zeese, pp. 417–22. Washington, D.C.: Drug Policy Foundation.

———, 1993. "From Marijuana to Heroin: The Potency of Illegal Drugs." In *The Faces of Change*. Washington, D.C.: Drug Policy Foundation.

Timberlake, James, H. 1963. *Prohibition and the Progressive Movement: 1900–1920*. Cambridge: Harvard University Press.

Towne, Charles Hanson. 1923. *The Rise and Fall of Prohibition*. New York: Macmillan.

Tyrrell, Ian R. 1979. *Sobering Up: From Temperance to Prohibition in Antebellum America, 1800–1860*. Westport, Conn.: Greenwood Press.

Warburton, Clark. 1932. *The Economics of Prohibition*. New York: Columbia University Press.

Yandle, Bruce. 1983. "Bootleggers and Baptists: The Education of a Regulatory Economist." *Regulation* 7 (May/June): 12–16.

# 9

# Predatory Public Finance and the Origins of the War on Drugs: 1984–1989

*Bruce L. Benson*
*David W. Rasmussen*

The Harrison Narcotics Act of 1914 is often cited as the law that made consumption of narcotics illegal in the United States. In reality, the Harrison Act only imposed very modest selective excise taxes on the sale of narcotics such as opiates. What was made illegal was the possession or sale of *untaxed* narcotics. Public policy against marijuana began in a similar fashion with passage of the Marijuana Tax Act in 1937.[1]

Selective excise taxes such as these inevitably lead to crime, however, as individuals attempt to avoid the tax through black markets, smuggling, and the violent forms of competition and contract enforcement that accompany such activities. An excise tax may reduce legal transactions in the product that is being taxed, but as occurred with narcotics and marijuana, it simultaneously creates new problems that are often much more costly for society. However, rather than recognizing of the proximate cause of the crime and eliminating of the taxes, full-blown criminalization of possession and sale of narcotics and marijuana evolved as bureaucrats who were given the authority to police these markets and collect the taxes propagated the belief that it was the "sin" of drug consumption that produced the crime, rather than the incentives to avoid the taxes being imposed on the "sin." This chapter's purpose is to demonstrate that bureaucratic self-interest and predatory public finance in the form of explicit or implicit selective taxes have been and continue to be the primary determinants of public policy in the area of illicit-drug control.

When tax-induced crime becomes a significant problem, the government entity imposing the tax has at least two options. One is to crack down on the criminals; another is to repeal the tax. Consider Quebec's recent experiences with taxes on cigarettes, for instance. An article in the 9 August 1993 issue of *Maclean's,* a leading Canadian newsmagazine, reports that "tax levels in excess of 60 per cent on cigarettes have convinced many smokers that they are justified in breaking the law." Roughly half the cigarettes in Quebec and some other Canadian provinces were being purchased in illegal black markets in order to avoid excise taxes; indeed, one in nine cigarettes consumed in the entire country was purchased illegally.

As one buyer of black-market cigarettes explained, "stupid laws are meant to be broken." As noted above, however, tax avoidance is not the only crime arising from selective taxes. Canada exported roughly 7.6 billion cigarettes to the United States in 1992, for instance, and police estimate that 80 percent were smuggled back across the border. Cigarette smuggling has been so lucrative that organized crime got involved. Rival smuggling gangs were exchanging gunfire as they competed for shares of the illegal market. Large boats were being stolen, armed with mounted guns, and painted black for nighttime smuggling.

Thus, an inevitable cost of high excise taxes is that crime rises and increases the demands for already crowded policing, court, prison, and other law enforcement services. Canadian police were forced to become involved in the same kinds of interdiction efforts against cigarettes that the United States is attempting today against illegal drugs. The results were also similar: the flow of illegal cigarettes into Canada continued unabated. Furthermore, a crackdown on excise-tax–induced crime means either that other taxes have to be raised to support a larger criminal justice system or that some of society's scarce criminal justice resources will have to be shifted away from efforts to deter burglars, robbers, rapists, and other criminals who threaten lives and property, in order to control black markets, smuggling, and the violence that is inevitably associated with these activities. Citizens of Quebec apparently recognized this, and in early 1994 their government announced a massive reduction in the provincial cigarette tax in an effort to end uncontrollable smuggling.

The negative consequences associated with the selective excise taxation of narcotics and marijuana were not as readily apparent to citizens of the United States as were the adverse effects of prohibitively high taxes on cigarettes to citizens of Quebec. The United States consequently took a different route. Crime control became the focus of public policy. Sin taxes nonetheless remain extremely relevant to this day, albeit in a different form. Asset seizure laws have been revised to allow law enforcement officials to "tax" those who participate in illicit-drug markets. Indeed, the opportunity to profit from asset seizures helps to explain why, after 1984, so many state and local elements of the criminal justice system responded to the federal call for the latest offensive in the "war on drugs."

The most recent offensive in the U.S. war on drugs was launched by President Reagan in October 1982 (Wisotsky 1991). But such an offensive has to be waged by state and local "troops," and the fact is that state and local law enforcement agencies generally did not intensify their efforts against drugs significantly until 1984, when a substantial reallocation of state and local criminal justice resources toward drug enforcement began. In fact, drug arrests relative to arrests for reported crimes against persons and property (the so-called Index I offenses of murder, manslaughter, sexual assault, assault, robbery, burglary, larceny, and auto theft) remained fairly constant at a one-to-four ratio from 1970 to 1984, and then the *relative* effort against drugs increased by roughly 45 percent over the next five years. By 1989, criminal justice resources were being allocated in such a way as to make only about 2.2 Index I arrests for every drug arrest.

There are a number of possible explanations for the upsurge in drug enforcement, of course. Perhaps local elected officials, representing median voter preferences across the nation, coincidentally demanded that their police departments escalate the war on drugs. There are strong indications that this explanation does not hold, however. For example, in 1985, "public opinion" surveys suggested that drug use was not considered to be an especially serious problem. Indeed, illicit-drug policy appears to be a case wherein policy changes led public opinion, at least during the escalation of the drug war over the 1984–89 period (Rasmussen and Benson 1994, 122–27).

Another explanation for the trends in the reallocation of local police resources over the 1984–89 period is that powerful interest groups demanded the war. It would, in fact, be surprising if this were not the case, since as Chambliss and Seidman (1971, 73) concluded, "every detailed study of the emergence of legal norms has consistently shown the immense importance of interest-group activity, not the public interest, as the critical variable." Similarly, Rhodes (1977, 13) pointed out that "as far as crime policy and legislation are concerned, public opinion and attitudes are generally irrelevant. The same is not true, however, of specifically interested criminal justice publics."

More-recent research reaches similar conclusions, but also makes it clear that one of the most important "specifically interested criminal justice publics" consists of law enforcement bureaucrats (e.g., Berk et al. 1977; Benson 1990, 105–26; Rasmussen and Benson 1994, 119–73).[2] In order to pursue the argument that police bureaucracies have considerable power in the game of interest-group politics, at least as it pertains to drug legislation, law enforcement influences on the emergence of illicit-drug legislation and subsequent criminalization is examined briefly in section I. Placed in the context of Breton and Wintrobe's (1982) model of bureaucratic efforts to establish policy, the significant role played by entrepreneurial public agencies in the development and evolution of drug policy is emphasized as a prelude to section II, where federal legislation during the 1980s is examined from the same perspective.

Section II provides an explanation for the involvement of state and local law enforcement agencies in the 1984–89 drug war. Specifically, state and local police officials faced what presumably was an exogenous change in bureaucratic incentives (although at least some of these officials were important sources of the demand for the change), which induced an increase in drug enforcement efforts. In particular, one section of the Comprehensive Crime Act of 1984 established a system whereby any local police bureau that cooperated with federal drug enforcement authorities in a drug investigation would share in the money and other property confiscated as part of that investigation. As a result, police in many states whose own laws or constitutions limited confiscation possibilities began to circumvent state laws by having federal authorities "adopt" their seizures.[3] Thus, under the 1984 federal statute, a substantial fraction of seized properties went back to the agencies that seized them, even if the state's laws mandated that the proceeds go someplace other than to law enforcement. This asset seizure law not only established a way to tax the "sin" of participation in illicit-drug markets, but required that the resulting revenue go to the tax collector, the law enforcement agency, thus creating relatively strong incentives to collect the tax. This legislation was demanded by federal, state, and local law enforcement bureaucrats, and largely reflects the bureaucratic competition and cooperation that Breton and Wintrobe (1982) model.

Of course, local police bureaucracies may have advocated such legislation and joined in the drug war because they perceived it to be in the "public interest." There is considerable evidence suggesting that the opportunity costs of resources allocated to the war on drugs have been very high,[4] however, and a good deal of evidence also indicates that many law enforcement bureaucracies engaged in misinformation campaigns in order to exaggerate the potential benefits of a drug war (Michaels 1987, 311–24). These considerations are relevant because if confiscations can be used at the discretion of local police bureaucrats to significantly enhance their own well-being, then the federal statute may explain a substantial portion of the changes in the allocation of local police resources after 1984.

Local interbureau competition for resources may lead government decision makers (bureau sponsors) to treat confiscations as a substitute for ordinary appropriations, of course. Therefore, an important theme of section II is the summary of a case study by Benson, Rasmussen, and Sollars (1995) of the budgetary impact of local police confiscations from the drug war. The findings are consistent with the hypothesis that confiscation legislation creates significant incentives to alter the allocation of police resources.

Not all states were equal participants in the 1984–89 war on drugs, however. Table 9.1 shows that in a few states, drug arrests accounted for a smaller portion of all arrests in 1989 than in 1984. But these are exceptions to the trend. The largest states, such as California, Florida, Michigan, Illinois, and Pennsylvania, increased drug enforcement to an extent that the drug arrest/ total arrest ratio rose 67 percent between 1984 and 1989—from 5.8 percent to 9.7 percent. Since there is significant variation in drug enforcement activity

## TABLE 9.1
### Drug Arrests per 100,000 Population by State, 1984 and 1989

| State | Rank | 1989 | 1984 | % Change | State | Rank | 1989 | 1984 | % Change |
|---|---|---|---|---|---|---|---|---|---|
| Alabama | 21 | 392 | 190 | 106.3 | Montana | 27 | 332 | 130 | 155.4 |
| Alaska | 44 | 162 | 120 | 35.0 | Nebraska | 32 | 283 | 150 | 88.7 |
| Arizona | 11 | 519 | 380 | 36.6 | Nevada | 42 | 170 | 110 | 54.5 |
| Arkansas | 30 | 311 | 230 | 35.2 | New Hampshire | 35 | 265 | 138 | 92.0 |
| California | 1 | 1,060 | 590 | 79.7 | New Jersey | 2 | 895 | 460 | 94.6 |
| Colorado | 33 | 279 | 230 | 21.3 | New Mexico | 13 | 454 | 300 | 51.3 |
| Connecticut | 8 | 647 | 270 | 139.6 | New York | 3 | 799 | 510 | 56.7 |
| Delaware | 28 | 329 | 230 | 43.0 | North Carolina | 20 | 411 | 261 | 57.5 |
| Florida | 6 | 675 | 360 | 87.5 | North Dakota | 49 | 107 | 160 | -33.1 |
| Georgia | 7 | 661 | 344 | 92.1 | Ohio | 17 | 426 | 190 | 124.2 |
| Hawaii | 25 | 355 | 420 | -15.5 | Oklahoma | 29 | 327 | 270 | 21.1 |
| Idaho | 39 | 221 | 140 | 57.9 | Oregon | 15 | 438 | 240 | 82.5 |
| Illinois | 14 | 446 | 120 | 271.7 | Pennsylvania | 34 | 274 | 130 | 110.8 |
| Indiana | 41 | 189 | 130 | 45.4 | Rhode Island | 19 | 422 | 380 | 11.1 |
| Iowa | 46 | 119 | 90 | 32.2 | South Carolina | 12 | 470 | 300 | 56.7 |
| Kansas | 37 | 233 | 140 | 66.4 | South Dakota | 47 | 118 | 190 | -37.9 |
| Kentucky | 9 | 528 | 300 | 76.0 | Tennessee | 36 | 263 | 160 | 64.4 |
| Louisiana | 10 | 526 | 270 | 94.8 | Texas | 16 | 433 | 360 | 20.3 |
| Maine | 38 | 229 | 130 | 76.1 | Utah | 31 | 291 | 320 | -9.1 |
| Maryland | 4 | 776 | 420 | 84.8 | Vermont | 48 | 109 | n.a. | n.a. |
| Mass. | 5 | 689 | 310 | 122.3 | Virginia | 26 | 341 | 200 | 70.5 |
| Michigan | 23 | 374 | 170 | 120.0 | Washington | 24 | 369 | 170 | 117.1 |
| Minnesota | 45 | 161 | 130 | 23.8 | West Virginia | 50 | 88 | 100 | -12.0 |
| Mississippi | 22 | 375 | 190 | 97.4 | Wisconsin | 40 | 207 | 200 | 3.5 |
| Missouri | 18 | 422 | 240 | 75.8 | Wyoming | 43 | 169 | 180 | -6.1 |
| | | | | | United States | | 538 | 312 | 72.4 |

*Source:* U.S. Department of Justice 1984, 1989.

across states and cities, as well as through time, it follows that if this "sin tax/bureaucratic self-interest" story actually provides a strong explanation for drug enforcement policy, it should help explain cross-sectional variation in enforcement policy as well as time series variation.

This question has been explored in a cross-sectional analysis of urban drug enforcement policies (Rasmussen et al. 1994). Since the proceeds of federally "adopted" seizures are only partially turned back to the local police (the federal authorities extract a 20 percent handling charge), police in states whose own laws allow them to fully retain seized assets are able to secure even greater benefits from seizures than police who must involve federal authorities in the process. Thus, a self-interest model of police behavior suggests that in states whose laws grant police exclusive rights to seizures, police will focus relatively greater efforts against drugs than police in states whose laws remove seized assets from the police departments' control. This expectation is supported by the empirical results in Rasmussen et al. (1994). These findings and their implications are explored in section III.

The escalation of the U.S. war on drugs ended in 1989. Indeed, since 1989, a substantial reduction in drug enforcement activity has occurred. The concluding section offers several potential explanations for this downturn in the drug policy cycle, all of which are consistent with the "sin tax/bureaucratic self-interest" arguments that explain the 1984–89 escalation of drug enforcement.

## I. Law Enforcement Bureaucrats,
## Interest-Group Politics, and Drug Policy

There are many models of bureaucratic behavior based on self-interest assumptions. Tullock (1965) saw bureaucratic behavior driven by a desire for security. Chant and Acheson (1972) contended that bureaucratic behavior was driven by a desire for prestige. Niskanen (1968, 1971) assumed that a bureau manager could be characterized as a budget maximizer. Migué and Belanger (1974) explained that the budget maximization assumption unduly limits the range of utility-maximizing efforts, however, and proposed that the bureaucrat seeks discretion ("slack"), reflected in a budget with excess revenues over actual costs.[5]

Public officials are presumably characterized by the same basic utility-maximizing behavior that motivates people operating in private markets. The institutional framework of public officials may differ from that of private-sector employees, but their fundamental objectives do not. Employment security is a desirable job attribute in the private sector, for instance. The U.S. Department of Health, Education, and Welfare Task Force (1973) found that job security, interesting work, and opportunity to develop special skills were considered to be the most important features of job quality. Not surprisingly, civil service bureaucrats are also very concerned about job security (Johnson and Libecap 1989). In fact, the public sector offers more job security and lower pay than comparable jobs in the private sector, on average, so self-selection appears to play a role in employment decisions.

A similar point can also be made about elected officials whose desire to be reelected is consistent with a broadly held desire for employment security. Surveys of private-sector employees identify other sources of job satisfaction that may be applicable to elected and appointed public officials as well as to civil servants: (1) good pay; (2) *discretionary* authority, information, and opportunity to get the job done; and (3) seeing the results of one's work. Discretion in controlling the intensity and pace of work is also an important job characteristic, and some research suggests that part of the wage premiums paid to workers in very large manufacturing plants is explained by the absence of these job attributes (Stafford and Duncan 1980). Thus, discretion may be a major source of satisfaction for bureaucrats and public officials (Parker 1992).

Job characteristics that people value in a private setting are not likely to lose their allure just because someone is engaged in public-sector employment. In this light, as Breton and Wintrobe (1982, 27) noted,

> In addition to size, budgets, discretion, prestige, and self-preservation, it has been suggested that security, the avoidance of risk or responsibility, secrecy, complexity, career promotion, leisure, internal patronage, and a bureaucrat's personal conception of the common...good are objectives of bureaucrats, either one at a time or in groups.

They suggested that all of these factors may enter into a bureaucrat's utility function and that no general theory of bureaucratic behavior can be built on only one particular objective.

Thus, Breton and Wintrobe assumed general utility maximization and focused on the institutional setting (e.g., the intensity of interbureaucratic competition for budget shares and intrabureaucratic competition for promotions; positions in networks; the existence of barriers to mobility; and the ability of superiors and sponsors to monitor performance) as the determinant of which particular objective will appear to dominate in a particular bureau. Breton and Wintrobe characterized the bureaucratic institutional process as one dominated by "entrepreneurial competition," wherein individual bureaucrats pursue their subjective goals by selectively seeking and implementing policy innovations.[6] This characterization fits the role played by law enforcement bureaucrats in the evolution of U.S. drug policy.

Actually, a number of self-interested political motivations for demanding drug legislation have been identified for both bureaucratic and nonbureaucratic interest groups. Some studies have noted the incentives of professional organizations such as the American Pharmaceutical Association to create legal limits on the distribution of drugs (historically there was significant competition between pharmacists and physicians for the legal right to dispense drugs, for example),[7] while others have focused on the disparate racial impacts of illicit-drug laws and the desire by some groups to control racial minorities through the enforcement of such laws.[8] More important from the perspective stressed here, however, still other studies have emphasized that law enforcement bureaucrats were a major source of demand for criminalization of narcotics after the Harrison Act was passed; the same groups lobbied for passage of the Marijuana Tax Act and played an important role in the subsequent criminalization of this illicit drug.[9]

Breton and Wintrobe (1982, 146–54) explained that one bureaucratic strategy for competing for resources is to "generate" demand for a bureau's own services through direct lobbying, policy manipulation, and the selective release of information to other interest groups and the media. These strategies are followed because bureaus must compete with one another for the support and attention of sponsors (and individual bureaucrats must compete with other bureaucrats for benefits within a bureau), and because control of resources is necessary before most of the subjective goals of bureaucrats can be achieved.[10] Indeed, Lindesmith (1965, 3) contended that the nation's program for handling the "drug problem" is one "which, to all intents and purposes, was established by the decisions of administrative officials of the Treasury Department."

Why would the Treasury Department care about drug criminalization? Because the Harrison Act established federal taxes on narcotics and the Treasury Department's Federal Bureau of Narcotics was responsible for its enforcement. For several years after its passage in 1914, the Harrison Act remained a rather unimportant source of taxes and regulatory measures (Reinarman 1983, 21). Indeed, the law's most important consequence may have been that a bureaucracy grew up to enforce it. Given their regulatory powers, agents of the Federal Bureau of Narcotics chose to instigate criminalization of opiate users with a series of raids on morphine treatment clinics in 1919.[11] King (1957, 122) maintained that "the Narcotics Division launched a reign of terror. Doctors were bullied and threatened, and those who were adamant [about treating addicts] went to prison."

Efforts by bureaucrats in the Narcotics Bureau led to a series of court decisions that reinterpreted the Harrison Act and became the pretext for criminalization of drug use (Reinarman 1983, 21). Furthermore, because of pressure from people in the same bureau, the Marijuana Tax Act was passed in 1937.[12] Some writers (e.g., Howard Becker 1963) have stressed moral entrepreneurship by Narcotics Bureau officials, but others (e.g., Donald Dickson 1968) have focused on bureaucratic fiscal self-promotion. The bureau was in need of a new raison d'etre for continued funding in 1937; after all, it faced stiff competition from the FBI for the attention of the public and of Congress (King 1978), which saw crime control to be within the domain of the FBI rather than the Treasury Department's Narcotics Bureau. Bureaucratic survival was certainly a probable motivation.

Breton and Wintrobe (1982, 39) emphasized that bureaucratic release of both true and false information, or "selective distortion," can play a significant role in bureaucratic policy advocacy.[13] This has clearly been the case in the evolution of drug policy. For example, the bureaucratic campaigns leading up to the 1937 marijuana legislation "included remarkable distortions of the evidence of harm caused by marijuana, ignoring the findings of empirical inquiries."[14] The "reefer madness" scare can be traced to the misinformation propagated by the Narcotics Bureau. Marijuana was alleged to cause insanity, to incite rape, and to trigger delirious rages in users making them irresponsible and prone to commit violent crimes. Factual distortions did not stop there, however. For instance, the bill was represented as one that was largely symbolic in that it would require no additional enforcement expenditures (Galliher and Walker 1977).

The evolution of drug policy since the initial legislation has also been, at least in part, shaped by bureaucratic competition, both between law enforcement and drug treatment bureaucrats over "ownership of the problem"—that is, over shares of federal, state, and local budgets (Gusfield 1980; Morgan 1983)—and between law enforcement bureaucracies themselves—that is, between the DEA and the FBI (King 1978) at the federal level, as well as between various local, state, and federal bureaucracies.

This evolution also reflects another aspect of the bureaucratic process emphasized by Breton and Wintrobe. As the perceived responsibility for some social ill (e.g., crime in this case, and inflation in Breton and Wintrobe 1982) is shifted from outside forces to the government and to the bureaucracy, bureaucrats seek to shift the blame elsewhere (Breton and Wintrobe 1982, 149). Blaming crime on people crazed by drugs takes advantage of such an opportunity.

A good deal of false or misleading information emanating from police bureaucrats about the relationship between drugs and crime has clearly characterized the evolution of drug policy.[15] In fact, police bureaucracies were key sources of the "information," much of which was inaccurate or unsubstantiated (Michaels 1987, 311–24), used to justify the 1984–89 phase of the war on drugs. It was chiefly as a result of information promulgated by police (Barnett 1984, 53) that drug crime came widely to be believed to be the root cause of much of what is wrong with society (see Office of National Drug Control Strategy 1990, 2).

In particular, drug use is claimed to be a leading cause of nondrug crime because, it is contended, property crime is a major source of income for drug users. This claim has been made to justify political demands for the criminal justice system to "do something" about the drug/crime problem, demands which largely emanate from the police lobbies (e.g., see Berk et al. 1977; Barnett 1984; Benson 1990; and Rasmussen and Benson 1994), and in turn, it has been used to justify an emphasis on control of illicit-drug traffic as a means of general crime prevention. State and federal legislators have been passing laws mandating increasingly strict sentences for drug offenders, police have shifted resources to make more drug arrests, and judges have sentenced ever larger numbers of drug offenders to prison.

Such a reallocation of resources would appear to be justified if drugs truly are the root cause of most other crime, but these causal relationships do not actually hold. In particular, increased drug enforcement efforts tend to cause increases in crime as other criminal activities are less effectively deterred.[16] Thus, the opportunity costs of the war on drugs appear to be quite high. This should not be surprising, of course, given the history of failure of drug and alcohol prohibition policies (Thornton 1991; Nadelmann 1993). Answers to the question "Why has this reallocation occurred?" would appear to be even more pressing under the circumstances.

Breton and Wintrobe (1982, 150–51) offer two reasons to explain why bureaucrats advocate a policy of directly controlling "a source of blame" for a problem such as crime (e.g., alcohol prohibition, criminalization and prohibition of various drugs after 1914 and 1937, and increased emphasis on drug control in the mid-1960s and then again in the mid-1980s), even though such policies have a history of failure. First, there is always opposition to such a policy, so when it fails, the opposition can be blamed for not allocating enough resources to combat the problem. And second, because policy outcomes depend jointly on the inputs of several different groups and bureaus and the set of possible control methods is very large, when the subset selected fails, the bureaucrats can argue that (1) while they advocated a control policy, they favored a different subset of control tools (e.g., more severe punishment of drug offenders or greater spending on interdiction efforts), so they are not responsible for the failure, (2) the other groups whose contributions were necessary to make the effort successful—witnesses, judges, legislators who approve prison budgets, other law enforcement agencies—dropped the ball, or both. Indeed, a policy can fail completely while at the same time entrepreneurial bureaucrats expand their reputations and end up being substantially better off.[17]

The ongoing competition for a share of the total budget is always an important motivating factor for a bureaucracy. After all, few of the subjective goals of bureaucrats can be achieved without a budget. Therefore, each bureau must demonstrate that it is doing a good job in serving its constituencies. The function of police in the minds of most citizens is to "fight crime," of course, but how can interest groups, voters, taxpayers, and elected representatives tell if police are doing a good job? The number of crimes prevented cannot be observed. Police therefore need statistical indicators of their "productivity" to use in their lobbying efforts for expanded budgets (Sherman 1983, 156).

The number of arrests is a natural measure of "effectiveness," and this is a primary "statistic" that police focus on in the budget negotiation process. Others include response times following emergency calls and, increasingly, asset seizures. Indeed, with drug prohibition, a source of arrests is created that does not require waiting for some victim to report a crime, *and* it provides a new statistical indicator of effectiveness: the value of drug seizures (and of nondrug property seizures, as discussed below).[18]

Police conduct may be even more "perverted" by drug prohibition than suggested so far: incentives actually exist to reallocate resources in order to avoid deterring Index I crimes. After all, while arrest statistics may be key indicators of police performance in the budget-bargaining process, they are not the only statistics relevant to such bargaining. As Milakovich and Weis (1975, 10) noted, police have a "vested interest" in keeping crime rates relatively high: if crime rates drop too much, then support for more police and larger budgets declines, and "like all bureaucracies, criminal justice agencies can hardly be expected to implement policies that would diminish their importance."

The literature on the economics of crime indicates that higher Index I crime rates are correlated significantly with more police resources in "demand for policing" equations, supporting the assumption that political demands for police services rise if reported crime rates are high. But if police do respond to the incentives outlined here, additional funding need not lead to any reduction in reported crime rates. Police can focus resources on drug control, which can lead to increased arrests and drug seizures as indicators of effectiveness, while simultaneously increasing Index I crime rates, thus implying a greater need for police services.

But these incentives have been in place since drugs were initially criminalized. Something else must have changed in 1984 to produce the significant reallocation of policing resources away from Index I crimes discussed earlier. Indeed, something else did change, at least for the police in many states. A bureaucratically motivated policy innovation appears to have created explicit incentives for shifting resources toward drug enforcement. This innovation allowed police agencies to benefit directly through the collection of an ersatz sin tax—the police were given the opportunity to impose a tax in the form of confiscations of money and other property used in or purchased with profits from the drug trade and, more important, to keep the proceeds from this tax.

## II. Police Interests in Federal Confiscations as a Sin Tax

Government seizure of property used in criminal activity is actually a long-standing practice. It was one stimulus for the king's involvement in law enforcement as early as the ninth and tenth centuries (Benson 1990), for instance, and was first used in the United States to combat smugglers who avoided import duties in the early nineteenth century. Nowadays it is being used to combat the supply of illicit drugs. Federal officials confiscated over $100 million worth of property in 1983, and the Comprehensive Crime Act of 1984 broadened support for the practice insofar as the law required the Justice Department to share the proceeds with state and local agencies participating in the investigations. Perhaps as a result of the cooperation this produced, federal forfeitures were projected to be valued at $700 million for 1991.[19]

The 1984 federal asset forfeiture law was a bureaucratically demanded innovation that allowed for an expanded interbureau cooperation. As Breton and Wintrobe (1982, 128) explained, cooperation through informal networks, both within and across bureaucracies, is an alternative to competition. A reduction in the intensity of competition allows bureaucrats greater discretion in the pursuit of their subjective goals.[20]

On the surface at least, this innovation allowed local law enforcement agencies to generate revenues that were not limited by the interbureaucratic competition for resources that arises in the local budgeting process. The statute mandated that shared assets go directly to law enforcement agencies rather than—as provided by many state forfeiture laws—into general funds, education funds, or other depositories.

An increase in the revenues from drug-related seizures creates the potential for bureau managers to expand their discretionary budgets, thereby enhancing their own well-being directly *and* indirectly by rewarding supporters in the managers' networks with various "perks" (Breton and Wintrobe 1982, 137). After all, police have considerable discretion in how they allocate the resources they control, and monitoring generally does not limit their discretion in any substantial way.[21] Therefore, inasmuch as this new source of revenue has increased the police's ability to control resources, it has probably increased their discretionary ability to generate perks.

From the criminal's point of view, forfeiture has an obvious potential deterrent value in that it raises the costs associated with drug offenses. Indeed, the justification for asset seizures is precisely the same as the justification for an explicit excise tax on drugs or any other politically incorrect product. The activity being taxed should be reduced as a consequence of the tax, whether the tax is explicit in the form of a levy on the legal sale of a "sinful" good or implicit in the form of the seizure of assets involved in illicit transactions in the good. Selective excise taxes are also justified as a source of revenue that can be used to help correct the problems arising from the consumption of the good. Thus, it is often contended that cigarette taxes are an appropriate source of revenue for financing the extra health care costs alleged to arise from smoking. Similarly, since drugs supposedly cause crime, forfeiture policies that earmark the resulting revenues to law enforcement are said to be justified as a way of defraying the costs of policing drug-related crime.

This practical aspect of asset seizures—treating the proceeds as something akin to a crime-fighting "user fee"—was emphasized in a manual designed to help jurisdictions develop a forfeiture capability (National Criminal Justice Association 1988, 40). Pointing out that less tangible law enforcement effects (such as deterrence) should be counted as benefits, the manual emphasized that the determining factor for pursuit of a forfeiture is "the *jurisdiction's* best interest" (emphasis added).

This interest, of course, is viewed from the perspective of law enforcement agencies—a perspective that might put somewhat more weight on benefits for bureaucrats and somewhat less weight on community-wide (and uncertain) deterrence effects. After all, as Stumpf (1988, 316) noted, we must "look past the external political and social determinants of criminal justice procedures and policies to understand the system in operation. The process is staffed by professionals and quasi-professionals who have their own agenda...[and] largely internal imperatives may be of even greater importance in explaining their outcomes." (See also Blumberg 1979; Benson 1990; and Rasmussen and Benson 1994.) Indeed, if forfeitures are in the "public interest" because of their deterrent effects, and if police are exclusively motivated to serve the public interest, then they should willingly cooperate in forfeiture efforts no matter what government agency's budget is enhanced by these seizures. The 1984 federal confiscation legislation directed that all shared seizures go to law enforcement, however, because of lobbying efforts by law enforcement bureaucracies. Subsequent efforts to overturn this provision of the legislation have been vehemently opposed by these same bureaucracies.

The 1984 federal confiscation legislation followed a period of active advocacy by federal, state, and local law enforcement officials who emphasized that it would foster cooperation between their agencies and increase the overall effort devoted to—and the effectiveness of—drug control. The law enforcement bureaus maintained, in other words, that they needed to be paid to cooperate, whether the cooperation was in the public interest or not.

In hearings on the Comprehensive Drug Penalty Act held before the Subcommittee on Crime of the Committee on the Judiciary of the U.S. House of Representatives on 23 June and 14 October 1983, for instance, much of the testimony focused exclusively on the issues of confiscation and forfeiture (U.S. House 1985). Among the organizations and bureaus testifying in support of the forfeiture-sharing arrangement were the U.S. Customs Service, various police and sheriffs' departments, the U.S. Attorney's Office of the Southern District of Florida, and the U.S. Drug Enforcement Administration. No witnesses representing local-government oversight authorities (mayors, city councils, county commissions) appeared either in support of or in opposition to such legislation.

Furthermore, when the legislation earmarking the proceeds of asset seizures for law enforcement was first introduced, it appears that most non-law-enforcement bureaucrats did not anticipate its implications, probably due to the poor quality of information selectively released by law enforcement bureaucracies and their congressional supporters to their rivals for resources. The only group that warned of problems with the legislation was the Criminal Justice Section of the American Bar Association. Two groups involved in drug treatment (the Therapy Committees of America and the Alcohol and Drug Problems Association) supported forfeiture sharing but proposed that a share also go to drug therapy programs. The law enforcement lobbies prevailed.

Following passage of the initial law, interbureaucratic competition for the rights to seized assets, as defined by federal statutes, intensified. It became clear to state and local bureaucrats who compete with the law enforcement sector for the control of resources that the federal legislation was being used to circumvent state laws and constitutions prohibiting certain forfeitures or limiting law enforcement use of seizures. For example, North Carolina law requires that all proceeds from the sale of confiscated assets go to the County School Fund. Law enforcement agencies in North Carolina, and in other jurisdictions where state law limited their ability to benefit from confiscations, began using the 1984 federal legislation to circumvent the restrictions by routinely arranging for federal "adoption" of forfeitures so that the assets could be shared with the state and local law enforcement agencies.

As education bureaucrats and others affected by this diversion of resources realized what was going on, they began to advocate changes in the federal law. They were successful, at least initially: the Anti-Drug Abuse Act of 1988 (passed on 18 November 1988) changed the asset forfeiture provisions that had been established in 1984. Section 6077 of the 1988 statute stated that the attorney general must ensure that any seized asset transferred to a state or local law enforcement agency "is not so transferred to circumvent any requirement of state law that prohibits forfeiture or limits the use or disposition of property forfeited to state or local agencies." This provision was to go into effect on 1 October 1989, and the Department of Justice interpreted it to mandate an end to all adoptive forfeitures (U.S. House 1990, 166).

State and local law enforcement officials immediately began advocating repeal of section 6077. Thus, on 24 April 1989, the Subcommittee on Crime heard testimony urging repeal of section 6077 from such groups as the International Association of Chiefs of Police, the Florida Department of Law Enforcement, the North Carolina Department of Crime Control and Public Safety, and the U.S. Attorney General's Office.

Perhaps the most impassioned plea for repeal was made by Joseph W. Dean of the North Carolina Department of Crime Control and Public Safety (U.S. House 1990, 20–28),[22] who admitted both that law enforcement bureaucracies were using the federal law to circumvent the state's constitution and that without the benefit of confiscations going to those bureaus, substantially less effort would be made to control drugs:

Currently the United States Attorney General, by policy, requires that all shared property be used by the transfer for law enforcement purposes. The conflict between state and federal law [given Section 6077 of the 1988 act] would prevent the federal government from adopting seizures by state and local agencies....

This provision would have a devastating impact on joint efforts by federal, state and local law enforcement agencies not only in North Carolina but also in other affected states....

Education is any state's biggest business. The education lobby is the most power-ful in the state and has taken a position against law enforcement being able to share in seized assets. The irony is that if local and state law enforcement agen-cies cannot share, the assets will in all likelihood not be seized and forfeited. Thus no one wins but the drug trafficker....

If this financial sharing stops, we will kill the goose that laid the golden egg.

This statement clearly suggests that law enforcement agencies focus resources on enforcement of drug laws because of the financial gains arising from for-feitures. Perhaps it was not the fact that drugs are illegal, or that the president declared war on drugs, which induced the massive post-1984 policy effort against them; rather, the stimulus seems to have been the 1984 legislation which mandated that forfeitures generate benefits for police.

The implication that law enforcement agencies benefit from the additional discretionary funds secured through the sale of forfeited assets was also cor-roborated by other testimony, including that of the commissioner of the Florida Department of Law Enforcement (U.S. House 1990, 13–14). In fact, a state-ment by the U.S. Attorney for the Eastern District of North Carolina, in sup-port of repealing section 6077, actually implied that law enforcement agencies were focusing on confiscations as opposed to criminal convictions (U.S. House 1990, 26): "Drug agents would have much less incentive to follow through on the asset potentially held by drug traffickers, since there would be no reward for such efforts and [they] would concentrate their time and resources on the criminal prosecution."

Indeed, forfeitures can be successful even if arrest and prosecution are not. Forfeiture laws are supposedly designed to protect lien holders and owners whose property is used without their knowledge or consent, but owners' rights are tenuous since most states prohibit suits claiming that the property was wrongfully taken. This prohibition, coupled with the fact that the procedure takes place in a civil forfeiture hearing, greatly diminishes the capacity of property owners to defend themselves. Generally, owners whose property is alleged to have been used in a drug offense or purchased with the proceeds from drug trafficking have the burden of proving that they merit relief from the forfeiture proceeding (National Criminal Justice Association 1988, 41). The owners must prove not only that they are innocent of the alleged crime, but also that they lacked both knowledge of and control over the property's unlawful use by others.

For example, if a drug dealer places a drug order by phone from a friend's place of business, that property can be seized unless the owner proves both lack of knowledge and control. Thus, forfeiture activity can be a lucrative source of revenue for a police agency, without regard to the actual criminality of the potential target of such seizures. The power of confiscation is illustrated by a March 1991 drug raid in which federal agents confiscated three University of Virginia fraternity houses after drugs valued at a few hundred dollars were seized there. The fraternity houses were valued at $1 million, and the rent from these buildings has subsequently been paid to the U.S. Justice Department.[23]

Many law enforcement agencies have benefited from asset seizure laws. Over 90 percent of the police departments with jurisdictions containing populations of 50,000 or more and over 90 percent of the sheriffs' departments serving populations of 250,000 or more received money or goods from drug asset forfeiture programs in 1990, for instance (Reaves 1992, 1). Furthermore, the Drug Enforcement Administration seizes assets worth millions of dollars at seaports, airports, and bus stations.

Congress began investigating alleged abuses by the DEA in May 1992. Indeed, asset seizure by law enforcement agencies has become increasingly controversial throughout the nation. Widely publicized horror stories in the print and electronic media have raised constitutional issues such as erosion of Fourth Amendment rights, protection of innocent parties, and proportionality of punishment to the crime. Whether a large fraction of the seizures involve assets owned by criminals themselves cannot be determined since many do not entail arrests, and the costs associated with recovering wrongfully seized assets from the federal authorities can run into thousands of dollars. Despite widespread abuse of the forfeiture laws,[24] the police lobbies won the battle over federal legislation. Section 6077 of the Anti-Drug Abuse Act of 1988 never went into effect. Its repeal was hidden in the 1990 defense appropriations bill, and the repeal was made retroactive to 1 October 1989. It appears that the police bureaucrats have won the competition over the property rights to forfeitures, at least as it has been waged at the federal level.

Rivals for budgets at the local level may more clearly see the significant discretionary gains police enjoy as a consequence of asset seizures, however. If so, they may be able to convince local sponsors that police budgets should be reduced accordingly; that is, proceeds from asset forfeiture do not necessarily represent a net gain to local police agencies even when the assets are given to the law enforcement agencies. Pressure from other local bureaucrats who are competitors for resources may lead administrators and politicians with whom bureaucrats bargain for agency budgets to view the flow of money from asset seizures as a substitute for regular budget appropriations.

After all, one alleged purpose of asset forfeitures is to make drug enforcement efforts to a degree self-financing. Becker and Lindsay (1994), for instance, have shown that government can "free ride" by reducing an agency's budgetary appropriations when the agency obtains funding from some other source. If the money from asset seizures is fungible in the budget bargaining and review process, and local commissions, councils, and mayors face strong pressures to take full advantage of this possibility, they could refuse to approve police budgets that are not reduced to offset expected confiscations.

Counteracting the incentive to reduce police budgets by the full amount of the money obtained from asset seizures is the fact that these seizures are visible indicators of law enforcement "output." Major seizures are media events that provide benefits to both police and their budgetary sponsors. If police officials are not allowed to retain at least some of the benefits from the production of this output, their incentives to engage in publicity-generating drug busts will be reduced. It can therefore be hypothesized that police budgets will not be reduced by the full value of the assets they seize.

*Asset Seizures and Police Discretionary Budgets*

The extent to which police agencies can increase their budgets through forfeiture activity is explored in Benson et al. (1995), using data from local Florida policing jurisdictions. Confiscations were found to have a positive and significant impact on police agencies' budgets after accounting for demand and local-government budget-constraint factors. As expected, the impact was larger in more populous jurisdictions. It appears that forfeitures offer police an attractive policy option: an activity that can be justified politically because of its potential as a strong criminal deterrent and because it suggests that drug enforcement is, to a degree, self-financing. At the same time, forfeitures generate direct benefits to the police bureaucracy by increasing its discretionary budget. Relatively small amounts of money from seized assets can mean substantial increases in budget discretion.

Florida data provide an indication of the importance of confiscations as a source of discretionary spending. The estimated elasticity of noncapital expenditures with respect to confiscations is .04 for all jurisdictions in Benson et al. (1995) and .07 for the larger ones. But this seemingly modest elasticity belies the potentially large impact of asset forfeiture on decision making, since only a small fraction of noncapital expenditures are discretionary. The elasticity of discretionary spending with respect to confiscations can be approximated by dividing the estimated elasticity by the proportion of all noncapital expenditures that are discretionary. Thus, if 10 percent of noncapital expenditures are discretionary, the relevant elasticity lies in the 0.4 to 0.7 range. Since the budget share that is committed to specific uses is probably larger than assumed here, these figures probably represent a significant underestimate of the impact confiscated assets can have on the discretionary budget. These results, combined with the evidence of more-intense drug enforcement after 1984, are consistent with the hypothesis that police have responded to the Comprehensive Crime Act of 1984 in ways predicted by economic theory.[25]

The asset forfeiture provisions of the federal statute represented an exogenous change in state and local law enforcement agencies' bureaucratic benefit-cost calculus, inducing them to join in the federally declared war on drugs. Police agencies seeking to increase their budgetary discretion were encouraged to use more of their resources against drug offenders, and to devote fewer resources to other crimes, *whether this reallocation was cost-effective from the standpoint of public safety or not*. The changes in police behavior observed since 1984 are consistent with the proposition that these agencies responded rationally to the incentives created by this law. The relative share of state and local law enforcement resources has shifted dramatically toward drug enforcement, the major source of asset confiscations.

Hence, selective taxes continue to be an integral part of public policy toward drug markets, despite the fact that the use of narcotics and marijuana has been criminalized. When an activity is legal, the tax is called an excise tax; when the activity is illegal, the tax is called asset seizure or asset forfeiture. Selective excise taxes are intended to alter the behavior of consumers, but as explained here, the disposition of the tax revenues can have a dramatic effect on the behavior of the tax collectors. The impact of what might be called predatory public finance can be seen by looking at the interstate variation in asset seizure laws and drug enforcement policies.

### III. Differences in Drug Enforcement across States and Cities

The federal confiscation statute appears to help explain the nationwide staging of a drug war, but it does not explain the large variation in drug enforcement activities across states that is detailed in table 9.1. However, under the federal adoption procedures, federal authorities keep 20 percent of the assets confiscated in adopted seizures, and there are other transaction costs associated with dealing with the federal authorities that tend to undermine the incentives for cooperation (Rasmussen et al. 1994). Thus, police have reasons to avoid federal adoptions if their state laws allow them to keep seized assets, as a number of state laws do. In fact, the importance of the federal statute had diminished greatly by 1990, as many state legislatures followed the federal government's lead—and police bureaucrats' demands—by incorporating the forfeiture process into their standard law enforcement procedures.

Many more states now have forfeiture statutes that both provide expanded opportunities for seizures and direct the proceeds toward law enforcement. Items most often subject to seizure include material used in drug production, paraphernalia, containers, motor vehicles, and money, but most states now also allow confiscation of real estate used in the "furtherance of illegal drug activity." Only seven states allowed confiscation of real estate in 1984, but statutory changes increased this number to seventeen by 1988, and it reached forty-three in 1991. Beyond that, a growing number of states have more general forfeiture provisions, allowing seizure for nondrug "contraband" offenses and felonies. State racketeering laws that authorize the forfeiture of property obtained as a result of numerous illegal activities are even more conducive to law enforcement interests. Nonetheless, state statutes are not all as accommodating to police as the federal statute, leaving the federal law a useful vehicle by which many police bureaucracies can enhance their discretionary budgets.

Given the variation in state laws regarding forfeitures and the transaction costs, including the 20 percent carrying charge, associated with using the federal authorities, it might be that these factors help to explain the cross-state variation in drug enforcement activities. Rasmussen, Benson, and Mast (1994) explored this issue using a reduced-form econometric model of the demand for and supply of drug enforcement in a sample of large U.S. cities. Included in the model are variables that control for the extent of drug use, the opportunity cost of police resources, and socioeconomic factors affecting the demand for drug enforcement.

The key variable of interest is the presence of a confiscation law that permits police to keep some of the proceeds from seized assets. Rasmussen, Benson, and Mast reported that the level of drug use, as measured by the percentage of arrestees testing positive for any illicit drug, is a highly significant determinant of drug arrests. More important for our purposes here, they found that a state law that allows the police to keep any portion of seized assets was associated with significantly more emphasis on drug arrests.[26] Indeed, the laws have a large and important impact on the allocation of police resources: the existence of a confiscation law that is favorable to the police raises the drug arrests/total arrests ratio between 35 and 50 percent, depending on the model specification. Allowing police to profit from the confiscation of assets seized from alleged drug offenders apparently provides a powerful incentive to law enforcement agencies that, as expected, changes agency behavior.

## Conclusions: The Drug War Winds Down

The main offensive of the war on drugs, when measured by drug arrests relative to Index I arrests, apparently ended in 1989. In the United States, the drug arrest/Index I arrest ratio fell from 0.46 in 1989 to a 1990 figure of 0.36, a decline of 24 percent. This decline in drug arrests is not inconsistent with bureaucratic incentives, however, including those created by asset forfeiture legislation. Police may simply be arresting "smarter," for example, concentrating on drug offenders with potentially more valuable forfeitable assets. For instance, if police agencies are seeking lucrative seizure opportunities, they are likely to reduce juvenile arrests relative to adult arrests, as youthful offenders are less likely to own property that can be seized.

This implication is particularly interesting because, from a theoretical perspective, rising juvenile participation in the drug trade can be expected during a period of rising drug enforcement. The war on drugs produced greater arrest rates for drug offenses, greater probabilities of conviction given arrest, and longer sentences, but these increased costs were primarily imposed on adults rather than juveniles, who generally received relatively lenient sentences for identical offenses. Therefore, major drug traffickers had stronger incentives to reduce their own risk both by lengthening the distribution chain and by employing more juveniles in the process.

Yet persons under age eighteen accounted for 11.95 percent of all U.S. drug arrests in 1984 but only 7.47 percent in 1990, a 37 percent decline. This reallocation of police effort is consistent with the hypothesis that police have been increasingly interested in the potential benefits of using asset seizures to enforce drug laws. As a high-ranking U.S. antidrug official noted in 1991: "Increasingly, you're seeing supervisors of cases saying, 'Well, what can we seize?' when they're trying to decide what to investigate. They're paying more attention to the revenues they can get...and it's skewing the cases they get involved in."[27]

It is also possible that the opportunities for asset seizures are being reduced as drug market entrepreneurs adjust to the emphasis on confiscations. For instance, marijuana growers are increasingly using national forests and other public lands rather than private land to grow their crops, because "this technique precludes the use by the government of the legal remedy of confiscation of the land on which the illegal activity is being perpetrated" (U.S. Department of Justice 1989, 12). Drug dealers can rent or lease houses, apartments, cars, and other assets rather than purchasing them, and shield assets by moving them abroad. Indeed, increasingly sophisticated efforts to hide assets (e.g., money laundering) make seizures more and more costly.

Another factor may be the growing recognition that the drug war has not been living up to its billings. Indeed, public support for the drug war has fallen since 1989. Opinion polls report a consistent public preference for tougher treatment of criminals. But importantly, opinions regarding drug policy are becoming much more ambiguous, and the public does not necessarily think that law enforcement should be the only approach to the problem. Public opinion might be expected to support "get tough" policies against drugs if the claims made by law enforcement interests (specifically, that such a strategy reduces other kinds of crime) were supported by the evidence. However, it is becoming increasingly clear that the war on drugs is not being won *and* that the negative consequences of the war are substantial.

Today, for example, many states are wrestling with a prison crowding problem that many citizens recognize is at least in part a consequence of the get-tough policies against drugs that occurred during the 1984–89 period, which included large increases in arrests and convictions as well as longer mandatory sentences. To illustrate, the Florida legislature was forced to hold a special session in 1993 in order to allocate more funds to prison construction and avoid the "gridlock" that was anticipated late that year when none of the prisoners in the system would be eligible for early release (many prisoners cannot be released early under statutes regarding habitual offenders and various specific crimes, many of which are drug related). The 1994 legislature allocated funds to expand the state's prison system by an additional 27 percent. Given widespread recognition that drug enforcement policy is a major cause of recent prison crowding, and that the drug war has not produced the benefits that its supporters claimed it would, public opinion may be turning.[28]

At any rate, it is clearly the case that the media has begun to focus on some negative consequences of the drug war, and the media's change in focus seems to be a reflection of changing public sentiments.[29] In the face of growing recognition on the part of taxpayers that the war on drugs has not achieved its announced goals, police may be reducing their drug control efforts in order to shift resources to non-drug-related crimes. After all, as Breton and Wintrobe (1982, 149) noted, as time passes the perceived responsibility for the failure of a policy (e.g., crime control through the suppression of drug market activity) shifts from outside forces (e.g., the drug dealers or the recession) to the government, and within the government, it shifts from politicians to the bureaucracy. Pressure increases for bureaucrats to account for what is going on. Indeed, prison officials are now starting to blame the war on drugs for the negative consequences of their early-release programs.

Consider the example of Frank Potts, who was released from the Florida prison system in 1988, after serving six years of a fifteen-year sentence for molesting an eleven-year-old girl. Early release was granted despite the report of a parole examiner who noted that there was a very good chance that Potts would repeat his crime if he were set free. Potts is now being held on charges of molesting another eleven-year-old girl; in addition, an intense investigation is under way regarding allegations that he has killed as many as thirteen people. A Florida Department of Corrections spokesperson justified the early release by noting that "the agency is bound by mandates from the courts and the legislature. In the mid-1980s, the prison system was inundated with inmates carrying minimum-mandatory sentences during the country's initial skirmishes in the war on drugs."[30]

Policies tend to cycle. An uninformed public can be misled by bureaucrats and policy makers for awhile, but if the policy does not work, it will ultimately have to be retrenched in recognition of its failure. This does not mean that a return to the pre-1984 level of drug enforcement is anticipated, but it does suggest that the increase in drug enforcement activity over the 1984–89 period could not be sustained forever.

Another important reason police have increasingly emphasized nondrug crime since 1989 is that "a growing number of states, such as Texas, Florida, and New Jersey, apply their forfeiture laws to any criminal activity" (Reed 1992, 2). Police have learned from their drug forfeiture experience that asset seizures can be very lucrative.

The 1984 federal confiscation statute pertained to drug crime alone, but with changes in state laws, seizures are increasingly targeted at property owners in general, not just criminally culpable property owners engaged in drug market activities. A family home is fair game in some jurisdictions, for instance, if anyone (e.g., a son, relative, or friend of the owner or of the owner's family) uses the property unlawfully. The spread of forfeiture activities to nondrug criminal offenses means "that property owners must police their property against all such activity, drug related or not" (Reed 1992, 2).[31]

In effect, property owners are being forced to act for the police in preventing all sorts of crime on their property, and failure to do so can result in a very high tax for the "sin" of failing in this regard—forfeiture of the property. With the ever-broadening scope of forfeiture possibilities, drug activity may become a less important target of police efforts (at the same time that it is probably becoming a more difficult target to attack), and drug enforcement may become a politically less viable policy to stress. Thus, a winding down of the drug war appears to be a product of the same forces that led to the war's escalation: changing incentives that affect police bureaucrats, including the opportunity to collect taxes on "sins" other than those associated with illicit-drug markets.

## Notes

1. The Marijuana Tax Act was nominally a revenue-producing act that imposed taxes on physicians who prescribed marijuana, pharmacists who dispensed it, and others who might deal in the drug. The nonmedical possession and sale of the drug were made illegal, however, and all those in the production and distribution chain for medical purposes were required to keep detailed records and pay annual fees. These onerous record-keeping requirements, taxes, and fees effectively ended the legal use of the drug for medical purposes as well.

2. Bureaucrats often try to influence the demand side of the political process (Berk et al. 1977; Congleton 1980; Breton and Wintrobe 1982; Benson 1983, 1990; Mbaku 1991). They have incentives to "educate" sponsors regarding interest-group demands that complement their own and to "propagate" their own agendas. Furthermore, they may have a relative advantage in the lobbying process because they have ready access to sponsors, with whom they are often informally networked (Breton and Wintrobe 1982, 41–42), and they are naturally called upon for advice, due to their expertise. This is clearly the case with law enforcement bureaucracies (Glaser 1978, 22). Additional discussion of the role of bureaucrats as demanders of legislative action appears in sections I and II.

3. Many states mandated that confiscated assets be turned over to a general government authority, while others required that some or all seized assets be used for specific purposes, such as drug treatment or education. Various states also limited the kinds of assets that could be seized. For instance, in 1984, only seven states allowed seizure of real estate used for illegal drug activities. The federal statute had no such limitation.

4. See Reuter (1991); Benson and Rasmussen (1991, 1992); Benson et al. (1992); Rasmussen et al. (1993); Sollars et al. (1994); Rasmussen and Benson (1994); and Zimring and Hawkins (1992).

5. This argument was subsequently accepted by Niskanen (1975). A large literature has developed following in this Niskanen/Migué-Belanger framework— see Toma and Toma (1980); Gonzalez and Mehay (1985); Benson and Greenhut (1986); Wyckoff (1988, 1990a, and 1990b); and Kress (1989).

6. This competition is multidimensional. It includes general competition for resources as well as competition for positions and promotions in the formal bureaucratic structure and membership in the informal networks that bureaucrats develop to facilitate non-market exchanges of benefits, information, and support between network members. Competitive strategies employed include: "(i) alterations in the flows of information or commands as these move through or across the hierarchical levels of the organization; (ii) variations in the quality or quantity of information leaked to the media, to other bureaus in the organization, to special interest groups, and/or to opposition parties and rival suppliers; and (iii) changes in the speed of implementation of policies as these are put into effect" (Breton and Wintrobe 1982, 37–38). These strategies and selective behavior in general are possible because of the way bureaucratic organizations and hierarchies work, including the fact that monitoring by sponsors is costly and the measurement of bureaucratic performance is generally difficult or impossible. Indeed, the use of such strategies can increase monitoring costs and make measurement of performance even more difficult.

7. See Musto (1987, 13–14 and 21–22); Thornton (1991, 56–60); and Klein (1983, 31–55).

8. Bonnie and Whitebread (1974); Helmer (1975); Musto (1987); Nadelmann (1993).

9. See Himmelstein (1983); Becker (1963); Bonnie and Whitebread (1974); King (1957); Dickson (1968); Oteri and Silvergate (1967); Lindesmith (1965); Hill (1971); and Reinarman (1983). In fact, as Thornton (1991, 62, 66) and Morgan (1983, 3) have stressed, all of the various self-interests mentioned above (bureaucrats, professionals from the American Medical Association and American Pharmaceutical Association, and groups attempting to suppress certain races or classes) interacted with still more groups (temperance groups, religious groups, etc.) to produce policies against drug use. Interest groups and bureaucratic entrepreneurs continue to dominate modern drug policy as well. These groups include "civil rights, welfare rights, bureaucratic and professional interests, health, law and order, etc." (Morgan 1983, 3). For instance, the pharmaceutical industry had a significant impact on the Comprehensive Drug Abuse Prevention and Control Act of 1970 (Reinarman 1983, 19): "In this case as in most others, the state's policy makers were buffeted by law enforcement interests and professional interests."

10. See Stutmann and Esposito (1992) for a very revealing examination of the actual activities of an agent in the Drug Enforcement Agency (DEA), and note the tremendous amount of time and effort that this agent spent in competing for resources. Also note the significant role that politics played in determining the allocation of drug enforcement resources. This entire book could easily be set in the context of the Breton-Wintrobe model of bureaucratic entrepreneurship.

11. King (1957); Lindesmith (1965); Klein (1983, 32).

12. Becker (1963); Dickson (1968); Oteri and Silvergate (1967); Lindesmith (1965); Hill (1971); Bonnie and Whitebread (1974).

13. This is suggested by the second strategy listed in note 6, and arises in part because of the high cost of monitoring bureaucrats.

14. Richards (1982, 164). For details, see Kaplan (1970, 88–136); Lindesmith (1965, 25–34); Himmelstein (1983, 60–62); Bennett and DiLorenzo (1992, 237–39).
15. Lindesmith (1965); Kaplan (1970, 1983); Richards (1982); Michaels (1987); Bennett and DiLorenzo (1992); Rasmussen and Benson (1994).
16. See Benson et al. (1992); Sollars et al. (1994), and Benson and Rasmussen (1991). Rasmussen et al. (1993) provide evidence that violent crimes may also be caused by drug enforcement. See also Reuter (1991) in this regard.
17. Note with Breton and Wintrobe (1982, 152) that "one need not assume Machiavellian behavior, deceit, or dishonesty on the part of bureaucrats, because in all likelihood the pursuit of their own interest will be, as it is for everyone else, veiled in a self-perception of dedication and altruism."
18. Once a prohibition policy is in place, police have incentives to make large drug seizures in order to demonstrate their effectiveness in controlling drug market activity. In fact, as one of their "selective distortions," police have incentives to exaggerate the magnitude of the seizures they make. Thus, drug seizures are always reported in terms of their "estimated street value" no matter at what stage of the distribution and processing chain the seizure is made. Claiming that pure cocaine has a value equal to its retail value after it has been processed and distributed as crack is like claiming that the two or three cents' worth of wheat that goes into a loaf of bread is worth the dollar that consumers pay for that loaf of bread—it ignores the other inputs that must be added to turn the wheat into a marketable loaf of bread, such as transportation costs, processing costs, packaging, distribution costs, and advertising.
19. "Turning Drug Busts into a Profit Center," *Washington Post Weekly Edition,* 19 April 1991.
20. The role of informal networks within and across bureaucracies is very important in the Breton-Wintrobe model (1982, 78–87, 99–106). These networks are the nonmarket institutions of exchange through which individual bureaucrats cooperate in order to obtain benefits. Thus, competition for positions in networks is also an important determinant of bureaucratic behavior (Breton and Wintrobe 1982, 99), and to the extent that this expanded network is able to generate more benefits for bureaucrats, competition to enter the network should intensify. However, competition for positions within a network actually tends to increase the potential for discretionary, or selective, behavior in Breton and Wintrobe's model (1982, 103). For instance, if the network gets larger, cooperation between two agencies can effectively become collusion, an example of which is explored in Higgins et al. (1987). They found that collusion between the Justice Department and the Federal Trade Commission after 1948 led to roughly a doubling of the cost of an average antitrust case. This suggests that discretionary funds increased through this "coordination" of bureaucratic law enforcement efforts.
21. Stumpf (1988, 327–32); Williams (1984, 77–105); Benson (1990, 132–46, 163–68); Rasmussen and Benson (1994, 32–37).
22. Recall that North Carolina requires that all forfeited assets go to education.
23. "Turning Drug Busts into a Profit Center," *Washington Post Weekly Edition,* 19 April 1991.
24. Dennis Cauchon and Gary Fields documented this in a series of articles on "Abusing Forfeiture Laws" in *USA Today,* beginning on 18 May 1992. Also, in a series of *Orlando Sentinel* articles during June 1992, Jeff Brazil and Steve Berry described, in vivid detail, an asset seizure program in Volusia County, Florida, that netted over $8 million in four years.
25. An examination of the expenditures made by some police departments from their asset seizure funds suggests that these funds are frequently spent on perks

to make police officers feel better about themselves and their jobs, as Breton and Wintrobe (1982) imply they might be. "Equipment" such as Stetson hats and fancy pistols are purchased frequently. Computers are another favorite purchase. Some seized assets, such as airplanes, sports cars, and helicopters, may not be sold but are instead retained by police (perhaps to be used in drug control activities) or turned over to police allies (perhaps in exchange for political support). An Illinois prosecutor, for instance, was found to be driving a Corvette seized from an alleged drug dealer.

26. Most states allow police to keep either 100 percent of the proceeds from seizures or 0 percent, so use of a continuous variable reflecting an 80 percent break point produces virtually the same statistical implications as a simple dummy variable indicating that police can keep some of the proceeds. Furthermore, the 80 percent break point is probably not as significant as it appears to be, because of the transaction costs associated with dealing with the feds, along with the fact that the feds are not particularly interested in adopting small seizures that may be attractive to local police if they can keep all of the proceeds (Rasmussen et al. 1994).

27. *Washington Post Weekly Edition,* 19 April 1991, 32.

28. When asked about the most effective way to deal with the drug problem, survey respondents generally favor treatment over incarceration. Fifty-seven percent of survey respondents in 1989 thought building more federal prisons would not reduce illegal drug use, for example, while 80 percent thought more money for drug treatment would be effective. Over 90 percent responded that more spending on drug education in schools would be effective in reducing drug use (U.S. Department of Justice 1991, table 2.95). A 1990 Gallup Poll revealed similar skepticism of the efficacy of arresting drug offenders. Only 4 percent believed the most money should be spent on arresting users, and 19 percent thought arresting sellers was the most effective use of resources. In contrast, 40 percent thought early education was the best way to combat drug use; treatment to overcome addiction was preferred by only 5 percent of respondents in this poll, however (U.S. Department of Justice 1991, table 2.96).

29. For example, the *Tallahassee Democrat* has picked up a number of stories from other newspapers and news services with themes such as those in the following sampling: (1) from Knight-Ridder's Washington Bureau: Aaron Epstein, "Tide of Opinion Turns Against Harsh Sentencing for Drug Offenders," 7 May 1993, 4-A; (2) from the Associated Press: Michael White, "Cases Indicate the War on Drugs May Be Overdoing It," 2 November 1992, 3-A; (3) from the *Chicago Tribune:* Jon Margolis, "Punishment Should Fit Drug Crime," 5 July 1991, 15-A; and (4) from the *Miami Herald:* Ronnie Greene, "Skip Town, Judge Tells Drug Suspect," 8 October 1992, 4-C. Furthermore, significant negative coverage has been given to asset seizure policies. It is not obvious whether the media is leading or following public opinion in this regard.

30. Associated Press, "Probe: Potts Granted Early Release," *Tallahassee Democrat,* 10 May 1994, 5-B.

31. As this volume was in press, news reports were circulating that environmental interest groups have begun lobbying for asset-forfeiture laws to be extended to cover environmental "crimes."

## References

Barnett, Randy E. 1984. "Public Decisions and Private Rights." *Criminal Justice Ethics* 3 (Summer/Fall): 50–62.

Becker, Elizabeth, and Cotton M. Lindsay. 1994. "Does Government Free Ride?" *Journal of Law and Economics* 37 (April): 277–96.

Becker, Howard. 1963. *Outsiders: Studies in Sociological Deviance.* New York: Free Press.

Bennett, James T., and Thomas J. DiLorenzo. 1992. *Official Lies: How Washington Misleads Us.* Alexandria, Va.: Groom Books.

Benson, Bruce L. 1983. "The Economic Theory of Regulation as an Explanation of Policies Toward Bank Mergers and Holding Company Acquisitions." *Antitrust Bulletin* 28 (Winter): 839–62.

———. 1990. *The Enterprise of Law: Justice without the State.* San Francisco: Pacific Research Institute for Public Policy.

Benson, Bruce L., and M. L. Greenhut. 1986. "Interest Groups, Bureaucrats and Antitrust: An Explanation of the Antitrust Paradox." In *Antitrust and Regulation,* edited by Ronald E. Grieson. Lexington, Mass.: Lexington Books.

Benson, Bruce L., Iljoong Kim, David W. Rasmussen, and Thomas W. Zuehlke. 1992. "Is Property Crime Caused by Drug Use or Drug Enforcement Policy?" *Applied Economics* 24 (July): 679–92.

Benson, Bruce L., and David W. Rasmussen. 1991. "The Relationship Between Illicit Drug Enforcement Policy and Property Crimes." *Contemporary Policy Issues* 9 (October): 106–15.

———. 1992. "Illinois' War on Drugs: Some Unintended Consequences. " *Heartland Policy Study* 48 (April): 1–36.

Benson, Bruce L., David W. Rasmussen, and David L. Sollars. 1995. "Police Bureaucracies, Their Incentives, and the War on Drugs." *Public Choice* 83 (April): 21–45.

Berk, Richard, Harold Brackman, and Selma Lesser. 1977. *A Measure of Justice: An Empirical Study of Changes in the California Penal Code, 1955-1971.* New York: Academic Press.

Blumberg, Abraham. 1979. *Criminal Justice: Issues and Ironies.* 2nd ed. New York: New Viewpoints.

Bonnie, Richard J., and Charles Whitebread II. 1974. *The Marijuana Conviction: A History of Marijuana Prohibition in the United States.* Charlottesville: University of Virginia Press.

Breton, Albert, and Ronald Wintrobe. 1982. *The Logic of Bureaucratic Control.* Cambridge: Cambridge University Press.

Chambliss, William, and Robert Seidman. 1971. *Law, Order, and Power.* Reading, Mass.: Addison-Wesley.

Chant, J. F., and K. Acheson. 1972. "The Choice of Monetary Instruments and the Theory of Bureaucracy." *Public Choice* 12 (Spring): 13–34.

Congleton, Roger. 1980. "Competitive Process, Competitive Waste and Institutions." In *Toward a Theory of the Rent-Seeking Society,* edited by James M. Buchanan, Robert D. Tollison, and Gordon Tullock. College Station: Texas A&M University Press.

Dickson, Donald. 1968. "Bureaucracy and Morality: An Organizational Perspective on a Moral Crusade." *Social Problems* 16 (Fall): 142–56.

Galliher, J., and A. Walker. 1977. "The Puzzle of the Social Origins of the Marijuana Tax Act of 1937." *Social Problems* 24 (February): 366–76.

Glaser, Daniel. 1978. *Crime in Our Changing Society.* New York: Holt, Rinehart & Winston.

Gonzalez, Rodolfo A., and Stephen L. Mehay. 1985. "Bureaucracy and the Divisibility of Local Public Goods." *Public Choice* 45: 89–101.

Gusfield, Joseph. 1980. *The Culture of Public Problems.* Chicago: University of Chicago Press.

Helmer, John. 1975. *Drugs and Minority Oppression.* New York: Seabury Press.

Higgins, Richard S., William F. Shughart II, and Robert D. Tollison. 1987. "Dual Enforcement of the Antitrust Laws. In *Public Choice and Regulation: A View from inside the Federal Trade Commission,* edited by Robert J. Mackay, James C. Miller III, and Bruce Yandle. Stanford, Calif.: Hoover Institution Press.

Hill, Stuart. 1971. *Crime, Power, and Morality: The Criminal Law Process in the United States.* Scranton, Pa.: Chandler Publishing, 1971.

Himmelstein, Jerome L. 1983. *The Strange Career of Marijuana: Politics and the Ideology of Drug Control in America.* Westport, Conn.: Greenwood Press.

Johnson, Ronald N., and Gary D. Libecap. 1989. "Agency Growth, Salaries and the Protected Bureaucracy." *Economic Inquiry* 27 (July): 431–51.

Kaplan, John. 1970. *Marijuana: The New Prohibition.* New York: World Publishing.

———. 1983. *The Hardest Drug: Heroin and Public Policy.* Chicago: University of Chicago Press.

King, R. 1957. "Narcotic Drug Laws and Enforcement Policies." *Law and Contemporary Problems* 22:113–31.

———. 1978. "Drug Abuse Problems and the Idioms of War." *Journal of Drug Issues* 8:221–31.

Klein, Dorie. 1983. "Ill and Against the Law: The Social and Medical Control of Heroin Users." *Journal of Drug Issues* 13 (winter): 31–55.

Kress, Shirley E. 1989. "Niskanen Effects in the California Community Colleges." *Public Choice* 61 (May): 127–40.

Lindesmith, Alfred. 1965. *The Addict and the Law.* New York: Vintage Press.

Mbaku, John M. 1991. "Military Expenditures and Bureaucratic Competition for Rents." *Public Choice* 71 (August): 19–31.

Michaels, Robert J. 1987. "The Market for Heroin Before and After Legalization." In *Dealing with Drugs,* edited by Robert Hamoway. Lexington, Mass: Lexington Books.

Migué, Jean-Luc, and Gerard Belanger. 1974. "Towards a General Theory of Managerial Discretion." *Public Choice* 17:27–43.

Milakovich, Michael, and Kurt Weis. 1975. "Politics and Measures of Success in the War on Crime." *Crime and Delinquency* 21 (January): 1–10.

Morgan, Patricia A. 1983. "The Political Economy of Drugs and Alcohol." *Journal of Drug Issues* 13 (Winter): 1–7.

Musto, David F. 1987. "The History of Legislative Control Over Opium, Cocaine, and Their Derivatives." In *Dealing with Drugs,* edited by Ronald Hamowy. Lexington, Mass.: Lexington Books.

Nadelmann, Ethan A. 1993. "Should We Legalize Drugs? History Answers Yes." *American Heritage* (February-March): 42–48.

National Criminal Justice Association. 1988. *Asset Seizure and Forfeiture: Developing and Maintaining a State Capability.* June. Washington, D.C.

Niskanen, William A. 1968. "The Peculiar Economics of Bureaucracy." *American Economic Review* 58 (May): 293–305.

———. 1971. *Bureaucracy and Representative Government.* Chicago: Aldine-Atherton.

———. 1975. "Bureaucrats and Politicians." *Journal of Law and Economics* 18 (December): 617–43.

Office of National Drug Control Strategy. 1990. *National Drug Control Strategy.* Washington, D.C.: U.S. Government Printing Office.

Oteri, Joseph, and Harvey Silvergate. 1967. "In the Marketplace of Free Ideas: A Look at the Passage of the Marihuana Tax Act." In *Marihuana: Myths and Realities,* edited by J. L. Simmons. North Hollywood, Calif.: Brandon House.

Parker, Glenn R. 1992. *Institutional Change, Discretion, and the Making of the Modern Congress.* Ann Arbor: University of Michigan Press.

Rasmussen, David W., and Bruce L. Benson. 1994. *The Economic Anatomy of a Drug War: Criminal Justice in the Commons.* Lanham, Md.: Rowman & Littlefield.

Rasmussen, David W., Bruce L. Benson, and Brent L. Mast. 1994. "Entrepreneurial Police and Drug Enforcement Policy." Working paper, Florida State University, Tallahassee.

Rasmussen, David W., Bruce L. Benson, and David L. Sollars. 1993. "Spatial Competition in Illicit Drug Markets: The Consequences of Increased Drug Enforcement." *Review of Regional Studies* 23 (Winter): 219–36.

Reaves, Brian A. 1992. "Drug Enforcement by Police and Sheriffs' Departments, 1990." In *Bureau of Justice Statistics: Special Report.* Washington, D.C.: U.S. Department of Justice, Bureau of Justice Statistics. May.

Reed, Terrance G. 1992. "American Forfeiture Law: Property Owners Meet the Prosecutor." *Policy Analysis* 17 (29 September).

Reinarman, Craig. 1983. "Constraint, Autonomy, and State Policy: Notes Toward a Theory of Controls on Consciousness Alteration." *Journal of Drug Issues* 13 (Winter): 9–30.

Reuter, Peter. 1991. "On the Consequences of Toughness." In *Searching for Alternatives: Drug Control Policy in the United States,* edited by Edward Lazear and Melvyn Kraus. Stanford, Calif.: Hoover Institution Press.

Rhodes, Robert. 1977. *The Insoluble Problems of Crime.* New York: John Wiley & Sons.

Richards, David A. J. 1982. *Sex, Drugs, Death, and the Law: An Essay on Human Rights and Overcriminalization.* Ottawa, N.J.: Rowman & Littlefield.

Sherman, Lawrence W. 1983. "Patrol Strategies for Police." In *Crime and Public Policy,* edited by James Q. Wilson. San Francisco: Institute for Contemporary Studies Press.

Sollars, David L., Bruce L. Benson, and David W. Rasmussen. 1994. "Drug Enforcement and Deterrence of Property Crime Among Local Jurisdictions." *Public Finance Quarterly* 22 (January): 22–45.

Stafford, Frank P., and Greg J. Duncan. 1980. "Do Union Members Receive Compensating Wage Differentials?" *American Economic Review* 70 (June): 355–72.

Stumpf, Harry P. 1988. *American Judicial Politics.* San Diego: Harcourt Brace Jovanovich.

Stutmann, Robert M., and Richard Esposito. 1992. *Dead on Delivery: Inside the Drug Wars, Straight from the Street.* New York: Warner Books.

Thornton, Mark. 1991. *The Economics of Prohibition.* Salt Lake City: University of Utah Press.

Toma, Mark, and Eugenia Froedge Toma. 1980. "Bureaucratic Responses to Tax Limitation Amendments." *Public Choice* 35:333–48.

Tullock, Gordon. 1965. *The Politics of Bureaucracy.* Washington, D.C.: Public Affairs Press.

U.S. Department of Health, Education, and Welfare Task Force. 1973. *Work in America.* Cambridge: MIT Press.

U.S. Department of Justice. 1989. Office of the Attorney General. *Drug Trafficking: A Report to the President of the United States.* Washington, D.C.: U.S. Government Printing Office.

U.S. Department of Justice. 1991. Bureau of Justice Statistics. *Sourcebook of Criminal Justice Statistics, 1990*. Washington D.C.: U.S. Government Printing Office.

U.S. House. 1985. Subcommittee on Crime of the Committee on the Judiciary. *Hearings on the Comprehensive Drug Penalty Act*. Held 23 June and 14 October 1983. Serial No. 136. Washington, D.C.: U.S. Government Printing Office.

U.S. House. 1990. Subcommittee on Crime of the Committee on the Judiciary. *Hearings on Federal Drug Forfeiture Activities*. Held 24 April 1989. Serial No. 55. Washington, D.C.: U.S. Government Printing Office.

Williams, Gregory H. 1984. *The Law and Politics of Police Discretion*. Westport, Conn.: Greenwood Press.

Wisotsky, Steven. 1991. "Zero Tolerance/Zero Freedom." Paper presented at the Seventh Annual Critical Issues Symposium, Florida State University, Tallahassee.

Wyckoff, Paul Gary. 1988. "Bureaucracy and the 'Publicness' of Local Public Goods." *Public Choice* 56 (March): 271–84.

———. 1990a. "Bureaucracy, Inefficiency, and Time." *Public Choice* 67 (November): 35–47.

———. 1990b. "The Simple Analytics of Slack-Maximizing Bureaucracy." *Public Choice* 67 (October): 35–47.

Zimring, Franklin E., and Gordon Hawkins. 1992. *The Search for Rational Drug Control*. Cambridge: Cambridge University Press.

# 10

# The Taxation of Alcohol and the Control of Social Costs

## Richard E. Wagner

The Tax Foundation calculates that Tax Freedom Day now comes to America only in early May.[1] Until then the average American must work to support government. Only after then can his work go to support self and family. Stated differently, the average person devotes nearly three hours out of each eight-hour working day just to pay taxes. It is hardly surprising in the face of such high tax burdens that resistance to proposed tax increases is stiff. Even the calculation of Tax Freedom Day understates the true tax burdens that Americans face, because this calculation ignores the implicit tax burdens that are contained in government regulations. The costs of complying with government regulations and mandates are truly taxes on people, only they are absorbed into the costs of doing business and embedded in market prices.[2]

Yet the business of politics remains the same, and an important element of this business requires the expansion of existing spending programs and the development of new ones. In the face of increased taxpayer resistance, the politics of taxation has become increasingly creative in developing justifications that allow taxes to be called something else. Many proposed taxes are now called "user fees," and are accompanied by claims that what is being proposed is not truly a tax but rather is simply a means of charging people marketlike prices for particular services they receive from government.[3]

The classic model of such revenue dedication is the use of gasoline tax revenues to finance highways. Up to now it has not been feasible to charge people directly for their use of highway services, save for a few toll roads and bridges.[4] There is, however, a close correlation between how much use people make of highways and how much gasoline they consume; an increased use of highways generally corresponds to an increased consumption of gasoline. When the revenues from a gasoline tax are dedicated to the construction and maintenance of highways, people who buy more gasoline make larger contributions to the support of highways. In this way, these tax payments are similar to the market payments that people make in situations where direct pricing is feasible. While the gasoline tax is called a tax and not a price, it has many of the features of a user fee, which in turn is similar to the market prices that consumers would have paid if highways could have been financed through market prices.

The political desire to increase government spending in the face of strong taxpayer resistance has led to great interest in situations where a tax might plausibly be labeled a user fee instead. Many of these situations correspond to what economists call "corrective taxation." In principle, a corrective tax is something that adjusts for what are presumed to be the false prices that would otherwise characterize certain markets. For instance, a producer of beverages must bear the cost of such things as containers, ingredients, labor, warehouses, and capital equipment. The market price of the product will reflect the costs of these inputs that the producer must employ. But there may be other costs of production that the producer might not have to pay and which may not be reflected in the market price of the product. Wastes may be allowed to seep into underground water supplies, thereby reducing the quality of the water available to others and increasing the costs of treatment that those people must bear. In addition, some have expressed concern over consumers who may leave beverage containers lying about the landscape, degrading the scenic value that would otherwise exist.

In such cases as these, the market price of the beverage might fall short of the full ("social") cost of production. If so, a tax on the beverage might serve to correct the erroneous market prices that could otherwise result. Such a tax would not be a source of burden but would be an instrument of benefit; it would act as a price for those resources that are used in production but which are not paid for by producers.[5]

In this chapter I shall examine the degree to which the principles of corrective taxation can be used to justify the taxation of alcoholic beverages. A necessary condition for such justification is that there are costs associated with the consumption of alcohol that are not reflected in the market prices of alcoholic beverages. If the prices of those beverages can be shown to be too low, it is possible that a tax on alcohol might correct the market failures that could otherwise result. If so, a tax on alcohol would be a tax in name only. In truth, it would be a user fee imposed on consumers of alcoholic beverages to charge them for their use of those resources associated with alcohol consumption that are not reflected in the market price of alcohol. After describing briefly how heavily alcoholic beverages are currently taxed within the United States, I will describe several efforts to apply the principle of corrective taxation to alcohol. I will then examine the various specific arguments for alcohol taxation that have been developed, explaining in the process why they cannot serve to justify the taxation of alcoholic beverages.

**TABLE 10.1**
**Federal Excise Taxes on Alcoholic Beverages (as of 1 January 1991)**

| Item | Tax Rate |
|---|---|
| Distilled Spirits (per proof gallon) | $13.50 |
| Still Wines (per wine gallon) | |
| Not over 14 percent alcohol | $ 1.07 |
| 14 to 21 percent alcohol | $ 1.57 |
| 21 to 24 percent alcohol | $ 2.25 |
| Beer (per 31-gallon barrel) | $18.00 |

*Source*: Tax Foundation 1993, 134.

## Alcohol Taxation in the United States

Alcoholic beverages are taxed by both the federal government and the individual states. In all instances, tax rates differ among distilled spirits, wine, and beer. The federal government taxes distilled spirits by the proof gallon, which is literally 64 ounces of pure alcohol, or, as usually stated, one gallon of liquor at 50 percent concentration. Thus, 10 gallons of 80 proof gin would constitute only 8 proof gallons. Table 10.1 shows that the federal government taxed distilled spirits at $13.50 per proof gallon as of 1 January 1991.

Table 10.2 shows that rates of taxation vary considerably among the states. So, too, does the method by which distilled spirits are sold, which clouds the interpretation of comparative tax rates. While most states permit ordinary retail distribution, on which taxes are imposed, quite a number of states operate state liquor monopolies, in which cases the announced tax rates understate the true tax because part of the true tax is collected through higher prices charged in the state monopoly stores. Of those states that permit ordinary retail distribution, New York has the highest tax rate, at $6.70 per proof gallon, followed closely by Florida, at $6.50. At the lowest tax end, Maryland imposes a tax of $1.50 per proof gallon, as does the District of Columbia. Among the eighteen states that operate retail monopolies, tax rates cannot be compared directly. In four of those states, there is no direct tax on distilled spirits, the entire tax being embedded in the retail price charged by the state liquor stores.

Both the federal government and the states tax wine by the gallon, typically with the rate of tax being lower on wine that contains less than 14 percent alcohol than on wine whose alcohol content exceeds 14 percent. Table 10.1 shows that the federal government taxes wine that does not exceed 14 percent alcohol at $1.07 per gallon, while it taxes wine whose alcohol content ranges between 14 and 21 percent at $1.57 per gallon. Wine taxes vary enormously among the thirty-four states where state monopoly is not involved:

## TABLE 10.2
### State Alcoholic-Beverage Tax Rates (as of 1 September 1992)

| State | Distilled Spirit (per gallon) | Wines (per gallon) | | Malt Beverages | |
|---|---|---|---|---|---|
| | | 14% or less alcohol | 14–21% alcohol | Draught (per gallon) | Package (per case of 24) |
| Alabama | M | M | M | $1.53 | $2.37 |
| Alaska | $5.60 | .85 | .85 | .35 | .79 |
| Arizona | 3.00 | .84 | .84 | .16 | .36 |
| Arkansas | 2.50 | .25 | .75 | .24 | .45 |
| California | 3.30 | .20 | .20 | .20 | .45 |
| Colorado | 2.55 | .33 | .33 | .08 | .18 |
| Connecticut | 4.50 | .60 | .60 | .20 | .45 |
| Delaware | 5.46 | .97 | .97 | 1.56 | .35 |
| Florida | 6.50 | 2.25 | 3.00 | .64 | 1.44 |
| Georgia | 4.80 | .43 | 1.06 | .48 | 1.08 |
| Hawaii | 5.75 | 1.30 | 2.00 | .89 | 2.00 |
| Idaho | M | M | M | .15 | .34 |
| Illinois | 2.00 | .23 | .60 | .07 | .16 |
| Indiana | 2.68 | .47 | .47 | .12 | .26 |
| Iowa | M | M | M | .19 | .43 |
| Kansas | 2.50 | .30 | .75 | .18 | .41 |
| Kentucky | 1.92 | .50 | .50 | .08 | .18 |
| Louisiana | 2.60 | .12 | .24 | .32 | .73 |
| Maine | M | M | M | .35 | .79 |
| Maryland | 1.50 | .40 | .40 | .09 | .20 |
| Massachusetts | 4.05 | .55 | .55 | .11 | .25 |
| Michigan | M | M | M | .20 | .45 |
| Minnesota | 5.03 | .30 | .95 | .08 | .18 |
| Mississippi | M | M | M | .43 | .97 |
| Missouri | 2.00 | .30 | .36 | .06 | .14 |
| Montana | M | M | M | .14 | .33 |
| Nebraska | 3.00 | .75 | 1.35 | .23 | .52 |
| Nevada | 2.05 | .40 | .35 | .09 | .20 |
| New Hampshire | M | .35 | .50 | .30 | .67 |
| New Jersey | 4.40 | .70 | .70 | .12 | .27 |
| New Mexico | 4.10 | .25 | .25 | .18 | .41 |
| New York | 6.70 | .20 | .20 | .21 | .47 |
| North Carolina | M | M | M | .53 | 1.20 |
| North Dakota | 2.50 | .50 | .60 | .16 | .36 |
| Ohio | M | M | M | .11 | .25 |
| Oklahoma | 5.70 | 1.46 | 1.46 | .40 | .90 |
| Oregon | M | M | M | .08 | .18 |
| Pennsylvania | M | M | M | .08 | .18 |
| Rhode Island | 3.75 | .60 | .60 | .10 | .23 |
| South Carolina | 2.72 | 1.08 | 1.08 | .77 | 1.73 |
| South Dakota | 3.93 | .93 | 1.45 | .27 | .61 |
| Tennessee | 4.00 | 1.10 | 1.10 | .27 | .61 |
| Texas | 2.40 | .20 | .41 | .20 | .44 |
| Utah | M | M | M | .36 | .80 |
| Vermont | M | M | M | .27 | .60 |
| Virginia | M | M | M | .28 | .64 |
| Washington | M | M | M | .15 | .35 |
| West Virginia | M | 1.04 | 1.04 | .18 | .40 |
| Wisconsin | 3.50 | .26 | .47 | .07 | .15 |
| Wyoming | M | M | M | .02 | .04 |
| Washington D.C. | 1.50 | .30 | .40 | .09 | .20 |

*Note: M* denotes some form of state monopolization of retail sales, which renders stated tax rates unsuitable for comparison with those of other states.    *Source*: Tax Foundation 1993, 256–57.

whereas Louisiana taxes wine whose alcohol content is less than 14 percent at twelve cents per gallon, Florida taxes such wine at $2.25 per gallon.

A similar situation exists with beer. Table 10.1 shows that the federal government taxes beer at $18.00 per 31-gallon barrel, which is just over fifty-eight cents per gallon. State tax rates vary considerably. For draught beer, table 10.2 shows that state taxes range from a low of two cents per gallon in Wyoming to a high of $1.56 in Delaware. Most states impose comparable taxes on beer sold in cans or bottles, for which a case of twenty-four 12-ounce containers would contain 2.25 gallons. The only significant exception is Alabama, where beer sold in containers is taxed about two-thirds as heavily as draught beer.

When taxes on alcohol are expressed in relation to the amount of alcohol they contain, tax rates vary considerably across the three categories of alcoholic beverages. At the federal level, distilled spirits are the most heavily taxed category, bearing a tax burden of $21.00 per gallon of pure alcohol. Under the assumption that the average alcohol content of beer is 4.5 percent, the federal government taxes beer at $12.89 per gallon of pure alcohol. As for wine, the federal tax rate runs around $9.00 per gallon of pure alcohol.

## Alcohol Taxation as Corrective Taxation?

A basic principle of economics is that the cost of one product is the value of the other products that could have been produced had not the product in question been produced instead. The cost of an alcoholic beverage, in other words, is the value of whatever else could have been produced with the various land, labor, and capital resources had not that alcoholic beverage been produced. The land might have been used for growing artichokes. Trucks that were used to ship that beverage might alternatively have been used to ship televisions or household goods. The wood used in the barrels used to store those beverages might have been used instead to produce rocking chairs.

To say that the market price of some quantity of an alcoholic beverage is $10.00 is equivalent to saying that the value of what could have been produced alternatively is also $10.00. A market economy tends to operate in such a fashion that one more unit of an alcoholic beverage is worth to consumers just as much as the value of whatever alternative products they must sacrifice for that beverage to be produced. The value of the alcoholic beverage is equal to its cost, and this in turn is equal to the value of those alternative products that would have been produced had not the alcoholic beverage been produced instead.

Placing an excise tax on alcoholic beverages—or any other good for that matter—destroys this equivalency. Such a tax increases the price of alcoholic beverages, while leaving the prices of alternative products unchanged. As a result, consumers will now value one more unit of an alcoholic beverage more highly than they value the alternative output that they would have to sacrifice to secure the production of that additional unit of alcoholic beverage. This gap between the market price of alcoholic beverages and the cost of those beverages constitutes an "excess burden" of taxation. The "excess" indicates that the tax imposes a burden on consumers beyond that indicated by the revenues the government collects. The government collects revenue from consumers, but the loss suffered by consumers exceeds the revenue collected by the government.

Such considerations of excess burden have informed the general preference of public-finance scholars for broad-based taxes over such narrow-based taxes as excise taxes. To be sure, this preference is only a general predisposition and not some inviolable principle.[6] For one thing, all taxes influence choices and exert excess burdens. The idea of a neutral tax is a conceptual construct that is used for theoretical purposes but which finds no counterpart in the world of practice. Furthermore, and directly relevant to the topic of this chapter, the standard argument about the excess burden of excise taxation may be offset by contrary arguments concerning corrective taxation. If the untaxed consumption of alcoholic beverages were to entail costs beyond those represented by the price consumers pay for their beverages, the taxation of those beverages might represent a form of corrective taxation.

Since the 1977 publication of Ralph Berry and James Boland's *The Economic Cost of Alcohol Abuse,* several studies have been published that present alternative estimates of the cost of consuming alcoholic beverages. These studies reflect an underlying presumption that the cost of consuming alcoholic beverages has two components: (1) a personal cost that is paid when someone buys an alcoholic beverage, and (2) a social cost that is revealed only subsequently as people miss work, incur medical expenses, and are involved in automobile accidents. It is this second category of cost that involves arguments that the consumption of alcoholic beverages imposes costs on others— on society in general, not just on those who drink alcoholic beverages.

Table 10.3 summarizes the initial estimates of the social cost of alcohol consumption compiled for 1971 by Berry and Boland (1977) and expresses those magnitudes in 1992 dollars. Those cost figures are truly substantial. In 1971 total consumer spending on alcoholic beverages was about $19 billion, which would convert to $69 billion in 1992 dollars. Berry and Boland's estimate of the social cost of alcoholic beverages was thus nearly twice as large as direct consumer spending on those beverages. Moreover, governments at all levels collected a little over $6 billion from taxes on alcoholic beverages in 1971, an amount that would have exceeded $20 billion at 1992 prices.[7] Hence, what Berry and Boland claimed to be the social cost of alcoholic beverages was about five times greater than the taxes collected on those beverages.

Most studies of the social cost of alcohol consumption use the same or similar cost categories as those presented in table 10.3, and they also generally report estimates of the same general magnitude. For instance, Adrian (1988) reports a social-cost estimate of $5.67 billion for Canada for 1981. If

Table 10.3
Estimates of the Social Cost of Alcohol Consumption (millions of dollars)

| Cost Category | Amount | |
|---|---|---|
| | 1971 | 1992 |
| Lost Production | $14,869 | $ 53,766 |
| Medical Care | 8,293 | 29,987 |
| Vehicular Accidents | 4,667 | 16,876 |
| Crime | 1,996 | 7,217 |
| Social Services | 1,329 | 4,806 |
| Fires | 270 | 976 |
| Total Cost | $31,424 | $113,628 |

*Source*: The column labeled "1971" is pulled together from various chapters in Berry and Boland 1977. The column labeled "1992" multiplies the 1971 amounts by 3.616 to convert them to 1991 dollars.

that magnitude is multiplied by ten to allow for the approximate difference in population between Canada and the United States, and then adjusted for inflation and exchange rate differences, a social-cost figure in the vicinity of $90 billion results. Indeed, Adrian also reports on a number of other studies for the United States, with the magnitude of estimated social cost ranging between $30 billion and $90 billion annually. While the magnitudes are large in any case, the threefold variation in the estimates is also large, and surely suggests the speculative nature of such estimates.

With the retail value of alcoholic beverages running around perhaps $60 billion annually, the social cost of alcoholic beverages might appear to be as much as twice as large as the amount that people now pay for those beverages. The social-cost argument might be used to claim that while consumers pay some $60 billion for their beverages, there is an additional cost to society of around $120 billion. And even the low-range estimate that the social cost is but $30 billion would imply that consumers currently pay only two-thirds of the costs associated with their consumption of alcoholic beverages.

The central idea behind the principle of corrective taxation is to impose a tax that is equal to the amount of the costs associated with production that are not incorporated through ordinary market processes into the price of the product. Some scholars have used these principles of corrective taxation to lend support for vastly higher taxation of all forms of alcoholic beverages. Pogue and Sgontz (1989), for instance, argue that the taxation of alcoholic beverages should be roughly doubled, on the basis of the corrective tax arguments.[8]

Even if it is accepted that the consumption of a product can entail costs that are not reflected in the price of the product or otherwise borne by the consumer of the product, it does not follow that the principle of corrective taxation calls for a tax on the product. There may be instances where external costs are equally inherent in every unit of a product that is consumed. In many cases, however, those costs might arise only with certain units of consumption or may result not from consumption per se but from a particular technique or process of production.

With respect to the latter, the owner of a landfill who incinerates appliances before burying them might cause toxic minerals to leach into underground water supplies. If so, the source of social cost would reside not in the output of the landfill per se, but in its particular method of operation. A tax on the landfill's volume of activity would be inefficient, as compared with a tax on the landfill's deposit of toxic minerals. The latter form of taxation would in turn give landfill owners incentives to consider such options as lining their landfills or reclaiming some of the minerals that might otherwise leach into water supplies.

With respect to the former, beverage containers sometimes have littered the landscape. A general tax on beverage containers may, however, be particularly inefficient as compared with other options. After all, most consumption takes place indoors, where littering is not a problem. A tax on beverage containers that was limited to those containers that were to be used at picnics or at other outdoor venues might come closer to some idealized corrective tax, but there is no practical way to levy such a tax. Moreover, such a tax would be imposed on people who would not litter in any case, as well as on those who might. A tax is not the best instrument for dealing with external costs; such instruments as fines would offer better precision in dealing with the claimed sources of social cost.

In short, even if a case where consumption of a product is alleged to be a source of social cost is stipulated as being accurate, it does not follow that an excise tax on that product is warranted by the principle of corrective taxation. The external cost might be attributable not to consumption per se but to particular techniques of production. In such a case, the tax should aim at the offending techniques, not at general consumption. Even in cases where external costs can be reasonably attributed to consumption, it does not follow that all acts of consumption are sources of external cost. It is possible that only some acts of consumption, or perhaps some consumers, are sources of external cost. If this is so, a tax targeted at the offending consumers or units of consumption would be clearly superior in principle to a tax on all consumption of the product in question. To be sure, there may be no realistic way to design and implement a tax in some instances. In such a case, it is necessary to compare a tax remedy for the social cost with such alternatives as penal or judicial remedies.

### The Lost-Production Costs of Alcohol Consumption

By far the largest component of the alleged social cost of alcohol consumption is attributed to lost production. In table 10.3, lost production accounts for about half of the alleged social costs of alcohol. There is no direct, censuslike tabulation of these cost magnitudes; they are projections or estimates based on various assumptions or conventions that may in some cases have little justification other than convenience. Consider Adrian's (1988) estimate of the economic cost of lost production that he attributed to the consumption of alcoholic beverages in Canada. Algebraically, he portrayed this cost figure as

$$C = M \times P \times D \times W \times L \times t.$$

Set aside for the moment consideration of the first variable, $M$, to consider the remaining five variables in the cost equation. $P$ denotes the percentage of the population who drink alcoholic beverages and are considered abusers of alcohol,[9] and $D$ represents the percentage of the population who drink alcoholic beverages. Thus, the product $PD$ is the percentage of the total population who would be defined as alcohol abusers.

The variable $W$ denotes the average weekly wage, $L$ denotes the number of workers employed, and $t$ is the number of work weeks in a year. Hence, the product $WLt$ simply represents total earnings in Canada for a particular year—1981 for the study under review. The product of the last five variables in the cost equation, $PDWLt$, would thus seem to represent the total earnings of alcohol abusers, under the assumption that the earnings of alcohol abusers are equal to the average earnings within the general population.[10]

It is the first variable in the cost equation, $M$, that bears the weight of estimating the lost-production cost of alcohol abuse, for it is a fraction that converts what would otherwise be an estimate of the total earnings attributed to people classified as alcohol abusers into an estimate of how much higher those earnings would have been had alcohol abuse not been present. It might seem as though this variable might be some estimate of a rate of absenteeism that is higher among abusers than nonabusers. Actually, $M$ is simply an estimate of the percentage of accidents, poisonings, and violence morbidity attributed to alcohol.[11] For Canada this percentage was 10.5. No argument was advanced as to why this percentage represents a reasonable estimate of the share of the total estimated earnings of alcohol abusers that can be attributed as lost because of alcohol abuse. Alcohol abusers may well have had 10.5 percent of all accidents while comprising only 6.4 percent of the population. Neither percentage, however, speaks to the amount of additional production that would otherwise have resulted had that abuse not been present.

It is very doubtful that these types of cost estimates represent an adequate characterization of what national income would have been if no one drank more than 10 centiliters of alcohol per day—the "abuse" threshhold. Among other things, illnesses and losses of work associated with alcohol need not be caused by alcohol. The direction of causation may be the reverse, as in the case of someone who misses work and then drinks more than 10 centiliters of alcohol. Furthermore, a great deal of arbitrary, administrative classification is involved in such efforts. For instance, where some estimates attribute about one-third of suicides to alcohol, others attribute them all to mental illness. I would affirm only the conclusions reached by Heien and Pittman (1989, 577) in their careful review of the literature on the social costs of alcohol: "The estimates currently used by the federal government are flawed empirically and conceptually. These problems are so pervasive and fundamental that the current and past estimates cannot be taken seriously."

I would emphasize that these costs, whatever their magnitude might happen to be, are personal and not social costs. Whatever the results of a correct accounting might happen to show those costs to be, they would not be costs to society at large. The reason is simple: whatever production is lost is lost to the person who loses it. The counting of lost productivity as a social cost of alcohol consumption involves a subtle confusion in economic reasoning. If people who take an extra three days off per year earn less than those who do not, this loss of earnings reflects a cost of alcohol consumption if the absences are *caused* by alcohol consumption, but this cost is borne by the workers who drink. This lost production is reflected in market-determined income payments; those payments already reflect the value of the lost output. Therefore, to count that lost production as a social cost of drinking is to count the same thing a second time. This is a fundamental confusion in many economic studies of the social costs of alcohol consumption.[12] The productivity costs, if any, have already been counted in the economy in market wage and compensation rates. To count them again as "social costs" is meaningless. These are not social costs at all; if such costs exist, they are fully borne by the consumers of alcoholic beverages as personal costs.

### Medical Costs of Consuming Alcoholic Beverages

The costs of treatment of alcohol-related illnesses were estimated in Berry and Boland (1977), as well as in several subsequent studies, to be the second-largest component of social cost. Table 10.3 shows those estimated costs to have been $8.3 billion for 1971, which would have been nearly $30 billion in 1992 dollars. As with lost production, there is no directly observable measure of the medical costs that stem from the consumption of alcoholic beverages. Some technique must be employed to construct an estimate. Adrian's (1988) estimate of the excess health care costs attributable to alcohol in Canada for 1981 is instructive. Total health care costs were estimated to be $24.5 billion. The problem is to reach a judgment about what portion of those costs would not have been incurred had there been no alcohol abuse. For Canada in 1981, it was estimated that 77 percent of the population drank alcoholic beverages, and that 8.34 percent of those who did so drank at least 10 centiliters per day, on average, of pure alcohol. This 10-centiliter standard was considered to constitute alcohol abuse. Among the total Canadian population, 6.4 percent were estimated to drink, on average, at least 10 centiliters of pure alcohol per day, and, hence, were considered to be alcohol abusers.

The problem then becomes one of forming some estimate of the excess health care costs incurred by abusers over those incurred by nonabusers. Such data, however, are not directly available, and some indirect approach to estimation must be taken. Adrian took data from a clinical study of death rates among a set of heavy drinkers, and compared them with the mortality rates within the general population for people of the same age and sex. The result was that the mortality rate among the sample of heavy drinkers was 2.33 times the general mortality rate. If among two groups of 1,000 people there were 100 deaths among the general population, there would have been 233 deaths among the heavy drinkers.

Following the standard reasoning, if those drinkers had not drank so heavily and had been like the general population instead, there would have been only 100 deaths among them. The factor 1.33, then, represents the excess mortality attributed to heavy drinking. Among the 6.4 percent of the population who are judged by the 10-centiliter standard to be alcohol abusers, 6.4 percent of Canadian deaths would be attributed to normal circumstances. But an additional 8.5 percent of Canadian deaths (6.4 percent multiplied by the 1.33 excess-death factor due to heavy drinking) would be attributed to alcohol abuse. With total health care expenditures of $24.5 billion, $2.11 billion (8.5 percent of $24.5 billion) would be treated as the excess health care cost of alcohol.

While other studies have used somewhat different methods because of differences in the availability of different types of data, there is an underlying similarity to these efforts. They all face the same problem of having to construct some hypothetical estimate of something that is not directly observable—what health care costs would have been had no one abused alcohol. What must be done to construct this estimate is to work with some alternative data that are available, and which seem to have some degree of plausibility as adequate substitutes for the unavailable data. In Adrian's study the death rate among heavy drinkers in a clinical setting was used to infer excess-death rates among heavy drinkers, and this excess-death rate was then presumed to be an accurate factor in the estimate of the excess health care costs incurred by heavy drinkers.

This procedure is highly speculative and without foundation. Save for a prejudgment in favor of wanting to find some number, some dollar magnitude, this procedure is groundless. There is simply no basis for thinking that the estimated $2.11 billion magnitude has anything at all to do with the task at hand: to form a reasonable hypothetical judgment about an unobservable event, namely, what would have happened to health care costs in Canada in 1981 had no one drank an average of at least 10 centiliters of pure alcohol daily. For one thing, the heavy drinkers in the clinical setting were almost surely *not* a random sample of all people who drank an average of at least 10 centiliters per day. Rather, those people almost certainly not only were at the upper end of the spectrum in terms of alcohol consumption, but also were self-selected into the clinic because they were experiencing health problems. Hence, there is strong reason to believe that the death rate among the heavy drinkers in that clinical setting was greater than that among all Canadians who fit the 10-centiliter standard.

And there are other considerations that render even more questionable the meaningfulness of such cost estimates. One is that there is no basis for assuming that comparative death rates are proportional to comparative health care costs. Some forms of death have relatively low health care costs associated with them, suicides and automobile accidents probably being good examples. Other forms would have relatively high health care costs.

Beyond these matters of particular detail, there is the important point made by Alan Woodfield (1986), namely, that the abolition of alcohol abuse would not transform those abusers into people who otherwise became indistinguishable from the population in general. This assumption clearly informs all of the efforts at cost calculation, but it is as implausible as it is widely used. To some extent this is because alcohol abuse is symptomatic of personal problems and the choices people make in response. The removal of alcohol will often lead to substitute forms of conduct, such as increased use of drugs. And how could alcohol abuse be halted anyway? It was tried during Prohibition. That clearly did not stop consumption. And more than this, it led to an increase in the quantity of impure alcohol on the black market, with associated increases in ill-health effects.[13]

The statistical bases for estimating the health care costs of alcohol abuse are dubious. And beyond this, those health care costs, whatever they may happen to be, are not costs to society in general but are costs to those alcohol abusers who happen to incur them. In the United States, about one-quarter of medical costs are paid directly by the patients who receive the services. These costs clearly are not borne by society at large, but are borne by those who receive the services. The analysis of the part of health care costs that are paid directly by patients is essentially the same as the analysis of lost production presented above.

The situation is more complex for the bulk of medical payments, which are made through insurance programs. If everyone pays the same premiums, it might seem as though the people who have relatively high claims are imposing costs on those who do not, for if those high claims could have been pared down, the total cost of the insurance program would have been less and those without claims would have paid lower premiums. If alcohol-related health claims are in addition to other health claims, it might thus seem that consumers of alcohol impose costs on others. However, it has not been demonstrated that any alcohol-associated costs are in addition to other medical costs. In other words, there is no support for the assertion that drinkers and nondrinkers have identical medical costs for everything unrelated to alcohol, so what are referred to as alcohol-related costs may be additional costs that are incurred solely by drinkers. If the costs of treating alcohol-related illnesses substitute for other medical costs that would otherwise be incurred, such figures as those represented by the $8.3 billion for 1971 and the $30 billion for 1992 do not represent some excess cost of treating people who drink alcoholic beverages, because those people incur lower medical costs in other respects.

When thinking of medical costs financed through insurance programs, it is important to take cognizance of the nature of insurance as a business. In doing so, perhaps the most significant distinction to make is that between anticipation and realization. During the course of a year, all participants pay premiums into an insurance program, but only a few people make claims during that year. But it would not be correct to say that the people who file claims are imposing costs on the remainder of the participants, who pay premiums but do not file claims, for it is in the very nature of insurance as a business that only a fraction of the total participants will file claims. People choose to buy insurance with the awareness that the most likely outcome is that they will pay premiums but will not file a claim. In effect, people are avoiding having to face a small chance of a relatively big loss by accepting a small but certain loss in the form of premium payments.

The correct perspective toward insurance is anticipation at the time of participation. People will choose to participate so long as they anticipate that the cost of their participation through the premiums they would have to pay is less than the value they place upon having the coverage the insurance offers. The fact that at the end of the year, a minority of people are observed to have received payments on claims in excess of the premiums they paid, while most people paid premiums but filed no claims, is simply irrelevant to any argument that the people who filed claims imposed costs on those who did not.

From the perspective of realization after the fact, recipients of insurance payments do indeed appear to impose costs on the remainder of the participants in the program. But people would never have chosen to participate in the program in the first place if they had truly known that they would make premium payments but would have no chance of having their claims paid. Insurance is an operation where all participants gain in the before-the-fact sense of anticipation, and it is meaningless to make inferences about social costs based on observations about realized payments on claims relative to premium payments during any particular year.

In comparing personal responsibility with insurance as forms of paying for medical care, it is important to distinguish between *ex ante* (before the fact) and *ex post* (after the fact) perspectives. When insurance payments are looked at after the fact, people who are sick more often would seem to be subsidized by those who are not. But this is true of all insurance programs when they are viewed after the fact. People who have automobile accidents seem to be subsidized by those who do not. People whose homes are damaged or destroyed by fire seem to be subsidized by those whose homes are not.

People who require medical care seem to be subsidized by people who do not. All insurance has the *ex post* property of appearing to subsidize some people at the expense of others.

But the appropriate perspective toward insurance is *ex ante*. From the *ex ante* perspective, all participants must look upon their participation as beneficial, for otherwise they would not have chosen to participate in the first place. People choose to participate in an insurance program because they judge the benefits of coverage in the event of accident or illness to be worth the price of participation, even though the most likely outcome is that their total premium payments will exceed their total claims. In principle there is little economic difference between a system where people pay for their medical expenses personally and a system where those expenses are covered by insurance.

## Drunk Driving and the Social Cost of Alcohol

Many images of the social cost of alcohol seem to involve an automobile, driven by a drunk, running through a red light and causing a three-car crash. Although the carnage is horrible, with three dead, including one pedestrian, and four injured, two critically, the drunken driver is unhurt. While the injuries and fatalities that occur among the drunk drivers themselves are personal costs to them and not costs to society, the mayhem wreaked upon other people *is* a social cost. Table 10.3 shows that Berry and Boland estimated this cost to be $4.7 billion for 1971, which would be $16.9 billion in 1992 dollars. While this amount is only about one-half of that attributed to medical care and about one-third of that attributed to lost production, it is still well in excess of existing tax revenues from alcoholic beverages. Vehicular accidents clearly involve the imposition of costs on people who do not consume alcoholic beverages, and so provide a possible justification for corrective taxation.

To be sure, the cost attributed to alcohol-related vehicular accidents is a constructed and not a directly observed figure. The assumptions involved in the construction of this cost estimate have several questionable features that might seem to impart an upward bias to those figures, though the principle of external cost would apply to such accidents in any case. Berry and Boland start with an estimate of the full costs of vehicular accidents in 1971, and then ask what share of those costs can be attributed to alcohol. They start with a total cost figure of $30.5 billion for 1971, and then estimate that 15.3 percent of that cost can be attributed to alcohol.

This construction involves several assumptions that are difficult to justify on grounds other than that of expediency in deriving a number. The $30.5 billion figure used for the total cost of vehicular accidents in 1971 is a hybrid of two different sources, and one that works out to be approximately an average of those two sources even though the method of construction was not simply to average the two figures. In any case, the National Highway Traffic

Safety Administration estimated the costs of vehicular accidents to be $46 billion in 1971, while the National Safety Council estimated those costs to have been $16 billion.

From this point of departure, the calculation of cost involves some determination of what share of that $30.5 billion figure to attribute to alcohol. The method used involved a comparison of people who were involved in vehicular accidents with a sample of people who were not. Alcohol abuse was attributed as the cause of an accident in all cases where the blood alcohol content (BAC) of a driver exceeded .05 percent. Suppose that 40 percent of the drivers who were involved in accidents had a BAC of .05 or more, while some alternative sample of drivers who were not involved in accidents showed only 10 percent of those drivers to have a BAC of .05 or more. This situation shows clearly that people with a BAC of .05 or more were involved disproportionately heavily in vehicular accidents. While they were estimated to have constituted only 10 percent of the relevant driving population, they were involved in 40 percent of the accidents. From this point of departure, it is a relatively simple step to estimate a figure for the additional number of accidents that can be attributed to a BAC of .05 or more. While Berry and Boland constructed different estimates of attributable cost for fatalities, personal injuries, and property damage, the weighted average across the categories was 15.3 percent. Starting with a $30.5 billion figure for the total cost of vehicular accidents in 1971, it was estimated that $8.3 billion could be attributed to alcohol.

Such attributions of cost involve a large degree of arbitrariness whenever vehicular accidents might be a joint product of two or more sources of influence. Indeed, in the case where a vehicular accident is fully a joint product of two influences, it is wholly arbitrary how the cost might be divided between those influences. To illustrate, suppose the analysis of vehicular accidents was extended to include the time of day as well, with the finding that nighttime drivers have a higher accident rate than daytime drivers. If both a BAC in excess of .05 and nighttime driving are positively correlated with vehicular accidents, the method used by Berry and Boland to construct an attribution of cost for alcohol will be inaccurate, for an accurate assessment would require the construction and estimation of a model of vehicular accidents, in which case BAC would be but one of many possible considerations.[14]

It is, of course, possible to question the precision of particular estimates of the social cost of alcoholic beverages without denying the validity of the claim that vehicular accidents involve external costs in all cases except those where accidents involve no damage to persons or property other than the drivers'. Injuries and deaths of third parties are the primary sources of possible social costs from alcohol. Unlike lost-production and medical costs, it is undeniable that these costs are social costs. But even here it does not follow that increased taxation is desirable. True, the increased taxation would reduce consumption by alcohol abusers, and this should translate into a reduction in fatalities caused by those abusers. This is precisely what a corrective tax is supposed to accomplish: reduce the damage imposed on innocent parties by reducing usage of the item that causes the damage. But that increased taxation would also reduce consumption by nonabusers, who would not cause fatalities anyway, or at least not because of alcohol abuse. Taxation penalizes these people as well.

An alternative approach is to restrict the harm the abusers are likely to inflict upon the innocent. It might be possible to make greater use of individual responsibility and liability by supplying incentives to potential abusers to refrain from driving, while not infringing upon the freedoms of the nonabusing majority of the population. In this respect, only a small portion of the people who drink alcoholic beverages would be considered abusers, candidates for DUI arrests, and more likely to cause accidents. The vast preponderance of those who drink alcoholic beverages do so safely and prudently. The corrective tax argument seeks to spread the liability across all consumers of the product. But if the damage is done largely by a relatively small number of abusers and dipsomaniacs, what is the basis for placing most of those costs upon the preponderant majority of consumers?

The corrective tax argument works best if everyone is alike and getting drunk is a random event that is equally likely to strike anyone who drinks alcoholic beverages. Once it is recognized that inebriated driving is not random and that becoming drunk is largely a product of individual choice for which people are themselves responsible, the standard case for corrective taxation becomes quite problematical, and must be grounded on some argument from expediency to the effect that a tax is the best of a set of poor options. This would be an argument grounded on second-best considerations, and taken in recognition that a better option is not attainable. An excise tax on alcoholic beverages to cover the costs imposed by abusers may reduce the drinking done and damage imposed by abusers, but it will also reduce the consumption opportunities available to nonabusers.

The corrective tax approach essentially assumes that people are guilty from the start, in that everyone is presumed to be as abusive as the population average. This might be a necessary working assumption if there are no other means available for controlling those costs. But other means of control are available: fines and jail sentences are already in place. The principles of efficient deterrence do not promise to deter all accidents or crimes, but promise only to achieve cost-effective deterrence.[15] How closely the existing fines and jail sentences fit with the principles of efficient deterrence is an open question. In any case, such deterrence targets the guilty, unlike the corrective tax approach, which strikes the guilty and the innocent alike.

Moreover, in the presence of a set of efficient penal sanctions, there is no place for corrective taxation. The penal sanctions achieve a cost-effective reduction of drunk driving, or at least have that capability. There is no scope for the taxation of alcoholic beverages to improve matters. In the presence of penal sanctions, excise taxes cannot serve as instruments of correction, but can serve only as instruments for raising revenue. To be sure, it might be argued that existing penal sanctions are not strong enough to achieve efficient deterrence. This argument, however, is a plea for stiffer sanctions, not a call for higher taxation.[16]

## Concluding Remarks

What is to be made of claims regarding the social cost of drinking alcoholic beverages? There is an almost universal acceptance in the economics literature that the consumption of alcoholic beverages entails significant social costs beyond the personal costs reflected in market prices. To be sure, the variation in those estimates is quite large, with there being as much as a threefold difference between low and high estimates. While this variation attests to the speculative and elusive nature of efforts to assess such social costs, there is nonetheless a strong consensus in the literature that significant social costs are associated with alcohol consumption.

I have sought to explain here why much of this consensus is unfounded, for much of what have been called social costs are actually private, or personal, costs. This is certainly true of the lost-production costs associated with illness and premature death. It is the drinkers and their families who suffer those losses, not the remainder of society. This point is beginning to get recognition in the scholarly literature, as some studies now distinguish between private and social costs and categorize lost production as a private cost.

Medical costs, even when paid by insurance, are also a private cost, although this point has not yet received the same degree of recognition in the scholarly literature. To some extent this is because the argument is more subtle. A finding that alcohol abusers incur higher medical costs than nonabusers would seem to suggest that insurance costs to nonabusers are higher than they would otherwise be because of the inclusion of abusers in the program. Yet there are ways insurance companies could charge higher premiums to alcohol abusers. Premiums based on DUI convictions would be one, random blood testing another. However, it would be costly to do so, and insurers may well judge that the added cost exceeds whatever benefits in terms of extra business they could expect. In this case alcohol abusers may well impose small costs on everyone else, yet those costs will be less than the costs of doing anything about them. In other words, insurance premiums would have to rise to cover the higher costs incurred in seeking to charge higher premiums for alcohol abusers, and those increased costs may well exceed the premium reductions for nonabusers that might result.

This leaves injuries and deaths of third parties as the primary source of alcohol-related social costs. In contrast to excise taxation, the penal approach to deterrence would penalize only the guilty. It would rely upon principles of individual responsibility and personal liability in supplying incentives for potential abusers to refrain from driving, while not infringing upon the nonabusing majority of the population. While alcohol seems generally to be exaggerated as a source of external cost, it cannot be denied that such costs exist. If the only instrument available to influence that cost were excise taxation, some such taxation might be warranted under $n$th-best types of arguments. But better, more precisely targeted instruments are available through penal sanctions. Thus, there is no good case for yet higher taxes on alcoholic beverages, and in the presence of penal sanctions, it could even be argued that existing taxes are too high.

## Notes

1. For a list of Tax Freedom Days going back to 1929, see Tax Foundation (1993, 19).
2. This theme is developed forthrightly in Posner (1971).
3. For a collection of essays that explore various facets of this theme concerning the political economy of user charges, see Wagner (1991).
4. To be sure, technological developments are now in the offing that may make it possible to charge people directly for their use of highways, much as they can be charged for their use of water or electricity.
5. For a strongly critical analysis of these conventional arguments about corrective taxation, see Cordato (1993).
6. See, for instance, the discussion in Atkinson and Stiglitz (1980, 366–93).
7. Actual tax collections in 1992 were about half of that amount.
8. See Phelps (1988), Grossman (1989), Adrian (1988), Coate and Grossman (1988), and Manning et al. (1989) for similar arguments.
9. An alcohol abuser is defined as someone whose average daily consumption is equal to 10 centiliters or more of pure alcohol.
10. Heien and Pittman (1989, 573) find that for the United States, the average income of alcohol abusers is about one–sixth lower than that of nonabusers, and from this draw the conclusion that abusers and nonabusers are drawn from different populations, statistically speaking, and so cannot be treated as identical in all other relevant respects, contrary to a presumption common to the various studies on the social cost of alcohol.
11. Even a statistic showing that people who consumed more than 10 centiliters of alcohol per day had a higher absenteeism rate than people who consumed less, including none, could not validly be used to infer that consuming large amounts of alcohol causes people to miss more work, because any of several other considerations might have accounted for the missed work. For further discussion with respect to similar claims about smoking and absenteeism, see Tollison and Wagner (1992, 111–17).
12. These pitfalls are generally avoided in Manning et al. (1989) and Pogue and Sgontz (1989), both of which distinguish internal from external costs and find the external costs to be much lower than such magnitudes as those reported in table 10.3.
13. The effect of Prohibition on the consumption of alcoholic beverages is explored in Miron and Zweibel (1991).

14. Indeed, following a line of argument initiated by Sam Peltzman (1975), it is conceivable that one partial effect of an increased BAC operates to reduce accidents because of an increased level of care taken by an impaired driver. Just as Peltzman found drivers rationally to exercise less caution as safety equipment was added to vehicles, so, too, might drivers with elevated BACs exercise more caution through such things as driving more slowly and changing lanes less often.
15. See the seminal articulation of the theory of deterrence in Becker (1968).
16. There might be an exception if there were some obstacle to the full imposition of penal sanctions, as noted in Safer and Grossman (1987, 374).

## References

Adrian, Manvella. 1988. "Social Costs of Alcohol." *Canadian Journal of Public Health* 79 (September/October): 316–22.

Atkinson, Anthony B., and Joseph E. Stiglitz. 1980. *Lectures on Public Economics.* New York: McGraw–Hill.

Becker, Gary S. 1968. "Crime and Punishment: An Economic Approach." *Journal of Political Economy* 76 (March/April): 169–217.

Berry, Ralph E., Jr., and James P. Boland. 1977. *The Economic Cost of Alcohol Abuse.* New York: Free Press.

Coate, Douglas, and Michael Grossman. 1988. "Effects of Alcoholic Beverage Prices and Legal Drinking Ages on Youth Alcohol Use." *Journal of Law and Economics* 31 (April): 145–71.

Cordato, Roy. 1993. *Welfare Economics and Externalities in an Open Ended Universe: A Modern Austrian Perspective.* Boston: Kluwer Academic Publilshers.

Grossman, Michael. 1989. "Health Benefits of Increases in Alcohol and Cigarette Taxes." *British Journal of Addiction* 84:1193–1204.

Heien, Dale M., and David J. Pittman. 1989. "The Economic Costs of Alcohol Abuse: An Assessment of Current Methods and Estimates." *Journal of Studies on Alcohol* 50(6):567–79.

Manning, W. G., Emmett B. Keeler, Joseph P. Newhouse, Elizabeth M. Sloss, and Jeffrey Wasserman. 1989. "The Taxes of Sin: Do Smokers and Drinkers Pay Their Way?" *Journal of the American Medical Association* 261:1604–9.

Miron, Jeffrey A., and Jeffrey Zweibel. 1991. "Alcohol Consumption during Prohibition." *American Economic Review Papers and Proceedings* 81 (May): 242–47.

Peltzman, Sam. 1975. "The Effects of Automobile Safety Regulation." *Journal of Political Economy* 83 (August): 677–725.

Phelps, Charles E. 1988. "Death and Taxes: An Opportunity for Substitution." *Journal of Health Economics* 7:1–24.

Pogue, Thomas F., and Larry G. Sgontz. 1989. "Taxing to Control Social Costs: The Case of Alcohol." *American Economic Review* 79 (March): 235–43.

Posner, Richard A. 1971. "Taxation by Regulation." *Bell Journal of Economics* 2 (Spring): 22–50.

Safer, Henry, and Michael Grossman. 1987. "Beer Taxes, the Legal Drinking Age, and Youth Motor Vehicle Fatalities." *Journal of Legal Studies* 16 (June): 351–74.

Tax Foundation. 1993. *Facts & Figures on Government Finance, 1993 Edition.* Washington, D.C.: Tax Foundation.

Tollison, Robert D., and Richard E. Wagner. 1992. *The Economics of Smoking.* Boston: Kluwer Academic Publishers.

Wagner, Richard E., ed. 1991. *Charging for Government: User Charges and Earmarked Taxes in Principle and Practice.* London: Routledge.

Woodfield, Alan. 1986. "Economic Cost of Alcohol-Related Health Care in New Zealand: An Interpretive Comment." *British Journal of Addiction* 83:1031–35.

# 11

# Excise Taxes, Social Costs, and the Consumption of Wine

*Paula A. Gant*
*Robert B. Ekelund, Jr.*

Wine consumption, production, and distribution have been subject to a wide range of political controls throughout history. Taxes and customs duties have consistently been levied on wine production and trade, providing revenue for governments as diverse as those of imperial Rome, medieval England and the contemporary United States. Alcoholic beverages in general have been the focus of a considerable amount of social concern and government regulation. Aside from the revenue-generating capabilities of the popular drink trade, the controversial effects of alcohol consumption have, over time, spawned much public debate and many temperance movements. With the implementation of the National Prohibition (Volstead) Act in 1920, the U.S. Congress went so far as to attempt to prohibit consumption of alcohol. The results of the fourteen-year experiment were not those intended. As history reveals, fashion may come and go, but there has never been an effective substitute, in terms of satisfaction, to the drinking of wines and spirits, even when they have been made scarce or illegal. Nevertheless, as governments struggle to address chronic budget deficits and "special projects," taxes on "sin" are a very attractive alternative to other, less popular taxes.

In the ongoing battle to balance the federal budget, proposals continually surface that would increase alcohol excise tax rates. These plans, those that preceded them, and future attempts to tax alcoholic beverages generally, and wine specifically, raise a number of interesting and important issues. Is the selective excise taxation of alcohol, past or present, an efficient or equitable way to raise federal revenues? In addition to the need for increased federal revenues, making consumers pay the full social cost of producing and consuming alcohol is often cited as justification for tax increases. The rationale for selective taxation of alcohol from a public-health perspective is based on the idea that taxation deters consumers from exposing themselves to the serious health hazards associated with alcohol abuse. Can taxes on wine specifically (and alcohol generally) be regarded as "corrective taxes"? The attempt to impose a corrective tax or an ersatz "user fee" on wine would be premised on the existence of substantial social costs from wine consumption.

What are the (alleged) social costs of alcohol consumption? If such social costs can be identified, what are their magnitudes? What lessons concerning product substitution between types of alcohol due to their differential tax treatment can be drawn from the most recent experience with selective excise taxes in the United States?

This chapter attempts to shed some light on these and related questions. Our first objective is to briefly examine the impact of selective taxes on the horizontal equity of the tax system. We then discuss the concept of user taxes on wine and investigate whether and in what manner wine taxes may be construed as corrective taxes or user fees. Next we investigate both the revenue potential and the social effects of increasing taxes on wine, using data from the recent past. In order for such taxes to be sufficiently lucrative from a revenue perspective, the demand for such products must be sufficiently inelastic. Proposals that would impose a disproportionate share of the alcohol tax increase on wine have much in common with the increase in the federal excise tax on alcohol products contained in the Omnibus Reconciliation Act of 1990 (and put into effect in 1991): the revenue projections assume no cross-substitution among alcoholic beverages and consequently ignore the revenue and cost effects associated with consumption shares being reallocated among product sectors.

Our study employs a simultaneous-equations model to estimate the price and cross-price elasticities for wine, beer, and liquor in response to the 1991 excise tax increase. The focus is on the impact of changing relative rates of taxation on consumption shares in the alcoholic-beverages commodity group, and on the relevance of these consumption changes to the purported social goals of such legislation. In interpretive and concluding sections, we evaluate the potential costs and benefits of new excise taxes on wine (and alcoholic beverages generally) as a means of generating government revenue for health care or, for that matter, any other purpose.

## I. The Wine Tax: Relevant Literature

Increases in taxes on alcohol consumption have been justified on both political and economic grounds. From an economic perspective, little social welfare is presumed lost in the markets directly affected by these taxes, because the demand elasticities are generally assumed to be low.[1] Even so, Cook and Tauchen (1982) find evidence that tax increases do reduce alcohol consumption. Using data from Australia in order to examine supply-side effects,

Tsolakis (1983) finds that even if the effects of wine taxation on consumption are small, a significant reallocation of resources from the wine production sector to other sectors is evident over a two- to three-year period. Such a conclusion would imply that in the long run, there is a tradeoff between revenue collected and quantity consumed. In accordance with the commonly accepted theory of excise tax incidence, Tsolakis also finds that the relative responsiveness of supply and demand, rather than the stage in the marketing chain at which the tax is imposed, dictates where the burden of the tax will ultimately be borne. A general equilibrium model is employed by Boyd and Seldon (1991) to extend the analysis beyond the sectors that are directly affected by the alcohol tax and to examine the secondary welfare effects of sin taxes on revenue and land use. Not surprisingly, the authors find that when one sector of the alcoholic-beverage market is taxed more heavily than others, "production and consumption will be diverted and consumption will move into sectors with lower taxes" (Boyd and Seldon 1991, 370).

The overall demand for alcoholic beverages is generally considered to be relatively unresponsive to price changes because there are no close substitutes for alcohol as a commodity. Clements and Johnson (1983) find unconditional own-price elasticities of −0.4, −0.4, and −0.7 for beer, wine, and spirits, respectively. However, individual types of alcoholic beverages are substitutable for one another and, therefore, are more responsive to price changes than alcoholic beverages as a group. Although Tsolakis et al. (1983) find the demand for wine to be relatively price inelastic in the short run, they do report estimates of long-run price elasticities for wine of between 1.2 and 1.6. Using data from the United Kingdom, Duffy (1983) estimates the price elasticity of the demand for wine to be 0.65–0.87.[2]

Of course, the ultimate impact of a tax on demand will depend on the form of the tax, the magnitude of the tax, and how much the relative prices of alcoholic beverages are affected. Wine, moreover, is a product of widely differing qualities. In an empirical analysis, Tsolakis (1983) finds that an ad valorem tax would have the same percentage price impact across all qualities of wine. From the viewpoint of the wine industry, therefore, a tax based on percentage of value would be the least distortional. Because higher-quality wines with an established image have been shown to be relatively price inelastic (White 1991, 167), an ad valorem tax would also have the capacity to raise substantial government revenue.

An excise tax, on the other hand, would affect different qualities of wine differently. A per unit tax would have a proportionately greater effect on the lower-quality bulk wines, a sector that is generally assumed to be more price sensitive than the upscale wine sector. With respect to the alcoholic-beverage market in general, tax increases in one sector can reallocate consumption shares among the other sectors. The method of taxation will no doubt have implications for the structure and stability of the sector on which it is imposed. Clements and Johnson (1983) apply a systemwide analysis of demand at the individual product level in order to evaluate the rapid growth of wine's share of the total alcohol consumed in Australia over the 1955–77 period. Given that beer is subject to a substantial tax in Australia, while wine is not, the authors conclude from several simulations of their model that wine's favorable tax treatment accounts for a large part of the observed growth in wine consumption over the period in question. According to their results, a tax rate on wine similar to that imposed on beer would have lowered the annual growth in wine consumption approximately 1.8 percentage points below the observed trend. As will be discussed at greater length below, a shift in consumption away from wine due to tax increases can have many undesirable effects, not only by directly affecting the wine-producing sector, but also by shifting consumption in favor of alcoholic beverages that may be associated disproportionately with the negative externalities related to alcohol abuse.

Whether the taxation of alcoholic beverages is an appropriate means of reducing the social costs supposedly associated with alcohol consumption is also a continuing policy issue. The corrective taxation argument serves as the basis for implementing public policies and social programs directed at reducing alcohol consumption. Sound estimates of these social costs are vital to designing such policies. Consequently, an abundance of studies have been conducted with the objective of providing some method of estimating the costs associated with alcohol use that are imposed upon society. In a survey of this literature, Adrian (1988) listed 139 references to studies on the social costs of alcohol consumption that were published between 1978 and 1985. Among these studies, Adrian refers specifically (on page 320) to ten studies estimating the social costs of alcohol use for the United States. The estimates ranged from $30 billion to $89.5 billion per year. The studies referenced include as elements of social costs some or all of the following: health care, social welfare, productivity losses, crime and law enforcement, traffic accidents, fire losses, and premature mortality. The wide range of the social-cost estimates reported in these studies raises serious questions about their methods of estimation, an observation that will be discussed more fully in section III.

In a critique of the methods and assumptions commonly employed in studies of the economic costs of alcohol abuse, Heien and Pittman (1989, 577) find the estimates to be "flawed empirically and conceptually." Of particular interest to our discussion of the corrective taxation principle, the authors are especially critical of the failure to distinguish "between externalities and costs that are internalized by alcohol abusers" (p. 578). Given the stated objective of corrective taxation measures (the internalization of some external cost), the relevance of studies that fail to make this distinction becomes all the more questionable. Employing a model that aims to construct an optimal tax in order to force consumers to internalize the social costs of alcohol abuse, Pogue and Sgontz (1989, 242) conclude that "the average tax rate should be at least as high, and probably double, the present rate of about 25 percent." The spurious nature of the methods of estimation and the policy implications that result from such studies are discussed at greater length below. After examining the impact of excise taxes in general and sin taxes specifically on the efficiency and horizontal equity of the tax system, we shall turn, in section III, to a discussion of the principle of corrective taxation and its relevance for the taxation of wine.

## II. Economic Aspects of Taxation

Taking a panoramic view, the relatively small size of the wine industry does not lend itself to high expectations regarding the revenue potential of wine taxes. Aside from the moderate importance of revenue associated with such taxation (alcohol taxes accounted for only $7.7 billion out of the $1,177 billion in total federal revenue in 1993 [U.S. Bureau of the Census 1993, 329]), there exist cogent theoretical arguments that reject selective excise taxation as inequitable and inefficient.

An excise tax is simply a per unit tax on the consumption of a selected good or service. The impact of such a tax depends on a number of factors, including the expenditure patterns of different income groups, the incidence of the tax, and the income distribution of consumers. A great deal of attention has been devoted to the partial equilibrium effects of selective excise taxes in the economics literature. Specifically, critics of excise taxes cite their regressivity and their differential impact on different segments of the population as major drawbacks (Ekelund and Long 1989, 1991).[3] There is widespread agreement regarding the desirability of adhering to the principle of horizontal tax equity, or ensuring that people of the same economic situation pay comparable taxes in support of governmentally provided services. The principle of horizontal equity attempts to treat equals as equals. Therefore, in accordance with this concept of equity, a fair consumption-based tax system is one that apportions equal tax liabilities to people whose consumption expenditures are the same. Selective, or discriminatory, taxation violates this principle by unfairly burdening certain groups of consumers due simply to differences in their tastes and preferences for different goods and services.

In order to assess the distributional impact of a tax, we must also be able to determine the incidence of taxation—or who actually pays. The theory of the impact of an excise tax on price and quantity is shown in figure 11.1. The curves represent the demand and supply for alcoholic beverages in general, under no taxation, with $P_o$ and $Q_o$ representing the original price and quantity. With the imposition of an excise tax of $t$ dollars per alcohol gallon sold, the marginal cost of producing and selling alcohol rises. Because the cost increase is constant for each and every gallon sold, the supply curve shifts up and to the left, from $S$ to $S + t$. Following the imposition of the tax, a new

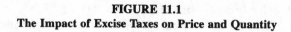

**FIGURE 11.1**
**The Impact of Excise Taxes on Price and Quantity**

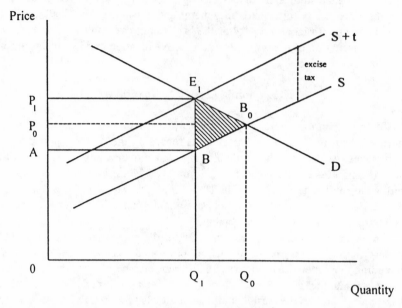

When consumers respond to price increases by decreasing consumption, excise taxation has the general effect of reducing equilibrium output and raising price. The extent to which an excise tax leads to a higher price depends on the relevant elasticities, that is, on how responsive consumption and production are to price changes. In the illustration above, the price rises, but not by the full amount of the tax, *t*.

market equilibrium results with producers supplying $Q_1$ gallons, for which consumers are willing to pay, at most, $P_1$ dollars per gallon; the excise has the ultimate effect of raising price and lowering consumption after equilibrium is reestablished.

The actual incidence of the tax depends on the supply and demand conditions that characterize the market under consideration. The common, but frequently erroneous, assumption of partial equilibrium analysis is that excise taxes are completely passed forward to consumers in the form of higher prices. Goods and services characterized by relatively inelastic demands are primary targets for excise taxation because consumption of these commodities is relatively unresponsive to price changes and, therefore, to taxation. Along with the question of who among consumers and producers pays a tax, we must also consider the impact of such taxes on the distribution of income.

In addition to the principle of horizontal equity, Americans also subscribe to the ability-to-pay principle of taxation. According to this view, taxes are levied on the basis of income. Those at higher levels of income are assumed to have a greater ability to pay and are, for that reason alone, required to pay higher taxes. The ability-to-pay criterion is often invoked when considering the fairness of tax systems. The vast majority of theoretical and empirical studies of specific excise taxes have characterized them as regressive in nature. Using a computable general equilibrium model to examine the effects of increases in selective taxes, Boyd and Seldon (1991, 371) found that "in percentage terms, the lower income classes tend to lose slightly more of their total income than higher income classes." In a study that employed a modified Lorenz-curve-based Gini ratio in constructing an index of tax progressivity, Suits (1977) found excise taxes to be borne disproportionately by those earning the lowest percentages of total income. Higher excise taxes can therefore be expected to result in a more regressive and less equitable tax structure if the items subject to taxation are consumed disproportionately by those in the lower income ranges of the population. Given these results, we can observe that reliance or increased reliance on regressive taxes, such as excise taxes, works against the long-held ability-to-pay principle of equity.

In addition to these equity considerations, there is the issue of the partial equilibrium efficiency effects of the excise. Here the objection to excise taxation is that it distorts normal buying patterns because the prices of the goods do not reflect their true production costs. An excise tax, in effect, distorts the signals transmitted by prices to consumers because those prices are artificially raised by taxes. Because consumers will purchase less of relatively more expensive goods and more of those goods that are relatively less expensive, consumer welfare is lost when the tax is imposed. The end result is that consumer expenditures are redirected in nonoptimal ways. An indirect effect of the tax-induced distortions in consumer spending patterns is that producers are induced to shift resources away from the production of the taxed good (which is being sold in smaller quantities) to the production of goods with lower-valued uses.

A rudimentary principle of economics tells us that the cost of one product is measured in terms of the next most valued product that could have been produced with the same resources. In a freely functioning market economy, the value (or market price) of wine is equal to its cost, which is in turn equal to the value of the next most valuable product whose production has been sacrificed. Imposing a specific tax on wine interferes with the market process by transmitting false information about the cost of wine. The result of the tax is to drive a "wedge" between the market price of wine and its cost of production.

Such distortions, often referred to by public-finance economists as the "excess burden" of a tax, provide the foundation for the argument that excise taxes are inefficient. The deceptive signals sent by artificial increases in the price of a good following the imposition of a tax cause distortions in consumers' choices and in producers' resource allocation decisions. The resulting "deadweight" loss is represented by the shaded area $E_1 B_0 B$ in figure 11.1. Deadweight loss, or excess burden, is the welfare cost to society associated with the tax. This loss represents the reduction in consumer and producer surplus over and above what is transferred to the government in the form of tax revenues. In his famous taxation theorem, Jules Dupuit ([1844] 1952) proved that the narrower is the base of the tax, the larger is the deadweight loss relative to the revenues generated by the tax. In other words, the loss in welfare resulting from the imposition of an excise tax is proportional not to the tax itself but to the square of the tax. Following Dupuit's theorem, economists in general have argued that the welfare loss resulting from excise taxation is significant enough to justify "spreading" taxes across many commodities (i.e., economists generally prefer broad-based taxes to narrow-based taxes on efficiency grounds).[4]

### III. Are There Social Costs to Wine Consumption?

Other rationales exist for selective taxes apart from revenue considerations. We live in a political environment of high taxation—one where politicians are horrified at the prospect of having voted for any "new tax." Although selective taxes of all types are somewhat easier to enact, especially if the burden is shifted to the politically weak, politicians have attempted to lump some of them under the rubric of corrective taxes or user fees. In this section we briefly examine the basis for such arguments with respect to wine.

New taxes, particularly in the present political environment, are increasingly called user fees or corrective taxes. A "user fee" tax, such as the excise tax on gasoline, is a charge for the use of some public resource, such as highways. According to the benefit principle of taxation, the more an individual derives benefits from highway use, the more she or he should pay in gasoline taxes. In this manner the taxes raised to finance the provision of some "public good" are levied under the more palatable name of "user fees."

A similar political strategy has developed around medical and environmental issues. New excise taxes on tobacco and alcohol—especially those earmarked to finance health care—are routinely rationalized by being called corrective taxes. The foundation for the corrective tax concept is that the untaxed market-determined prices of some goods do not fully reflect the social costs of production or consumption. As pointed out in an important study on the social costs of alcohol:

> On the surface, it is easy to see how corrective tax ideas might be applied to wine. To do so it would be necessary to show that there are costs associated with the consumption of wine that are not reflected in the market price of wine. If the price of wine can be shown to be too low, it is possible to argue that a tax on wine might be a way of correcting for some of the market failures that could otherwise result. (Tollison and Wagner 1991, 4)

Wine sales and tax receipts were estimated by Tollison and Wagner. The federal excise taxes on wine of $1.07 per gallon (where alcohol percentage does not exceed 14 percent) and $1.57 per gallon (for alcohol percentages between 14 and 21 percent) yielded revenue amounting to approximately half a billion dollars in 1991. State wine taxes vary considerably, but on the basis of a standardized calculation, Tollison and Wagner estimated that the states collect a total of about $1.1 billion each year. Based on this estimate, with sales of $42 billion annually on all alcoholic beverages sold wholesale (and assuming retail markups of about 30 percent), wine sales would account for about 40 percent of the total (Tollison and Wagner 1991, 9).[5] (The importance of differential taxation and relative shares within the alcoholic-beverage market are discussed in the next section of this chapter.)

The case for expansion of corrective taxes on wine must rest upon the (alleged) social costs that pertain to alcohol in general. This case, as Tollison and Wagner suggest, is fragile and rests on the market's supposed inability to account for the full costs to society of alcohol consumption. Most particularly, estimates of social costs are vastly overstated when they are subjected to even cursory economic analysis. Statistics compiled by the National Institute of Alcohol Abuse and Alcoholism (NIAAA) present both the categories and cost estimates of the supposed market failure. For 1983, the NIAAA's estimates of the social costs of consuming alcohol (in billions of dollars) were as follows: lost production ($70.9); premature death ($18.2); medical care ($15.0); vehicular accidents ($3.3); crime ($5.8); and welfare administration ($3.7). Extrapolated to 1991, total social costs would be about $146 billion (Tollison and Wagner 1991, 14)—double the estimate of total alcohol sales for 1991. If this estimate is correct, the social costs of alcohol consumption are substantial and highly relevant for public policy and corrective taxation.

But, as Tollison and Wagner clearly show, most of these cost estimates are highly speculative, if not simply unbelievable. More than 91 percent of the estimated social cost of alcohol is attributed to lost production, premature death, and medical care. As even partisans of the social-cost argument are beginning to realize (Manning et al. 1989), these costs, especially those relating to lost production and premature death, are not social costs at all but are private costs. The NIAAA, for example, places an estimate of $1.6 million (in 1991 dollars) on lost production for each life lost due to alcohol abuse. But who loses these earnings? Clearly it is the unfortunate "victim" of death by alcohol. He or she will not be earning income or paying taxes in the future (an apparent social cost), but neither will he or she be making claims on scarce resources or public expenditures. Clearly these costs are private costs, just as the so-called social costs of absenteeism from smoking or drinking beer are (Ault et al. 1991). Calculation errors will consequently abound where researchers fail to make the correct distinction between the external costs of alcohol abuse and those that are internalized by the abuser.

The social costs claimed to be associated with health care are even more frequently cited as a social cost of alcohol consumption than are the costs associated with lost production. But estimates of what health care costs *would be* in the absence of alcohol consumption are practically impossible to obtain. Moreover, medical costs—to the extent that they are borne directly by those who consume health care services—are private costs, not social costs. The same conclusion is reached when private insurance premiums are considered in *ex ante* rather than *ex post* fashion.[6] As Tollison and Wagner (1991, 29) note, it is wrong to claim that insurance costs are costs

> to society at large. From the perspective of realization after the fact, recipients of insurance payments do indeed appear to impose costs on the remainder of the participants in the program. But people would have never chosen to participate in the first place if they truly knew that they would make premium payments but would have no chance of having their claims paid. Insurance is an operation where all participants gain in the before-the-fact sense of anticipation, and it is meaningless to make inferences about social costs based on observations about realized payments on claims relative to premium payments during any particular year.

In other words, individuals choose to insure because they expect the utility of the eventual benefits to exceed the present value of the anticipated costs (in case of illness or accident) even though it is likely that their premium payments will exceed the total value of their claims. (Risk-neutral or risk-averse individuals are by definition willing to pay premiums that, in monetary terms, are greater than the expected monetary value of the benefits.) In this manner, externalities are internalized within the contract setting. When all things are considered, even if the difficult link between the size of health expenditures and alcohol consumption could be established, it is not clear that these costs could be characterized as social costs rather than private costs.

More than any other category of costs, property losses and drunk-driving accidents are most closely associated with alcohol consumption. If such property losses, injuries, and deaths were borne solely by the drunk driver, all the costs would be private costs. But clear and tragic social costs exist when drunk drivers destroy property or kill or injure others. While taxation may not be the preferred solution to this problem (Tollison and Wagner 1991, 31, 35–36), these social costs are real.[7] Even so, there may be a case for lower taxes on wine relative to other alcoholic beverages. Tollison and Wagner (1991, 31–32), using data on DUI arrests from the U.S. Department of Justice (1988) and assuming that drunk-driving accidents are proportional to DUI arrests, estimated that only 9 percent of the social costs of drunk driving can be attributed to wine. Using the NIAAA's vehicular-accidents figure of $3.3 billion for 1983, Tollison and Wagner's calculation would put wine's share of the total at $297 million or less—considerably *less* than the total tax revenues collected by federal and state governments from wine sales.

While the costs imposed on society by alcohol abuse would be defended by no one, studies such as Tollison and Wagner's suggest that the standard social-cost estimates for alcohol are grossly exaggerated.[8] Moreover, there are a number of reasons why even prohibitive taxation would probably not reduce the social costs that can be legitimately credited to alcohol (principally those related to drunk driving). The psychophysiological forces that create addictions to alcohol generally (and to particular types of alcohol) are not fully understood. A ban on alcohol, which was tried before and did not work (Thornton 1991), would not have the desired effects but would likely either drive production and consumption underground or cause some individuals to shift to other forms of antisocial behavior—illicit drugs, for example. In their study of beverage choice, Klatsky et al. (1990, 1287) note that "presumably the total psychosocial situation of an individual plays a dominant role in usual choice of beverage." That assessment would apply, in all likelihood, to all types of beverages, alcoholic and nonalcoholic alike, and to addictive behavior generally.[9]

An important point relates to the relative social costs of wine drinking and to the relevance of the tax structure to any social costs that are attributable to wine. We discuss the latter question in the following section of this chapter, but it is important to note that wine drinking has been found to have positive effects, which must modify any cost assessment. In their study of the demographics of alcohol drinkers, a study that replicates an earlier one by Cahalan et al. (1969), Klatsky et al. (1990, 1287, 1279) note that "the traits of persons who prefer wine are, in general, most favorable to health" and that "persons who prefer wine are likely to be women, temperate, young or middle-aged, non-smokers, better educated and free of symptoms or risk of illness."

The personality and demographic profiles of wine drinkers are indicative of healthy lifestyles, and positive medical benefits are increasingly associated with wine drinking. Well-designed scientific studies suggest that the organic components present in wine are associated with reduced heart disease risk (Frankel et al. 1993), reduced stress (Klein and Pittman 1993), and other health benefits (Fitzpatrick et al. 1993). Such benefits must be set against costs in the case of wine consumption. Indeed, evidence is accumulating that the moderate consumers of *any* alcoholic beverage "have above-average health—above the average of both abusers and nondrinkers alike" (Heien 1996, 62).

Clearly, the social costs of alcohol use are overstated. Moreover, the *relative* tax treatment of various types of alcoholic beverages is an important issue in dealing with the social costs that do in fact exist. The importance of this issue becomes apparent when we consider the effect of tax biases on consumption within the alcoholic-beverage sector. We therefore ask the following question: Does the current tax structure influence consumption in such a way as to exacerbate the "market failure" associated with alcohol abuse? In order to study this question more fully, we consider the impact of alcohol taxation with a case study of the federal excise tax increase imposed in 1991.

### IV. The 1991 Alcohol Excise Tax Increase:
### Distributional Effects

Of primary concern when considering any tax measure are its revenue potential and its social-welfare effects. New selective excise taxes on alcohol must act upon sufficiently inelastic demands in order to be effective as revenue sources. But our discussion of the social costs of alcohol consumption and the relative contribution of wine to such costs indicates that an analysis of the *relative* consumption effects and efficiency of taxes within the broader "alcohol" category is also of critical importance in assessing the actual welfare costs of selective taxes.

To this end, we analyzed the increase in the federal excise tax on alcoholic beverages that went into effect on 1 January 1991. This new tax schedule, contained in title XI of the Omnibus Budget Reconciliation Act of 1990, marked the first federal excise tax increases on beer and wine since November 1951, although there was a small increase in the liquor tax in 1985. As a result of inflation during this period, federal excise tax rates had maintained only about 20 percent of their real values. The 1991 tax increases temporarily reversed this long-term trend: the real value of the liquor excise was restored to its 1989 value, and the beer tax to its 1978 value. The increase in the tax on wine was, however, more than enough to restore its 1951 value.

The changes in the tax schedule are summarized in table 11.1. Because the brunt of the 1991 tax increase fell on wine, it is expected that wine became more expensive *relative* to beer and liquor even though wine taxes were very much lower from the outset.[10] Due to the resulting substitution effects among alcoholic beverages, the tax increase would be expected to lead to increased consumption of beer and liquor relative to wine. If such substitution effects are significant, then revenue projections that assume no cross-substitution among alcoholic-beverage groups would be misleading. The impact of changing relative tax rates on consumption shares in the alcoholic-beverages sector, along with the implications of the changes in consumption patterns for the (alleged) social goals of such taxation, is the focus of the following analysis.

To capture shifting revenue and social effects, we analyzed the impact of the federal excise tax increase on the consumption of wine. The model we employ attempts to account for variables other than tax rates that are likely to affect wine consumption as a share of total alcoholic-beverage consumption. Among such factors, we include the price of wine, as well as the prices of substitutes and per capita income. As we are attempting to isolate the effects of changes in federal excise tax rates, individual states' tax rates are assumed to remain unchanged and are not included in our model. The empirical model can be stated as follows:

**TABLE 11.1**
**Federal Excise Tax Rates**

|  | Before January 1991 | Since January 1991 |
|---|---|---|
| Liquor* | $12.50 | $13.50 |
| Beer** | 9.00 | 18.00 |
| Wine*** | 0.17 | 1.07 |

   * Rate is given per proof gallon. A proof gallon contains 50% alcohol by volume.
   ** Quoted rate is per barrel of 31 gallons.
   *** Rate quoted is applicable per gallon for wines that do not exceed 14% alcohol by volume.

$$WINESHARE = \beta_1 + \beta_2 NPWINE + \beta_3 PBEER + \beta_4 PLIQ + \beta_5 PERINC + \beta_6 WINETAX,$$

where the variables are defined as follows:

$WINESHARE$ = per capita wine consumption as a share of total alcohol consumption

$NPWINE$ = the retail price of wine net of federal excise taxes

$PBEER$ = the retail price of beer

$PLIQ$ = the retail price of liquor

$PERINC$ = per capita income

$WINETAX$ = the federal excise tax on the wine product surveyed

The regression model was estimated using a data set comprised of observations from forty-six states.[11] The variables employed were obtained for the calendar years 1988, 1989, and 1992. The years 1990 and 1991 were omitted in order to eliminate spillover effects associated with short-run adjustments in consumption patterns attributable to expectations regarding the tax hike, along with pre-adjustment based on the rational-addictions theory. Theoretical expectations concerning the influence of the explanatory variables on the dependent variable include positive relationships for all the variables except $NPWINE$ and $WINETAX$, which are expected to be inversely related to $WINESHARE$.

*Per Capita Wine Consumption.* Estimates were obtained from annual reports published by the Distilled Spirits Council of the United States (DISCUS).

*Retail Price of Wine.* The *ACCRA Cost of Living Index,* published on a quarterly basis by the American Chamber of Commerce Researchers Association (ACCRA), provides a comprehensive survey of the prices of fifty-nine items in almost 300 U.S. cities. Prices were averaged for all sources reporting within a particular metropolitan or urban area. The survey specifies the price of a 1.5-liter bottle of Gallo Sauvignon Blanc. Quarterly price reports from 1988, 1989, and 1992 were averaged to yield one observation for each state for each year.[12] *NPWINE,* price net of federal excise taxes, is used along with *WINETAX* in order to isolate the effect of the tax increase on wine consumption. In line with the first law of demand, *NPWINE* is expected to have a negative effect on *WINESHARE.*

**Retail Price of Beer.** Prices of relatively close substitutes for wine are expected to influence the demand for wine. The price of beer is included in the model to account for this influence. Prices for a six-pack of Budweiser beer were taken from the *ACCRA Cost of Living Index.*

**Retail Price of Liquor.** Price quotes for a 750-milliliter bottle of J&B Scotch were obtained from the ACCRA report cited above, and the same reporting methods were employed. Assuming that wine and liquor are substitutes, *PLIQ* is expected to have a positive relationship with wine consumption.

**Per Capita Income.** Personal per capita income estimates, measured in dollars, were obtained from various issues of *Survey of Current Business* (May 1992, 69–87; May 1993, 67–87). Expectations are that wine is a normal good and, therefore, that *PERINC* will exhibit a positive relationship with wine consumption.

**Federal Excise Taxes on Wine.** A summary of the federal excise tax schedule for wine was obtained from DISCUS. From this schedule, the per unit tax applicable to a 1.5-liter bottle of Gallo Sauvignon Blanc (which contains 11 percent alcohol by volume) was calculated for the period prior to the tax increase as well as for the period following the tax increase. The tax per 1.5-liter bottle increased from \$0.07 in 1989 to \$0.42 in 1991, a 500 percent increase. An important point is that the tax hike did not fall as heavily on beer and liquor in percentage terms. Given that the price of wine rose relative to its substitutes following the tax increase, a negative relationship is posited between *WINETAX* and *WINESHARE.*

In order to estimate the magnitude of the hypothesized substitutions among alcoholic beverages resulting from the tax hike, a regression model was also specified to explain cross-state variations in beer consumption as a share of total alcoholic-beverage consumption. The same variables were employed as in the *WINESHARE* equation, with the exception of *BEERTAX* being substituted for *WINETAX.* The empirical model, including expected signs of the variables, is as follows:

$$\overset{(+)}{} \quad \overset{(?)}{} \quad \overset{(+)}{} \quad \overset{(+)}{} \quad \overset{(?)}{}$$
$$BEERSHARE = \beta_1 + \beta_2 PWINE + \beta_3 NPBEER + \beta_4 PLIQ + \beta_5 PERINC + \beta_6 BEERTAX$$

Generally speaking, the same expectations as those in the previous model hold regarding the relationships between the explanatory variables and *BEERSHARE.* A price for beer net of federal excise taxes, *NPBEER,* is substituted for *PBEER* in the second equation. *BEERTAX,* as computed for a six-pack of Budweiser, doubled from \$0.16 in 1989 to \$0.32 in 1991. In line with the hypothesized substitution away from wine due to its being disproportionately targeted by the federal excise tax increase, expectations are reserved

**TABLE 11.2**
**OLS Regression for *LWINESHARE***

| Regressors | Coefficient Estimates | t-ratio |
|---|---|---|
| Intercept | −22.760 | −11.947 |
| LNPWINE | −0.5842 | −3.181** |
| LPBEER | 0.3478 | 1.337 |
| LPLIQ | 0.5167 | 1.921*** |
| LPERINC | 1.9186 | 11.356* |
| LWINETAX | −0.0005 | −6.622* |

n = 46 states x 3 years = 138; R-squared = .571; D-W statistic = 1.919·
Significance: * = .001 level; ** = .01; *** = .1

**TABLE 11.3**
**OLS Regression for *LBEERSHARE***

| Regressors | Coefficient Estimates | t-ratio |
|---|---|---|
| Intercept | 1.9569 | 9.735* |
| LPWINE | 0.0340 | 1.703*** |
| LNPBEER | −0.0375 | −1.459 |
| LPLIQ | −0.0254 | −0.903 |
| LPERINC | −0.2051 | −11.582* |
| LBEERTAX | 0.0005 | 7.013* |

n = 138; R-squared = .578; D-W statistic = 1.986
Significance: * = .001 level; ** = .01; *** = .1

regarding the relationships between variables affecting beer prices and the dependent variable, beer consumption. The aim of the analysis is to isolate the impact of a tax-induced price change on the relative consumption shares of beer, wine, and liquor. The model is estimated in log-linear form in order to obtain slope coefficients that gauge the ceteris paribus elasticities of the dependent variables with respect to the explanatory variables.

Ordinary Least Squares (OLS) regression analysis yielded the results in tables 11.2 and 11.3. The signs on the estimated regression coefficients are as expected.

Wine consumption has an own-price elasticity of −0.58, and positive cross-price elasticities with beer and liquor indicate that the three types of alcoholic beverages are relatively good substitutes. Several points concerning the cross-price elasticities are worth noting. The OLS estimates reveal that both beer and wine prices are positively related to *WINESHARE*, although only liquor prices are statistically significant at the 10 percent level. (A reversal of these results is obtained in a more elaborate test discussed below.) Furthermore, a positive income elasticity of 1.92 indicates that wine is a normal good; in other words, wine consumption rises along with increases in per capita income. As expected, the tax increase had a negative impact on *WINESHARE,* meaning that consumption shifted away from wine and in favor of other alcoholic beverages following the implementation of the new federal excise tax structure in 1991.[13]

The results of estimating the *BEERSHARE* model by OLS regression appear in table 11.3. Although the cross-price elasticities of liquor are negative and wine are positive, only wine prices attain statistical significance in the *BEERSHARE* regression. The negative coefficient on *PERINC* implies that beer is an income-inferior good. Of some concern is the positive coefficient on the tax variable, which implies that beer's share of total consumption rises with increases in the tax rate on beer. This result would be disturbing if we were seeking to explain the effect of an increase in the beer tax on beer consumption in isolation from other effects. However, in the present analysis, we are interested in disentangling the tax-induced reallocation of consumption shares among alcoholic beverages. Given the disproportionate burden imposed on wine by the 1991 tax increase, consumers would be expected to shift their purchases away from wine and toward other alcoholic beverages. The results of the *BEERSHARE* model appear to be in accord with this expectation.

However, given that the *SHARE* variables are most likely determined simultaneously with our price variables, it became necessary to correct for possible simultaneous equations bias in the previous estimates by employing Two-Stage Least Squares (2SLS) regression. The second-stage estimates obtained from applying 2SLS regression to the *WINESHARE* and *BEERSHARE* models are reported in tables 11.4 and 11.5.

The 2SLS estimation of *WINESHARE* and *BEERSHARE* produced even more precise coefficient estimates than those obtained with OLS. In particular, the two-stage estimates show highly significant and positive relationships between *WINESHARE* (*BEERSHARE*) and the price of beer (wine). These results indicate that beer is highly substitutable for wine, a finding

**TABLE 11.4**
**2SLS Regression for *LWINESHARE***

| Regressors | Coefficient Estimates | T-ratio |
|---|---|---|
| Intercept | −20.929 | −9.981* |
| LNPWINE | −0.7715 | −3.846* |
| LPBEER | 1.1147 | 3.497* |
| LPLIQ | −0.0798 | −0.252 |
| LPERINC | 1.8111 | 9.860* |
| LWINETAX | −0.0009 | −7.964* |

n = 138; R-squared = .489; D-W statistic = 1.861
Significance: * = .001 level; ** = .01; *** = .1

**TABLE 11.5**
**2SLS Regression for *LBEERSHARE***

| Regressors | Coefficient Estimates | T-ratio |
|------------|----------------------|---------|
| Intercept | 1.7657 | 8.038* |
| LPWINE | 0.0525 | 2.430** |
| LNPBEER | –0.1071 | –3.445* |
| LPLIQ | 0.0350 | 1.067 |
| LPERINC | –0.1956 | –10.256* |
| LBEERTAX | 0.0008 | 8.110* |

n = 138; R-squared = .506; D-W statistic = 1.892
Significance: * = .001 level; ** = .05; *** = .1

which may, as we shall argue, have important implications for the social costs attributable to alcohol consumption. These cross-price elasticities are in contrast to the insignificant relationships (one negative, one positive) between *WINESHARE* and *BEERSHARE* and the price of liquor (*PLIQ*).[14]

Other aspects of these results are equally interesting. The negative coefficient on *WINETAX* in table 11.4 can be interpreted to mean that the 1991 federal excise tax increase contributed to a shift in consumption away from wine and toward beer and liquor. The 2SLS estimates of the *BEERSHARE* equation shown in table 11.5 reinforce this conclusion. The negative coefficient on *PERINC* suggests that beer is an inferior good, while the positive coefficient on *BEERTAX* again shows substitution effects working to rearrange consumption shares in the alcoholic-beverage market. It is worth reiterating in this regard that although the 1991 tax increase affected beer prices, wine bore a disproportionate share of the tax increase. As wine became more expensive relative to beer and liquor, consumption shifted away from wine. Given that total alcoholic-beverage consumption consists of beer, wine, and liquor, a decrease in the consumption share of one beverage implies an increase in one or both of the others. The substitution effect appears to override the income effect associated with higher beer prices, resulting in a positive relationship between the excise tax and consumption of beer. Indeed, in terms of the *retail* market, beer sales increased in 1990, reaching a peak from which they fell slightly in 1991 and then again in 1992. By contrast, sales of wine and spirits remained roughly constant over the same period.

## V. Empirical Implications

Our evidence from the most recent increase in the federal excise tax on alcohol suggests caution in the future applications of such taxation methods for at least two reasons. First, questions of equity and efficiency aside, the ability of excise taxes to provide new revenues is problematical. Second, the distributional effects of alcohol taxes have important implications for the magnitude of any social costs actually generated by alcohol consumption. Consider each of these issues with reference to our empirical results.

### Equity, Efficiency, and Revenue Considerations

Recourse to selective excises as instruments of public finance ignores the efficiency and equity effects of such taxes. In this chapter we have reiterated the long-known point that excise taxes in general and alcohol taxes in particular tend to be highly regressive. Selective excise taxes—especially those applied to goods consumed disproportionately by low-income individuals—single out particular groups of people to be taxed simply because of differences in tastes and preferences for particular bundles of goods and services. All excises, including those levied on all kinds of alcoholic beverages, are regressive and create inequities in the tax structure. Tobacco products and alcoholic beverages are selected as special objects of taxation because of their (supposed) ability to generate revenue at minimal social cost. A growing literature (e.g., Becker et al. 1991) suggests, however, that the long-run elasticities for smoking, heavy drinking, and gambling might be sizable and much larger than short-run elasticities. Such estimates, if pertinent to alcohol in general, would raise important questions about relying heavily on selective tax revenue as a predictable source of government finance.[15]

Our results suggest that tax revenues from wine and beer are not dependable sources of revenue at the federal level. To be sure, the estimated short-run price elasticities for WINESHARE and BEERSHARE are less than 1.0. The WINESHARE elasticity is between –0.58 and –0.77 in our alternative formulations. Short-run BEERSHARE elasticities are even lower, ranging from –0.03 to –0.10 in the OLS and 2SLS formulations, respectively. Elasticities of such magnitudes would undoubtedly produce revenue increases, but long-run elasticities calculated from our regression estimates suggest that alcohol taxes may not be a reliable revenue source. In additional empirical work not reproduced here, we calculated simultaneous short-run and long-run elasticities for our WINESHARE equation for 1989–92, and found long-run share elasticities that were on the order of ten times the corresponding short-run elasticities. These values, while tentative, are in full accordance with those reported in the literature on addictions and related work. Elasticity estimates of this magnitude should, at the very least, give pause to governments who would count on taxes on wine or other alcoholic beverages as steadfast sources of revenue.[16]

### The Social-Cost Issue

The rationale for taxing alcohol consumption has even deeper roots than the revenue-raising rationale put forth in the contemporary literature. Such taxes, as we have discussed in this chapter, have been characterized as user fees or corrective taxes. We have analyzed the validity of this characterization by employing the logic of Tollison and Wagner (1991). Although a clear social cost exists in the case of property damage, injuries, and deaths due to drunk driving, the case for basing corrective taxation on production losses, absenteeism, or medical care of alcohol users is weak or nonexistent. At any rate, the taxation of alcohol (in general) on the basis of social costs does not carry much weight.

For these reasons, new taxes on alcohol cannot be advocated as a trustworthy tool in financing health care reform or any other government venture. *Lower taxes* are in fact called for when the true total social costs of drinking are assessed. But while the taxation of alcohol as a user fee carries little appeal from an economic perspective, the relative tax structure on *kinds* of alcohol has important implications for the magnitude of any social cost that *might* be attributed to alcohol. Our proposition is the following: *If wine consumption imposes a disproportionately lower cost on society in terms of lost life and property due to drunk driving, and if new tax levies fall disproportionately on wine, then an alternative tax structure could be devised that would raise the same amount of revenue at a lower social cost.*

Cross-price elasticity estimates indicate a good deal of substitutability between types of alcohol, especially between beer and wine. This point has special relevance for the drunk-driving component of social costs. In their important study of the relation between beverage preference and drinking-driving violators, psychologists Berger and Snortum (1985, 235) note the following:

> The picture that emerges is one of beer drinkers differing markedly from wine drinkers on many dimensions, with spirits drinkers generally falling between. Beer drinkers typically drink to higher levels of intoxication, are less likely to express moral objections to driving after drinking and report much higher DWI rates than the other two groups.

Their research further shows "wine drinkers to be the most responsible of the three beverage groups in their attitudes and behavior concerning drinking and driving" (p. 238).[17] Our estimates suggest that public-policy makers should reexamine the taxation of wine generally and the relative taxation of wine vis-à-vis other alcoholic beverages in particular. This is especially so if the goal of corrective taxation is to minimize social costs where *actual* social costs are incurred.

## Conclusions

The selective tax increase on alcoholic beverages contained in the Omnibus Reconciliation Act of 1990 may be used to gauge the relative impacts on consumption. Clearly, the form and rate of taxation levied on particular kinds of alcohol have important implications for both the revenues raised and the social costs generated by the new tax structure. The brunt of the federal excise tax increase fell on wine, making it more expensive relative to beer and liquor. Wine taxes increased more than fivefold, whereas beer taxes only doubled and liquor taxes rose by less than 10 percent. As wine became relatively more expensive, the predictable substitution effects took place. The responses of consumers to the tax increase suggest that high and significant cross-price elasticities exist between kinds of alcoholic beverages, particularly between wine and beer.

Naturally, such relative consumption shifts have important revenue implications. With long-run price elasticities for wine estimated at between 1.2 and 1.6 (Tsolakis et al. 1983), total revenues from the differential tax on alcohol imposed in 1991 may well decline in the future. This result would of course depend on a number of factors, including relative share changes (cross-price elasticities), changes in state taxes, and so on. But a critical point relating to social costs is that a declining share of wine consumption in overall alcohol use may, according to estimates of wine's impact on social cost, actually exacerbate any earlier estimated social costs that apply to alcohol consumption generally. A reduction in the share of the total alcohol market accounted for by wine (estimated at about 40 percent) will, *if* estimates of the social costs of consuming *types* of alcoholic beverages are anywhere near correct, create *greater* losses of property and human life from drunk driving. This conclusion is strengthened when any other social benefits (including the health benefits now recognized to be associated with alcohol consumption) are taken into account.

At all odds, selective excise taxes, aside from being unpredictable and unreliable forms of government finance, are inefficient and inequitable. The corrective tax argument does not apply to alcohol (see chapter 10). The application of differential excise tax rates to alcoholic beverages makes even less sense. We argue that taxes of the form implemented in the tax increase of 1991 may actually be counterproductive if redressing social costs is the aim of public policy.

## Notes

1. However, it is worth noting that where demand elasticities are assumed to be low, estimates of the welfare cost of a tax must take into account the consumption effects observed in markets indirectly affected by the tax.
2. Selective taxes may be related to the rational-addictions model, which has important implications for demand elasticities. We do not attempt to include these considerations in the present study. See Becker and Murphy (1988) and the associated literature that article has spawned, including Becker et al. (1991).
3. In their studies of excises for the years 1984 and 1989, Ekelund and Long (1989, 1991) found general regressivity for alcohol and other selective taxes. Utilizing

expenditure patterns of rural and urban consumers, they showed that low-income urban consumers paid the highest proportion of excises on alcohol as a class. The type of alcohol consumed most in rural areas probably differs from the type consumed most in urban areas, but data limitations prohibited a study of rural-urban incidence by kind of alcohol. Anecdotally, the incidence of the beer tax would probably fall heaviest on rural consumers, while the incidence of the wine tax would probably fall heaviest on urban dwellers. We know of no formal study that yields these conclusions, however.

4. Generalizing the Dupuit taxation theorem from partial to general equilibrium analysis, Harold Hotelling (1938) demonstrated that excise taxes are economically inefficient compared to lump-sum taxes raising the same revenue.

5. This figure may be too high, though. For instance, 1995 estimates of retail sales of alcoholic beverages were: distilled liquor, $32.7 billion; beer, $51.6 billion; and wine, $12.05 billion (personal communication). Wine sales would account for approximately 12.5 percent of the total on this basis.

6. Of course, not all medical costs are paid directly or through private insurers. An important share is provided by government in the form of Medicare to retirees or Medicaid to the indigent. Typical studies link these expenditures to social costs of alcohol, without very much foundation in fact.

7. Tollison and Wagner suggest a variety of alternative solutions. Higher legal penalties and the posting of bonds are two possibilities.

8. In a relevant study on smoking and absenteeism, Ault et al. (1991) found that smokers miss no more work than nonsmokers *because they smoke*. Rather, smokers tend to be younger, heavier drinkers, employed in blue-collar jobs, and so on— characteristics that make them more likely to miss work regardless of whether or not they smoke.

9. For additional criticisms of the methodology used to estimate the external costs of alcohol consumption, see Heien and Pittman (1989) and Heien (1996).

10. Although wine taxes were increased relatively more than those on beer and liquor in 1991, it is nevertheless true that wine is still taxed at a lower rate than other alcoholic beverages. Wine taxes are currently about 28.3 cents per liter. This represents approximately 5.5 percent of the current average retail price of wine. A similar calculation indicates that beer taxes represent about 8.8 percent of the retail price, and liquor taxes are higher yet.

11. Alcohol price data were available for only forty-six states.

12. The prices reported are exclusive of state and local sales taxes but not state excise taxes.

13. Part of this reduction in wine consumption may have been due to the declining popularity (and lower sales) of wine coolers over this period. The data do not allow us to determine the magnitude of this "taste" effect, though.

14. The insignificant relationship observed between our dependent variables and the price of liquor may be attributable to the small change in the federal excise tax on liquor relative to that imposed on other sectors. The impact of liquor prices may also have been muted by the secular decline in the consumption of spirits (28 percent over the past 15 years).

15. It is worth noting that if long-run elasticity prevails, state governments must face revenue *reductions* in response to additional federal selective taxes. In the past many states have "retaliated" by imposing new taxes of their own in response to the new federal tax. This policy may backfire in a number of respects. Shughart and Tollison (1991) provide a case in point with their analysis of cigarette taxation. They find that when governments compete for tax revenues from the same commodities, overtaxation is likely to result. When cross-border ca-

sual smuggling is taken into account, overenthusiastic revenue projections by state revenue seekers may be much inflated. See, for example, Saba et al. (1995).
16.  Calculations of short-run and long-run elasticities are not reported in this chapter but are available from the authors upon request.
17.  More recent evidence (Klatsky and Armstrong 1993) suggests that the relative risk of dying in a motor vehicle accident is highest for liquor drinkers, then wine drinkers, then beer drinkers.

## References

Adrian, Manuella. 1988. "Social Costs of Alcohol." *Canadian Journal of Public Health* 79 (September/October): 316–22.
American Chamber of Commerce Researchers Association (ACCRA). 1988, 1989, and 1992. *ACCRA Cost of Living Index.* Quarterly reports. Alexandria, Va.
Ault, Richard W., Robert B. Ekelund, Jr., John D. Jackson, Richard S. Saba, and David S. Saurman. 1991. "Smoking and Absenteeism." *Applied Economics* 23:743–54.
Becker, Gary S., Michael Grossman, and Kevin M. Murphy. 1991. "Rational Addiction and the Effect of Price on Consumption." *American Economic Review Papers and Proceedings* 81 (May): 237–41.
Becker, Gary S., and Kevin M. Murphy. 1988. "A Theory of Rational Addiction." *Journal of Political Economy* 96 (August): 675–700.
Beer Institute. 1994. *Brewer's Almanac 1994: The Brewing Industry in the United States.* Washington, D.C.
Berger, Dale E., and John R. Snortum. 1985. "Alcoholic Beverage Preferences of Drinking-Driving Violators." *Journal of Studies on Alcohol* 46:232–39.
Boyd, Roy, and Barry J. Seldon. 1991. "Revenue and Land-Use Effects of Proposed Changes in Sin Taxes: A General Equilibrium Perspective." *Land Economics* 67 (August): 365–74.
Cahalan, D., I. H. Cisin, and H. M. Crossley. 1969. *American Drinking Practices: A National Study of Drinking Behaviour and Attitudes.* Monograph No. 6. New Brunswick, N.J.: Rutgers Center of Alcohol Studies.
Clements, Kenneth W., and Lester W. Johnson. 1983. "The Demand for Beer, Wine, and Spirits: A Systemwide Analysis." *Journal of Business* 56 (July): 273–304.
Cook, Philip J., and George Tauchen. 1982. "The Effect of Liquor Taxes on Heavy Drinking." *Bell Journal of Economics* 13 (Autumn): 379–90.
Distilled Spirits Council of the United States (DISCUS). Various publications. Washington, D.C.
Duffy, M. 1983. "The Demand for Alcoholic Drink in the United Kingdom." *Applied Economics* 15 (February): 125–40.
Dupuit, Jules. [1844] 1952. "On the Measurement of the Utility of Public Works." Translated by R. H. Barback from the *Annales des Ponts et Chaussees,* 2nd ser., 7 (1844) in the *International Economic Papers,* no. 2. Reprint, London: Macmillan.
Ekelund, Robert B., Jr., and James Long. 1989. *The Impact of Excise Taxes on Rural Americans.* Washington, D.C.: American Agriculture Movement.
———. 1991. *Consumer Excise Taxes and the Rural Taxpayer: Losing Ground in the '80s and '90s?* Washington, D.C.: American Agriculture Movement.
Fitzpatrick, David F., Steven L. Hirschfield, and Ronald G. Coffey. 1993. "Endothelium-Dependent Vasorelaxing Activity of Wine and Other Grape Products." *American Journal of Physiology* 265 (August, pt. 2): 774–78.

Frankel, E. N., A. L. Waterhouse, and J. E. Kinsella. 1993. "Inhibition of Human LDL Oxidation by Resveratrol." *Lancet,* North American Edition 341 (24 April): 1103–4.

Heien, Dale M. 1996. "Do Drinkers Earn Less?" *Southern Economic Journal* 63 (July): 60–68.

Heien, Dale M., and David J. Pittman. 1989. "The Economic Costs of Alcohol Abuse: An Assessment of Current Methods and Estimates." *Journal of Studies on Alcohol* 50 (November): 567–79.

Hotelling, Harold. 1938. "The General Welfare in Relation to Problems of Taxation and Railway and Utility Rates." *Econometrica* 6 (July): 242–69.

Klatsky, Arthur L., and Mary Anne Armstrong. 1993. "Alcohol Use, Other Traits, and Risk of Unnatural Death: A Prospective Study." *Alcoholism: Clinical and Experimental Research* 17:1156–62.

Klatsky, Arthur L., Mary Anne Armstrong, and Harold Kipp. 1990. "Correlates of Alcoholic Beverage Preference: Traits of Persons Who Choose Wine, Liquor or Beer." *British Journal of Addiction* 85:1279–89.

Klein, Hugh, and David J. Pittman. 1993. "The Relationship Between Emotional State and Alcohol Consumption." *International Journal of Addictions* 28:59–67.

Manning, Willard G., Emmett B. Keeler, and Joseph P. Newhouse. 1989. "The Taxes of Sin." *Journal of the American Medical Association* 261 (17 March): 1604–9.

Phares, Donald. 1980. *Who Pays State and Local Taxes?* Cambridge, Mass.: Oelgeschlager, Gunn & Hain.

Pogue, Thomas F., and Larry G. Sgontz. 1989. "Taxing to Control Social Costs." *American Economic Review* 79 (March): 235–43.

Saba, Richard P., T. Randolph Beard, Robert B. Ekelund, Jr., and Rand W. Ressler. 1995. "Estimating Border Crossing Demands: Methodology and an Application to Casual Smuggling of Cigarettes." *Economic Inquiry* 33 (2): 189–202.

Shughart, William F. II, and Robert D. Tollison. 1991. "Fiscal Federalism and the Laffer Curve." *Journal of Public Finance and Public Choice* 1:21–28.

Suits, Daniel B. 1977. "Measurement of Tax Progressivity." *American Economic Review* 67 (September): 747–52.

Thornton, Mark. 1991. *The Economics of Prohibition.* Salt Lake City: University of Utah Press.

Tollison, Robert D., and Richard E. Wagner. 1991. *Claims About the Social Cost of Wine: An Assessment.* Prepared for the National Wine Coalition.

Tsolakis, D. 1983. "Taxation and the Consumption of Wine." *Review of Marketing and Agricultural Economics* 51 (August): 155–63.

Tsolakis, D., P. Riethmuller, and G. Watts. 1983. "The Demand for Wine and Beer." *Review of Marketing and Agricultural Economics* 51 (August): 131–53.

U.S. Bureau of the Census. 1993. *Statistical Abstract of the United States.* Washington, D.C.: U.S. Government Printing Office.

U.S. Department of Justice. 1988. *Drunk Driving.* Bureau of Justice Statistics special report.

White, G. B. 1991. "Recent Developments in Wine Markets in the United States." In *Wine Economy,* edited by E. P. Botos. New York: Elsevier.

Wine Institute. Various publications.

# 12

# Bordering on Chaos:
# Fiscal Federalism and Excise Taxes

*Richard K. Vedder*

The federal nature of the United States has important implications for excise taxation. At this writing, a significant proportion of the so-called sin taxes are levied by state and local governments. Yet large percentages of the populations of many states live within short distances of other states, and some live near Canada or Mexico. Given the lack of major barriers to interstate commerce incorporated in the U.S. Constitution, it is possible for millions of Americans to buy goods and services in other jurisdictions. A jurisdiction that heavily taxes, say, cigarettes, will pay a price in lost business to jurisdictions where taxes are less onerous.[1]

There are numerous examples where interstate excise tax differentials are substantial. To illustrate, the state of Kentucky imposes only modest taxes on cigarettes (three cents a pack), but its neighbors to the north all tax cigarettes at least five times as much. For example, Ohio imposes taxes that are eight times higher than those in Kentucky, a difference of over twenty cents a pack. Until recently, consumers living in areas of the United States bordering Canada paid dramatically lower cigarette taxes than their Canadian neighbors.

The ability to cross borders to avoid high excise taxation has impacted immensely on human behavior. Canada, with taxes on cigarettes several times those of any American state, found that its citizens were traveling to the United States in such large numbers to buy cigarettes that sales losses were having a devastating impact on Canadian businesses and, in fact, retarding excise tax revenues. These revenue losses actually led the government to reduce cigarette excise taxation. The same cross-border phenomenon is common within the United States.

---

The author was assisted in the preparation of this study by Virin K. Vedder.

## The Economics of Cross-Border Effects of Excise Taxation

Economists assume typically that individuals attempt to maximize their utility, or satisfaction in life, subject to the constraints imposed by limited resources (income). A person buying a standardized product, say, cigarettes, would buy that product at the lowest price existing anywhere in the world *if there were absolutely no costs associated with buying goods in different locales*. In reality, of course, there are several forms of what we generally call "transaction costs," expenses associated with the purchasing of goods.

In the absence of transaction costs, if a given brand of cigarettes cost $1.50 in Paris and $1.55 in Chicago, the Chicagoan would buy his or her cigarettes in Paris. The empirical evidence, of course, is that few Chicagoans buy their cigarettes in Paris or, for that matter, at locations even 50 miles away. Why? Simply because the costs of obtaining cigarettes by traveling long distances exceed the savings from lower prices on cigarettes elsewhere.

People will buy their cigarettes at the location offering the lowest price, but price includes not only the market price of the good, but also the transaction costs. A major component of these transaction costs is the cost of transportation. Buying gasoline in Paris, for example, would not be economical, simply because the cost of transporting a gallon of gas from Paris to the United States is very high in relation to the value of the product. However, it might make sense to fly to Russia to buy a $30,000.00 fur coat, simply because the transportation costs associated with that transaction would be low in relation to the value of the product.

Yet transportation costs are only one component of transaction costs. The late economist George Stigler won the Nobel Prize in part for his work pointing out the importance of information costs (Stigler 1961). People likely do not know whether cigarettes are cheaper in Paris, and to acquire that information takes time and money. The cost of learning about bargains often is so great that people forgo them. Thus bread may sell for fifty-five cents a loaf at supermarket A but for fifty-one cents at supermarket B; aside from transportation costs, it simply is not worth spending half an hour scouring newspaper advertisements to find out where bread is cheapest, because the potential savings are measured in pennies or nickels, not dollars, and because people place some value on their own time. Time spent scouring for bargains in supermarkets is time not available to spend reading a favorite book, watching a television show, and so forth. People value their leisure.

In short, people will buy a product if the expected benefits exceed the expected costs. In order to maximize benefits, people will buy identical goods at the particular location that minimizes costs, where "costs" includes four components: the market asking price of the good, including taxes, and the three parts of transaction costs: transportation costs, information costs, and the cost of time.

Will people cross borders to buy products in a state imposing lower excise or sales taxes? The answer depends on several factors:

1. the extent of the tax-driven interstate price differential;
2. the cost of getting to and from the location selling the good;
3. the cost of learning about the alternative location, how to get there, and so forth;
4. the amount of time it takes to obtain the product; and
5. the probability that law enforcement officials in the home jurisdiction of the purchaser may try to intercept the goods and claim additional tax payments.

The last point requires some elaboration. Some states, in order to minimize revenue losses to lower-tax jurisdictions, employ revenue agents to attempt to stop the flow of what is, from a legal perspective, smuggling or bootlegging. For example, historically it has been common for revenue officials from the state of Virginia to stake out liquor stores in Washington, D.C., looking for purchasers with Virginia license plates, who are then followed to the state border. This is merely an interstate application of the international practice of having customs agents inspect incoming luggage of tourists to assure compliance with tax (tariff) laws.

Given the material size of these various costs of attempting to avoid taxes, why would anyone engage in much interstate movement of goods for tax avoidance reasons? For example, suppose the tax differential on a pack of cigarettes is twenty cents between two states (a relatively large differential). Surely the costs of going to another state to purchase a pack of cigarettes exceed twenty cents! Almost always, of course, that is true. However, a cigarette smoker who might buy one or two packs when shopping at home may buy five cartons when shopping in other states, since volume buying lowers the per pack transaction costs of out-of-state purchases.

Assume, for example, that the total costs associated with transactions (including the possibility of getting caught) amount to $5.00 per purchase, and that the *marginal* transaction costs beyond the first pack of cigarettes (or six-pack of beer) purchased are zero over a large range, a not unreasonable assumption. It costs no more time or gas money, and requires no more information, to buy five cartons than to buy one pack of cigarettes. The marginal benefit of shopping out of state may be a tax-induced price differential of twenty cents per pack of cigarettes. The marginal transaction cost of the first pack is $5.00, so buying one or two packs of cigarettes is uneconomical. However, it would pay to buy twenty-six packs or more because the total marginal benefits equal $5.20 ($0.20 times 26) or more, while the total marginal costs (falling entirely on the first pack purchased) equal $5.00.

The same principle, of course, applies to goods other than cigarettes. The sheer volume or weight of the commodity and some possibility of product deterioration over time suggest that for some products, marginal transaction costs rise beyond the first unit, thus limiting the incentive for bulk purchases. Hence, people who cross borders to save on motor fuel taxes seldom buy more than one tank of gasoline. Similarly, a purchaser of beer living in a small apartment might be reluctant to buy more than, say, five twelve-packs of beer, simply because of limited storage space, fear of theft, and so forth. Such considerations, along with liquidity constraints, keep even purchasers of cigarettes from buying enormous (say, 100-carton) quantities: at some point marginal transaction costs do rise above marginal benefits.[2]

To this point, the discussion has been concerned with individuals purchasing products for their own use. The possible financial advantages of large-volume cross-border purchases, however, opens the door for professional smuggling operations. Smugglers have to make the same marginal benefit–marginal cost calculation as individual cross-border purchasers, yet there are different dimensions on the cost side of the equation. Where large-volume smuggling operations exist, transportation costs usually become somewhat less important. The cost-of-getting-caught factor looms much larger, as the penalties are likely to involve felony charges, large fines, and possible incarceration. Legal expenses become a potentially significant cost item. Also, smugglers have an important problem (cost) of disposing of their illicit cargo to individuals who will sell the products at retail to ordinary citizens.

Until recently, interstate excise tax differentials have been modest enough that the rather high potential legal costs of smuggling overcame the potential revenue benefits for most potential black-market participants. That, however, is no longer the case in some jurisdictions. A semitrailer truck filled with cigarettes purchased legally in Kentucky or North Carolina (state and federal taxes paid) but transported into Pennsylvania should be able to evade at least $50,000.00 in taxes (I am assuming that a semitrailer can carry 20,000 cartons and that the tax advantage is at least $2.50 per carton). That is a sum large enough to induce some individuals into the business of illicit commerce in cigarettes. When per carton tax differentials were $1.00 or less, however, the revenue potential ($20,000.00 or less per semitrailer load) typically was not great enough to overcome potential costs.

## The Extent of Cross-Border Activity in the United States

All discussion of the relative benefits of cross-border transactions becomes moot if the transaction costs of such activity are high for virtually all Americans. While it is probably impossible to measure these transaction costs with precision for each American, there is considerable evidence that for millions of citizens, these costs are relatively low, suggesting that cross-border tax avoidance activity is a serious issue.[3]

Most transaction costs are positively related to distance. It costs more to transport a good 50 miles than it does to ship it 10 miles. Information on price and availability is more likely to be readily (cheaply) available for goods located a few miles away than for goods located 50 miles away. It is probably also true that a smuggler moving goods 10 miles is less likely to get caught than one transporting them hundreds of miles. Citizens will therefore engage in short-distance cross-border activity much more extensively than they will engage in long-distance transactions.

An important empirical question, then, is: What percentage of Americans live within close physical proximity to another tax jurisdiction? Because most excise taxes are levied by state and federal governments, the relevant borders are between states and nations. What percentage of Americans live near another state or nation?

To get an approximate answer to this question, I calculated for each state and the nation as a whole the proportion of the population living in counties that border another state or nation (see table 12.1). In a typical case of a border county, most individuals within that county live within 15 miles or so of the adjacent state or country. Assuming decent transportation access, this suggests that most of the residents are within a 20- or 25-minute drive of another major taxing jurisdiction.

There are exceptions, to be sure. California's San Bernardino County is huge, and most of its population lives a long distance from the Nevada border. Offsetting this, there are people living in nonborder counties within 20 minutes or so of another tax jurisdiction. In a few states, counties or cities have enacted their own cigarette taxes, creating intrastate border counties. A special problem exists where counties border on bodies of water that also have another state or nation bordering on them. Where the water distance to the adjacent state or nation is short (usually well under 10 miles) and highway maps indicate bridges across the water, I counted them as border counties.

With these caveats in mind, table 12.1 shows that three out of every eight Americans live in a border county. In some forty states, at least one-fourth of the population lives in a county adjacent to another state or nation; in a solid majority of jurisdictions, the proportion exceeds 40 percent. All told, more than 95,000,000 Americans (as of 1990) live in border counties. Thus the issue of cross-border tax activity is real and substantial.

Moreover, table 12.1 almost certainly understates the potential tax competition between jurisdictions. Probably millions of Americans living in nonborder counties work in border counties or even other states. Others travel frequently on business to other states, allowing them the opportunity to buy goods (e.g., cigarettes and liquor) that may be more lightly taxed. Additional millions live within reasonably close proximity to Indian reservations, where often they can buy cigarettes and other goods without paying state excise taxes. Adding these to the 38 or 39 percent of Americans living in border

## TABLE 12.1
### Percent of Population Living in Border Counties, 1990*

| State or District | Border County Population | Border County Population As % of Total Population |
|---|---|---|
| Alabama | 1,579,359 | 39.1% |
| Arizona | 1,252,353 | 34.2 |
| Arkansas | 987,499 | 42.0 |
| California | 5,710,348 | 19.2 |
| Colorado | 646,915 | 19.6 |
| Connecticut | 2,340,701 | 71.2 |
| Delaware | 666,168 | 100.0 |
| District of Columbia | 606,900 | 100.0 |
| Florida | 950,539 | 7.3 |
| Georgia | 1,696,404 | 26.2 |
| Idaho | 533,094 | 53.0 |
| Illinois | 7,904,369 | 69.2 |
| Indiana | 2,350,303 | 42.4 |
| Iowa | 959,351 | 34.5 |
| Kansas | 983,655 | 39.7 |
| Kentucky | 2,064,677 | 56.0 |
| Louisiana | 1,141,489 | 27.0 |
| Maine | 418,208 | 34.1 |
| Maryland | 3,985,566 | 83.4 |
| Massachusetts | 4,566,419 | 75.9 |
| Michigan | 2,954,653 | 31.8 |
| Minnesota | 1,159,371 | 26.5 |
| Mississippi | 993,698 | 38.6 |
| Missouri | 3,537,239 | 69.1 |
| Montana | 385,003 | 48.2 |
| Nebraska | 825,952 | 52.3 |
| Nevada | 1,128,619 | 94.0 |
| New Hampshire | 939,661 | 84.7 |
| New Jersey | 4,846,611 | 62.7 |
| New Mexico | 666,464 | 44.0 |
| New York | 7,572,233 | 42.1 |
| North Carolina | 2,060,727 | 31.1 |
| North Dakota | 323,635 | 50.7 |
| Ohio | 3,314,993 | 30.6 |
| Pennsylvania | 5,969,059 | 50.2 |
| Rhode Island | 1,003,464 | 100.0 |
| South Carolina | 1,553,278 | 44.5 |
| South Dakota | 465,205 | 66.8 |
| Tennessee | 2,541,835 | 52.1 |
| Texas | 2,620,473 | 15.4 |
| Utah | 289,087 | 16.8 |
| Vermont | 488,095 | 86.7 |
| Virginia | 3,806,414 | 61.2 |
| Washington | 1,159,558 | 23.8 |
| West Virginia | 952,316 | 53.1 |
| Wisconsin | 874,190 | 17.9 |
| Wyoming | 315,243 | 69.5 |
| **Contiguous U.S.** | **95,754,759** | **38.8** |

*Alaska and Hawaii do not have counties; some independent cities in some states (e.g., Virginia) were treated as if they are border counties.
Source: Author's calculations from U.S. Bureau of the Census data.

counties probably brings the total population with relatively easy access to other tax jurisdictions to roughly 50 percent of the U.S. population.

## Taxes and Variations in Interstate Cigarette Consumption

There is an enormous variation between states in per capita purchases of cigarettes on which state taxes have been paid (table 12.2).[4] Per capita annual tax-paid purchases of cigarettes in fiscal year 1991 ranged from fewer than 59 packs in Utah to well over double that—144 packs—in New Hampshire. Purchases are relatively high in the states with very low excise taxes (e.g., Kentucky and the Carolinas). Purchases are also high in some states along the Canadian border (e.g., New Hampshire, Vermont, and Maine), but low in states bordering Mexico (e.g., Arizona, New Mexico, California, and Texas). States with significant Indian reservations similarly tended to have relatively low levels of tax-paid purchases (e.g, Arizona and Oklahoma).[5]

To more systematically attempt to explain these wide variations in indicated purchases, I formulated a regression model to explain per capita cigarette purchases as a function of five independent (explanatory) variables. I hypothesized that the per capita volume of taxed cigarettes would be greater

1. the lower the state excise tax on cigarettes;[6]
2. the smaller the presence of Indian reservations in the state;[7]
3. the greater the average cigarette tax in bordering states or countries;[8]
4. the greater the importance of border activity, as measured by the percent of population living in a state's border counties or, alternatively (model 2), by the population living in border counties on *both* sides of the border as a percent of a state's population;[9] and
5. the lower the per capita income in the state.

Lower internal cigarette taxes should result in greater sales to out-of-state residents, as well as somewhat higher in-state sales resulting from lower overall cigarette prices. Access to Indian reservations should reduce taxed sales as residents shift their purchases to reservations for tax avoidance purposes. Previous studies have shown that the incidence of cigarette smoking is quantitatively greater among lower-income Americans.

Respecting the border variables, their impact depends in part on having a significant percentage of the population living on borders, and in part on the level of taxation in the border states. If taxes are high in bordering jurisdictions relative to the state in question, per capita sales should be increased by the in-migration of out-of-state smokers.

The results of estimating two variants of the regression model are presented in table 12.3. The results are relatively robust. All the variables behave as expected, and all but one are statistically significant at the 1 percent level

**TABLE 12.2**
**Estimated Per Capita Purchases of Cigarette Packages, FY 1991\***

| State or District | Per Capita Cigarette Packages |
|---|---|
| Alabama | 103.2 |
| Arizona | 83.1 |
| Arkansas | 126.2 |
| California | 72.5 |
| Colorado | 92.8 |
| Connecticut | 87.4 |
| Delaware | 119.1 |
| District of Columbia | 101.1 |
| Florida | 97.6 |
| Georgia | 109.6 |
| Idaho | 84.2 |
| Illinois | 93.0 |
| Indiana | 128.1 |
| Iowa | 99.2 |
| Kansas | 91.8 |
| Kentucky | 129.1 |
| Louisiana | 101.4 |
| Maine | 115.2 |
| Maryland | 96.8 |
| Massachusetts | 92.3 |
| Michigan | 111.6 |
| Minnesota | 91.5 |
| Mississippi | 109.9 |
| Missouri | 117.3 |
| Montana | 88.6 |
| Nebraska | 91.4 |
| Nevada | 119.6 |
| New Hampshire | 144.0 |
| New Jersey | 89.2 |
| New Mexico | 68.2 |
| New York | 86.0 |
| North Carolina | 114.6 |
| North Dakota | 81.5 |
| Ohio | 108.5 |
| Oklahoma | 84.4 |
| Oregon | 104.6 |
| Pennsylvania | 99.8 |
| Rhode Island | 101.8 |
| South Carolina | 124.3 |
| South Dakota | 86.8 |
| Tennessee | 85.3 |
| Utah | 58.8 |
| Vermont | 118.8 |
| Virginia | 99.5 |
| Washington | 77.8 |
| West Virginia | 104.1 |
| Wisconsin | 93.0 |
| Wyoming | 100.2 |
| **United States** | **100.2** |

\*Excludes Alaska and Hawaii.                    *Source:* U.S. Bureau of the Census 1992.

### TABLE 12.3
### Regression Results: Model Explaining Per Capita Taxed Cigarettes*

| Variable or Statistic | Model 1 | Model 2 |
|---|---|---|
| Constant | 127.959 | 131.914 |
| | (11.488)** | (11.905)** |
| Indian reservation dummy | –28.528 | –28.696 |
| | (6.127)** | (6.293)** |
| Average cigarette tax, | 0.191 | 0.210 |
| bordering states | (2.757)** | (3.097)** |
| Income per capita, 1991 | –0.002 | –0.002 |
| | (2.123)* | (2.169)* |
| Percentage of state's population | 0.288 | |
| living in border counties | (3.663)** | |
| Border population on both | | 0.072 |
| sides as % of state's population | | (3.984)** |
| State excise tax | –0.629 | –0.638 |
| on cigarettes | (3.181)** | (3.320)** |
| F-statistic | 13.884 | 14.863 |
| $R^2$ | 0.573 | 0.591 |

Note: For fiscal year 1991. See text for details. Numbers in parentheses are $t$-statistics (absolute values). Asterisks denote significance at the 1 percent(**) and 5 percent(*) levels

(the income variable is statistically significant at the 5 percent level). The hypothesis that cigarette sales are negatively related to local taxes is strongly confirmed. Even more striking is the sharply negative relationship between per capita sales and the variable indicating the significant presence of Indian reservations. Tax-paid sales in the major Indian reservation states are reduced by 25 percent or more by their presence. Likewise, there is a strong negative relationship between cigarette sales and income per capita, confirming the findings of many other studies that cigarette taxation tends to be highly regressive.

The results support the importance of cross-border activity. If bordering states raise their cigarette excise taxes by fifteen cents per pack, yearly cigarette sales in the state in question are estimated to rise by about three packs per person, all else equal. Since those increased cigarette sales will be concentrated in border counties, which typically comprise roughly one-third of a state's population, a state excise tax increase of fifteen cents per pack is estimated to increase per capita cigarette sales in bordering counties by perhaps eight or nine packs per year. Given that only about 25 percent of the adult population smokes, the coefficient estimate translates into tax-paid consumption of about two extra cartons per year per smoker. This figure probably significantly understates the cross-border effects, owing to the definitional problems in measuring the populations truly having low-cost access to alternative tax jurisdictions for cigarette purchases.

### Cigarette Taxation and Cross-Border Activity: The Case of Ohio

The author, along with David Klingaman and Lowell Gallaway, has attempted to measure the impact of differential excise taxation, particularly of cigarettes, with respect to economic behavior in Ohio (Klingaman et al. 1992). Over 30 percent of Ohioans live near borders with other states, a fairly typical figure. At the time the study was conducted, in late 1991 and early 1992, the excise tax on cigarettes in the state of Ohio was eighteen cents, compared with only three cents in Kentucky. A major metropolitan area, Cincinnati, straddles the two states, with the Ohio River serving as the border. Numerous bridges provide quick transportation between the two states. There was a $1.50 differential per carton in state cigarette taxes between the two states. Does a tax difference of this magnitude have a material impact on cigarette sales by jurisdiction?

To examine behavior, we actually visited stores in both states where cigarette sales were important, including convenience stores, liquor stores, and supermarkets. We recorded the state of residence of shoppers from automobile license plates. Our sample included nearly 1,000 cars. The first issue was whether differential tax rates were shifted forward to consumers. The average price of a carton of a leading brand of cigarettes in the stores visited was $15.87 in Ohio, but $14.27 in Kentucky. The $1.50 additional tax burden in Ohio was in fact fully (actually, slightly more than fully) shifted forward to consumers.

We calculated that 16 percent of the Ohioans we observed purchased their cigarettes in Kentucky, whereas only 6 percent of Kentuckians bought cigarettes in Ohio. Moreover, these observations grossly understate the impact of cross-border activity because, as mentioned above, when customers are induced by taxes to cross borders, usually they make large purchases to overcome transportation costs, whereas in-state purchases involve lower transportation costs and thus tend to be smaller in magnitude. This theoretical expectation was in fact fulfilled, as verified by interviews with customers and store managers.

Based on our survey, we estimated that 42.9 percent of the cigarettes purchased by Ohioans living in the Cincinnati area in December 1991 were bought in Kentucky; in contrast, only 1.6 percent of the cigarettes purchased by Kentuckians living in the Cincinnati area were bought in Ohio. We calculated that the elasticity of demand for cigarettes in the border counties was an extraordinary 5.66. A 10 percent increase in the price of cigarettes, other things equal, would lead to a 56.6 percent decline in the quantity of cigarettes demanded *in the area raising prices*.

This cross-border elasticity of demand is remarkably consistent with that observed in several other studies. Michael Walsh and Jonathan Jones (1988), looking at West Virginia, observed a slightly higher (5.9) elasticity. Looking at durable goods, the state of Washington's Department of Revenue has obtained a border elasticity of 4.8 (State of Washington 1990). An older study implicitly found elasticities of demand in border counties varying with the good or service, with the median estimate being 6.3 (Mikesell 1970, 1971).

The extraordinary sensitivity of customers to price owing to the opportunity of making cross-border purchases means that the revenue potential of higher taxes in border areas is extremely small. To use the Cincinnati example, we calculated that if Ohio's cigarette excise taxes had been increased by twelve cents per pack (67 percent of the original excise tax), as was being proposed at the time, tax-paid sales of cigarettes on the Ohio side of the Kentucky-Ohio border would have fallen by 41 percent. The decrease in the tax base would have more than completely offset increases in the tax rate, so the actual amount of tax revenue raised in the Ohio border areas would have actually shown a slight *decrease*. The Laffer curve evidently works outside the area of income taxation.

This finding is remarkably consistent with what one leading textbook on public finance stated:

> Although the price elasticity of demand for cigarettes is low, it is not low for sales within a single state when the price there differs greatly from that in other states. The extent of cigarette smuggling is evidence of this. (Browning and Browning 1987, 479)

The authors conclude:

> Cigarette smuggling should serve as a warning: taxing goods that are easily transported across state boundaries at rates higher than those of other states may produce little revenue and a great deal of illegal activity. (Browning and Browning 1987, 480)

Moreover, the analysis above probably understates the adverse economic and fiscal consequences of excise tax increases in border areas. People who stop to buy cigarettes often buy, sometimes on impulse, other products (milk, beer, newspapers, soft drinks, and so forth). These products are typically at least partly subject to sales taxation. Taking into account the potential loss of sales tax revenues, the financial impact of excise tax increases becomes even more clearly negative.

The adverse effect of reduced retail sales activity is not confined to tax revenues. In the specific case of Ohio examined, we estimated that a twelve-cent increase in the cigarette tax would have led to a loss of about 2,000 jobs in border counties as declining sales activity led to reduced employment opportunities in retail establishments.

To be sure, Ohio's loss to a considerable extent is Kentucky's gain. The broader geographical impact of a tax increase is clearly far less than the narrower intrastate effects. Nonetheless, people making decisions about taxes are typically almost entirely concerned about the impact on their own jurisdiction, and do not consider any positive effects that an increased tax may have on business activity in other jurisdictions.

## Policy Issues Relating to Excise Taxation

From a policy perspective, there is a tendency to assume that the demand for goods such as cigarettes and beer is price inelastic. Tax-induced price increases will lead to modest sales declines. Moreover, since taxes are only a fraction of the price of the good sold, a given percentage increase in taxes should have a dramatically smaller negative impact on sales, increasing total tax revenues. What the cross-border analysis shows is that the assumption of low price elasticity is dubious because *the elasticity of demand for products varies inversely with the extent of the market.* The elasticity of demand for cigarettes may be relatively low for the entire United States: if all retailers raised prices by 10 percent, sales would fall less than proportionately (say, 5 percent). However, if a single retailer or, for that matter, a group of retailers in a single county were to raise their prices 10 percent, the decline in sales would be much more substantial.

My research with others suggests that the practical significance of this theoretical point is substantial for two reasons: First, roughly half of Americans have relatively low-cost access to products in other tax jurisdictions on a fairly routine basis. Second, the sensitivity of consumers to tax differentials in cross-border situations is in fact very large. State governments often do not raise the money they initially expect to when they raise excise taxes, simply because they underestimate the cross-border phenomenon.

The discussion above suggests that *state*-induced increases in excise taxes lead to behavior modification that often thwarts the revenue objectives of government, but what about increases in *federal* taxes? This is particularly relevant given recent proposals to substantially increase the federal excise tax on cigarettes.

It is true that a much smaller proportion of Americans live near international borders, so the adverse tax revenue effects of federal excise tax increases are likely to be smaller than those associated with state tax increases. However, when retail customers are far from borders, higher transportation costs lead to changes in the nature of smuggling. Most interstate tobacco smuggling involves small purchases of cigarettes that are transported by users across borders for personal consumption. Where distances are great, the suppliers rather than the demanders incur the costs of transporting the illicit cigarettes. Instead of five cartons of cigarettes traveling across the Ohio River or some imaginary state line, 20,000 cartons travel in semitrailer trucks on interstate highways.

The Canadian experience is very instructive in this regard. Federal and provincial excise taxes several times the magnitude prevailing in the United States led to a dramatic decline in legal tobacco sales, with tax revenues falling dramatically from 1991 to 1993.[10] It has been estimated that at the beginning of 1994, some 75 percent of the cigarettes consumed in Quebec and 40 percent in Canada as a whole were contraband (Lemieux 1994). In February 1994, a major joint federal-provincial tax reduction in Quebec reduced the price of legal cigarettes by 50 percent. The result? A dramatic (80 to 90 percent) decline in smuggling. This experience later led to the extension of tax reductions to the national level.

If large increases in U.S. federal taxes were imposed, it is likely that smuggled cigarettes would enter the United States in large numbers from across international borders, especially the one with Mexico. Already, California's state excise tax of thirty-seven cents per pack, along with federal excise taxes, has encouraged a significant amount of contraband cigarette business in the Golden State.[11] A large federal excise tax increase would expand this underground activity enormously.

Students of public finance have long had serious problems with excise taxes. They violate the principle that taxes should not distort the allocation of resources, but rather should be neutral in their impact on consumer decisions. They also violate the ability-to-pay principle of taxation, hurting the poor more than the more affluent. In addition, the administrative problems associated with interstate or international trade in cigarettes prompted by tax avoidance considerations are very substantial, and further add to the arguments against continued increases in tobacco taxation.

It (almost) goes without saying that the cross-border effects identified herein do not apply solely to tobacco and liquor. Any time any one jurisdiction imposes or raises a selective excise tax on any commodity, be it cigarettes, soft drinks, or high-fat snacks, it creates incentives for consumers—and smugglers—to make their purchases elsewhere to avoid the tax.

## Notes

1. The academic literature tends to confirm that cross-border activity to avoid taxes is relatively common. Most modern studies deal with sales taxation. (See, for example, Fox 1986 and Vedder 1993.) As two preeminent authorities put it, "For cities, strong empirical evidence shows that a rate differential causes significantly lower per capita sales" (Due and Mikesell 1983, 326).
2. For truly large bulk purchases, another transaction cost relates to the opportunity cost of having resources tied up in commodity inventories, rather than earning interest in a bank account or financial security.
3. The Price Waterhouse firm has done considerable research on cross-border activity. See, for example, Price Waterhouse (1991, 1992a, and 1992b). These

studies consistently observed strong cross-border consumer reaction to excise tax increases.

4. There are some minor problems with the data. The reported per capita cigarette purchases were calculated by taking fiscal-year tax revenues and dividing by the per pack tax and then by the 1990 population. Tax revenue information was obtained from the U.S. Bureau of the Census (1992). The most significant problem arises because some states reported sales for "tobacco products," including noncigarette items, thus leading to a moderate overstatement of cigarette purchases for those states. Payments to distributors of cigarette products for tax collection vary between states, and the calculations make no attempt to correct for these payments.

5. Another factor that no doubt impacts on tax-paid cigarette purchases is the presence of military bases. This factor was excluded from this analysis in part because of some difficulties in precisely measuring military presence by state. Moreover, the Pentagon has taken action recently to raise cigarette prices at military commissaries and base exchanges by $4.00 per carton (35 percent). This action narrows the price differential with civilian retailers considerably (Associated Press, 11 November 1996).

6. Several states increased their excise taxes during fiscal year 1991. Accordingly, I calculated the average tax in effect during the twelve-month period.

7. To qualify as a major Indian reservation state, a state had to have at least 5,000 persons living on reservations, and the reservations had to contain at least 0.1 percent of the state's population. The eight states meeting these criteria were: Arizona, Montana, New Mexico, North Dakota, Oklahoma, South Dakota, Utah, and Wyoming.

8. The figures used were a weighted average of cigarette taxes in bordering states, the weights being determined by the numbers of persons on the border of each jurisdiction.

9. The population in other states living on a state's border was added to the state's own border population in model 2 to estimate the number of persons in each state who might potentially shop across borders because of taxes; unfortunately, data limitations prevented including the Canadian and Mexican border populations.

10. See Lemieux (1994). The most substantial recent study was prepared by Fred O'Riordan, the acting director general of Excise Duties and Taxes, Revenue Canada. See his "Increased Tobacco Taxes and Smuggling: The Canadian Experience," a presentation for the Federation of Tax Administrators, Austin, Texas, September 1993.

11. This information was provided by tobacco industry sources.

## References

Browning, Edgar K., and Jacquelene M. Browning. 1987. *Public Finance and the Price System*. 3rd ed. New York: Macmillan.

Due, John F., and John L. Mikesell. 1983. *Sales Taxation: State and Local Structure and Administration*. Baltimore: Johns Hopkins University Press.

Fox, William F. 1986. "Tax Structure and the Location of Economic Activity Along State Borders." *National Tax Journal* 39 (December): 387–401.

Klingaman, David, Lowell Gallaway, and Richard K. Vedder. 1992. *Business on the Edge: The Economic Impact of Excise and Sales Taxation in Ohio*. Columbus, Ohio: Border Coalition Against Taxes.

Lemieux, Pierre. 1994. "Canada's Taxing Pols Outwitted by Underground Economy." *Wall Street Journal,* 8 April, A-13.

Mikesell, John L. 1970. "Central Cities and Sales Tax Differentials." *National Tax Journal* 23 (June): 206–13.

———. 1971. "Sales Taxation and the Border Tax Problem." *Quarterly Review of Economics and Business* 11 (spring): 23–29.

Price Waterhouse. 1991. *An Estimate of Cross-Border Cigarette Activity on the Ohio-Pennsylvania Border.* New York: Price Waterhouse. September.

———. 1992a. *An Analysis of Cross-Border Activity Patterns in Maryland.* New York: Price Waterhouse. February.

———. 1992b. *Voting with Their Feet: A Study of Tax Incentives and Economic Consequences of Cross-Border Activity in New England.* Washington, D.C.: American Legislative Exchange Council. August.

State of Washington. 1990. Department of Revenue. *The Effects of Tax Rate Differences on Retail Trade in Washington Border Counties.* Research Report 90–5 (revised).

Stigler, George J. 1961. "The Economics of Information." *Journal of Political Economy* 64 (June): 213–25.

U.S. Bureau of the Census. 1992. *State Government Tax Collections: 1991.* Washington, D.C.: U.S. Government Printing Office.

Vedder, Richard K. 1993. *Economic Impact of an Oregon Sales Tax.* Portland, Oreg.: Cascade Policy Institute. October.

Walsh, Michael, and Jonathan Jones. 1988. "More Evidence on the 'Border Tax' Effect: The Case of West Virginia, 1979–84." *National Tax Journal* 41 (June): 261–65.

# Part IV

# Constitutional Liberties and Excise Taxation

# 13

# Wealth Creation as a "Sin"

*Jonathan R. Macey*

It is not yet clear how favorably history will treat the economic and social developments of the 1980s. That decade saw the longest peacetime expansion in U.S. history, with the nation's GNP nearly doubling from $2.7 trillion to $5.3 trillion. During that time, nearly 100,000 Americans became millionaires every year, and the top 20 percent of American families saw their average income increase more than $9,000.00, rising to $85,000.00 per year. Over 20 million new jobs were created, and full employment was maintained for much of the decade (Friedrich 1990, 76). It is certainly true that for many, the 1980s were a remarkable period of economic prosperity.

However, the 1980s are not so fondly remembered by everyone. In fact, much criticism and scorn has been directed at the economic developments of the 1980s and the "greed is good" attitude that many say characterized the period. Some label the 1980s as the "decade of greed," and suggest that "conspicuous consumption, cold careerism and self-centered spirit" were pervasive (Henkoff 1989, 40). Indeed, the media has devoted much effort to destroying any positive memories that some might have of the 1980s (Friedrich 1990, 76; Henkoff 1989, 40; Faltermeyer 1991, 58).

Critics are quick to point out that although the GNP nearly doubled, the national debt tripled. Also, the gains in income made by the top 20 percent of families were accompanied by a $576.00 decrease in the average income of the lowest 20 percent of families. Nearly 1.4 percent of the population, amounting to about 2 million people, joined the ranks of the impoverished (Friedrich 1990, 76). Critics seem to match every positive aspect of the decade to a concomitant negative aspect that served to "make the rich richer and the poor poorer."

Particular attention has been paid to the heavy merger and acquisition (M&A) activity of the decade. The M&A activity during the 1980s was indeed unprecedented in volume: Between hostile and friendly takeovers, over one-third of the companies in the Fortune 500 were engulfed by other firms (or went private). Buyers paid out over $1.5 trillion in order to consummate their acquisitions, and firms spent billions in order to defend against hostile takeovers. It is estimated that $60 billion in fees were paid to deal makers, attorneys, and commercial banks (Faltermeyer 1991, 58).

Those who view the M&A activity of the 1980s favorably point out that the threat of a hostile takeover can force the management of companies to work harder and smarter in order to keep share value high and thereby protect their jobs. Also, the activity has been credited with "undoing some of the early conglomerate silliness, stripping corporations back to products and markets they knew" (Faltermeyer 1991, 58).

The media consensus, however, seems to be that the M&A activity was a bad thing. The media has characterized the participants in the transactions of the "deal decade" as greedy corporate raiders and financiers obsessed with the accumulation of wealth and power. Michael Milken, the "junk-bond king at Drexel Burnham Lambert," is often held up as representing the 1980s mentality that money should be made at any cost, skirting the laws if necessary to make a profit. Critics frequently assert that the shady and greed-driven deals of the 1980s caused or contributed to the economic woes that the country experienced in the early 1990s (Friedrich 1990, 76).

It is in light of these conflicting views of the 1980s that this chapter will analyze four Internal Revenue Code (I.R.C.) provisions enacted by Congress over the period 1984–92. The first two provisions are I.R.C. sections 4999 and 280G, imposing a 20 percent excise tax on "excess golden parachute payments" received by individuals, and disallowing corporate deductions of the "excess golden parachute payments" as a business expense.[1] The third provision is I.R.C. section 5881. This section imposes a 50 percent excise tax on greenmail payments received by those attempting to acquire a corporation through a hostile takeover. The fourth and most recent provision is I.R.C. 162(m), which provides that compensation paid to certain executives in excess of $1 million yearly cannot be deducted as a business expense by the corporation.

This chapter will argue that Congress, in enacting the above-mentioned tax code provisions, has clearly embraced the more critical and politically popular view of the economic and social developments of the 1980s. Congress, during and after the 1980s, sought to curb the perceived greed and excesses of the corporate world by creating tax disincentives to discourage certain arguably legitimate and rational corporate compensation policies. Particularly, Congress targeted compensation paid to corporate executives, through enactment of I.R.C. sections 4999, 280G, and 162(m), and greenmail payments made in defense of hostile-takeover bids, through I.R.C. section 5881. These tax code provisions, this chapter argues, are, in effect, sin taxes that impose a sanction on highly compensated individuals who have legally and legitimately earned income in the form of very high salaries or greenmail.

This chapter includes sections dealing with golden-parachute payments, greenmail, and executive compensation over $1 million. The first part of each section will describe the nature of these forms of compensation and detail their merits. The second part will discuss the legislative history of each tax provision and will summarize the arguments advanced by Congress to justify its actions in each case.

The third part of each section will analyze critically Congress's purported justifications for each tax provision to determine if they are rational and credible. Each of these parts will conclude that despite Congress's vague and fundamentally weak justifications, the legislation serves mainly to impose Congress's (and, concededly, much of society's) moral judgment that it is wrong for executives and corporate takeover specialists to make "too much money." The chapter will conclude that I.R.C. sections 4999, 280G, 5881, and 162(m) are indeed types of sin taxes imposed by Congress as a gesture to punish highly paid individuals who are able to successfully take advantage of the opportunities made available by the corporate world.

### Golden Parachutes

Section 280G of the Internal Revenue Code defines a golden-parachute payment as a payment that "is contingent on a change (I) in the ownership or effective control of the corporation, or (II) in the ownership of a substantial portion of the assets of the corporation."[2] Generally, corporations offer golden parachutes to executives as part of their pay packages in order to provide them with a certain degree of financial security in the event of a takeover of the corporation. If another firm takes over the corporation and the executive is displaced from her job, the golden parachute provides the executive with a large sum of money to "cushion her fall" from the ranks of the highly compensated corporate elite. The golden parachute is, in essence, a form of "layoff insurance" for the executive, meant to protect her from an abrupt loss of employment resulting from a merger or acquisition of her firm.

In addition to their primary purpose of compensating executives for the loss of their jobs (and the power and prestige that accompany them), there are several additional justifications for golden-parachute payments. The first justification is that golden parachutes function to reduce some of the agency costs associated with the market for corporate control. The existence of the golden parachute allows an executive to evaluate a potential takeover more objectively, because she need not fear substantial pecuniary loss resulting from a loss of employment. The argument is that executives often selfishly deploy defensive tactics in efforts to thwart takeover attempts that may be in the best interests of the shareholders. The golden parachute may effectively create a counterbalancing incentive to executives that will make the prospect of losing their jobs less repugnant.

A second argument in favor of golden parachutes is that they are necessary to attract and retain top management talent. The insurance-like character of golden parachutes makes them very attractive to an executive, especially during periods of heavy merger and acquisition activity such as the decade of the 1980s.[3] Moreover, as golden parachutes become more and more popular among Fortune 500 corporations,[4] firms not offering such "insurance" will be less attractive to an experienced, proven executive. Golden parachutes, therefore, make it more likely that a corporation will be able to lure a high-quality executive and keep her in the face of a takeover threat or an attempt by another firm to draw her away. For these reasons, golden parachutes can benefit a corporation and its shareholders by promoting stability within the corporation's leadership.

A third, rather questionable argument made in support of golden-parachute payments is that they actually discourage attempts to take over a firm. The idea is that the cost of assuming the golden-parachute obligations of an acquired firm creates a disincentive for a potential acquirer to target that firm (Maurer 1984, 354–55). This notion that golden parachutes somehow raise the cost of a takeover will arise later in this chapter in relation to Congress's justifications for measures against golden parachutes. At that point this chapter will discuss how this argument does not square with the facts concerning hostile-takeover bids. In any event, the argument is that a firm can insulate itself from undesirable hostile-takeover bids by providing executives with generous golden-parachute payments.[5]

## Congressional Taxation of Golden Parachutes

In the Deficit Reduction Act of 1984, Congress included two new provisions that impose punitive taxes on corporations making "excess golden parachute payments" to their executives and on the executives receiving the payments. Section 280G denies a corporate income tax deduction for golden-parachute payments that have a present value in excess of three times an executive's "base amount" of pay.[6] Further, section 4999 imposes a 20 percent excise tax on the recipient of such "excess" parachute payments.[7] These harsh measures, in effect, treat golden-parachute payments that are in excess of three times an executive's base pay as per se unreasonable under the tax code.[8] The 20 percent excise tax is particularly harsh in that it is applied in addition to the normal amount owed through the income tax.[9]

Congress adopted these measures near the beginning of the 1980s, when M&A activity was high[10] and golden parachutes were becoming commonplace. The provisions were most likely a response to the harsh criticisms in the media concerning golden parachutes (Morrison 1983; Moore 1982; Klein 1982).

A typical criticism of golden-parachute arrangements is that the payments are ridiculously high, far above what would be adequate compensation for losing one's job. Moreover, it is asserted that nearly all employment involves the risk of job loss, and that executives were already paid more than enough money to compensate for such a risk (Maurer 1984).

Congress, in justifying sections 280G and 4999, avoided relying on the general arguments that the payments were too high and unfair. Rather, in its explanation of the provisions, Congress put forth several more theoretical arguments concerning the effects of the payments on shareholders and the market for corporate control in general. However, even assuming that the tax code is an appropriate tool for regulating corporate activity (a proposition with which this author disagrees), nearly all of Congress's justifications for discouraging golden parachutes are based upon questionable arguments.

The House and Senate Joint Committee on Taxation provided three reasons for imposing the taxes: (1) "golden parachutes...hindered acquisition activity in the marketplace and, as a matter of policy, should be strongly discouraged"; (2) "Congress was concerned that the existence of such arrangements tended to encourage the executives and other key personnel involved to favor proposed takeovers that might not be in the best interests of the shareholders and others"; and (3) "Congress decided to discourage transactions that tended to reduce the amounts which might otherwise be paid to target corporation shareholders."[11]

The Senate Committee on Finance issued a separate report detailing its rationale for approving sections 280G and 4999. In its report, the committee explained that there was concern "that in many instances golden parachute contracts do little but assist an entrenched management team to remain in control. They also provide corporate funds to subsidize officers or other highly compensated individuals."[12] These justifications put forth by the joint committee and the Senate committee will be analyzed in depth in the following part of this section.

*Analysis*

The second rationale mentioned by the Senate committee, that excessive parachute payments subsidize executives at shareholder expense, is the only tax policy rationale put forth by Congress for sections 4999 and 280G.[13] Although the report is vague as to how executives are subsidized, Congress is probably implying that in many cases parachute payments are too high and not supported by adequate consideration; thus they are like "gifts." However, section 162(a) of the I.R.C. has always provided that only "ordinary and necessary" expenses are deductible in calculating taxable income.[14] The code goes on to clarify that this includes only allowances for reasonable salaries and compensation to employees for "services actually rendered."[15]

Thus, if Congress was really concerned about the reasonableness of golden-parachute payments, it is not clear why it did not leave it to the IRS to do its job of enforcing section 162(a) on a case-by-case basis, looking at the particular payments in question.[16] There is ample authority for the IRS to challenge the reasonableness and deductibility of executive compensation.[17] There are many cases in which the IRS has argued that certain executive compensation is unreasonably high and constitutes a disguised dividend payment.[18] Thus, it is more plausible that Congress was concerned more with remedying a perceived corporate governance problem than with refining the definition of an ordinary and necessary business expense.[19] However, with regard to its obvious objective of regulating corporate behavior, Congress did not put forth any factually or theoretically solid reasons why golden-parachute payments that exceed base pay by a certain amount constitute a corporate governance problem with which they should be concerned.

The joint committee stated that it was concerned that golden parachutes "hindered acquisition activity in the marketplace," and the Senate committee made essentially the same point, speaking in terms of management entrenchment. These arguments presume that golden-parachute payment obligations are generally high enough to make a firm a less desirable takeover target than otherwise. The joint committee also stated that it was concerned about shareholders receiving less for their shares. Their rationale presumably was that the golden-parachute payments owed to management of target firms are so high as to materially reduce the maximum amount an acquirer is able to tender for shares of stock. Therefore, the House and Senate relied on the weak position that golden parachutes raise the costs of acquisitions enough to significantly affect the takeover decision of a potential acquirer or the takeover price he is able to pay.

The weakness of this argument lies in the fact that the many millions of dollars required to pay off ousted managers usually amount to a very small percentage (usually less than 1 percent ) of a typical offer.[20] For example, in Allied's takeover of Bendix, the $4 million golden-parachute obligations that Allied acquired amounted to only three-tenths of 1 percent (0.29 percent) of the $1.4 billion takeover price (Maurer 1984, 354). Further, the takeover market of the 1980s involved over $1.5 trillion in purchases and highly leveraged deals where firms arguably overpaid for companies anyway.[21] Investment bankers and lawyers made over $60 billion just for putting the deals together (Faltermeyer 1991, 58). In such a market, it is unlikely that deals turned on the presence or absence of several million dollars' worth of golden-parachute obligations. Thus, the justifications that rely on the assumption that golden-parachute payments significantly affect takeover decisions and takeover prices are questionable at best.

The second justification mentioned in the joint committee's report is that golden-parachute agreements may actually encourage an executive to acquiesce in a hostile takeover that is not in the best interests of the shareholders. This proposition relies on the assumption that an executive making hundreds of thousands of dollars (possibly millions) per year would be eager to relinquish his job completely for a payoff of three years' base salary.[22] This is questionable at best. It may be more likely for older executives approaching retirement, but the existence of stock options and hefty pensions makes this not so clear. Such arguments fail to take account of the value to executives of the power and prestige of their positions in the ranks of the corporate elite. It seems more plausible that the payments would constitute a factor that allows an executive to evaluate a takeover more objectively.

Thus, Congress failed in its attempt to justify sections 280G and 4999 in terms of necessary tax policy and in terms of regulating corporate behavior to protect shareholders or the economy. Moreover, if Congress were actually concerned about protecting shareholders, denying the corporation a tax deduction for golden-parachute payments and taxing the recipient would be a poor means of protecting them. Indeed such action has tended to harm them more than help them. Since provisions 280G and 4999 were passed, corporations desiring to make parachute payments falling within the tax code's definition of "excess" have merely taken the tax penalty imposed by 280G and "grossed up" the amounts paid in order to compensate the executives for the 20 percent excise tax imposed by 4999.[23] These actions taken by corporations in response to the golden-parachute tax provisions have served to increase shareholders' costs rather than reduce them.[24] This situation additionally serves to illustrate how Congress's use of tax policy to regulate corporate behavior can backfire or be ineffective.

Notwithstanding Congress's purported justifications, the best explanation for sections 280G and 4999 is that Congress intended to levy a punitive tax on a corporate compensation practice that it considered to be excessive. Congress could not have liked the fact that executives were benefiting so greatly from the hostile takeovers of their companies and the loss of their jobs; and the vast amount of negative publicity concerning golden-parachute payments no doubt put pressure on Congress to act.

However, Congress could not come up with any strong arguments for why it needed to act on this perceived problem. The parachute arrangements were the result of legitimately bargained contracts and involved no breach of duties to shareholders, and the tax code already disallowed tax deductions for unreasonable compensation packages. Therefore, Congress was forced to put forth the five rather transparent arguments mentioned above in order to justify what was essentially a sin tax on a type of executive compensation. This sin tax was intended to punish the corporation and the recipient for legitimately but "unfairly" making "too much money."

### Greenmail Payments

Greenmail payments are defined by the Internal Revenue Code as

consideration transferred by a corporation...to directly or indirectly acquire stock of such corporation from any shareholder if...such shareholder held such stock...for less than 2 years before entering into the agreement to make the transfer, [and]...at some time during the 2-year period ending on the date of such acquisition...such

shareholder [or any person related to or acting in concert with such shareholder]
...made or threatened to make a public tender offer for stock of such corporation,
and such acquisition is pursuant to an offer for stock not made on the same terms
to all shareholders.[25]

More simply, greenmail is payment from a corporation to a person or persons
intended to induce them to abandon an attempt at taking over that corporation. Typically, the managers of the target pay a premium above market price
for the shares of the potential acquirer, yielding him a large profit on his
investment in the firm's shares.

Assuming that the directors of the corporation are not acting solely to entrench themselves (an issue that will be addressed below), greenmail can serve
a legitimate corporate purpose. Greenmail, by giving a corporation some power
to control its destiny, may allow a corporation to stave off a takeover attempt
that is not in the best interests of the firm or its shareholders. This theory, called
the "shareholder-welfare hypothesis," holds that greenmail can benefit shareholders and society by facilitating an auction for the shares of a corporation,
thus allowing corporations to be controlled by the highest-valued user.[26]

For example, suppose that a potential acquirer, M, conducts extensive research and determines that a corporation, B, is undervalued. M then initiates
a two-tiered takeover of B. This action signals other potential acquirers that
B is undervalued and that a profit can be made from a takeover. Suppose that
another potential acquirer, T, then enters the picture and expresses an interest
in B, but needs time to put together an offer. If B calculates that its value
would be less under the control of M than it would be under the control of T,
B should pay greenmail to M to prevent his taking control.[27] As a consequence, B will eventually be acquired by T or an even higher-valued user that
subsequently enters the picture. In any case, the corporation, the shareholders
of B, and society benefit because B's resources will end up under the control
of a user more highly valued than M.[28]

In addition to allowing firms to create an auction for their shares, greenmail
also rewards a potential acquirer for discovering an undervalued firm and
providing such information to the market. Rewarding those who produce
important information will encourage the production of such information and
lead to a more efficient market for corporate control (Macey and McChesney
1985). A more efficient market for corporate control works as an important
check on managers and directors and, as mentioned above, leads to the most
efficient use of a firm's resources. Thus greenmail, if utilized wisely and in
good faith, can clearly be desirable.

## Congressional Taxation of Greenmail

The Omnibus Budget Reconciliation Act of 1987 contained I.R.C. section
5881, which imposed a 50 percent excise tax on greenmail payments received

(Lustig 1988, 791). This tax is levied regardless of whether the greenmail is taxable under normal income tax rules.[29] Moreover, when the greenmail is taxable as income, section 5881 can result in nearly a 90 percent cumulative tax rate on the payments (Zelinsky 1990). This tax, similar to the one imposed on recipients of golden-parachute payments, is quite onerous and was clearly a part of Congress's efforts, during the 1980s, to curb perceived excesses in the hostile-takeover market and within corporations.

These provisions were enacted during a time when greenmail payments were frequent and highly criticized. In a one-year period in the mid-1980s, corporations paid out over $4 billion to repurchase blocks of stock from individual shareholders (Macey and McChesney 1985). Several well-publicized cases, such as Warner Communications' repurchase of 5.6 million shares of its stock from Rupert Murdoch for 33 percent above its market price, drew much attention to and criticism of the practice of greenmail (Kirkland 1984, 152). Critics of greenmail usually characterize the payments as a tool for management to entrench itself at shareholders' expense. It is also asserted that the payments to raiders are unfair because similar repurchase terms are not offered to all shareholders (Lustig 1988, 791).

Oddly, Congress justified section 5881 primarily as a tactic to discourage takeovers in general. The section was passed during a period when antitakeover sentiment in Congress was strong.[30] For example, Representative Byron Dorgan, a vocal critic of greenmail and hostile takeovers in general, is quoted in the Congressional Record:

> [Legislation is needed] in response to the spate of hostile takeovers and the devastation that they bring.... Obviously,...legislation will not stop hostile takeovers, but it will discourage these manipulative raids. It's time that Congress acted to protect American workers, American competitiveness, and the American economy from the greed and crimes of these raiders.[31,32]

In any event, Congress purportedly enacted section 5881 to discourage the practice of greenmail, which in turn might discourage raiders from launching their initial attacks on corporations.[33] To the extent that these taxes can deter attacks by raiders, they might accomplish Congress's stated purpose of avoiding the "devastation" associated with hostile-takeover activity.

In addition, Congress stated that it had a problem with raiders making a profit from greenmail, though it did not state specifically why. The legislative history contains the following explanation: "[T]he committee believes that taxpayers should be discouraged from realizing short-term profits by acquiring stock in a public tender offer and later being redeemed by the corporation in an effort by the corporation to avert a hostile takeover."[34] Presumably, Congress was persuaded that greenmail represented some evil to shareholders or society and that it needed to be regulated. The next part of this section will analyze critically Congress's justifications for section 5881.

*Analysis*

From the legislative history of section 5881, it is fairly clear that Congress had no true tax policy justifications for the 50 percent tax on greenmail. Section 5881 does not serve to define the tax base, to raise revenues, or to meet any of the other traditional justifications for a tax (Zelinsky 1990). Therefore, it can only be concluded that section 5881 was a naked measure to regulate the behavior of corporations and corporate raiders.

Indeed, as mentioned above, Congress made no secret of its general disapproval of hostile takeovers and the payment of greenmail. So what is wrong with Congress protecting shareholders and society from the effects of such practices it deems harmful? The answer is that section 5881 is too broad to actually protect anyone; it deters all hostile takeovers and greenmail payments regardless of whether they cause any harm. Surely Congress could not have rationally believed that all hostile takeovers and greenmail payments were objectionable and needed to be discouraged in order to protect shareholders and the public from harm.[35]

The theory that a robust market for corporate control has positive effects in terms of disciplining managers is well established. The basis of this theory is that a high market price for a corporation's shares is the best deterrent to a hostile takeover. A low share price relative to a firm's potential going-concern value or actual liquidation value is precisely what a corporate raider is looking for. It follows that managers who are interested in keeping their jobs will strive to keep the value of the firm's shares high, and the best way to do so is through responsible and effective management. Thus the self-interest of managers will lead to healthier and more efficient corporations, which are beneficial to the general economy, society, and, of course, shareholders.

This is a well-known and widely accepted principle of corporate law. Despite the fact that some hostile takeovers may not be in the best interests of shareholders, employees, or society, Congress must have been cognizant of the above theory and could not have rationally believed that it needed to deter all hostile takeovers.[36]

In the same vein, the payment of greenmail is clearly not in all cases a bad thing. The shareholder-welfare hypothesis, discussed above, posits a situation where the payment of greenmail results in an increase in the value of a firm due to the reallocation of a corporation's resources to a higher-valued user.[37] A more efficient allocation of resources and a stronger, more valuable firm is clearly in the best interests of society and shareholders.

As further support for the proposition that Congress could not have rationally believed that discouraging greenmail would benefit society by discouraging takeover activity, it should be noted that one of the main criticisms of greenmail payments has always been that they help entrench existing management. Critics contend that corporate executives who fear losing their jobs in a hostile takeover will pay out corporate assets to finance purely self-interested defensive tactics (Macey and McChesney 1985). However, by discouraging the acceptance of greenmail through a hefty tax on such payments, hostile takeovers may indeed be facilitated. As discussed above, greenmail is an effective means for a corporation to protect itself from the kind of attack, acquisition, and liquidation that Representative Dorgan alluded to.[38] If a raider is discouraged from accepting the "payoff" because of the large tax, then management's ability to avert a hostile takeover by "buying off" the raider is impaired. Thus, in this situation a harmful hostile takeover may be unavoidable, a result Congress purportedly intended to discourage.

This is not to assert that a better outcome will always be produced by a robust market for corporate control and the ability of managers to pay greenmail. Rather, the argument is that Congress could not have rationally justified a blind punitive tax on *all* greenmail payments by asserting that greenmail generally leads to harmful results in the form of increased hostile takeovers and injury to shareholders.[39]

Thus, this analysis concludes that Congress did not intend to discourage all greenmail payments in an honest attempt to minimize harm to society and to shareholders. It is likely that Congress did perceive that greenmail in some instances encouraged harmful takeover activity, but there is a much more plausible explanation for section 5881. Considering the bad press aimed at corporate raiders such as Carl Icahn and T. Boone Pickens, it is most likely that Congress was disturbed by the large premiums that raiders were making in the greenmail deals. Although Congress must have recognized that greenmail in some instances could be beneficial to a corporation and to society, it must have seen the payments to greenmailers as too high. Greenmailing a firm is not an illegal or illegitimate activity,[40] so Congress resorted to the tax code to implement antigreenmailer policies because of a tax's ability to cut away benefits deemed "ill-gotten." The 50 percent excise tax, therefore, is most plausibly explained mainly as a sin tax designed to strip raiders of legally obtained profits associated with locating undervalued firms and initiating takeovers.

### Taxation of Executive Compensation over $1 Million

It is undeniable that corporate executives, CEOs in particular, are very well compensated these days. For example, in 1990, John Sculley of Apple, Paul Fireman of Reebok, and Michael Eisner of Walt Disney each made over $10 million in salary, bonuses, and long-term compensation.[41] In addition, at least seven other CEOs made over $10 million and at least twenty-five made over $5 million in salary, bonuses, and long-term compensation.[42] Indeed, it is not unusual for a CEO to make over thirty-five times the salary of a manufacturing employee, and in some cases the figure has been as high as 1,000 times (Nelson-Horchler 1990, D-3).

However, it should be noted, and it infrequently is, that many of these huge figures that are quoted include millions of dollars in benefits from stock option redemptions. These options are accumulated over many years and, if redeemed all at once in one year, can increase the CEO's compensation that year manyfold. For example, John A. Shirley, president of Microsoft, had reported earnings of $26.008 million in 1990. Of that amount, only $414,000 was in salary and bonuses, with $25.594 million coming from stock option redemptions. Also, $17.151 million of the $18.301 million Stephen M. Wolf of UAL Corp., the parent of United Airlines, earned in 1990 was in long-term compensation.[43] In fact, of the twenty highest-paid CEOs of 1990 (all receiving over $5 million for the year), only two actually earned more than $5 million in salary and bonuses.[44] A strong argument can be made that it was more the "staggering" market performance of the 1980s than irresponsible pay practices that has led to the very high levels of total yearly compensation reported today (Brownstein and Planner 1992, 28). Despite the large profits many CEOs reap from redeeming stock options, few would deny that stock options are an important tool for reducing agency costs within the modern publicly held corporation.[45]

Those who would be so bold as to defend current executive pay levels make several arguments. First, it is pointed out that the executive compensation is generally set by the directors of a corporation. In the absence of any conflicts of interest, these directors are able to exercise their sound business judgment in setting the compensation of the executives in the corporation. It can be persuasively argued that directors generally have no personal stake in setting salaries and that the market for executive talent determines what a corporation must offer an executive to lure him to the firm or to prevent him from leaving.[46]

Second, it is pointed out that top executives are burdened with a tremendous amount of responsibility. The CEO of a major corporation must manage thousands of employees and millions or billions of dollars in assets and debts. In order to induce one to take on such a stressful, high-profile, and high-accountability position, the pay needs to be very high.

Third, it is argued that the skill and knowledge that it takes to responsibly manage a multibillion-dollar corporation are as rare and as valuable as the ability to bat over .300 for an entire season in baseball, or to put on an impressive performance in a major motion picture. However, few are outraged to hear that a top baseball player is going to earn $6 million a year or that a major film actor has earned over $10 million for barely a year of work.

Critics respond to such arguments by asserting that the market for executive talent is severely flawed and that executive pay is simply not correlated with how an executive performs. Although there is conflicting empirical evidence concerning the correlation between executive pay and performance, it seems that those critics claiming little or no correlation, such as Graef Chrystal, have louder voices.[47]

Also, critics argue that executives are merely managers of an enterprise and are unlike professional athletes or entertainers, who are products that directly generate revenue. Further, critics cite salaries of CEOs in Japan and Germany and assert that U.S. CEOs are paid much more for lesser or equal performance.[48] A final point made is that the United States' lack of competitiveness internationally is due in part to the large gap between the salaries of low-level workers and executives. Critics assert that "the widening gap between executive compensation and the earnings of workers at the lower end is sapping morale and reducing commitment."[49]

### Congressional Taxation of Executive Compensation

In the 1992 Budget Reconciliation Act, Congress responded to the controversy surrounding executive compensation by adding section 162(m) to the Internal Revenue Code. Basically, this provision denies corporations the right to include certain "excessive employee remuneration"[50] as a business expense in calculating their taxable income. The section provides that "no deduction shall be allowed under this chapter for applicable employee remuneration...to the extent that the amount of such employee remuneration for the taxable year with respect to such employee exceeds $1,000,000."[51] There are many stipulations and exceptions to the general rule, but the basic premise is that for publicly held corporations, the CEO and the four other highest-paid employees (deemed "covered employees") may not receive non-performance-related compensation above $1 million.

Undoubtedly, section 162(m) was a response by Congress to the vast amount of criticism aimed at executive compensation in the early 1990s. Evidence of this can be found in the report issued by Congress justifying the new tax provision. The committee stated that "[r]ecently, the amount of compensation received by executives has been the subject of scrutiny and criticism."[52] Moreover, this is the *only* comment the committee makes with regard to its rationale in the "Reasons for Change" section of the report. Interestingly, Congress made no attempt to justify the provision in terms of tax policy or of protecting shareholders, the economy, or society.

### Analysis

For reasons similar to those put forth above concerning the tax on golden parachutes, it would be difficult for Congress to assert that section 162(m) was necessary to clarify the concept of net income in the tax code. As noted, section 162(a)(1) of the I.R.C. already disallowed deductions for "unreasonable" salaries or compensation, and the IRS had ample precedents with which to attack compensation that it believed patently unreasonable or equivalent to a "disguised dividend."[53] In any event, Congress apparently thought it appropriate to set a bright-line limit on what can be considered reasonable compensation for corporate executives.

However, similar to the consequences of the tax on golden parachutes, section 162(m) is likely to result in increased costs to shareholders in terms of executive salaries. Just as the golden-parachute tax did not deter corporations from providing executives with golden-parachute payments above a certain level, section 162(m) is not likely to affect what a corporation is going to offer its most valuable executives in order to secure their services. The denial of a tax deduction will lead to a higher tax liability for the corporation, which will lead to lower profits for shareholders.[54] Thus, as a bright-line rule intended to protect shareholders from the excesses of corporate officers, the measure is likely to prove rather ineffective.

Despite the fact that Congress was not very explicit concerning its justifications for I.R.C. section 162(m), some insight into the motivations and general attitude of Congress concerning the section can be gained from the words of Senator Levin spoken on the floor of the 102nd Congress:

> [T]here appears to be an unusual consensus [in the Senate] on the issue of CEO pay. Most of us are in agreement that there has been unacceptable excess and that the brakes should be applied. Measured against corporate profits, cost of living, worker salaries, and the salaries of CEOs in other countries, the pay of American CEOs is exorbitant. Not only has CEO pay become an issue in and of itself, but it has become a symbol of the deepening discomfort that we are feeling about the values of our society, the fear that many of us have that the social disruption that we are experiencing is due in part because the rich are indeed getting richer and the rest of us are getting nowhere.[55]

Senator Levin's words seem to indicate that Congress was won over by the arguments that executive pay is out of proportion to corporate performance and out of line with the compensation of executives in other countries. However, the senator neglects to mention who is harmed and why Congress should be concerned.

Most telling are his words blaming exorbitant executive salaries for creating "social disruption" and a "discomfort" with "the values of our society." These phrases seem to indicate a general feeling that executive salaries represent some kind of serious social defect. It seems he believes that by curbing the salaries of executives, a more acceptable and morally correct result can be achieved.

Considering the lack of other significant societal interests, this kind of thinking, correct or not, was most likely the true motivation of Congress in enacting section 162(m). Coincidentally, the measure was passed in the early 1990s, when there was much criticism in the media concerning "the excesses" of the 1980s and the widening gap between the rich and the poor. This analysis argues that critics of section 162(m) have been correct in describing the policy behind it as "misguided populism," and in questioning the significance of the societal interest concerning executive salaries (Brownstein and Planner 1992, 28; Sheppard 1993, 454; Levinson 1992, 44). It does not take much presumptuousness to conclude that section 162(m) was basically a gesture by Congress in response to pressure from the public and the media.[56] Congress showed its concern for the average worker by punishing corporations in order to discourage them from paying "too much" to their executives. Of course, "too much" was defined in terms of what is morally or ethically correct rather than with concern for what the law allows or the market dictates.

## Conclusion

After careful analysis of the four Internal Revenue Code provisions, their legislative history, and the political and social environment in which they were enacted, it seems rather clear that Congress did not enact these provisions chiefly to further legitimate tax policy goals or to protect some group or groups of citizens that could not fend for themselves. Rather, a much more plausible explanation for provisions 280G, 4999, 5881, and 162(m) is that Congress felt obligated to take action as a gesture to show its concern for the unfairness of some legal and legitimate corporate compensation policies. It was logical for Congress to choose the tax code, primarily because of its ability to discourage and punish without directly prohibiting an activity.

This approach parallels very closely the approaches taken by Congress in imposing selective excise taxes on cigarettes, alcohol, and other perceived evils in society. Those taxes punish users of certain substances by making them pay extra for their consumption choices. This involves the government making judgments as to how citizens should conduct themselves and discouraging activities it finds unwise or morally incorrect.

The golden-parachute, greenmail, and excess-executive-compensation provisions similarly work to impose the government's view as to how much certain highly compensated individuals should be able to make without it being too "unfair." The government, in effect, punishes individuals and corporations in order to discourage them from engaging in certain legal and legitimate practices that involve the payment of large sums of money—large relative to the income of the average American worker or small-business owner anyway. In many cases, individuals are merely taking advantage of their skills and intelligence (in full compliance with the laws), and corporations' directors are exercising their business judgment in good-faith efforts to adequately reward employees or protect the corporations against undesirable takeovers. Such interference by the government with the lives of citizens and the operation of the free market is of questionable wisdom and arguably has no place in a free society.

## Notes

1. I.R.C. § 162(a) (West 1988).
2. I.R.C. §§ 280G(b)(2)(A) (West 1988).

3. During the period 1981–84, over 4,000 mergers and acquisitions took place (Morrison 1983, 82).
4. By 1983, 15 to 30 percent of the largest U.S. firms provided golden parachutes to key executives. A survey by Howard International found 15 percent, and a survey by Pearl Meyer found 30 percent (Morrison 1983, 82).
5. One problem with this argument is that it is not clear that a corporation insulating itself from hostile takeovers in general is a good thing. Some takeovers, though hostile, may be in the best interests of the shareholders and should not be deterred. Additional problems will be discussed below.
6. I.R.C. §§ 280G(a),(b)(1),(b)(2)(A)(ii) (West 1988). The base amount of pay is defined as the "average annual income in the nature of compensation...with respect to the acquired corporation in the disqualified individual's gross income over the 5 taxable years [prior to the takeover year]" (U.S. Congress 1984, 200).
7. I.R.C. § 4999(a) (West 1988).
8. The tax code denies tax deductions for salaries that are in excess of a "reasonable allowance for salaries or other compensation for personal services actually rendered." I.R.C. § 162(a)(1) (West 1988).
9. I.R.C. § 4999(c)(1) (West 1988).
10. See note 3.
11. U.S. Congress (1984, 199).
12. U.S. Senate (1984, 1:195).
13. It should be noted that the most basic rationale for a tax, that of raising revenues, is inapplicable here because Congress acknowledged when it passed sections 280G and 4999 that the revenue effect of such provisions was less than $5 million per year (U.S. Senate 1984, 1:196).
14. I.R.C. § 162(a) (West 1988).
15. I.R.C. § 162(a)(1) (West 1988).
16. According to one commentator, "[t]here are no unusual difficulties applying the Code's general rules...about unreasonable compensation to parachute payments. In the case of the normal golden parachute payment, it is easy to find the normal indicia of nondeductible compensation under section 162.... This is a classic situation in which the regular rules under section 162 adequately identify unreasonable compensation. It is not clear why these rules would require augmentation in the form of section 280G" (Zelinsky 1990, 163).
17. Kowalchuk (1992); Sheppard (1993, 454).
18. Kowalchuk (1992).
19. "Rather than refining the notion of income, [sections 4999 and 280G] evidently constitute penalties for engaging in corporate behavior Congress sought to restrict" (Zelinsky 1990).
20. "The amounts involved [in golden-parachute arrangements], while often large, are not large enough compared to the size of tender offers to affect decisions made by those making tender offers" (Maurer 1984, 354). See also Herzel (1982, 22); and Comment, "Golden Parachutes: Ripcords or Rip Offs?" *John Marshall Law Review* 20 (237): 254–56.
21. "Ready-to-go money...drove takeover prices beyond what [could] be justified by a company's earnings.... In the Eighties...'funny paper' pushed prices too high" (Faltermeyer 1991, 58).
22. As mentioned previously, parachute payments above three times an executive's base salary trigger the taxes.
23. "[The golden parachute taxes have] failed in practice. Corporations [have] simply added a 'gross up' to their pay packages for executives—that is, companies

paid an additional tax on behalf of the individual receiving the golden parachute" (Brownstein and Planner 1992, 28).

24. "Rather than eliminate golden parachutes or reduce their size, the excise tax just made them more expensive for the company and ultimately the shareholder" (Brownstein and Planner 1992, 28).

25. I.R.C. § 5881(b) (West 1988).

26. For a more detailed discussion of the shareholder-welfare hypothesis, see Macey and McChesney (1985).

27. Of course, the greenmail price needs to be less than the expected increased value of the firm in the hands of the third party. See Macey and McChesney (1985, 27).

28. Specifically, if T ultimately acquires B, the shareholders of B will receive a higher share price than they would if M had acquired the firm. This is because T expects to make B more valuable than M did, and therefore is willing to pay a higher price than M to acquire it.

29. I.R.C. § 5881(d) (West 1989). "The [50 percent] tax imposed by [section 5881] shall apply whether or not the gain or other income referred to in subsection (a) is recognized." Ibid.

30. The House Committee on Ways and Means stated in its report that "the Committee believes that corporate acquisitions that lack the consent of the acquired corporation are detrimental to the general economy as well as to the welfare of the acquired corporation's employees and community." H. Rept. 391, 100th Cong., 1st Sess., reprinted in 1987 *U.S. Code Congressional and Administrative News,* 2313–701, p. 1086.

31. H.R. 2995, 100th Cong., 1st Sess., 133 *Congressional Record* E3043 (1987). Interestingly, this type of rhetoric contrasts with the language used to justify the provisions taxing golden-parachute payments. In justifying the tax discouraging golden-parachute payments, one of Congress's statements was that "golden parachutes...hindered acquisition activity in the marketplace and, as a matter of policy, should be strongly discouraged" (U.S. Congress 1984, 199). Thus, it appears that within a few years, Congress shifted its stance on the desirability of a robust market for corporate control and began to look for ways to discourage corporate raiders from taking over unwilling corporations.

32. See text accompanying note 11 above.

33. "The Committee...believes that it is appropriate not only to remove tax incentives for corporate acquisitions, but to create tax disincentives for such acquisitions." Legislative History-P.L. 100–203, 1987 *U. S. Code Congressional and Administrative News,* 2313–701, p. 1086.

34. Ibid.

35. In addition, even if Congress did believe that hostile takeovers were generally bad for the economy, why did it not enact legislation to directly address the problem? A 50 percent excise tax on the recipient of greenmail is surely a roundabout approach. In 1984, four bills to outlaw greenmail were introduced in Congress; all of them failed. See "Greenmail: Targeted Stock Repurchases and the Management Entrenchment Hypothesis," *Harvard Law Review* 98 (1985): 1045.

36. As noted above, the legislative history of the golden-parachute provisions mentions Congress's concern about measures that "hindered acquisition activity in the marketplace."

37. Indeed, the message of Macey and McChesney (1985) is that greenmail should not be outlawed based on the assumption that it is always a bad thing; rather,

any regulation of the activity should be aimed at ensuring that the shareholders benefit regardless of management's motivations for the greenmail payment.

38. Of course, it is possible that management will raise funds for greenmail by doing the same sorts of things that a raider would do if the takeover were successful, such as sell off high-cost operating divisions, close outmoded production facilities, and lay off workers. To the extent that these actions actually make the firm more efficient and profitable, they are economically desirable, and thus not deserving of per se discouragement. However, it should be noted that management does not have the same incentives as a raider to liquidate the firm in a haphazard, destructive fashion. A raider is going to be a residual claimant of the firm's assets and stands to benefit directly from any liquidation that generates large amounts of cash. Moreover, the raider is typically going to be in need of a lot of cash in order to deal with the tremendous amount of leverage that is usually necessary for a hostile takeover. Therefore, the raider is more likely to use its power after the takeover to liquidate parts of the firm in order to effect large payments to itself as a shareholder, with less concern for long-run efficiency and profitability. Management, on the other hand, is typically not going to represent a very large shareholder interest standing to benefit directly from large-scale liquidation. Also, management is more risk-averse due to its status as a fixed claimant on the corporation's assets, and is less likely to act to hurt its firm's overall strength. Thus, management is much more likely to have the long-term interests of the corporation in mind if it chooses to raise money for greenmail by selling off parts of the corporation.

39. Harmful in terms of encouraging takeover activity that is "detrimental to the general economy as well as to the welfare of the acquired corporation's employees and community" (see note 30 above).

40. And, as stated above, it actually may reward a speculator for locating an undervalued firm. See Macey and McChesney (1985).

41. Sculley at $16.73 million, Fireman at $14.822 million, and Eisner at $11.233 million. "The Flap Over Executive Pay," *Business Week,* 6 May 1991, 91.

42. Ibid.

43. Ibid.

44. Ibid.

45. "'[I]f managers are to be persuaded to act in the interests of those they represent,' said Prof. Kevin Murphy of the Harvard Business School, 'it's crucial to use executive compensation to mimic the incentives of ownership'" (Passell 1992, A-1).

46. However, critics of current levels of executive compensation argue that corporate boards "are often loaded with other high-paid CEOs. 'It's a cozy you-scratch-my-back-I'll-scratch-yours arrangement'" (McCarroll 1992, 46, quoting Graef S. Chrystal).

47. See Chrystal (1992a and 1992b). But also see Kesner (1993).

48. The average Japanese CEO, for example, earns about $400,000.00 a year, whereas the average U.S. CEO earns around $1,000,000 million in base salary alone (Nelson-Horchler 1990). This difference, however, may not be as significant as the statistics suggest. "When perks and other cultural features are taken into account, U.S. executives do not appear to be paid more than their Japanese counterparts.... Japanese executives benefit from extensive perquisites, lifetime job security, and lifetime pay. Also,...Japanese companies typically use a team-management approach that places less emphasis on a CEO's individual abilities and importance than U.S. companies do" (Brownstein and Planner 1992). In addition, "American executives do not benefit from cross-ownership with suppliers,

customers and lenders that ensures the availability of capital, sales, and product in good and bad times.... [And] one has to consider cost-of-living, tax structures and currency exchange rates, among other things" (Kesner 1993).

49. Reich (1992). But even he notes that "[t]he problem is not that American businessmen are draining the company treasuries. Even absurdly high salaries rarely make up a major percentage of corporate revenues."

50. I.R.C. § 162(m) (West 1994 Supp.).

51. I.R.C. § 162(m)(1) (West 1994 Supp.).

52. Budget Reconciliation Act, Legislative History, P.L. 103–66, H.R. No. 103–111, p. 646.

53. See notes 16–19 above and accompanying text.

54. In addition, the denial of a deduction gives rise to an unfair "double taxation of officers' salaries—once at the individual level...and once at the corporate level (as the result of the denial of the deduction)" (Kowalchuk 1992).

55. 138 *Congressional Record* S214 (23 Jan. 1992, daily ed.; statement of Senator Levin).

56. In a different speech, Senator Levin implied that he felt such pressure. He said that "hardly a week has gone by without another article detailing another example of sky-high executive pay.... The public and many members of the business community want...executive pay related to corporate performance." 138 *Congressional Record* S2907 (30 January 1992, daily ed.; statement of Senator Levin).

## References

Brownstein, Andrew R., and Morris J. Planner. 1992. "Who Should Set CEO Pay? The Press? Congress? Shareholders?" *Harvard Business Review* (May/June): 28.

Chrystal, Graef S. 1992a. "Does Money Matter? Not For America's Vastly Overpaid Executives." *Washington Post,* 9 August, C-1.

———. 1992b. "Perspectives on Executive Pay." *Los Angeles Times,* 25 February, 7

Faltermeyer, Edmund. 1991. "The Deal Decade." *Fortune,* 26 August, 58.

Friedrich, Otto. 1990. "Freed from Greed." *Time, 1* January, 76.

Henkoff, Ronald. 1989. "Is Greed Dead?" *Fortune,* 14 August, 40.

Herzel, Leo. 1982. "Golden Parachute Contracts: Analysis." *National Law Journal* 4 (15 February): 22.

Kesner, Michael S. 1993. "Are Executives Paid Too Much?" *Prentice-Hall Law and Business Corporations* 65 (sec. 2).

Kirkland, Richard I., Jr. 1984. "When Paying Off a Raider Benefits Shareholders." *Fortune,* 30 April, 152.

Klein, Frederick C. 1982. "A Golden Parachute Protects Executives, But Does It Hinder or Foster Takeovers?" *Wall Street Journal,* 8 December, 56.

Kowalchuk, Reginald W. 1992. "Memorandum from TEI President Reginald E. Kowalchuk to Members of the Congressional Tax-writing Committees. *Tax Executive* 44 (July-August): 296.

Levinson, Marc. 1992. "Lay Off the Pricey CEO." *Newsweek,* 10 February, 44.

Lustig, Eric A. 1988. "The Emerging Role of the Federal Tax Law in Regulating Hostile Takeover Defenses: The New Section 5881 Excise Tax on Greenmail." *University of Florida Law Review* 40:789–91.

Macey, Jonathan R., and Fred S. McChesney 1985. "A Theoretical Analysis of Corporate Greenmail." *Yale Law Journal* 95:16–27.

Maurer, David V. 1984. "Golden Parachutes—Executive Compensation or Executive Overreaching?" *Journal of Corporate Law* 9:354–55.

McCarroll, Thomas. 1992. "Executive Pay: The Shareholders Strike Back." *Time,* 4 May, 46.

Moore, W. John. 1982. "Golden Parachute Arrangements Shelter Displaced Executives." *Legal Times of Washington,* 25 October, 1.

Morrison, Ann M. 1983. "Those Executive Bailout Deals." *Fortune,* 13 December, 82.

Nelson-Horchler, Joani. 1990. "What's Your Boss Worth? 35 Times Your Salary? 1,000 Times? The Workforce Gets Angry." *Washington Post,* 5 August, D-3.

Passell, Peter. 1992. "Those Big Executive Salaries May Mask a Bigger Problem." *New York Times,* 20 April, A-1.

Reich, Robert B. 1992. "Executive Salaries: From the Absurd to the Grotesque." *San Francisco Chronicle,* 17 May, 16/Z-1.

Sheppard, Lee A. 1993. "The Misguided Populism of the Executive Compensation Limit." *Tax Notes,* 26 April, 454.

U.S. Congress. 1984. Staff of the Joint Committee on Taxation. *General Explanation of the Revenue Provisions of the Deficit Reduction Act of 1984.* 98th Cong., 2nd sess.

U.S. Senate. 1984. Committee on Finance. *Report on the Deficit Reduction Act of 1984.* 98th Cong., 2nd sess.

Zelinsky, Edward. 1990. "Greenmail, Golden Parachutes and the Internal Revenue Code: A Tax Policy Critique of Sections 280G, 4999 and 5881." *Villanova Law Review* 35:163.

# 14

# Gun Control, Strict Liability, and Excise Taxes

*Bruce H. Kobayashi*

Legislative proposals to limit the private ownership of firearms have proven a popular tool for lawmakers attempting to convince their constituents that they are fighting crime. Recent state and federal legislation has proposed to tax or otherwise restrict the private ownership of certain "styles" of firearms,[1] to limit the availability of certain types and calibers of ammunition,[2] to impose liability on manufacturers and retailers of firearms,[3] and to increase the transaction costs of purchasing firearms.[4]

However, such piecemeal attempts at regulating the private ownership of firearms often make little economic sense as serious crime-fighting tools. Many proposed regulations target firearms that are rarely used in crime, and are based on arbitrary distinctions that leave close substitutes unregulated.[5] The restrictions do little to limit the sources of firearms most used by criminals[6] and in some cases have the perverse effect of causing criminals to switch from less-lethal to more-lethal firearms.[7] Further, little evidence exists to suggest that states or localities that have passed restrictive laws have experienced reductions in crime.[8]

While the production of piecemeal legislation seems counterproductive from an efficiency standpoint, its political popularity is not surprising. While advocates of gun control would prefer broad-based uniform federal restrictions on the private ownership of firearms, such broad-based bans, which would likely require the confiscation of private property, currently do not have popular support.[9] Such a widespread prohibition on the private ownership of firearms would require costly expenditures on law enforcement, and

Michelle Burtis, Don Kates, and Nelson Lund provided helpful comments on this chapter, and Will Loeffler contributed valuable research. Any remaining errors are the author's.

would likely face constitutional challenges under the Second,[10] Fourth,[11] and Fifth[12] Amendments to the Constitution of the United States.[13]

Given the political and legal problems facing those wishing to enact widespread federal restrictions on firearms, proponents instead demand narrowly defined piecemeal legislation, hoping to expand its scope administratively after passage[14] or to argue for more sweeping restrictions when the narrow restrictions fail to produce any observable benefits. Legislators, facing a myopic constituency, routinely dismiss the intangible benefits of general firearm ownership (e.g., the effect widespread firearm ownership has on the general deterrence of crime and tyranny) and then supply gun control legislation in order to avoid being accused of "doing nothing" about the tangible costs of firearm ownership (deaths and injuries caused by firearms). Further, the production of piecemeal legislation produces a greater demand for the services of legislators, and for the opposing groups lobbying for and against the passage of the legislation (McChesney 1987). Last, but not least, the passage of legislation that encourages the disarmaming of private citizens tips the balance of power away from individuals and toward the government.[15]

The difficulties of enacting widespread restrictions on the private ownership of firearms through the legislative process have led advocates of gun control to seek alternatives to bald restrictions on private ownership and to use the legislative process to enact *indirect* restrictions on gun ownership. Specifically, proponents of restrictions on the private ownership of firearms recently have suggested "taxing" rather than banning firearms and ammunition. Further, given the likely difficulties they would face in obtaining direct taxation through legislation, they suggest that a similar result might be achieved through the courts[16] by imposing strict liability on manufacturers and distributors of firearms.[17]

In either case, proponents of the taxation of firearms suggest that such taxes are appropriate because firearms cause uncompensated externalities (i.e., that such taxes are corrective taxes). Until recently, the externalities argument has been implicit, but it is now being used explicitly in academic literature (see below) and by members of Congress to justify restrictive gun policies.[18] In adopting the externalities argument, the proponents have explicitly adopted an economic framework for discussing this issue—imposing taxes would cause gun purchasers to internalize the externalities caused by firearms, and would move this market closer to economic efficiency.[19]

This chapter critically examines the economic case for broad-based taxes on firearms as a method for controlling the criminal misuse of firearms. Section I examines the economic and legal case for strict liability for the manufacture and sale of firearms. Economic analysis suggests that the general taxation of firearms, whether directly or through the imposition of strict liability on manufacturers of firearms, is not an efficient means of reducing crime. Relative to an approach that distinguishes between legal use and misuse of firearms and punishes only the latter, generally taxing firearms provides weaker disincentives to misuse firearms and punishes those who do not misuse them. Further, a general tax on firearms may result in the commission of more violent crimes if widespread and legal ownership of firearms serves as a general deterrent to crime.

Thus, contrary to the claims of its proponents, the case for taxation and strict liability rules for the sale and manufacture of firearms is not based on economic efficiency—rather, it is rooted in a desire to reduce general firearm ownership or to provide a system of social insurance.[20] And as has been noted generally, use of strict liability or direct taxes to provide social insurance for persons injured or killed by firearms invariably distorts economic incentives and is likely a relatively inefficient means of providing such insurance (Kaplow and Shavell 1994).

Section II examines current attempts to regulate firearms and suggests reasons why such regulation is at best ineffective, and more likely to be counterproductive in reducing violent crime. The current status of constitutional protection of the right to keep and bear arms is summarized, and the economic role of constitutional protection—placing strict burdens on a government wishing to regulate the individual ownership of firearms—is examined. Existing evidence on the effects of gun ownership on the rate of violent crime and the effects of current gun laws on the rate of violent crime suggests that most government regulation of firearms would not pass a cost-benefit test, and certainly would fail the high standards of rationality and tailoring requirements applied to government regulation of other constitutional rights. Further, given that the difference between the imposition of a selective excise tax and an absolute prohibition on the ownership of firearms is largely a matter of degree (a de facto absolute prohibition can be achieved by a draconian tax or liability award[21]), a generalized excise tax imposed through the courts can raise the same type of constitutional issues that would be raised by direct prohibition. Further, even if court-imposed liability verdicts that only moderately increase the price of firearms present less general danger to the Second Amendment,[22] such price increases can raise equal-protection issues if their primary effect is to disarm the law-abiding poor—arguably the population that would benefit the most from the generalized private ownership of firearms.[23]

## I. An Economic and Legal Analysis of Strict Liability on Firearms

In this section, economic cases are presented for and against placing an excise tax on firearms by imposing strict liability on the manufacture of firearms. Part A examines the economic question at the heart of the public-policy debate: whether effective control of the *misuse* of firearms is best achieved by a generalized tax on the sale and manufacture of firearms or by taxing the misuse of firearms. Part B then examines existing legal treatment of policies placing liability for third-party injuries on firearm manufacturers.

For clarity of exposition, the analysis in this section generally addresses the criminal misuse of firearms, and does not address self-inflicted gunshot wounds or accidental injuries (of either firearm owners or third parties) caused by defective firearms. The case of injury due to defective firearms does not present any issues unique to the case of firearms, and such injuries are currently dealt with by the legal system.[24] As for suicides, even analyses advocating strict liability of firearm manufacturers have suggested that a defense of contributory negligence—a standard that would almost certainly include suicide—should be allowed.[25]

## A. *Externalities and Corrective Taxes*

According to proponents of imposing strict liability for third-party injuries on the manufacturers of firearms, the economic case for corrective taxes or the imposition of strict liability on firearms is a straightforward application of the standard Pigouvian analysis of an uncompensated externality. Proponents of placing excise taxes on firearms argue that the negligent use or the misuse of firearms causes uncompensated harm to innocent victims. Thus, absent taxes or liability, the prices of firearms will not reflect this externality, and are therefore too low. The implication of this type of analysis is that a corrective tax should be applied to the sale and manufacture of firearms to correct this distortion.[26]

The economic argument for the imposition of selective taxes or liability on firearms can be illustrated by using the familiar Pigouvian diagram. Figure 14.1 shows the private demand and supply of firearms in an unregulated market. The analysis assumes that users of firearms do not differ (or cannot be identified) according to their *ex ante* or *ex post* probabilities of committing a crime. Thus the demand for firearms, $D^0$, includes demands generated by legal and illegal uses of firearms. The analysis also assumes that firearms are homogeneous. The supply curve S(P) represents the marginal private cost of producing and selling a firearm. The price of guns in the market is $P_0$, and the quantity of guns produced and sold is $Q_0$.

Critics of private gun ownership argue that increased numbers of guns create external social costs, and are of little positive social value. The most oft mentioned costs include the costs of deaths and injuries caused by firearms.[27] In terms of figure 14.1, the assumption that firearms cause external social costs implies that the true marginal social cost of firearms (MSC) is above the marginal private cost of production (MC). This assumption is made for illustrative purposes only. As noted below, the mere existence of external social costs such as deaths and injuries from firearms does not imply, nor does empirical evidence suggest, that the private ownership of firearms imposes *net*

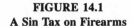

**FIGURE 14.1**
**A Sin Tax on Firearms**

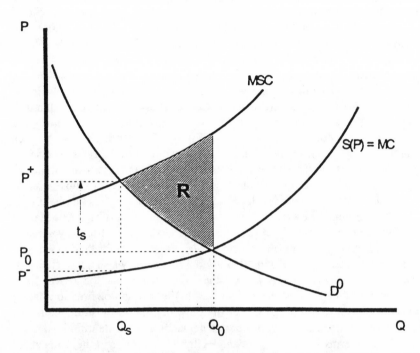

social costs on society. In the case illustrated in figure 14.1, the efficient level of production, $Q_s$, is less than the free-market quantity of firearms, $Q_0$. Absent regulation, this analysis suggests that too many guns are produced and sold.

In order to rectify this situation, a corrective Pigouvian tax equal to $t_s$ per unit should be applied to the sale of firearms. All purchasers of firearms pay $P^+$ for their firearms, and the manufacturers' price, net of taxes or expected liability awards, equals $P^-$. Application of such a tax reduces the number of firearms produced and sold to the efficient level, $Q_s$, and reduces social costs by an amount equal to the area R.

Such a tax could be applied directly. Alternatively, such a tax could also be imposed by forcing manufacturers of firearms to internalize these external social costs by placing liability for gun-related injuries on them. Manufacturers facing liability costs from selling firearms that are misused or otherwise cause externalities will incorporate these expected liability costs into their private marginal costs of producing and selling the firearms. Thus, to the extent that courts correctly impose liability for the externalities caused by firearms, the effective private marginal cost of manufacturing a firearm faced by individual manufacturers of firearms will equal the marginal social cost. Use of the court system, rather than having a legislatively set tax, would have the added benefit of a less centralized form of imposing the tax liability—implying both informational advantages and a less immediate threat to liberty. Further, if courts and liability awards are used, such a result will be automatically imposed by private suits against manufacturers (i.e., those firearms most used in crimes will suffer the greatest expected liability).

Thus, under the assumptions of the above model, the traditional Pigouvian rationale for the imposition of taxes or liability is obtained. However, the above analysis contains strong assumptions. For example, the analysis assumes that firearms create net negative externalities—an issue we will return to below. What is more important, the analysis assumes that legitimate and illegitimate uses of firearms cannot be distinguished. If these types of uses can be distinguished, a general tax or the imposition of liability unnecessarily punishes those who do not misuse firearms as much as those who do; that is, imposing taxes or liability will increase the price of firearms to those who do not misuse them. If, however, legitimate and illegitimate uses can be differentiated, economic efficiency does not imply imposition of a general tax or liability on the manufacture of firearms. Instead, economic efficiency *requires* that liability be placed on those who *misuse* firearms rather than those who manufacture them.[28] By placing liability only on those who misuse firearms, the system can more directly address the actions that create the losses.[29]

Figure 14.2 depicts the issues involved in the taxation of firearm misuse, as opposed to taxation of the sale of firearms. In order to illustrate the issues involved, we assume that two separate demands can be identified—the demand for firearms for responsible and legitimate use, $D^L$, and the demand for firearms for illegal use, $D^I$. The horizontal sum of these two demands represents the total demand for guns shown in figure 14.1, $D^0$. For simplicity, assume that only the demand for illegal use, $D^I$, generates social costs. In the absence of regulation, the market for guns again results in price $P_0$ and quantity $Q_0$ of firearms sold.

Now consider the effect of imposing the tax $t_s$ on manufacturers of firearms. As before, the total quantity of guns falls from $Q_0$ to $Q_s$. As shown in the left-hand panel of figure 14.2, illegitimate use of firearms is reduced from $Q_0^I$ to $Q_s^I$, resulting in a reduction of social costs equal to the shaded area R'. However, legitimate firearm use is also reduced (from $Q_0^L$ to $Q_s^L$ in the right-hand panel of figure 14.2), causing a deadweight loss to responsible firearm owners equal to the shaded area L'. The sum of areas R' and L' equals the area R depicted in figure 14.1.

However, the deadweight loss placed on the lawful users of firearms, L', is avoidable. Specifically, if the tax $t_s$ can be placed only on those who cause the external harm, the reduction in social costs R' can be achieved without imposing the loss L' on those with legitimate uses of firearms.[30] Further, the optimal tax on the illegitimate use of firearms should be increased from $t_s$ to $t_s + d$, raising the full price of purchasing a firearm for unlawful purposes (to

**FIGURE 14.2**
**A Tax on the Misuse of Firearms**

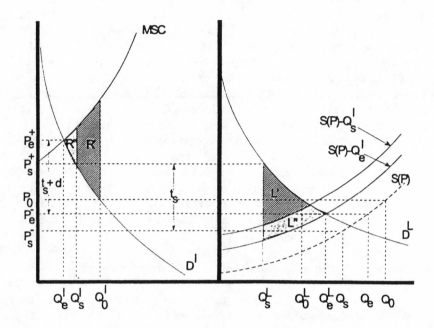

$P_e^+$), and resulting in an additional decrease in the quantity of firearms purchased for unlawful purposes (to $Q_e^l$) and an additional decrease in the social costs from firearm misuse (area R"). This also increases the supply of guns available to legitimate users (to $Q_e^L$) and lowers the price of firearms in the legitimate market (to $P_e^-$), thus increasing economic welfare by the shaded area L".

Thus, the above analysis suggests that in contrast to a generalized tax on the manufacture and sale of firearms, a tax on the misuse of firearms would increase welfare. Rather than suggesting that a tax or liability be placed on the manufacture and sale of firearms generally, economic analysis suggests that taxes or liability be placed only on those who misuse firearms.[31]

Several objections to the economic analysis just presented have been raised. One objection to the use of penalties on individuals who misuse firearms is that such individuals are judgment-proof—and thus are unlikely to be affected by the imposition of liability.[32] The major fallacy of this line of argument is that such an analysis ignores the existence of the criminal law. Solvency is not required to impose penalties for misuse of firearms—a more vigorous enforcement of the criminal law and its nonmonetary penalties would concentrate the costs of misuse on those committing crimes. Nor does it matter that not all misusers of firearms are caught and punished—such issues can be addressed through increasing the criminal penalty placed on misuse.[33]

It is unlikely that the proponents of liability of handgun manufacturers are unaware of the criminal law. A more likely explanation is an underlying desire to provide compensation for victims of criminal acts or a desire to impose a general tax on firearms.[34] If compensation of victims is a goal, then the insolvent criminal presents a problem. However, the goal of providing social insurance through the courts is not, as the proponents often claim, based on principles of economic efficiency. Indeed, such claims are likely to be at odds with economic efficiency. Scholars examining uses of the court system to provide social insurance have shown that such attempts generally result in a costly distortion of market incentives. Further, they argue that the expansion of liability has generally failed to provide such insurance, has increased the costs of doing business, has increased the demands placed on our court systems, and has lowered the efficiency of both. This line of reasoning has led these critics to conclude that the expansion of enterprise liability, largely carried out by the courts, was largely inconsistent with economic efficiency.[35]

## B. The Legal Treatment of Liability against Firearm Manufacturers

This part examines the legal treatment of liability for third-party injuries caused by nondefective firearms and compares the courts' treatment of this issue to that suggested by the economic analysis presented in part A. The question of under what circumstances firearm manufacturers should be liable for injuries caused by their products is part of the larger debate over the expansion of enterprise liability that has occurred in both academic and popular literature. Prior to the early 1960s, manufacturer liability for injuries was largely controlled by contract law and its privity requirement.[36] However, in the early 1960s, the courts rapidly moved away from contract law in expanding the scope of enterprise liability to include, among other things, enterprise liability for production and design defects.[37]

However, this expansion stopped short of holding firearm manufacturers strictly liable for injuries to third parties caused by misuse of their products. Because injuries caused by the misuse of a firearm do not involve either a production or design defect, holding firearm manufacturers liable under these circumstances would further expand enterprise liability by eliminating the requirement that plaintiffs show *any* type of defect exists. Examination of the courts' decisions suggests a general rule that rejects the doctrine of liability without defect, both generally (Henderson and Twerski 1991) and in the case of firearms.[38] Even proponents of holding firearm manufacturers strictly liable for third-party injuries suggest that "taken at face value these cases appear to present a firm and consistent line of authority" that has refused to hold the manufacturer liable (Bogus 1991).

As noted above, economists have criticized the general expansion of enterprise liability as inconsistent with economic efficiency. Commentators have argued that the expansion of liability to include "liability without defect" would further decrease the economic efficiency of the tort liability system for similar reasons (Henderson and Twerski 1991). Given that many of the courts have suggested that the appropriate focus is on placing liability on those who misuse the firearms, the current case law is broadly consistent with the efficiency rule suggested by the economic analysis presented above.[39]

In contrast to the views expressed by many economists, proponents of placing strict liability on the manufacture of firearms have suggested that the recent expansion of enterprise liability "is an accepted part of American common law, and many believe it is a great success story about which the courts can be justly proud"; they suggest that enterprise liability for third-party injuries caused by well-functioning firearms is the next logical step in the expansion.[40] Matching the courts' near unanimity in refusing to impose strict liability on handgun manufacturers is the call by academics to ignore the courts and to impose such enterprise liability.[41] Proponents of holding manufacturers liable have suggested that plaintiffs attempting to recover damages from manufacturers proceed under two theories—the negligent-entrustment theory, and a theory of strict liability under a risk-utility test.

Under the *negligent-entrustment theory,* plaintiffs argue that failure to prevent distribution of firearms to obviously incompetent persons, in addition to any defects in the product's design or manufacture, is negligence. Such suits have generally failed because the plaintiffs are not able to show that the defendant (the manufacturer or dealer) knew or had reason to know of the acquiring party's incompetence. Cases that have succeeded have been based on evidence of a dealer's failure to comply with statutory procedures.[42] Such cases can be limited to negligent dealers, and can be distinguished from cases where the dealers complied with statutory procedures.[43] What is more important, these cases can be easily distinguished from cases involving the manufacture of firearms. Further, many of the ambiguities involved in this type of case will be remedied by the Brady Act requirement that criminal background checks be done by the dealers.[44]

Under the *theory of strict liability* based on a risk-utility test, firearm manufacturers would be held strictly liable if the plaintiff can prove (1) the firearm caused the injuries, and (2) the cost of placing the firearm in the stream of commerce outweighs its benefits.[45] Under this theory, the plaintiff first must prove causation, a task that proponents of handgun liability suggest can, in many cases, easily be accomplished by showing that the firearm injured or killed the victim. Once causation is proven, risk-utility balancing occurs with the burden of proving "social utility" falling on the firearm manufacturer. Proponents of strict liability often cite studies and statistics on the number and frequency of firearm-related deaths and injuries, suggesting that many types of firearms easily fail the risk-utility test.

However, it is not clear that firearms would fail either prong of the risk-utility test. In considering the causation issue, courts generally have ruled in third-party-victim cases that causation was eliminated by a misuse or a superseding cause (i.e., the courts generally have found that the criminal's negligence is an intervening force that supersedes other causative factors on the part of the manufacturer).[46] As noted above, such a finding is consistent with the economic analysis presented in part A, namely, that efficiency requires a focus on the criminal act rather than the firearm. More generally, it embodies the concept of the least-cost avoider—the focus is on penalizing the act of misuse precisely to alter (reduce) the probability that such misuse will occur.[47]

Another assumption made by proponents of strict liability is that the act of placing firearms in the stream of commerce will not pass a risk-utility or cost-benefit test. An analysis of the type presented in part A assumes that increased private ownership of firearms creates net negative externalities, and that courts or legislatures will correctly identify the true marginal social costs and benefits of firearms. Proponents of strict liability of firearm manufacturers assert that "a review of the data leads ineluctably to one conclusion—the costs that handguns impose on society overwhelmingly outweigh their benefits" (Bogus 1991, 1122). These authors generally cite studies published in medical journals that claim to show the net social costs of firearm ownership. Frequently cited are three articles that appeared in the *New England Journal of Medicine*,[48] suggesting that firearms are much more likely to be used to kill a family member or an acquaintance than to kill an intruder (Kellerman and Reay 1986), that firearms increase the risk of homicide by a factor of three (Kellerman et al. 1993), and that firearms kept in the home are unlikely to be used to deter crime (Sloan et al. 1988).

A closer examination reveals significant flaws in the research cited by proponents of restricting private ownership of firearms. Kellerman et al. 1993 is a retrospective study that claims to show an increase in the risk of homicide from firearm ownership. However, the study fails to hold the characteristics of the case and control samples constant. For example, the study fails to consider that subjects in the case sample were more likely to have substance abuse problems than those in the control sample.[49] The study also fails to consider the possibility that the direction of causality between firearms and homicides is the reverse of that assumed by the authors—for example, the case sample, consisting largely of substance abusers, may have been more likely to experience violence and thus more likely to be armed than the control sample.

Even setting aside problems of selection and controls, basing conclusions on the use of "mortality data" (i.e., studies that consider only homicide data to define the cases) is likely to overstate the overall harm from the presence of firearms and understate the benefits from firearms. When one broadens one's perspective by considering the probability of attack in a threatening situation, rather than focusing only on mortality data, the evidence suggests that the presence of firearms does not increase the probability of injury or death. Generally, "the more lethal the weapon used in the attack is, the less likely it is that it will be used to actually inflict an injury"; that is, although firearms are more lethal if used in an attack, they are used less frequently per attack. On net, the two effects "almost exactly cancel each other out" (Kleck 1990, 183). Similarly, because both the Kellerman et al. (1993) study and the Kellerman and Reay 1986 study are based on mortality data, they do not consider defensive uses of firearms that do not result in homicides—an omission criminologist Gary Kleck estimates to account for approximately 2 million uses per year.[50]

Sloan et al. (1988) examine crime rates in two "similar" cities, Seattle and Vancouver. The authors find Seattle to have a higher homicide rate than Vancouver, with the difference between the two cities due to a difference in gun homicides. However, these results have also been the subject of academic criticism.[51] For example, as Kopel (1992) notes, the ethnic and cultural makeup of the two cities' minority groups, while similar in terms of overall percentages of the population, differ markedly in terms of composition. The difference in homicide rates is due entirely to the difference in the rates of minority homicides. Nonminority homicide rates are the same across the two cities despite higher gun ownership rates and fewer firearm restrictions in Seattle. Further, the argument that the Sloan et al. results demonstrate the effectiveness of Canadian gun control laws is inconsistent with a large number of time series studies that find no effect on either crime or suicide from the passage of these laws (Kopel 1991, 1992; Mundt 1990; Centerwall 1991).

Thus, the Sloan et al. and Kellerman et al. studies both suffer from similar problems resulting from unobserved or unexplained differences between the case and control populations.[52] A more serious problem plaguing all three studies is the failure to seriously account for the beneficial uses of firearms. Thus, far from leading "ineluctably" to one conclusion, the studies do little more than suggest that there are costs of firearm ownership. From an economic standpoint, the question is not whether there are social costs involved in the private ownership of firearms—there are. However, there are clearly benefits from private firearm ownership, including a large number of uses of guns for defense, for general deterrence of crime, for recreation and hunting, and for ensuring liberty. Thus, the relevant question is whether the benefits from firearm ownership outweigh the costs—a question to which no definitive answer has appeared (and which, in general, has not been asked). Comprehensive studies of the relationship between crime rates and rates of gun ownership suggest that there is little valid statistical evidence to support a claim that the private ownership of firearms significantly increases or decreases the rate of violent crime.[53]

## II. The Restriction of Firearms and the Second Amendment

The previous section suggests that, contrary to the claims of proponents of increased regulation of firearm ownership, little compelling evidence exists to suggest that the private ownership of firearms causes increased homicide rates, that the ownership of a firearm by an individual for purposes of self-defense is counterproductive, or that the private possession of firearms results in a net loss to society. Further, these studies and the articles that rely on them commit the "nirvana" fallacy (Demsetz 1969) by failing to address a second issue: will the regulation of firearms be effective in reducing violent crime? That is, the authors relying on such studies to conclude that increased regulation of firearms would increase societal welfare have failed to consider several paramount issues: First, as noted above, these authors have not adequately considered the benefits of firearm ownership, including the benefits from force being held in a decentralized fashion as a check on the power of the state. Further, these authors have failed to address the actual as opposed to the theoretical efficacy of firearm restrictions. Finally, they have generally ignored issues relating to the costs of enforcing gun laws.

This section examines whether there is any evidence that existing attempts at regulating firearms have reduced the rate of violent crime. Examination of common forms of firearm regulation suggests few positive effects. This result, coupled with the scant evidence suggesting that the private ownership of firearms creates net social losses, provides an extremely tenuous case for the regulation of firearms. In addition, this section examines the issue of whether an individual constitutional right to keep and bear arms exists, and its relation to the current debate over increased firearm regulations. It is argued that a strong case can be made for the existence of an individual right to keep and bear arms, and that much of existing firearm regulation would not pass constitutional tests of rationality.

### A. Partial Bans and Unintended Results

Proponents of gun control suggest that the problem of unfairly punishing innocent and responsible gun owners is overstated, and can be largely alleviated by taxing only those firearms that are commonly used in crimes (e.g., Saturday Night Specials and "assault style" weapons).[54] These analyses suggest that rational public policy should focus on partial bans—enacting laws restricting specific types of weapons or passing legislation restricting firearms in high-crime areas.

Partial bans affecting cheap handguns and automatic weapons have been the primary focus of recent legislative activity. However, the observed operation of partial bans has not been consistent with the goal of identifying and targeting the types of weapons commonly used in crimes. Instead, the types of weapons that have been the recent focus of legislative activity are not disproportionately used in crimes. The recent bans on the further sale to civilians of fully automatic weapons and "assault style" semiautomatic weapons in fact target weapons rarely used in crimes.[55]

One of the most commonly proposed forms of firearm regulation is a ban on handguns defined to be "Saturday Night Specials," firearms defined generally to be of small caliber and low cost. Support for such restrictions is generally based on the assertion that such firearms are disproportionately used in crime. However, as noted by Kleck (1990) and even by proponents of restrictions on the private ownership of firearms, most handguns used in crimes are not weapons that would be classified as Saturday Night Specials, and such firearms are not disproportionately used in crime.[56] Further, to the extent such bans are useful in banning inexpensive and small-caliber handguns, they are likely to have two pernicious effects. First, since such bans focus their effects on inexpensive guns, such laws will have a disproportionate effect on law-abiding, low-income consumers. This group of law-abiding citizens may be the most affected by crime, and may be afforded the least effective protection by police.[57] Thus, such regulations may disproportionately harm the segment of the law-abiding population that would benefit the most from firearm ownership.

Second, even if the bans are successful in increasing the average price of firearms and reducing the number of Saturday Night Specials purchased by criminals, the number of deaths caused by the illegal use of firearms may rise. Because such bans generally focus on small-caliber firearms, criminals will substitute away from less-lethal, small-caliber firearms toward more-lethal, large-caliber firearms.[58] Thus, even with a moderate reduction in the number of firearms purchased by criminals, the switch by criminals to larger–caliber handguns, or to shotguns, will increase mortality rates.[59]

The other type of commonly imposed partial ban is a geographic ban. Cross-sectional evidence does not find any correlation between the existence of restrictive gun laws and lowered crime rates. In fact, because such laws are likely to be enacted in urban areas with high crime rates (i.e., high crime rates cause more gun laws to be passed), simple correlations can actually show a positive relationship between crime rates and the number or severity of gun laws.[60] This problem of inferring causality from simple correlations (also a problem with the studies in the medical literature discussed in section I) renders many early cross-sectional studies invalid. And when omitted-variable and simultaneity biases are corrected, there is little evidence that gun laws reduce violent crime. Kleck's (1990) comprehensive survey of the literature suggests that, with the exception of laws that increased penalties for using a firearm in the commission of a crime, most types of gun control have not been found to significantly affect the rate of violent crime. Further, there is little evidence that such laws significantly reduced levels of gun ownership (Kleck 1990, 398).

Problems of causality and omitted variables theoretically can be alleviated by performing time series studies where the event (a change in the law) is not confounded by other factors. However, in practice, time series studies also suffer from confounding events. Recent time series evidence based on reduced total homicide rates in the District of Columbia (absolutely and relative to the surrounding suburbs) has been put forward as evidence of the effectiveness of that city's handgun freeze (Loftin et al. 1991). Apart from the prima facie absurdity of this claim, this study can be critiqued on two grounds. First, over the time period examined, the District experienced a large net outflow of residents to the suburbs of Maryland and Virginia. When one corrects for this out-migration from the District, the results cited in the article are reversed: the per capita homicide rate in the District of Columbia actually rose relative to the surrounding suburbs.[61]

Second, even if one accepts the conclusions of the study in the short term, the long-term experience with homicide in the District of Columbia presents a rather bleak picture. Quite separate from the claimed short-term gains of the handgun prohibition, the longer-term experience of the District of Columbia, which has included record homicide rates in the past few years, suggests that such laws are at best ineffective, and more likely result in higher crime rates due in part to the gradual disarming of the law-abiding population, leaving them more vulnerable to armed criminals.[62] In fact, these adverse selection problems are likely to be generic: because criminals are unlikely to be deterred by local boundaries, and are less likely to be deterred by relatively small penalties for the possession of firearms (in relation to the penalties for committing a violent crime), geographic bans generally disarm the law-abiding residents much more than they disarm the criminals.[63]

## B. Complete Bans and the Costs of Prohibition

Those advocating national gun prohibition strategies often cite the inability of localities that have enacted strict firearm laws to prevent the inflow of firearms from localities with relatively lax restrictions on firearms. Thus, to those conceding that partial bans seem ineffectual or even counterproductive, a complete national ban on the ownership of firearms seems like an attractive solution to these enforcement problems. However, advocates of a prohibition policy fail to note that the problems plaguing strict gun laws at the local level, including the inability to enforce current gun laws and the inability to keep firearms out of the hands of criminals, also will be present at the national level; that is, any attempts to enforce strict prohibitions on the private ownership of firearms, either local or national, will likely be costly, and will generally result in the adverse selection problems mentioned above.

The experiences with other episodes of national prohibition, such as the prohibition of alcohol in the 1920s and the current prohibition on certain drugs, illustrate the dual problems of the costs of enforcement and adverse selection.[64] As these episodes illustrate, prohibition does not result in elimination of the targeted activity, despite substantial expenditures of state and federal resources.[65] Further, such attempts at prohibition result in a shift away from the legal (and regulated) distribution of the commodity to illegal market activity. Because contracts relating to the distribution of illegal commodities cannot be legally enforced, disputes in illegal markets are often settled violently. The fact that large criminal penalties are placed on distribution of the prohibited commodity amplifies the tendency for violence, because the marginal penalty for violent crime falls as the absolute penalty for illegal distribution rises.[66]

Prohibitions of firearms will generate similar adverse selection problems. If laws banning the possession of firearms are enforced with large criminal penalties, citizens not engaged in criminal activity will face larger penalties at the margin, and are more likely to be disarmed. Thus, the effect of attempting to prohibit the private possession of firearms will be to disarm law-abiding citizens rather than criminals, resulting in a reduction in the deterrence from general firearm ownership.[67]

There are also reasons to think that prohibition of firearm ownership would be even less successful than the prohibition of alcohol or other drugs. As Kates (1984, 149) notes, alcohol and other drugs are consumed, while a firearm is a durable good that, "with proper care, will endure throughout the life of its owner and far beyond the seventh generation of descendants." Thus, firearms do not require the multiple and continuous transactions that increase the probability that the illegal distribution of alcohol or other drugs will be detected. And while ammunition is consumable, a small amount of ammunition can sustain a criminal for a long time (unlike target shooters, who may expend thousands of rounds per year). Criminals can usually commit many crimes by simply threatening their unarmed victims. Even when a firearm is discharged in the commission of a crime, the criminal does not, on average, consume a large amount of ammunition (Kates 1984, 150). For example, a purchase of 200 rounds of handgun ammunition (four standard boxes) would last ten years even if the criminal fired his weapon an average of twenty times a year.

## C. The Second Amendment and the Economics of Constitutional Rights

The final issue to address is the role of the Second Amendment to the Constitution of the United States, which states: "A well regulated militia, being necessary to the security of a free State, the right of the people to keep and bear arms, shall not be infringed." The question of whether the Second Amendment does or does not serve to protect an *individual's* right to keep and bear arms has been at the center of much of the gun control debate. From the standpoint of a legal and economic analysis of governmental restrictions of firearms, whether the Constitution protects an individual's right to keep and bear arms affects the burden placed on governments in attempting to impose such restrictions. As James Buchanan notes, the economic purpose of constitutional rights is to set out the "rules under which ordinary politics is to be allowed to operate" (Buchanan 1975).[68] Constitutional rules have been set out as the most durable form of legal contract, due to the supermajority required for constitutional change.[69] Further, the Supreme Court, in First Amendment cases, has limited the government's ability to regulate constitutional conduct by imposing higher standards of rationality,[70] by requiring more than "unsupported assertion" that the restriction serves a government purpose,[71] and by requiring that any attempts to regulate constitutionally protected conduct must be narrowly tailored.[72] Furthermore, the Supreme Court has chosen to limit liability in cases where the "possibility of suit and frequent recovery"[73] or taxation of inputs[74] would interfere with the exercise of constitutional rights under the First Amendment.

Thus, if an individual's right to keep and bear arms is preserved by the Second Amendment to the Constitution, and if this right is to be treated in a manner consistent with the treatment of other constitutional rights,[75] attempts to regulate the private possession of firearms would have to pass the higher standards of rationality required for regulation of constitutionally protected conduct. Under such a standard, both the federal government and the state governments (through the Fourteenth Amendment) would shoulder the burden of affirmatively demonstrating that any proposed regulation of firearms achieves its goal in a tailored fashion.[76]

Given the analysis in section I, this set of constraints on governmental regulation arguably would include attempts to regulate the availability of firearms by directly taxing firearms or ammunition or by holding firearm manufacturers strictly liable for injury caused by the misuse of their products. As noted above, there is little evidence to suggest that proposals to reduce crime by regulating firearms, including the imposition of strict liability on firearm manufacturers, are narrowly tailored to address the criminal misuse of firearms (strict liability imposes costs on both law-abiding and law-breaking users of firearms), or would pass a cost-benefit test. Thus, such regulations would fail to meet the strict scrutiny and tailoring requirements set out for regulations of constitutional conduct, and may even fail the less strict rational-basis test applied to regulation of nonconstitutional conduct.

Despite the centrality of the issue, the question of whether the Second Amendment protects individuals' rights to keep and bear arms has been largely ignored in studies of constitutional law[77] and by the Supreme Court.[78] While supporters of private firearm ownership see the Second Amendment as preserving an individual right, proponents of governmental restrictions of firearms have concentrated on the "militia clause," interpreting its inclusion as a restriction that limits the scope of the Second Amendment to a right that is a collective right, a state's right, or a right that accrues to an individual only in connection with his duties with the official state militia. The proponents of the "exclusively states' rights" view argue that the Second Amendment was solely a desire on the part of the framers to place "organized state militias" beyond the reach of the federal government's power to disarm at a time when such organized units were designed to be the nation's basic military defense.[79] Further, they argue, the fact that organized state militias do not currently represent the basic military defense has made the amendment a mere historical curiosity.[80]

However, recent scholarship on the Second Amendment suggests that a strong case can be made for rejecting the states' rights viewpoint.[81] As these scholars have noted, showing that one of the purposes of the amendment was to protect state militias is not sufficient to reject the individual rights view— to do this, one must show that this was the sole purpose of the amendment, and that there was no intention to protect the individual. As Kates (1983) notes, this latter task is "a particularly difficult burden to bear" given the large amount of evidence suggesting that protection of the individual was one of the purposes of the amendment.

Scholars argue that the wording and the historical origins of the Second Amendment cast doubt on the states' rights view, and suggest that the Second Amendment protects an individual right to keep and bear arms. As noted above, proponents of the states' rights view concentrate on the term *militia*, assuming that the term referred to an organized military force. However, during the eighteenth century, the primary meaning of the term *militia* was not to denote an organized military force. Rather, the dominant use of the term was to denote "the whole body of able-bodied citizens declared by law as being subject to call to military service" (Kates 1983). The colonies' adoption of the English militia system[82] and statements of the founding fathers, who referred to organized military units pejoratively as the "select militia," also support this latter definition.[83] Further, the states' rights view of the militia is inconsistent with clause 3 of section 10 in article I of the U.S. Constitution, which forbids the states to "keep troops" without the consent of Congress.

In addition, interpreting the phrase "the right of the people" as "the right of the states" would be inconsistent with the way in which similar clauses in the First, Fourth, and Ninth Amendments have been interpreted.[84] Such an interpretation also would be inconsistent with the Tenth Amendment, which explicitly distinguishes the powers of the people from the powers of the states, and as Kates noted, would "present a truly grotesque reading of the Bill of Rights."[85]

Further, historical evidence and an examination of the debate over the Bill of Rights supports the individual rights view. Debate over the Constitution suggests that the founding fathers were necessarily influenced by a universal belief in an armed citizenry as a check on the power of the government, and as a means to provide generally for self-defense. For example, the proponents of ratification of the Constitution buttressed their arguments for a strengthened federal government by denying that such a government could ever be strong enough to destroy the liberties of an armed populace (Kates 1983, 223–24). The antifederalists, noting that the Constitution offered citizens no protection against disarmament by the federal government, sought to ensure that this deterrent against the government would be preserved by insisting on a Bill of Rights that would guarantee an individual right to arms.[86]

The proponents of the states' rights view also argue that even if one agrees that the academic debate over the meaning of the Second Amendment supports the individual rights interpretation, this position has not been adopted by the federal courts. However, closer examination of the case law reveals that the exclusively states' rights position has not been adopted by the Supreme Court. The only Supreme Court case that directly addresses the Second Amendment, *U.S. v. Miller* (see note 78), certainly does not support the exclusively states' rights interpretation that "militia" in the militia clause is the National Guard. Although the decision is often cited by opponents of gun ownership because the Supreme Court failed to uphold the lower court's dismissal of an indictment based upon a finding that the defendant's Second Amendment rights had been violated,[87] the case is not a repudiation of the Second Amendment as an individual right.

If *U.S. v. Miller* stands for anything, it stands for the proposition that it is not within judicial notice that a "sawed-off shotgun" is a militia weapon. And to the extent that *U.S. v. Miller* defines the term *militia,* it suggests that the whole of the people comprise the militia, and is in fact supportive of the individual rights view.[88] The decision goes to great lengths to distinguish between the "Militia," or "all males physically capable of acting in concert for the common defense," and "Troops," or standing armies.[89] Further, although the Court clearly suggests that rational limitations may be placed on the kind of arms the amendment guarantees the individual, the Court also suggests that such arms must be both of the kind "in common use" and provably part of the ordinary military equipment—a standard that would certainly include many "assault style" weapons, such as the AR-15, M1A, HK-94, and high-capacity 9-millimeter and .45-caliber handguns.[90]

Three other Supreme Court cases—*Miller v. Texas, Presser v. Illinois,* and *U.S. v. Cruikshank* (see note 78)—are also cited in favor of the proposition that there is no individual right granted by the Constitution to keep and bear arms. These cases do not, however, address the scope of the right possessed by an individual under the Second Amendment. At most, they address the issue of whether or not the Second Amendment is to be applied to the states.[91] Similarly, subsequent cases in the lower courts, often cited as rejecting the individual rights interpretation of the Second Amendment, also hold only that the Second Amendment has not been incorporated to apply against the states by the Fourteenth Amendment.[92]

However, as scholars have noted, *Miller, Presser,* and *Cruikshank* all predate the first decision incorporating a provision of the Bill of Rights through the Fourteenth Amendment.[93] Thus, it is unclear if the *Miller, Presser, and Cruikshank* judges were willing to concede that any of the amendments comprising the Bill of Rights applied to the states as well as to Congress. And even considered under the doctrine of selective incorporation,[94] there is ample evidence that preservation of an individual's right to keep and bear arms, especially for recently freed slaves, was one of the driving forces behind passage of the Fourteenth Amendment.[95] The antebellum history of both the northern and the southern states restricting gun ownership by both free blacks and slaves, as well as the southern states' postbellum efforts to disarm recently freed slaves, were in the background when the Thirty-ninth Congress debated the Fourteenth Amendment.[96] Further, instances of the states' use of firearm laws to discriminate against minorities are not limited to the nineteenth century.[97]

However, in the period following the passage of the Fourteenth Amendment, the Supreme Court, beginning with the *Slaughterhouse* case,[98] severely weakened the amendment—a trend exhibited by the Second Amendment cases of the time. In *Cruikshank,* which involved federal prosecution of a white individual accused of violating the First and Second Amendment rights of two black men, the Court held that the First and Second Amendments were limitations on Congress, not on private individuals. The Court held that for such protection, the men threatened by the white racists were required to look to the state government, the very same government that the Fourteenth Amendment was designed to protect them from (Cottrol and Diamond 1991). The case starkly illustrates the inconsistency of the courts' subsequent treatment of the First and Second Amendments. Even though the First and Second Amendments are treated identically in *Cruikshank,* the decision is still regarded as a precedent for the proposition that the Second Amendment does not apply to the states, despite the fact that no one would seriously suggest that its identically reasoned passage regarding the First Amendment has any precedential value.[99]

Further, a close reading of *Presser* and *Miller* suggests even less authority for the proposition that the Second Amendment is not incorporated to apply against the states through the Fourteenth Amendment. *Presser* involved an Illinois state statute that prohibited bodies of men "other than the regular organized volunteer militia" of the state to drill or parade with arms without a license. As noted above, *Presser* preceded the first decision incorporating the Bill of Rights to apply to the states. Further, in the majority opinion, the Court ruled that the Illinois statute did not infringe upon the right to keep and bear arms. The Court then went out of its way in dicta (part of an opinion not necessary to the holding and therefore not part of legal precedent) to declare that the Second Amendment was a limitation on the federal and not the state governments. In *Miller*, the Court dismissed a defendant's appeal of a conviction because it found that no federal question was properly presented by the record of the case. Although the Court did proclaim that "it is well settled that the restrictions of these amendments operate only upon the Federal power," it did so once again in dicta.

In sum, an examination of the constitutional issues regarding the Second Amendment does not support claims that the Supreme Court has ruled that the Second Amendment is not an individual right. Interpreting the Second Amendment in a way other than as an individual right is inconsistent with the intent of the framers that the Bill of Rights generally, and the decentralized holding of arms protected by the Second Amendment in particular, provide a check on the federal government. Further, the claim that the Court has ruled that the Second Amendment has not been incorporated to apply against the states relies upon decisions that treat the First Amendment identically, or on decisions where such statements appear as dicta. Not enforcing the Second Amendment against the states also is directly in conflict with the history of the Fourteenth Amendment and its concern over the need to protect recently freed slaves from being disarmed by the southern states.

## Conclusion

While federal, state, and local laws restricting the private ownership of firearms continue to proliferate, close examination finds no rational basis for imposing such regulations. In many cases, assertions about the negative social utility of private firearm ownership are not proven or are provably false. Further, in many cases, little evidence exists to suggest that the proposed regulations will address the perceived problems in a rational and tailored fashion.

This chapter has argued that the above passage accurately describes efforts to impose excise taxes on firearms. Economic analysis suggests that placing a generalized excise tax on firearms is inconsistent with the goal of providing correct incentives to those who would misuse firearms, and is an inefficient way to provide compensation or social insurance for victims of firearm violence. More important, the operation of many gun control laws, including the imposition of strict liability on firearm manufacturers for third-party injuries caused by the misuse of their products, disproportionately affects law-abiding citizens, and may not severely affect the availability of firearms to criminals. In fact, such laws, which operate primarily by increasing the price of firearms to all, disproportionately affect law-abiding, low-income citizens—exactly the set of citizens most often victimized by crime and afforded the least protection by the professional police.

# Notes

1. See *Violent Crime Control and Law Enforcement Act of 1994*, P.L. 103–322, 103rd Cong., 2nd. sess, § 110102-4 (federal restrictions fixing the supply of some types of semiautomatic rifles and ammunition-feeding devices with a capacity of greater than ten rounds).
2. Senator Moynihan proposed large taxes on certain types of ammunition in conjunction with the Clinton administration's Health Care Reform Bill, suggesting that "we could tax [ammunition] out of existence." Proponents of health care reform have also suggested less draconian taxes on ammunition as a source of revenue, and have argued that such taxes are appropriate ways to cover the costs caused by firearm injuries. See "Moynihan to Add Handgun-Bullets Tax to Health Care Bill in His Committee," *Wall Street Journal*, 11 November 1993, B-6.
3. The District of Columbia has passed an ordinance that imposes strict liability on the manufacturers of "assault weapons" for all direct and consequential damage that arises from the discharge of these weapons in the District, without "regard to fault or proof of defect." See *The Assault Weapon Manufacturing Strict Liability Act of 1990*, Law 8-263, D.C. Code 6-2393 (1994). Imposition of liability on firearm manufacturers and retailers by the courts is discussed in part I.B of this chapter. For an analysis of strict liability for the manufacture and sale of firearms defined as "assault weapons," see Kobayashi and Olson (1996).
4. Under the Gun Control Act of 1968, all dealers and manufacturers of firearms must be federally licensed. See section 101 of P.L. 90-618, 82 Stat. 1213. For a summary of federal gun control legislation through the 1968 Gun Control Act, see Zimring (1975). Advocates of gun control have proposed legislation that would expand the regulation of firearm sales by increasing fees charged for federal firearm licenses, and by severely restricting or prohibiting private sales. See "Brady 2," H.R. 3932, H.R. 4300, 3 May 1994, 103rd Cong., 2nd. sess. Many purchaser waiting-period laws, including early versions of the recently enacted Brady Act, would not or do not require criminal background checks to be performed. See *Brady Handgun Prevention Act of 1993*, P.L. 103–159, 107 Stat. 1536, and its legislative history. The state of Virginia recently enacted a bill limiting purchasers of firearms to one a month. See *The Cavazos-Draughn Law*, VA ST § 18.2-308.2:2 (1993).
5. See Kobayashi and Olson (1996). See also "What Is an Assault Weapon?" *Wall Street Journal*, 25 August 1994, A-12. The article notes that "assault weapons are used in 0.14 percent of all violent crimes," and according to the FBI's 1992 *Uniform Crime Report*, only 698 individuals were killed with any type of rifle. In contrast, 1,114 persons were killed by beatings. The article also illustrates that functionally identical rifles are treated differently under the crime bill. For example, although the Colt AR-15 and the Ruger Mini-14 are both semiautomatic .223-caliber rifles capable of accepting detachable magazines, the supply of the former has been fixed, while the supply of the latter has not. The types of weapons regulated under the Violent Crime Control and Law Enforcement Act of 1994 have not been widely used in homicides involving police officers. In the last two years where information is available, only 23 of 121 deaths involved rifles of any type, and at most 5 of the incidents involved weapons affected by the provisions of the 1994 crime bill. In contrast, during the same time period, 12 officers were slain with their own weapons. See U.S. Department of Justice, *Uniform Crime Reports, Law Enforcement Officers Killed and Assaulted*, 1991 and 1992. For a discussion of similar results from an earlier time period, see

Kleck (1990, 77–82). In addition, of the 950 homicides that occurred in the District in 1990 and 1991, not one involved a rifle of any sort, let alone an "assault weapon" of the type that was the focus of the liability law discussed in note 3 above. See "Police Reports Show Criminals Don't Favor 'Assault Weapons,'" *American Rifleman* 20 (August 1992): 140. See also "Eight Months Later, No Suits Filed Under D.C. Gun-Liability Law," *Washington Post,* 26 August 1992, B-3; and "Assault Weapons Said to Play Small Role in Violent Crime," *Washington Times,* 27 June 1992, B-1 (noting similar issues with regard to California's experience under the Roos-Roberti Assault Weapons Ban).

6. According to research by Wright and Rossi (1986), a large proportion of criminals do not acquire their firearms legally.

7. For example, laws banning inexpensive small–caliber handguns (Saturday Night Specials) cause criminals to switch to more–lethal, larger–caliber firearms. See Kleck (1990). Further, the types of firearms regulated under "assault weapon" bans are not particularly lethal. Because military strategists have found that wounds produce more of a strain on enemy resources than deaths, military weapons are generally designed to wound rather than kill. This observation has also been empirically verified in ballistic tests and by recent experiences with battlefield casualties. See Martin L. Fackler, "Getting Your Guns Straight," *Washington Post,* 24 April 1993, A-25; and Fackler et al. (1990).

8. For a summary of the empirical evidence on the effectiveness of gun control laws, see Kleck (1990) and the discussion in part II.A of this chapter.

9. Senator Chafee of Rhode Island has recently sponsored a bill that would outlaw the private ownership of handguns, and would include provisions for confiscating the existing stock of handguns. See "Representative Owens and Senator Chafee Seeking to Disarm Americans," *American Rifleman* 68 (1992): 140.

10. "A well regulated militia, being necessary to the security of a free State, the right of the people to keep and bear arms, shall not be infringed." U.S. Constitution, amend. 2.

11. "The right of the people to be secure in their persons, houses, papers, and effects, against unreasonable searches and seizures, shall not be violated, and no warrants shall issue, but upon probable cause, supported by oath or affirmation, and particularly describing the place to be searched, and persons or things to be seized." U.S. Constitution, amend. 4.

12. "...nor shall private property be taken for public use, without just compensation." U.S. Constitution, amend. 5, takings clause.

13. Issues relating to the costly enforcement of and to the constitutional questions raised by firearm regulation are discussed in section II of this chapter.

14. See Niskanen (1975) for a general discussion of why bureaucrats would supply such expansion, sometimes with disastrous consequences. Recent actions by the Bureau of Alcohol, Tobacco, and Firearms (BATF), including its highly publicized raid in Waco, Texas, its actions in the Randy Weaver case, and its recent actions regarding street sweeper shotguns, are consistent with this hypothesis. See "ATF Top Officials Told Deliberate Lies about Waco Raid," *Wall Street Journal,* 1 October 1993, B-9; "BATF Gains New Attention following Waco, Texas Disaster," *Wall Street Journal,* 26 March 1994, A-14; and "Ambush at Ruby Ridge," *Reason,* October 1993, 25. See also "Treasury Classifies Certain Shotguns as Destructive Devices," *ATF News,* 28 February 1994.

15. In commenting on legislation prohibiting firearms by others than the high nobility instituted under the aegis of the English Game Act of 1671, ostensibly enacted to protect England's dwindling game resources, Blackstone noted that the "prevention of popular insurrections and resistance to the government, by dis-

arming the bulk of the people...is a reason oftener meant than avowed." 2 W. Blackstone, Commentaries 412. Many of the provisions of the Violent Crime Control and Law Enforcement Act of 1994 (see note 1 above), are consistent with both the interest-group theory and the tendency of such laws to weaken citizens vis-à-vis the government. Most notable is the provision that exempts sales to both active and *retired* police from manufacturing restrictions contained in the law.

16. For an explicit treatment of using courts as substitutes for enacting legislation, see Christopher Curran and Paul H. Rubin, "Private Law and Public Choice," mimeo., Emory University, 1993. For an argument that the use of courts for such arguably legislative purposes is inappropriate, see "Note" 1984.

17. In contrast to Posner's (1971) theory of taxation by regulation, this is a theory of regulation by taxation. For an article arguing for the use of the courts as an alternative to legislatively imposed gun control, see Mackarevich (1983): "Whether the plaintiffs win or lose, gun control advocates have an ulterior goal. They hope that the cost of litigation and any resulting increased insurance costs will force firearms manufacturers to increase handgun prices. Ideally, increased prices will deter sales and help stem the proliferation of handguns, thus reducing handgun injuries and deaths." See also Bonney (1985): "A related issue is whether a court, rather than...a legislature, is the appropriate body to establish a rule of strict liability for handgun manufacturers. Some have argued that the legislature is the preferred forum. Legislatures, however, have been unable to act on handgun issues, and many commentators contend that the courts should not wait.... Adoption of a strict liability rule...is the kind of judicial activism that is needed." See also Iveson (1983): "Current gun control legislation has not been effective in reducing handgun violence. Therefore it is particularly appropriate in this context for courts to supplement statutory duties with those imposed by the common law."

18. See the discussion in note 2 above.

19. For an explicit treatment, see Bonney (1985). He states: "Holding manufacturers liable rather than leaving victims without remedies would promote an economically efficient solution to the problem of handgun injury.... The economic analysis suggests that only if courts hold manufacturers liable will the efficient level of handgun sales be realized."

20. See Bonney (1985, 1450): "Strict liability makes the manufacturer an insurer for victims of unavoidable accidents." See also Iveson (1983): "Strict products liability law developed for two principal reasons: (1) to spread risk of loss while compensating the victim; and (2) to provide incentives for increased product safety." But see "Note" 1984: Strict liability was not designed to make manufacturers insurers of their products.

21. Senator Moynihan has suggested that some types of ammunition be taxed at a rate of 10,000 percent. (See the discussion and references in note 2 above.) The taxation of ammunition rather than firearms increases the costs of using firearms. Given that most criminal uses of firearms infrequently involve the expenditure of large amounts of ammunition, while most legitimate uses of firearms do (e.g., proficiency or target uses), such a tax seems to disproportionately tax legitimate uses. Further, to the extent such a tax deters law-abiding users from regularly using a firearm, such a tax may increase the rate of accidents, and decrease the effectiveness of legitimate firearm ownership as a crime deterrent.

22. Limitations on the role of the courts have been recognized. For example, Judge Cudahy, in his concurrence in *Martin v. Harrington and Richardson,* 743 F.2d 1200 (1984), stated: "The imposition of strict liability on the manufacture or sale of handguns should not be viewed as an attempt to drive handguns from the

market—for the courts, an improper goal. Rather it is an effort to place the costs inherent in handguns on the users rather than on the victims." However, concern over product liability suits has caused many products to be withdrawn from the market. Under these circumstances, liability suits may circumvent more-appropriate legislative procedures and interfere with constitutional rights. The issue of the constitutionality of the right to keep and bear arms is discussed in detail below.

23. See Cottrol and Diamond (1991) and "Note" 1984. Cottrol and Diamond conclude: "The history of blacks, firearms regulations, and the right to bear arms should cause us to ask new questions regarding the Second Amendment. These questions will pose problems both for advocates of stricter gun controls and for those who argue against them. Much of contemporary crime that concerns Americans is in poor black neighborhoods and a case can be made that greater firearms restrictions might alleviate this tragedy. But another, perhaps stronger case can be made that a society with a dismal record of protecting a people has a dubious claim on the right to disarm them. Perhaps a re-examination of this history can lead us to a modern realization of what the framers of the Second Amendment understood: that it is unwise to place the means of protection totally in the hands of the state, and that self-defense is a civil right" (p. 361).

24. See, e.g., *Sturm Ruger & Co. v. Day*, 594 P.2d 38 (1979); *Bender v. Colt Ind.*, 517 S.W.2d. 705 (1974); and *Phiilippe v. Browning Arms*, 375 So.2d 151 (1979).

25. A third category of third-party harm, injuries caused by the noncriminal negligence of firearm owners, is a special case of the analysis set out in part A of this section: liability placed on the negligent owner will produce better incentives than general liability placed on the manufacturer. Further, since the defendants in such a system are likely to be more solvent than those criminally misusing firearms, use of such a system will not involve the costs of imposing nonmonetary criminal sanctions. In cases of potential insolvency, the problem can be alleviated by imposing the criminal sanction, or by mandating insurance. For an analysis of the latter option, see Lund (1987).

26. For example, see Cochran (1993): "If bystanders do not recover for their injuries, these losses are external costs—the losses are not included in the cost of the products and do not affect the decision of manufacturers and consumers. These external costs create economic inefficiency. If courts imposed liability, the cost of bystander injury would be internalized in the cost of the products, and the price would more accurately reflect the costs that they create." See also *Martin v. Harrington and Richardson* (see note 22 above), which held that firearm manufacturers are not liable for third-party injuries, but suggested that doing so would be economically efficient. In his concurrence, Judge Cudahy stated that the "only question is who should bear [the costs]," and suggested that users of handguns bear them.

27. Segments of the medical profession have played a large role in backing regulations of firearms, arguing that handgun injuries are a public-health problem. For example, ammunition taxes have been suggested as sin taxes to pay for health care costs. (See the discussion in note 2 above.) In fact, much of the research cited by proponents of firearm regulations that alleges to show the negative social utility of firearms has appeared in medical journals. This literature is critically discussed below. Bans on firearms have also been supported by the American Medical Association, whose board of delegates has adopted a number of resolutions urging stricter legislation on the manufacture and sale of firearms. In addition, former Surgeon General Koop, former Surgeon General Elders, and the top injury prevention official at the Centers for Disease Control have been outspo-

ken supporters of broader restrictions on private firearm ownership. See "Gun Control Is Bad Medicine," *American Hunter* 22 (February 1994): 54.

28. See Landes and Posner (1987, 301): "The economic objection to [use of liability as a] method of crime control is that it raises the price to all users of guns, the lawful and unlawful alike (indeed, it increases the costs of the police!), whereas more vigorous enforcement of the criminal law would concentrate those costs on the criminals."

29. Bonney (1985) attempts to show that strict liability is the "economically efficient" rule by assuming (i) that the rate of misuse is exogenously determined, (ii) that consumers underestimate the risks of firearm ownership, and (iii) that firearm owners have complete information about these same risks. However, in making these assumptions, Bonney assumes away the primary issue: because the rate of misuse is assumed to be fixed, such analyses cannot address the deterrence function that is central to this chapter and to general law enforcement concerns. Further, unlike Bonney's analysis, the analysis in this chapter does not assume that the manufacturer can costlessly determine the price of the good that internalizes the external costs created by the exogenously determined firearm misuse. Arguably, the individual purchasing the firearm will have much more information about his intended use than either the dealer or the manufacturer. For a similar point, see "Note" 1984: "manufacturer [is] not the best able to prevent distribution of handguns to people who misuse them." Finally, a failure to impose strict liability on firearm manufacturers does not preclude the use of screening devices. Current liability rules do impose duties on dealers who "negligently entrust" firearms to minors or known felons in violation of state or federal laws, and the recently passed Brady Act mandates screening for criminal records. See the discussion in note 44 below.

30. Note that under both systems (i.e., taxation of the manufacture and taxation of misuse), *ex post* sanctions are being used to affect *ex ante* behavior. The analysis in this part does not compare the use of *ex post* liability with *ex ante* regulations such as firearm bans. For a discussion of this issue, see Wittman (1977).

31. Bonney (1985) would allow a defense of contributory negligence; that is, a manufacturer that is able to prove that the customer used the product in a negligent manner causing injury would be able to avoid liability for such injury. However, such a defense would not be allowed if an innocent victim that did not act in a contributorily negligent fashion was harmed by a consumer who did; that is, despite recognizing that strict liability must be refined to preserve incentives for users and potential victims to take appropriate care, he fails to note that a similar and, perhaps, much more important issue exists for the customer who intends to intentionally misuse the product. In addition, forcing the manufacturer to mount a defense of contributory negligence may be inefficient. Such inquiries are costly, and may not significantly alter manufacturers' efforts to reduce the probability that their products will be misused. For a general discussion of this issue, see Epstein (1973) and Chelias (1976).

32. For example, Bonney (1985, 1454) notes that "even where the purchaser's action provides a valid claim for victim recovery, the victim may not be able to recover because the purchaser cannot be found or is judgement proof." See also *Martin v. Harrington and Richardson* (see note 22 above): "[users are] frequently unreachable or judgement proof.... Plaintiff did not seek recovery from users of handguns who had little money."

33. See Becker (1968) and Kobayashi and Lott (1992). Statutes imposing large marginal penalties for use of a firearm in commission of a felony, as well as for the possession of a firearm by a felon, exist at both the state level and the federal

level. Such increased penalties are also part of the past and current sentencing practice of the courts. See, e.g., U.S. Sentencing Commission, *Guidelines Manual,* part A (increased sentencing levels for use of a firearm in commission of violent crimes). See also *U.S. Code,* vol. 18, sec. 924 (minimum mandatory penalties for use of a firearm in commission of certain violent crimes).

34. As has been pointed out in the economics literature, the driving force behind the general expansion of tort liability has been the desire to provide social insurance. See Priest (1985) and (1991).

35. See Priest (1985 and 1991), Kaplow and Shavell (1994), Epstein (1985), and Rubin (1993). Using what they have called the positive theory of law, Landes and Posner (1985, 1987) have shown that legal rules in general, and current liability rules in particular, are consistent with the efficient rules predicted by economic analysis. However, as noted above, Landes and Posner (1987, 301–2) suggest that the use of "more vigorous enforcement of the criminal law," not enterprise liability, for injuries caused by the misuse of firearms is consistent with economic efficiency.

36. Priest (1985, 1991) suggests that although the privity requirement was repudiated by Judge Cardozo in *MacPherson* over four decades earlier, the holding had been limited, until the early 1960s, to cases where negligence had been shown. See *MacPherson v. Buick,* 217 N.Y. 382 (1916).

37. Major developments in the expansion of enterprise liability occurred in the early 1960s; they included the adoption of strict liability for production defects, the expansion of strict liability to include design in addition to production defects, and the countenance of inadequate warnings as a form of design defect. In *Henningsen v. Bloomfield Motors,* 32 N.J. 358, 161 A.2d 169 (1960), the New Jersey Supreme Court invalidated a disclaimer of any implied warranties. In *Greenman v. Yuba Tool Co.,* 59 Cal.2d 57 (1963), the California Supreme Court announced a standard of strict liability in torts. The rules set out in these decisions subsequently were incorporated into section 402-A of the American Law Institute restatement on torts.

38. Among cases that have rejected manufacturer liability for injuries caused to third parties by firearms, see *Bennet v. Cincinnati Checker Cab,* 353 F.Supp. 1206 (ED Ky, 1973); *Patterson v. Roehm Gesellschatt,* 608 F.Supp. 1206 (ND Tex, 1985); *Perkins v. F.I.E. Corp.,* No. 82-3982 (ED La, 1983); *Richman v. Charter Arms,* 571 F. Supp. 192 (ED La, 1983); *Mauilia v. Stoeger Ind.,* 574 F.Supp. 107 (1983); *Riordan v. International Armament Corp.,* No. 81L27923 (Cir. Ct., Cook County, Ill, 1983); *Maliva v. Stoeger Ind.,* 574 F. Supp. 107 (D Mass, 1983); *Kloster v. High Standard,* No. 83-1690 (SD Fla, 1984); *Linton v. Smith & Wesson,* 469 N.E.2d 339 (1984); *Martin v. Harrington & Richardson,* 743 F.2d 1200 (1984); *Moore v. R.G. Ind.,* 789 F.2d. 1326 (Cal, 1986); *Rhodes v. R.G. Ind.* 325 S.E.2d 465 (Ga, 1984); *Shipman v. Jennings Firearms, LTD.,* 791 F.2d 1532 (1986); *Trespalacios v. Valor,* 486 So.2d 649 (Fla, 1986); and *Delahanty v. Hinkley,* 564 A.2d 758 (DC, 1989). *Perkins* and *Richman* were both decided at the appellate level in 762 F.2d 1250 (1985). In *Kelley v. R.G. Industries,* 479 A.2d 1143 (1985), the Court of Appeals in Maryland held that sellers of handguns were strictly liable for injuries to third-party victims. However, the holding was to be limited to factual situations where the court determined that the handgun was a "Saturday Night Special," the shooting was a criminal act, and the plaintiff was not a participant in the criminal activity. *Kelley* was overturned by the Maryland state legislature, which subsequently banned the sale of named handguns designated as Saturday Night Specials. See MD. ANN. CODE., art. 3-A, sec. 36-I(L) (1988 Supp.). For a more detailed discussion of Saturday Night Special bans, see part II.A of this chapter.

39. Bonney (1985) suggests that the current legal rule that does not hold manufacturers strictly liable for third–party injuries "should be abandoned for a rule that preserves economic efficiency." In contrast, the analysis presented in this chapter suggests that the current legal rule is consistent with economic efficiency. See also Landes and Posner (1987).

40. See Bogus (1991). For the economic critique of this trend, see Priest (1985 and 1991), Epstein (1985), and Rubin (1993).

41. See Bonney (1985), Bogus (1991), Iveson (1983), Cochran (1993), and Mackarevich (1983). See also Jett (1985). This is by no means an exhaustive list.

42. See *Franco v. Bunyard*, 547 S.W.2d 91 (Ark, 1977) (dealer liability for illegally selling a firearm to a convicted felon); *Olson v. Rutzel*, 278 N.W.2d 239 (1979) (firearm illegally sold to a minor); and *Moning v. Alfono*, 254 N.W. 2d 759 (1977) (slingshot sold to minor). But compare *Robinson v. Howard Bros.*, 372 So.2d 1074 (Miss, 1979) (dealer not liable for illegally selling firearm to minor); and *Hulsman v. Hemmeter Dev. Corp.*, 647 P.2d 113 (1982). Dealers have generally prevailed over plaintiffs when constructive knowledge of endangerment cannot be shown. See *Stephan v. Marlin Firearms Co.*, 353 F.2d 819 (1965); and *Pepper v. Hottecks*, 192 A.2d 213 (1963). See also *Heatherton v. Sears Roebuck*, 593 F.2d 526 (1979) (dealer not liable for misrepresentation by purchaser); *McMillen v. Steele*, 275 Pa.584; 119 A. 721 (1923); and *Decker v. Gibson Prod.*, 679 F.2d 212 (1982).

43. Recent cases include a jury holding Kmart liable for third-party injuries for selling a firearm to an obviously intoxicated purchaser who had difficulty completing the federal form. See "Jury Rules Against Kmart in 1987 Shooting," *Wall Street Journal*, 11 October 1993, B-2. Wal-Mart was sued for third-party injuries for selling a firearm to a purchaser who was told he would be denied if he truthfully revealed he had been treated for a mental illness. See "Retailer Wal-Mart Stops Handgun Sales Inside Its Stores," *Wall Street Journal*, 23 December 1993, B-1.

44. See *Brady Handgun Prevention Act of 1993* in note 4 above. The debate over the enactment of the Brady Act demonstrates many of the economic issues in the regulation of firearms. Under the assumption that the purpose of the law is to prevent criminals from purchasing firearms from licensed firearm dealers, a system that allows a timely background check of an applicant's criminal record would allow screening of purchasers without increasing the transaction costs of purchasing a firearm. However, the addition of waiting periods over and above the minimum time period necessary to complete a background check is, for the purposes of the criminal screening function, simply a device to increase the transaction costs of purchasing a firearm. The first seems rationally related and narrowly tailored to the purpose of screening potential purchasers for a criminal record. The latter does not seem to advance this goal.

45. For a general discussion of the risk-utility test, see Wade 1973. The application of a risk-utility test is essential to a third-party claim against a handgun manufacturer, as under the alternative "consumer expectations" test, recovery will not be allowed (i.e., the handgun, in causing the injury or death, is performing exactly as was expected).

46. See, e.g., *Sturm Ruger & Co. v. Bloyd*, 586 S.W.2d 19 (Ky, 1979); *De Rosa v. Remington Arms*, 509 F.Supp. 762 (1981); and *Dias v. Daisy-Heddon Ind.*, 390 N.E.2d 222 (1971).

47. See "Note" 1984: claim may also fail due to inability to show specific causation. Bogus (1991, 1111) argues that defenses of misuse, superseding cause, and unavoidably unsafe products are a "variety of masks worn by the same rough no-

tion of equity." Our analysis, however, is not based on equity considerations, and he does not consider the economic arguments contained in this chapter.

48. These studies are discussed mainly because of the uncritical media attention given to them. For a comprehensive survey of the relationship between gun ownership and violence, see Kleck (1990, chap. 5). For a critique of the publication process in the medical journals relating to firearm issues, see Don B. Kates, "A Controlled Look at Gun Control," prepared for oral testimony before the Select Committee of the Pennsylvania Legislature to Investigate the Use of Automatic and Semi Automatic Firearms, 20 September 1994.

49. Kellerman et al. (1993) began with a sample population of homicide victims and then matched this sample with a control sample of non-homicide victims. The relative odds ratio calculated and reported in the paper equals [Prob(Gun|Homicide)/Prob(No Gun|Homicide)]/[Prob(Gun|No Homicide)/Prob(No Gun|No Homicide)], which equals [Prob(Homicide/Gun)/Prob(No Homicide/Gun)]/[Prob(Homicide|No Gun)/Prob(No Homicide|No Gun) only if the underlying characteristics of the two populations are both equal to the characteristics of the general population. As noted in the text, there are significant differences in characteristics of the case and control samples. For example, the subjects in the case sample were much more likely to rent rather than own a home. In fact, if one is to take this methodology seriously, renting a home increases the homicide risk (measured by the odds ratio) by 4.4. However, the authors do not advocate banning rental contracts. More realistically, the authors' methodology suggests that alcohol-related factors are much more important in determining the probability of homicide (e.g., the authors' methodology suggests that trouble at work from drinking increases the homicide risk by a factor of 20). Yet no mention of a prohibition on alcohol is mentioned. Further, subjects in the case sample were much more likely to have substance abuse problems. The disparity between the case and control samples is not surprising given that the failure to use relevant matching criteria generally leads to a failure to hold constant the characteristics of the cases and controls, and given that the authors used criteria such as age, race, and sex, rather than more relevant socioeconomic criteria, such as history of substance abuse, to find the controls. For a detailed critique of the Kellerman et al. methodology, see Henry Schafer, "Serious Flaws in Kellerman et al. (1993)," mimeo., North Carolina State University, 1994. For other critiques of the methodology used in the Kellerman et al. study, see letters to the editor, *New England Journal of Medicine* 330 (1993): 365–66.

50. See interview with Gary Kleck by Neil Schulman, *Orange County Register*, 19 September 1993. See also Kleck (1990, chap. 4). Kleck suggests that "gun use by private citizens against violent criminals is common and about as frequent as legal actions like arrest, is a more prompt negative consequence of crime than legal punishment, and is more severe, at its most serious, than legal system punishments." The ignorance of this issue is also at the center of criticisms of the Kellerman and Reay (1986) study, which found that the odds that a person kills himself or an acquaintance is 43 times the odds that he kills an intruder. Of the 43 cases, 37 of them are due to suicide. This result is often reported to state that a person is 43 times more likely to kill himself or an acquaintance than he is to use the firearm in self-defense. As Kellerman and Reay themselves caution, "Mortality studies like ours do not include cases in which burglars or intruders are wounded or frightened away by the use or display of a firearm. Cases in which would be intruders may have purposely avoided a house [in which the occupant is] known to be armed are not identified." Wright and Rossi (1986) found that gun ownership by an occupant was a primary worry of convicted

felons. Perhaps the most convincing evidence of this phenomenon is found in comparing the rate of "hot" residential burglaries (cases where the resident is home) in countries with high and low firearm ownership rates. Kleck (1990, 140) noted that the hot-burglary rate in the United States was 12.7 percent of all burglaries, while the same rate for three low-gun-ownership nations averaged 45 percent.

51. Mauser (1992), citing the Sloan et al. (1988) article as "a particularly egregious example," suggests that "it is not too strong to say that many [gun control] studies are an abuse of scholarship, inventing, selecting or misinterpreting data in order to validate a priori conclusions."

52. Finkelstein and Levin (1990) note that "ensuring that controls are similar to cases with respect to potentially confounding factors is notoriously difficult, and many epidemiological studies are fatally flawed because of failure to adjust adequately for such factors, either by design or in the analysis."

53. Chapter 5 of Kleck (1990) contains a comprehensive review of the existing literature on the relationship between levels of gun possession and violent crime. Kleck concludes that "aggregate level analysis of violent crime rates indicated that the net impact of all the various individual effects of gun possession, among prospective victims and aggressors combined, was not significantly different from zero." For a similar conclusion, see Wright, Rossi, and Daly (1983), stating that existing studies show "no strong causal connections between private gun ownership and the crime rate.... There is not compelling evidence that private weaponry is an important cause of, or a deterrent to, violent criminality.... [T]he contradictory evidence and inconsistent interpretations of evidence...demonstrate only that existing knowledge about weapons, crime, and the relationship between them is, in general, not adequate as a basis for policy formulation." See also Reynolds and Caruth (1992) and Toch and Lizotte (1990).

54. See, e.g., Landes and Posner (1987, 302): "If, however, it were possible to identify a class of guns used mainly for illegal purposes ('Saturday Night Specials'?), a stronger case could be made for strict liability as a method of trying to price them off the market."

55. Civilian sales of newly produced fully automatic, or Class III, firearms were prohibited in 1986 under the Firearms Owners' Protection Act (P.L. 99-308, 19 May 1986, 100 Stat. 449), and civilian sales of newly produced semiautomatic rifles classified as "assault style" weapons (except to retired police officers) were banned for ten years under the Violent Crime Control and Law Enforcement Act of 1994 (see note 1 above). Possession and transfer of the existing stock of Class III firearms, "assault style" firearms, and high-capacity ammunition-feeding devices is legal. As noted above, rifles classified as "assault weapons" in the 1994 act are rarely used in crimes (see the discussion in note 5 above). The record of felonious use (more accurately described as nonuse) of legally possessed fully automatic weapons is an even more dramatic illustration of the irrationality of recent firearm legislation. Civilian possession of such weapons has been regulated under the 1934 Firearms Act, and requires payment of a $200.00 transfer tax, an FBI fingerprint check, and compliance with stringent BATF and state record-keeping and notice requirements. Not surprisingly, the class of persons willing to submit to such draconian requirements to purchase a firearm would not include many known or would-be felons, and would rarely use these weapons for felonious purposes. Kleck (1990, 68) reports that the director of the BATF testified that he knew of fewer than ten crimes of any kind (including violations of the regulations) involving a registered Class III weapon. In a December 1992 study, Reynolds and Caruth (1992) report: *"Over the past*

*50 years, no civilian has ever used a legally owned machine gun in a violent crime"* (emphasis in original). Despite this exemplary record under draconian regulations, additional restrictions on the sale of Class III firearms were enacted—restrictions guaranteed to have zero impact on crime.

56. See page 1103 of Bogus (1991), which notes that in *Kelley v. R. G. Industries* (see note 38 above) the court erroneously relied on the assumption that "Saturday Night Specials are particularly attractive for criminal activity, and generally unfit for legitimate uses.... [T]he manufacturer or marketer of a Saturday Night Special knows or ought to know that he is making or selling a product principally to be used in criminal activity." Kleck (1990, 83–91) notes that Saturday Night Specials, defined to be small and cheap handguns, constitute 10 to 27 percent of all crime handguns. More important, the Saturday Night Specials' share of crime handguns does not appear to be larger than their share of the general civilian stock of handguns.

57. Thus, bans targeting inexpensive firearms raise the same type of equal-protection issues associated with generally increasing the price of firearms through excise taxes. See "Note" 1984 and the discussion in part C of this section.

58. This is an application of the Alchian and Allen theorem discussed in chapter 1 of this book. Zimring (1972, 107–8) suggests large (62 percent) increases in fatalities from gun assaults if attackers switch from firearms below .38 caliber (firearms targeted by Saturday Night Special bans) to .38-caliber firearms. See also Kleck and Bordua (1984, 25).

59. The total effect of such bans on the number of fatalities will of course depend on criminals' elasticity of demand for firearms. Such bans are likely to be counterproductive in reducing fatalities when criminals' demand for firearms is inelastic—not an unreasonable assumption. For a similar argument, see Kleck 1990 and Kleck and Bordua (1984, 33).

60. For a similar discussion of this "reverse causality," see, e.g., Polsby (1986 and 1994).

61. See David P. Kopel, "Reply," *Heritage Foundation Policy Review* (April 1993). The population of the District of Columbia fell about 20 percent during the 20-year period of the study, and the surrounding suburbs' rate of growth exceeded 20 percent. Unless the authors wish to claim success because the law caused law-abiding citizens to move to safer jurisdictions, this study does not seem to provide strong support for handgun regulations. Other problems with the study include the seemingly arbitrary time windows chosen for the comparison: the study fails to explain why the city's homicide rate fell sharply between 1974 and 1976 (the two years prior to the handgun freeze) and why, according to FBI *Uniform Crime Report* data, the homicide rate in 1976 was lower than in each and every year in the postlaw time period except 1985. Further, the study does not include data from 1987–90, years that included record homicide rates in the District.

62. Paul Blackman (1992), a statistician working for the National Rifle Association (NRA), notes that the number of deaths reported in National Center for Health Statistics (NCHS) data used by the authors declines relative to the FBI data. The difference is that the FBI data exclude justifiable homicides, while the NCHS data do not. This suggests that the primary effect of the law was to reduce justifiable homicides. For a similar critique, see Jones 1981.

63. Kleck (1990, 408) examined the handgun ban enacted in Evanston, Illinios. Contrary to the Washington, D.C., handgun law, which froze gun ownership levels, the Evanston law applied to current gun owners. Kleck found little evidence that the law had any effect on violent-crime rates.

64. For an explicit comparison of the prohibition of alcohol and firearms, see Kates (1984). Kates notes that the link between alcohol and violent crime and mortality is often greater than the link between handgun ownership and violent crime. And as noted in note 49 above, a stronger link between alcohol and homicide was found by Kellerman et al. (1993) in their pro-gun-control study. Yet few, including these authors, publicly advocate a return to alcohol prohibition. However, Kellerman et al. had no problem simultaneously using weaker relationships to advocate the banning of firearms.

65. Posner (1992, 533) notes that the supporters of the prohibition of alcoholic beverages "were able to obtain a constitutional amendment—normally a particularly durable form of legislation. But prohibiting the sale of alcoholic beverages required a massive law enforcement effort that subsequent Congresses were unwilling to appropriate enough money for, with the result the constitutional amendment was effectively nullified, and it was repealed in 1933 after having been in effect for only 13 years." Kates (1984, 141) states that proponents of firearm bans have not generally addressed the enforcement cost issue; he notes, among other things, a plea by a gun control advocate for Congress to outlaw handguns "and then figure out how to seize them in the days ahead."

66. In economic terms, there is a loss of marginal deterrence. See Becker (1968), Stigler (1970), and Friedman and Sjostrom (1993). Large penalties placed on those engaged in illegal drug distribution can have other unintended effects. For example, drug organizations may actively recruit young juveniles who would not be tried as adults. These individuals would face much shorter sentences, and thus would require less compensation. For a discussion of the economics of this issue, see Faith and Tollison (1983).

67. If current owners are able to keep their firearms, this adverse selection effect will not be immediately felt. However, as is suggested by the discussion of the District of Columbia handgun freeze, the long-term adverse effects of such a restriction will be similar to a confiscatory ban as the ratio of firearm ownership by law-abiding citizens to firearm ownership by criminals falls over time.

68. See also Buchanan (1987) and Posner (1992), chap. 23.

69. George Will and Michael Kinsley, both opposed to individual firearm ownership, have concluded that the Second Amendment protects an individual right, and suggest that an appropriate way to limit firearm ownership would be to repeal the Second Amendment. See George F. Will, "The Right to Bear Arms Is in Stone," *Washington Post*, 21 April 1991; and Michael Kinsley, "The Embarrassing Second Amendment," *Washington Post,* 8 February 1990. Congressman Owens of New York has sponsored bills to repeal the Second Amendment. See 1993 H.J. Res. 81 (29 January 1993).

70. See *Central Hudson Gas and Electric Co. v. Public Service Comm. of New York*, 447 U.S. 557, 566 (1980): "regulation will not be sustained if it provides only ineffective or remote support for the government purpose."

71. See *Zauderer v. Office of Disciplinary Counsel of the Supreme Court of Ohio*, 471 U.S. 626 (1985): "unsupported assertion insufficient to support prohibition on commercial speech in violation of the first amendment."

72. See *Central Hudson* (note 70 above), at 566: "regulation directly and materially advances a substantial state interest in a manner no more extensive than necessary to serve that interest."

73. See *New York Times v. Sullivan*, 376 U.S. 254 (1964): "possibility of suit and frequent recovery would chill the right to criticize public conduct and create an atmosphere in which First Amendment freedoms cannot survive."

74. See *Minneapolis Star and Tribune Co. v. Minnesota Commissioner of Revenue,* 460 U.S. 575 (1983): imposition of a use tax on the cost of paper and ink products consumed in the production of publications violated the First Amendment by imposing a burden on freedom of the press. See also *Grosjean v. American Press Co., Inc.,* 297 U.S. 233, 250 (1936): "[The tax] is seen to be a deliberate and calculated device in the guise of a tax to limit the circulation of information."

75. In a recent takings case, *Dolan v. City of Tigard,* 114 S. Ct. 2309 (1994), Chief Justice Rehnquist argued for the consistent application of the Bill of Rights:

    We see no reason that the Takings Clause of the Fifth Amendment, as much a part of the Bill of Rights as the First Amendment or Fourth Amendment, should be relegated to the status of a poor relation in these comparable circumstances.

76. That is, the Second Amendment, interpreted as an individual right, does not preclude all regulations of firearms, just as the First Amendment does not proscribe all regulation of speech (e.g., the First Amendment does not protect a person that yells "fire" in a crowded theater from prosecution). A constitutional right to keep and bear arms sets out criteria that the government must overcome to regulate firearms. For example, many pro-Second Amendment scholars supported instant background checks for criminal records as rational (and constitutional) gun controls, and the NRA supported the Uniform Revolver Act, which, among other things, limited the ability of felons to possess firearms. See, e.g., Kleck (1990). However, imposition of arbitrary "waiting periods" that are not necessary to perform background checks are not tailored to the purpose of preventing felons from acquiring firearms, and likely would be unconstitutional under the standards applied to the First Amendment.

77. For example, the constitutional-law textbook used at George Mason Law School, Stone et al. (1991), does not even list the Second Amendment in the index. Other treatises on constitutional law often take the states' rights view. See, e.g., Tribe (1988).

78. The last time the Supreme Court addressed the Second Amendment was more than half a century ago, in *U.S. v. Miller,* 307 U.S. 174 (1939), and that was the only twentieth-century Supreme Court case addressing the Second Amendment. The Second Amendment and its relationship to the Fourteenth Amendment were taken up in three late-nineteenth-century cases. See *Miller v. Texas,* 153 U.S. 535 (1894); *Presser v. Illinois,* 116 U.S. 252 (1886); and *U.S. v. Cruikshank,* 92 U.S. 542 (1876). These cases are discussed in more detail below.

79. Advocates of the states' rights interpretation of the Second Amendment argue that the amendment was a countervailing response by the states to clauses 15 and 16 in section 8 of article I in the Constitution, which give Congress the power to call out the militia and to provide for organizing, arming, and disciplining it.

80. Proponents of restrictions on firearms have suggested a second reason for relegating the Second Amendment to historical-curiosity status—the inability of a disorganized militia to defeat a modern organized force. The argument fails for many reasons. First, a dispersed force is useful even if it is not likely to defeat a standing army. What matters is that the costs of achieving this victory are increased enough to make the net benefits of engaging in such an action negative. (See Lund 1987.) One needs only to consider recent actions by the vastly superior U.S. armed forces (e.g., Vietnam, Lebanon, and Somalia) to understand the empirical relevance of this point. Further, the history of standing armies, and their superiority to the militia, was well recognized at the time of the framers.

For example, Adam Smith, in his *Wealth of Nations* (published in the same year as the Declaration of Independence), noted the necessary superiority of standing armies over the militia.

81. See Kates (1983), Lund (1987), and van Alstyne (1994). Similar arguments are made by Levinson (1989).

82. Under this system, the colonists were not simply allowed to keep their arms, but affirmatively required to do so. See Kates (1983, 213).

83. Additional support can be found in section 13 of article I of the 1776 Virginia Constitution, which states: "[A] well regulated militia, composed of the body of the people...". For a more detailed description, see Kates (1983, 216–17).

84. See Kates 1983 and Lund 1987. See also *U.S. v. Verdugo–Urquidez,* 494 U.S. 259, 265–6 (1990), Rehnquist, C.J., holding that "the term 'the people' means the same thing in the First, Second, and Fourth Amendments."

85. See Kates (1983, 218). Proponents of the exclusively states' rights view have also concentrated on the term *bear arms*, which referred to the militiamen carrying their arms when mustered to duty. As Kates notes, support for the exclusively states' rights view falls apart when one considers that the term *keep arms* denoted a personal right to possess arms in the home for any lawful purpose, and that the amendment protects the right of the people to "*keep and* bear" (p. 220).

86. See Kates (1983, 223–24). The states' rights view is also weakened by James Madison's notes on the organization of the Bill of Rights. In drafting the Bill of Rights, Madison intended to attach each amendment to the relevant section of the original Constitution. If he had intended the right to arms as merely a limitation on Congress's control over the militia, the logical place for the Second Amendment would be in section 8 of article I, immediately after clauses 15 and 16. Instead, Madison's organization placed the right to arms with other personal rights in section 9.

87. For example, see Jett (1985): "The Supreme Court has interpreted the Second Amendment to protect only the existence of a state militia and not the individual right to bear arms."

88. Far from reversing the lower court's decision, the Supreme Court remanded the case to determine whether the weapon involved in the case was a "militia weapon." However, Miller, after being set free by the lower court, was not returned to custody to face trial on charges of illegally possessing a sawed-off shotgun.

89. In the decision the Court noted:

> The Militia which the States were expected to maintain and train is set in contrast with Troops which they were forbidden to keep without consent of Congress. The sentiment of the time strongly disfavored standing armies; the common view was that adequate defense of country and law could be secured through the Militia—civilians primarily, soldiers on occasion....
>
> The significance attributed to the term Militia appears from the debates in the [Constitutional] Convention, the history and legislation of colonies and states, and the writings of approved commentators. They show plainly enough that the Militia comprised all males physically capable of acting in concert for the common defense. "A body of citizens enrolled for military discipline." And further, that ordinarily when called for service, these men were expected to appear bearing arms supplied by themselves and of the kind in common use at the time. (*U.S. v. Miller* at 179)

The decision also cites passages from Blackstone and from Adam Smith's *Wealth of Nations* to characterize the militia.

90. This view has not been adopted by the lower courts that have interpreted *U.S. v. Miller*. See, e.g., *U.S. v. Hale*, 978 F.2d 1016 (1992), which held that no individual right exists in upholding convictions for possession of machine guns, and *Cases v. United States*, 131 F.2d 916 (1942), which upheld the conviction of a felon in possession of a firearm. See also *U.S. v. Warin*, 530 F.2d 103 (1976); *U.S. v. Oakes*, 564 F.2d 384 (1977); and *U.S. v. Nelsen*, 859 F.2d 1318 (1988). But see the concurrence by Beam in *U.S. v. Hale*, 978 F.2d 1016, 1021 (1992). While the absence of a definitive Supreme Court opinion on the Second Amendment has lead many legal scholars to an examination of first principles, Herz (1995) asserts that these lower-court cases, together with the incorporation cases (discussed below) and the Supreme Court's refusal to grant certiorari in Second Amendment cases, present a well-settled case against an individual right to bear arms under the Second Amendment.

91. For excellent discussions of the incorporation issue, see Kates (1983, 244–47); and Cottrol and Diamond (1991).

92. See, e.g., *Quilici v. Village of Morton Grove*, 695 F.2d 261 (1982), upholding a local ordinance prohibiting the possession of handguns: "Since we hold that the Second Amendment does not apply to the states, we need not consider the scope of its guarantee of the right to bear arms." The court does go on to address this issue; however, in light of the aforementioned holding, the court's opinions on this subject (the panel does not consider individually owned handguns to be military weapons) are dicta (not necessary to the holding). See also *Fresno Rifle & Pistol Club, Inc. v. Van De Kamp*, 965 F.2d 723 (1992), upholding California's Roberti-Roos Assault Weapons Control Act of 1989 (Cal. Penal Code sections 12275–12290): "The Supreme Court, however, has held that the Second Amendment constrains only the actions of congress, not the states [citing *Cruikshank* and *Presser*].... We are therefore foreclosed from considering these arguments."

93. The first incorporation decision was *B&O RR Co. v. Chicago*, 166 U.S. 226 (1897), which applied the Fifth Amendment's takings clause against the states.

94. This doctrine rejects the uniform application of the Bill of Rights against the states. In addition to the Second Amendment, the Third and Seventh Amendments and parts of the Fifth Amendment have not been incorporated. See, e.g., *Duncan v. Louisiana*, 391 U.S. 145 (1968), which held that the Seventh Amendment right of trial by jury did not apply to the states. See also Stone et al. (1991, 784).

95. See Aynes (1993), Amar (1992), and Curtis (1986).

96. See Cottrol and Diamond (1991). They describe the long history of restrictions on ownership of firearms imposed on black, but not white, citizens. Antebellum restrictions by southern states on the ownership of firearms by blacks were aimed at both free blacks and slaves. The series of statutes known as the "Black Codes," passed by southern states after the Civil War, also placed restrictions on the ownership of firearms, restrictions not placed on whites. Perhaps the most famous example of the unequal treatment of blacks and whites with respect to the right to keep and bear arms is Chief Justice Taney's opinion in *Dred Scott v. Sanford*. Taney declared that blacks could not be recognized as citizens because this would imply that southern laws requiring their disarmament could not stand in the face of constitutional guarantees of the right to arms:

> It would give to persons of the Negro race, who were recognized as citizens in any one State of the Union, the right to enter every other State whenever they pleased,... and it would give them the full liberty of speech...and to keep and carry arms whenever they went. (*Dred Scott v. Sanford*, 60 U.S. 393, 417 [1857])

97. See Kopel (1992). For example, Kopel reports that in the first three years after New York City's 1911 Sullivan Law, which required handgun owners to obtain police permits, went into effect, 70 percent of those arrested had Italian surnames.

98. In *Butcher's Benevolent Ass'n v. Crescent City Live-Stock Landing & Slaughterhouse Co.*, 83 U.S. (16 Wall.) 36 (1872), the Court severely limited the Fourteenth Amendment's privileges and immunities clause.

99. *Cruikshank* is often quoted for its holding that "[t]he right...of 'bearing arms for a lawful purpose'...is not a right granted by the Constitution. Neither is it in any manner dependent upon that instrument for its existence. The Second Amendment declares that it shall not be infringed; but this, as has been seen, means no more than that it shall not be infringed by Congress." However, in an identically reasoned holding two paragraphs earlier, the Court also held that "[t]he first amendment to the Constitution prohibits Congress from abridging 'the right of the people to assemble and to petition the government for a redress of grievances.' This, like the other amendments proposed and adopted at the same time, was not intended to limit the powers of the State governments in respect to their own citizens, but to operate upon the National Government alone."

## References

Amar, Akhil R. 1992. "The Bill of Rights and the Fourteenth Amendment." *Yale Law Journal* 101:1193–1284.

Aynes, Richard L. 1993. "On Misreading John Bingham and the Fourteenth Amendment." *Yale Law Journal* 103:57–104.

Becker, Gary S. 1968. "Crime and Punishment: An Economic Approach." *Journal of Political Economy* 76 (March-April): 169–217.

Blackman, Paul. 1992. "NRA Ridicules *Journal* 'Study' on Washington, D.C., Gun Ban." *American Rifleman* 140 (January): 69.

Bogus, Carl T. 1991. "Pistols, Politics, and Product Liability." *University of Cincinnati Law Review* 59:1103–64.

Bonney, Paul R. 1985. "Manufacturer's Strict Liability for Handgun Injuries: An Economic Analysis." *Georgetown Law Journal* 73:-1437–63.

Buchanan, James M. 1975. *The Limits of Liberty: Between Anarchy and Leviathan*. Chicago: University of Chicago Press.

———. 1987. "The Constitution of Economic Policy." *American Economic Review* 77 (June): 243–50.

Centerwall, Brandon. 1991. "Homicide and the Prevalence of Handguns: Canada and the United States, 1976 to 1980." *American Journal of Epidemiology* 134:1245–65.

Chelius, James R. 1976. "Liability for Industrial Accidents: A Comparison of Negligence and Strict Liability Systems." *Journal of Legal Studies* 5:293–309.

Cochran, Robert F., Jr. 1993. "Dangerous Products and Injured Bystanders." *Kentucky Law Journal* 81:687–725.

Cottrol, Robert J., and Raymond T. Diamond. 1991. "The Second Amendment: Toward an Afro-Americanist Reconsideration." *Georgetown Law Journal* 80:309–61.

Curtis, Michael K. 1986. *No State Shall Abridge: The Fourteenth Amendment and the Bill of Rights*. Durham, N.C.: Duke University Press.

Demsetz, Harold. 1969. "Information and Efficiency: Another Viewpoint." *Journal of Law and Economics* 12:1–22.

Epstein, Richard A. 1973. "A Theory of Strict Liability." *Journal of Legal Studies* 2 (January):151–204.

————. 1985. "Products Liability as an Insurance Market." *Journal of Legal Studies* 14 (December): 645–69.

Fackler, Martin L., J. A. Malinowski, S. W. Hoxie, and A. Jason. 1990. "Wounding Effects of the AK-47 Rifle used by Patrick Purdy in the Stockton Schoolyard Shooting of 17 January 1989." *American Journal of Forensic Medicine and Pathology* 11:185–90.

Faith, Roger L., and Robert D. Tollison. 1983. "The Pricing of Surrogate Crime and Law Enforcement." *Journal of Legal Studies* 12 (June): 401–11.

Finkelstein, Michael O., and Bruce Levin. 1990. *Statistics for Lawyers.* New York: Springer-Verlag.

Friedman, David D., and William Sjostrom. 1993. "Hanged for a Sheep: The Economics of Marginal Deterrence." *Journal of Legal Studies* 22 (June): 345–66.

Henderson, James A., and Aaron D Twerski. 1991. "Closing the American Products Liability Frontier: The Rejection of Liability without Defect." *New York University Law Review* 66:1263–1331.

Herz, A. D. 1995. "Gun Crazy: Constitutional False Consciousness and the Dereliction of Dialogic Responsibility." *Boston University Law Review* 75:57–153.

Iveson, H. Todd. 1983. "Manufacturer's Liability to Victims of Handgun Crime: A Common Law Approach." *Fordham Law Review* 51:771.

Jett, Rick L. 1985. "Do Victims of Unlawful Handgun Violence Have a Remedy against Handgun Manufacturers?: Overview and Analysis." *University of Illinois Law Review,* 967–95.

Jones, Edward D. III. 1981. "The District of Columbia's Firearms Control Regulations Act of 1975: The Toughest Handgun Control Law in the United States—Or Is It?" *Annals of the American Academy of Social and Political Sciences* 455:138–49.

Kaplow, Louis, and Steven Shavell. 1994. "Why the Legal System Is Less Efficient than the Income Tax in Redistributing Income." *Journal of Legal Studies* 23 (June): 667–81.

Kates, Don B. 1983. "Handgun Prohibition and the Original Meaning of the Second Amendment." *Michigan Law Review* 82:204–73.

————. 1984. "Handgun Banning in Light of the Prohibition Experience." In *Firearms and Violence: Issues of Public Policy,* edited by Don B. Kates. Cambridge, Mass.: Ballinger.

Kellerman, Arthur L., and Donald T. Reay. 1986. "Protection or Peril? An Analysis of Firearm-Related Deaths in the Home." *New England Journal of Medicine* 314:1557–60.

Kellerman, Arthur L., Frederick P. Rivara, Norman B. Rushforth, Joyce G. Banton, Donald T. Reay, Jerry T. Francisco, Ana B Locci, Janice Prodzinski, Bela B. Hackman, and Grant Somes. 1993. "Gun Ownership as a Risk Factor for Homicide in the Home." *New England Journal of Medicine* 329:1084–91.

Kleck, Gary. 1990. *Point Blank: Guns and Violence in America.* Chicago: Aldine de Gruyter.

Kleck, Gary, and David J. Bordua. 1984. "The Assumptions of Gun Control." In *Firearms and Violence: Issues of Public Policy,* edited by Don B. Kates. Cambridge, Mass.: Ballinger.

Kobayashi, Bruce H., and John R. Lott, Jr. 1992. "Low-Probability-High-Penalty Enforcement Strategies and the Efficient Operation of the Plea-Bargaining System." *International Review of Law and Economics* 12:69–77.

Kobayashi, Bruce H., and Joseph E. Olson. 1996. "In re 101 California Street and a Tale of Two Statutes: A Legal and Economic Analysis of Strict Liability for the Manufacture and Sale of Firearms Defined as 'Assault Weapons.'" *Stanford Law and Policy Review* 8 (forthcoming).

Kopel, David P. 1991. "Canadian Gun Control: Should the United States Look North for a Solution to Its Firearms Problem?" *Temple International and Comparative Law Journal* 5:1–50.

————. 1992. *The Samurai, the Mountie, and the Cowboy: Should America Adopt the Gun Controls of Other Democracies?* New York: Prometheus Books.

Landes, William M., and Richard A. Posner. 1985. "A Positive Analysis of Products Liability." *Journal of Legal Studies* 14 (December): 535–67.

————. 1987. *The Economic Structure of Tort Law*. Cambridge: Harvard University Press.

Levinson, Sanford. 1989. "The Embarrassing Second Amendment." *Yale Law Journal* 99:637–59.

Loftin, Colin, David McDowall, Brian Wiersems, and Talbert J. Cottey. 1991. "Effects of Restrictive Licensing of Handguns on Homicide and Suicide in the District of Columbia." *New England Journal of Medicine* 325:1615–20.

Lund, Nelson. 1987. "The Second Amendment, Political Liberty, and the Right to Self-Preservation." *Alabama Law Review* 39:103–30.

Mackarevich, Gerard M. 1983. "Manufacturers' Strict Liability for Injuries from a Well-Made Handgun." *William and Mary Law Review* 24:467–501.

Mauser, Gary. 1992. "Gun Control in the United States." *Criminal Law Forum* 3:147.

McChesney, Fred S. 1987. "Rent Extraction and Rent Creation in the Economic Theory of Regulation." *Journal of Legal Studies* 16 (January): 101–18.

Mundt, Robert J. 1990. "Gun Control and Rates of Firearms Violence in Canada and the United States." *Canadian Journal of Criminology* 32:137–54.

Niskanen, William A. 1975. "Bureaucrats and Politicians." *Journal of Law and Economics* 18:617–43.

"Note: Handguns and Product Liability." 1984. *Harvard Law Review* 97:1912.

Polsby, Daniel D. 1986. "Reflections on Violence, Guns, and the Defensive Use of Lethal Force." *Law and Contemporary Problems* 49: 89–111.

————. 1994. "The False Promise of Gun Control." *Atlantic* 273 (March): 57–63.

Posner, Richard A. 1971. "Taxation by Regulation." *Bell Journal of Economics and Management Science* 2:22–50.

————. 1992. *The Economic Analysis of Law*. 4th ed. Boston: Little, Brown & Co.

Priest, George L. 1985. "The Invention of Enterprise Liability: A Critical History of the Intellectual Foundations of Modern Tort Law." *Journal of Legal Studies* 14 (December): 461–527.

————. 1991. "The Modern Expansion of Tort Liability: Its Sources, Its Effects, and Its Reform." *Journal of Economic Perspectives* 5:31–50.

Reynolds, Morgan O., and W. W. Caruth. 1992. *Myths About Gun Control*. Center for Texas Studies Policy Report No. 176. Dallas, Tex.: National Center for Policy Analysis. December.

Rubin, Paul H. 1993. *Tort Reform by Contract*. Washington, D.C.: AEI Press.

Sloan, John Henry, Arthur L. Kellerman, Donald T. Reay, James A. Ferris, Thomas Koepsell, Frederick P. Rivara, Charles Rice, Laurel Gray, and James LoGerfo. 1988. "Handgun Regulations, Crime, Assaults and Homicide: A Tale of Two Cities." *New England Journal of Medicine* 319:1256–62.

Stigler, George J. 1970. "The Optimum Enforcement of Laws." *Journal of Political Economy* 78:526–36.

Stone, Geoffrey R., Louis M. Siedman, Cass R. Sunstein, and Mark V. Tushnet. 1991. *Constitutional Law*. Boston: Little, Brown & Co.

Toch, Hans, and Alan J. Lizotte. 1990. "Research and Policy: The Case of Gun Control." In *Psychology and Social Advocacy,* edited by Peter Suedfeld and Phillip Tetlock. New York: Hemisphere.

Tribe, Lawrence. 1988. *American Constitutional Law*. 2nd ed. Mineola, N.Y.: Foundation Press.

Van Alstyne, William. 1994. "The Second Amendment and the Personal Right to Arms." *Duke Law Journal* 43:1236–55.

Wade, John W. 1973. "On the Nature of Strict Liability for Products." *Mississippi Law Journal* 44:825–51.

Wittman, Donald. 1977. "Prior Regulation versus Post Liability: The Choice Between Input and Output Monitoring." *Journal of Legal Studies* 6:193–211.

Wright, James D., and Peter H. Rossi. 1986. *Armed and Considered Dangerous: A Survey of Felons and Their Firearms*. New York: Aldine de Gruyter.

Wright, James D., Peter H. Rossi, and Kathleen M. Daly. 1983. *Under the Gun: Weapons, Crime and Violence in America*. Chicago: Aldine de Gruyter.

Zimring, Franklin E. 1972. "The Medium Is the Message: Firearm Caliber as a Determinant of Death from Assault." *Journal of Legal Studies* 1:97–123.

———. 1975. "Firearms and Federal Law: The Gun Control Act of 1968." *Journal of Legal Studies* 4:133–98.

# 15

# Civil Forfeiture as a Tax

*Donald J. Boudreaux*
*Adam C. Pritchard*

Miguel Alvarez was arrested in October 1985 on a criminal drug charge. His bond was set at $50,000.00. American Bankers Insurance Company loaned Alvarez the bail money, taking a mortgage for $50,000.00 as security, and thus gaining an ownership interest in Alvarez's house. Several months later (but before Alvarez's criminal trial), the U.S. government brought a civil proceeding against Alvarez's house, alleging probable cause for suspecting that illegal drugs had once been harbored there. The government claimed title to the house, relying on the federal Comprehensive Drug Abuse Prevention and Control Act of 1970 ("Drug Act"), which forfeits to the government "[a]ll real property...which is used, or intended to be used, in any manner or part, to commit, or to facilitate the commission of, a violation of [federal drug laws] punishable by more than one year's imprisonment."[1]

When Alvarez failed to appear at his June 1986 trial, American Bankers paid the $50,000.00 bond to the government. The company then sought to exercise its ownership interest in the house (which under commercial law now belonged to American Bankers because Alvarez was a no-show at his trial). However, the government claimed to own the house under the Drug Act's forfeiture provisions. In response, American Bankers advanced the Drug Act's "innocent-owner" defense, which is intended to protect unwitting prop-

The authors thank Bruce Benson, Karol Ceplo, Dwight Lee, Jody Lipford, Hugh Macaulay, Roger Meiners, Bill Shughart, and Bruce Yandle for instructive discussion and comments. The following statement is inserted for the record: "The S.E.C., as a matter of policy, disclaims responsibility for any private publication or statement by any of its employees. The views expressed herein are those of the author and do not necessarily reflect the views of the Commission or of the author's colleagues upon the staff of the Commission. This article was written before Pritchard became employed by the Securities and Exchange Commission."

erty owners from having their assets seized by government agents fighting the "war on drugs." This innocent-owner defense says that "no property shall be forfeited...by reason of any act or omission established by that owner to have been committed or omitted without the knowledge or consent of that owner."[2] Because the alleged illegal acts took place prior to American Bankers' obtaining the mortgage—and because the government had not alleged any subsequent illegal acts—the company urged the court to find that the government had no right to take title to the house. American Bankers argued that title to the house vested in the company when Alvarez defaulted on his bond by not showing up for trial.

The court ruled in favor of the government, holding that because the statute places the burden on the owner to prove his innocence or lack of knowledge of wrongdoing, American Bankers failed to show that it did not know that the house once (allegedly) contained contraband drugs. Consequently, American Bankers lost both the $50,000.00 it paid when Alvarez skipped bail and its $50,000.00 security interest in the forfeited house. The government pocketed the $50,000.00 as well as the entire value of the house.[3]

American Bankers' experience demonstrates three frightening features of modern civil forfeiture law.[4] First, owners who have never even been charged with wrongdoing—much less tried and convicted of a crime by a jury—can lose sizable property interests through government seizures. Second, although the Drug Act provides a defense for innocent property owners, the owners themselves bear the burdens of proving that they are innocent of any wrongdoing and lack knowledge of wrongdoing; that is, if law enforcement agencies have probable cause for believing that felonious drug activity occurred on a piece of property, the government can immediately seize the property. The law then presumes that the property's owner is guilty unless and until the owner proves otherwise. Third, the government keeps the proceeds from the liquidation of forfeited properties. In practice, the various law enforcement agencies participating in drug arrests share in the proceeds from selling forfeited properties.

Civil forfeiture may not appear threatening to those committed to eradicating illegal drug use. After all, civil forfeiture acts as an implicit tax on undesirable behavior, raising drug dealers' costs as well as increasing the incentives of law enforcement agencies to hunt down and destroy illegal drugs. But such rosy first impressions about civil forfeiture prove illusory upon closer examination of the details of this crime-fighting tool. Though very much a sin tax, civil forfeiture does not promote more efficient law enforcement; it does the opposite. And in the process of clearing the way for more extensive use of civil forfeitures, courts have freed the government from the constitutional tethers created by America's founders to harness Leviathan.

In this chapter, we analyze civil forfeiture from the perspective of both economics and legal history. First, we argue that civil forfeiture creates an inefficient bias in favor of prohibition. Second, we show that permitting enforcement agents to retain proceeds from civil forfeiture promotes inefficient law enforcement decisions. Third, we review the history of civil forfeiture law as well as constitutional issues posed by the modern practice of civil forfeiture. Finally, we argue that the use of civil forfeiture as a sin tax has had the unintended and unfortunate consequence of reducing one of the few genuinely desirable sin taxes around: the Bill of Rights. The Bill of Rights acts as a tax on the propensity of government agents to violate citizens' liberties and confiscate their wealth. The Bill of Rights should be retained; repealing this particular sin tax—the Bill of Rights—would repeal the liberty of the people.

## Civil Forfeiture, Taxation, and Prohibition

Consider a politician's choice between prohibition and taxation. Why would politicians ever prohibit the possession of goods demanded by large numbers of people? The economic answer, of course, is that influential interest groups demand such statutes. If prohibition is effective (i.e., if commerce in the prohibited commodity is reduced or stopped altogether), politicians gain votes by removing from the streets goods intensely disliked by a sufficiently large bloc of voters. But even if prohibition is ineffective, voters may still be swayed by the posturing of politicians, who often stumble over each other in their efforts to "get tough on crime." Prohibition creates an instant crime problem, as market participants attempt to evade the prohibition. Politicians can milk votes and contributions by purporting to be solving the problem.

Political benefits from prohibition, however, are never free. When prohibition is effective, it carries a real cost to politicians: outlawed goods yield no tax revenues. Thus, legislators have fewer resources to (re)distribute in ways that enhance their reelection prospects. Ineffective prohibition also imposes costs on politicians. It may not be politically feasible to explicitly tax a good whose possession and sale have been made formally illegal, even though underground transactions in the prohibited commodity continue.[5] In short, legislators feel the pain of forgone tax revenues when they consider banning certain substances. Thus, prohibition is not a generally preferred strategy. Only those commodities intensely disliked by large numbers of voters will be outlawed, for only with such commodities will the political benefits of prohibition outweigh the forgone revenues.[6]

Civil forfeiture loosens this political constraint on the use of prohibition. Forfeiture surreptitiously imposes taxes on substances that have been formally prohibited. It permits seizure of contraband, and more important, it permits the seizure of valuable items used as "instrumentalities" in the commission of crimes (many of which are perfectly legal goods, such as automobiles used to transport marijuana). The government retains the proceeds when seized items are liquidated. By varying the intensity of its enforcement efforts, government can control the amount of revenues extracted through civil forfeiture. A government staffed by self-interested politicians will choose the level of enforcement that yields the highest net revenues. In this way, government can extract revenues from black-market transactions in the prohibited substances. Thus, civil forfeiture reduces the political cost of voting for outright prohibition. Politicians receive kudos for voting in favor of prohibition, while avoiding the complete sacrifice of tax revenues ordinarily extracted from legal markets.[7] When government can rely on civil forfeiture laws, politicians can more readily vote to prohibit those substances that will give rise to forfeiture opportunities. Accordingly, in legal regimes that can readily use civil forfeiture, there will be more formal prohibitions than in regimes where the use of civil forfeiture is narrowly confined.

Legislators benefit from civil forfeiture in two distinct ways: (1) civil forfeiture provides additional revenues, and (2) civil forfeiture increases the cost of prohibited substances, hence fostering more violence in the outlawed industry, which politicians can exploit to gain votes. They do so by adopting ever more draconian criminal sanctions that are peddled to voters as solutions to the problem of increased crime, notwithstanding politicians' role in fostering the increased amount of criminal activity.

Civil forfeiture poses other problems as a form of taxation. These problems stem from the interplay of the particular methods used to collect these taxes and the political effects on the government agencies that receive them. Specifically, additional problems with civil forfeiture emerge from the following facts:

- Law enforcement agencies keep part of the proceeds from civil forfeitures.
- Civil forfeiture proceeds are collected from only a small and politically unorganized subgroup of the population.
- Constitutional protections against government abuses are too often ignored in the civil forfeiture context.

As a consequence of allowing law enforcement agencies to retain the proceeds from disposing of seized assets, members of these agencies coalesce into an interest group favoring, and lobbying for, civil forfeiture statutes (as well as their attendant prohibitions).[8] Empirical studies of the effect of civil forfeiture upon the size of enforcement agencies' budgets indicate that forfeitures "have a significant positive impact on non-capital expenditures by police agencies"; that is, participation in civil forfeiture actions increases the discretionary budgets of law enforcement bureaus (Benson, Rasmussen, and Sollars 1995, 22). Law enforcement officials thus campaign to expand the reach of prohibition, and fight to minimize constitutional and statutory restraints on the use of the forfeiture power.[9]

Moreover, civil forfeiture is a grossly inequitable form of taxation. It may initially appear to be a useful revenue source in that it imposes a larger share of the fiscal burden on criminals. But appearances here are deceiving. Because of their civil nature, civil forfeiture laws permit government to confiscate and liquidate assets without abiding by constitutional restrictions designed to protect innocent citizens from overly vigorous government execution of laws. Civil forfeiture *would* impose a greater burden on criminals if the owners of property were in fact proved to have engaged in criminal conduct, but the procedures used afford no such assurance. For example, law enforcement agencies need only have probable cause for believing that the property has been used unlawfully in order to seize it; once seizure has occurred, the burden falls on the property owner to prove his or her innocence.[10] The burdens placed on the government to prove its case are slight indeed relative to the burden imposed on the government in criminal prosecutions. In a criminal case, the accused enjoys a presumption of innocence, and can be convicted and punished only if the government proves beyond a reasonable doubt—to the satisfaction of a jury—that he or she has committed a crime.

Thus, the government has a much easier time confiscating and liquidating properties under civil forfeiture statutes than it has convicting people of criminal offenses. Minimal procedures inevitably lead to many erroneous determinations. Civil forfeiture, by eliminating these procedural safeguards, creates a situation in which too many innocent people will be burdened by taxes not shared by their fellow citizens. The procedural safeguards afforded citizens accused of crimes exist not to make life easier for criminals, but to reduce to tolerable levels government error and overexuberance in arresting, prosecuting, convicting, and punishing *non*criminals. In consequence, civil forfeiture results in too many innocent people having their properties seized, liquidated, and transformed into government revenues, while similarly situated (i.e., equally innocent) people escape this tax.

The random manner in which civil forfeiture taxes are levied hides from taxpayers a part of the cost of government's operations. A disproportionate share of these costs are foisted upon owners whose properties law enforcement agencies only *suspect* were used in the commission of drug offenses. This group of property owners is politically unorganized and, hence, generally cannot adequately defend itself against more cohesively organized lobbies—such as law enforcement agencies—who clamor for liberalized civil forfeiture powers. Property owners at risk of forfeiture remain unorganized because they do not know who they are before having their properties confiscated under civil forfeiture statutes. The potential loss of property due to forfeiture is typically a one-time, low-probability event for each property owner. Thus, they have little incentive to form or to join lobbying groups pressing for repeal or reform of civil forfeiture statutes (Pritchard 1991).

The proceeds from civil forfeiture actions thus relieve the general body of taxpayers from some of the burden of paying collectively for the public good of law enforcement.[11] Because the general population of taxpayers does not feel the full cost of government as readily as it would if government were financed entirely by direct tax payments, the result is excessively large government in general, and overly aggressive drug law enforcement in particular.[12]

## Civil Forfeiture and the Nonoptimality of Law Enforcement

In the previous section, we showed the biases civil forfeiture creates in the legislature; these biases result from exploitation of a revenue source that is at least partially hidden from general taxpayers. In this section, we explore the consequences of civil forfeiture for decisions made in the executive branch, where law enforcement agencies get to keep all or part of the proceeds from such seizures.

As a preliminary step, however, we must first review some basic economics of law enforcement. Law enforcement, like other goods, is scarce. Resources used to enforce laws have alternative valuable uses, such as building more bridges and highways, providing more education, staffing larger social-service agencies, or keeping taxes lower so that private citizens can individually make their own resource allocation decisions. After some point, the gains from using additional resources to police against crime—even heinous crimes such as murder and rape—become smaller than the gains available from using these same resources elsewhere. Thus, completely wiping out all criminal activity would not be socially desirable.

As with all economic choices, the optimal amount of law enforcement occurs when the marginal benefit from an additional unit of enforcement just equals the marginal cost of the resources used to produce that additional enforcement. And what is true for law enforcement in general holds also for choices among alternative areas of law enforcement activity. Each type of crime fighting entails costs. Devoting more crime-fighting resources to vice offenses means that fewer resources are available to police against murder and other illegal activities.[13]

Figure 15.1 depicts the costs and benefits of enforcing drug prohibition. In the top panel, the horizontal axis measures the quantity of drug law enforcement, while the vertical axis shows the dollar value of the costs and benefits of such enforcement. The marginal-benefit curve (MB) shows the gains to society of each additional unit of drug law enforcement; the marginal-cost curve (MC) shows the costs of the additional units of enforcement. Enforcement beyond $E^*$ is excessive because the benefits from further reductions in drug crime are worth less to society than are all the goods and services sacrificed to generate these further reductions. Similarly, enforcement less than $E^*$ is suboptimal because the gains from additional enforcement would exceed the costs. Therefore, any institutional arrangement affecting law enforcement should be assessed by how likely it is to encourage the optimal amount of enforcement.

**FIGURE 15.1**

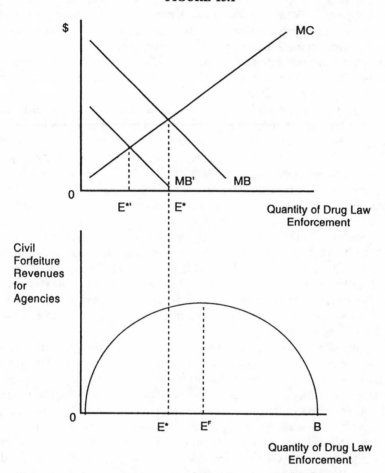

Civil forfeiture works *against* achieving the optimal amount of law enforcement. The reason is that civil forfeiture reduces the incentives law enforcement officials have to attain $E^*$ by giving law enforcement agents a disproportionate stake in the enforcement of drug prohibitions.

The lower part of figure 15.1 shows the totals of civil forfeiture revenues that law enforcement agents retain as funds for their agencies.[14] These revenues can be depicted using the familiar Laffer curve, which shows the relationship between tax rates and tax receipts. If the agency engages in no drug law enforcement, it will gain no revenues from drug-related civil forfeiture actions. This result is shown at point 0. At the other extreme, if the agency enforces drug laws with such vigor as to eliminate illegal drug operations totally, the amount of civil forfeiture revenues will also be zero. With no drug crime, there is no opportunity for drug-related civil forfeitures. This result is shown at point B. Between points 0 and B, however, civil forfeiture revenues are positive. Civil forfeiture revenues increase as drug law enforcement is expanded from point 0 (no enforcement) toward greater enforcement. After some point, however, a greater intensity of enforcement reduces the number of drug offenses to such an extent that the dollar amounts available from seizures will also be reduced.

Revenues from seizures are maximized at $E^F$, the "optimal" level of enforcement for law enforcement agencies allowed to keep proceeds from civil forfeiture seizures. Law enforcement agencies will determine the intensity of their drug law enforcement efforts—and, by implication, the intensity of their efforts to enforce laws against nondrug crimes—by how such efforts affect their civil forfeiture revenues. The revenue effects, rather than social-welfare consequences, of drug law enforcement determine the extent of police efforts in attacking various kinds of criminal behaviors.

No necessary correlation exists between $E^F$ (revenue-maximizing enforcement) and $E^*$ (socially optimal enforcement). $E^F$ could be to the right or to the left of $E^*$; only by chance will $E^F$ be at the same level of enforcement as $E^*$. Allowing law enforcement agencies to retain proceeds from civil forfeitures affords agencies discretion over their budgets. As a consequence, agencies supply either sub- or supraoptimal amounts of drug law enforcement, thus leaving society worse off.

An alternative to giving government agencies discretion over their budgets is to place budget decisions solely in the hands of legislatures. When legislatures determine the entire budgets for law enforcement agencies, legislatures in effect choose a quantity of law enforcement. With their budgets set by legislatures, law enforcement agencies allocate their money among different types of activities, for example, drug law enforcement versus policing against burglaries. In this scenario, no one type of activity has a "revenue advantage" over others in attracting law enforcement resources.[15] The heads of law enforcement agencies will thus make more-rational enforcement decisions.

The legislature is the most appropriate branch of government for selecting the *budget* for law enforcement agencies. The legislature confronts a large number of constituencies vying for public funds. Therefore, legislatures are better positioned than any of the specialized bureaucracies to determine if an additional dollar of public revenue should be used for law enforcement or for schooling or for social-welfare programs or for any other of the multitude of items on which governments spend money. The economics of public choice make clear that legislatures are hardly likely to tax, spend, and regulate in ways that maximize society's well-being.[16] Even so, legislatures are better placed to rationally allocate resources extracted from civil forfeiture proceeds than are individual enforcement agencies.[17]

Can we be more precise and say whether the current civil forfeiture regime causes over- or underenforcement? We believe that *over*enforcement of drug laws is the more likely result. Overenforcement is more likely because of the victimless nature of drug use.[18] While all but a small handful of sociopaths prefer effective enforcement of laws curbing violent or fraudulent behaviors aimed at nonconsenting parties, it is much less obvious that a large number of Americans approve of the war on drugs. In 1990, in the midst of drug war hysteria, the Drug Policy Foundation discovered that more than one in three Americans (36 percent) supported legalization.[19] And more recently, in January 1994, *NBC Nightly News* conducted a telephone call-in poll asking callers if drugs should be legalized. A majority (52.2 percent) favored legalization.[20]

As popular support for a particular law decreases, it is plausible to assume that the social benefits of enforcing the law also decrease, especially in the case of victimless crimes. In figure 15.1, this fall is shown by a marginal-benefit curve (MB') closer to the origin than MB. The socially optimal level of enforcement falls as well (to $E^{**}$). Naturally, $E^F$ is more likely to be to the right of $E^*$ the further to the left is $E^*$; that is, the weaker the consensus for outlawing a particular behavior, the more likely it is that legal prohibitions will be excessively enforced if enforcement agents derive personal benefits from their enforcement efforts. If no consensus exists for drug prohibition, then civil forfeiture probably leads to overenforcement of drug laws.

## The Legal Pedigree of Civil Forfeiture

The constitutionality of modern civil forfeiture statutes does not depend on their efficiency. Many ill-thought statutes remain on the books with no one questioning their constitutionality. Nevertheless, there are solid arguments tending to show that most civil forfeitures under the Drug Act are unconstitutional. In this section, we briefly review the history of civil forfeiture, emphasizing germane Supreme Court decisions. After many years of deference to legislative choices in the realm of civil forfeiture, the Court now seems to be coming around, albeit slowly, to the view that civil forfeiture poses a grave and unconstitutional threat to American liberties.

The roots of American forfeiture law are found in England. The predominant kind of forfeiture in England was not *civil* forfeiture at all; it was *criminal* forfeiture (which remains on the statute books). Criminal forfeiture occurs only after a person has been convicted of a criminal offense. The convict's property is seized and liquidated by government, following a criminal conviction, as part of the punishment visited upon those proven guilty.

The strict procedural requirements of the criminal law (e.g., trial by jury, a presumption of innocence, the privilege against self-incrimination, and protection against double jeopardy) help thwart unjustified seizures by government. With a criminal conviction as a necessary prerequisite to forfeiture, criminal forfeiture affords greater assurance that people paying fines or restitution to government are actually guilty of antisocial behaviors. Moreover, the Eighth Amendment's protection against excessive fines helps keep property loss under criminal forfeiture from growing out of proportion to the seriousness of the crime.

When government prosecutes someone for a crime, the suit is said to be *in personam,* which is legal jargon for a suit against an identifiable person. The individual accused of criminal wrongdoing can be punished only after government wins a conviction in court. Criminal forfeitures are always *in personam* prosecutions.

Contrast criminal forfeiture with civil forfeiture. In civil forfeiture, the government sues the offending *items* rather than any human being. In legal jargon, the government proceeds *in rem;* that is, the government sues the thing (rather than the thing's owner).[21] All civil forfeiture suits are *in rem* suits. For example, if Mr. Smith's house at 159 Elm Street is thought by the police to have been the site of a cocaine sale, then the government will sue the house at 159 Elm Street, charging it with wrongdoing. Because criminal law protections are available only to people, the defendant in this hypothetical civil case—formally, the house at 159 Elm Street—can be found liable for wrongdoing and confiscated and liquidated by government without the usual constitutional formalities. If Mr. Smith complains that he has been deprived of his property without ever having been charged with a crime, the government resorts to the legal fiction that the house was punished, not Mr. Smith, so that Mr. Smith has no cause to complain.

Understanding the origin of civil forfeiture (i.e., of *in rem* legal proceedings) will shed light on contemporary practice. In pre–Civil War America, as under English common law, *in rem* forfeiture proceedings were used in only two related contexts: (1) to enforce customs law (customs duties being the main source of federal revenue), and (2) to enforce admiralty laws (such as laws against piracy). If the government found smuggled goods, it could seize and liquidate them for revenue. The government was not obliged to convict the owner of the goods of a criminal offense prior to forfeiture. Likewise, a seized pirate ship was forfeitable without securing a criminal conviction of the vessel's owner. Practical concerns justified dropping the requirement of criminal conviction of property owners in these cases. Owners were likely to be in foreign lands, beyond the jurisdiction of domestic courts. Rather than let these defendants break the law without penalty, the government cleverly devised the legal fiction of *in rem* civil suits to govern those classes of cases in which defendants were not likely to be within the jurisdiction of domestic courts.

Historically, in England and in the United States until the second half of the nineteenth century, civil forfeiture suits were limited to the narrow class of cases (having to do with customs or admiralty law) in which the overwhelming impracticality of gaining *in personam* jurisdiction over property owners dictated an alternative means of penalizing wrongdoers. Augmenting government revenues with confiscated valuable properties was not the rationale for the civil (*in rem*) proceedings in these special cases; rather, evenhanded enforcement of the customs and admiralty laws required proceeding without the owners' consent or participation. Under common law, real property was subject to forfeiture only after a criminal conviction of the owner—and the first U.S. Congress, by statute, abolished criminal forfeiture altogether. With the Civil War, however, came the beginning of government efforts to use civil forfeiture proceedings as a general method of avoiding the procedural requirements of the Constitution. Rather than being limited to those instances when it was practically impossible to gain jurisdiction over an owner, civil forfeiture came to be used as a device by which the government sought to evade constitutional restrictions.

Beginning in August 1861, Congress enacted the Confiscation Acts authorizing the seizure of property owned by Confederates and those aiding the rebellion.[22] These acts permitted *in rem* proceedings for the confiscation of both personal *and* real property. The acts' coverage of real property is particularly noteworthy. Until the Civil War, civil forfeiture was limited to personal property (mainly ships and contraband goods); it did not extend to real property. The reason it did not is a straightforward one: real property (unlike personal property) cannot be contraband. Moreover, the owners of real properties used in unlawful ways are more likely to be within the jurisdiction of domestic courts than are the owners of the personal properties traditionally subject to civil forfeiture. Unlike personal property, real property cannot flee during the time it takes to find and establish jurisdiction over the owner.

But wartime exigencies notoriously serve as pretexts for expansion of government power.[23] The Supreme Court upheld the Confiscation Acts as a legitimate exercise of the war power, rejecting the argument that the acts violated the Fifth and Sixth Amendments. The Court also dismissed the contention that due process requires a criminal conviction before forfeiture.[24] By labeling such punishments "civil," despite their obviously punitive nature, the government succeeded in nullifying constitutional protections against criminal punishment. The war power served as the excuse for doing so.

The upholding of the Confiscation Acts encouraged Congress to expand *in rem* forfeiture further beyond its traditional domain—customs and the admiralty jurisdiction—to enforce revenue provisions unrelated to the maritime trade or to the war power.[25] In *Dobbins's Distillery v. United States,* the Court upheld the civil forfeiture of a distillery, and the real property upon which it stood, for liquor tax violations.[26] The tenant on the property was accused of defrauding the government of the excise taxes due on the liquor distilled there.[27] The Court held that it was not "necessary that the owner of the property should have knowledge that the tenant was committing fraud on the public revenue, in order that the information of forfeiture should be maintained."[28]

The Court reasoned that the proceeding was civil in nature, and that any "conviction of the wrong-doer must be obtained, if at all, in another and wholly independent proceeding."[29] But no precedent is cited for the proposition that a forfeiture of real property, as opposed to the personal property traditionally subject to forfeiture in *in rem* proceedings, can be accomplished without a prior criminal conviction;[30] indeed, the opinion nowhere indicates that the Court even considered that real property might be distinguished from personal property. The Court affirmed the judgment of forfeiture, despite the absence of wrongdoing by the owner, because "the offence...is attached primarily to the distillery, and the real and personal property used in connection with the same, without any regard whatsoever to the personal misconduct or responsibility of the owner."[31]

The Confiscation Acts cases, along with *Dobbins's Distillery,* thus mark a watershed in the Court's treatment of civil forfeiture statutes. The Court has opened the door so that any kind of property is subject to civil forfeiture as long as the government labels its enforcement actions "civil." The initial limited rationale for allowing forfeitures in civil rather than criminal proceedings was ignored or forgotten. Civil forfeiture became a generally available weapon for use by government against wrongdoers, and the Constitution's guarantee of certain rights and privileges to the criminally accused would not block government's way if the legislature took care to *label* a particular forfeiture action "civil" rather than "criminal."

During the next century, the Court never seemed quite sure what to do with civil forfeiture statutes. Although the genie of civil forfeiture was out of the bottle, every now and then the Court would declare a specific application of this or that civil forfeiture statute unconstitutional. But such declarations never amounted to any wholesale scaling back of the use of civil forfeiture. For example, in *Coffey v. United States,* the Court held that a prior acquittal of the crime of violating internal-revenue laws barred a subsequent civil forfeiture suit based on actions for which the defendant was earlier found innocent;[32] that is, civil forfeiture defendants were thus extended the constitutional protection against double jeopardy. And later in the same term, the Court held in *Boyd v. United States* that both the Fourth and Fifth Amendments protected the defendant against compulsory production of his private books and papers in a civil forfeiture proceeding. The Court declared the proceedings to be "quasi-criminal," reasoning that "proceedings instituted for the purpose of declaring the forfeiture of a man's property by reasons of offences committed by him, though they may be civil in form, are in their nature criminal."[33] *Boyd* thus promised that the Court would no longer be duped into treating the forfeiture of property as a civil matter simply because the legislature labeled it "civil."

*Boyd*'s promise was quickly abandoned. Subsequent decisions served to limit *Boyd*'s reach to the narrow Fourth and Fifth Amendment grounds on which it was decided. The Constitution's other protections of the criminally accused were held not to apply in civil forfeiture actions because these actions are "civil" and not "criminal." For example, in *United States v. Zucker,* the Court held that the right of a criminal defendant to confront his accusers does not apply to civil forfeiture.[34] Also, proof beyond a reasonable doubt was found by the Court not to be required in civil forfeiture proceedings.[35] Finally, the Court declared that there is no constitutional requirement that a jury find the defendant guilty in civil forfeiture proceedings; judges are free to direct verdicts in favor of government.[36]

Ominously, *Coffey*'s protection against double jeopardy in the civil forfeiture context is no longer good law. In 1984, the Court declared that the double-jeopardy clause does not bar "a civil, remedial forfeiture proceeding initiated following an acquittal on related criminal charges. To the extent that *Coffey v. United States* suggests otherwise, it is hereby overruled."[37] And *Boyd* has been all but overruled. In *United States v. Ward,* the Court accurately noted that it "has declined…to give full scope to the reasoning and dicta in *Boyd*."[38]

The most notable recent refusal of the Court to restrain civil forfeiture is the 1974 case of *Calero-Toledo v. Pearson Yacht Leasing Co.*[39] In *Calero-Toledo,* a yacht worth $20,000.00 was leased by Pearson Yacht Leasing to a party who subsequently smoked or transported marijuana on the yacht. Upon the discovery of two marijuana cigarettes on the vessel, local authorities— under a Puerto Rican civil forfeiture statute—seized the yacht without a prior judicial hearing or without notice being given to Pearson. All parties admitted that Pearson had no knowledge that marijuana was used or carried on the vessel. However, the Supreme Court upheld the forfeiture on the grounds that Pearson had failed to prove that it had done "all that reasonably could be expected to prevent the proscribed use of [its] property."[40] The Court ruled that Pearson's right to due process had not been violated.

In effect, *Calero-Toledo* reversed the presumption of innocence that is the Constitutional right of persons subject to criminal prosecution. The government was presumed to have behaved properly, and the burden of proving that the government overstepped its authority by seizing a vessel whose owner had done no wrong was foisted upon the owner. If the Puerto Rican statute had been labeled "criminal" rather than "civil," of course, this reversal of the presumption of innocence would have been held unconstitutional. But, as it had so often in the past, the Court simply trusted the legislature to choose the correct labels for its actions: the Puerto Rican legislature *said* that this action was civil, so it must *be* civil, and thus, constitutional protections available to the criminally accused are inapplicable.

Fortunately, a trend against unchecked use of civil forfeiture is just now emerging in the Court. During two recent terms (1992–93 and 1993–94), the

Court heard four civil forfeiture cases to which the United States government was a party. The government lost all four.[41] Each of these cases exhibits intensified judicial skepticism of the use of civil forfeiture in fighting the war on drugs. We focus here on the last two of these cases, *Austin* and *James Daniel Good*.

In *Austin*, the government sought the civil forfeiture of Richard Austin's mobile home and auto-body shop after he was convicted of distributing 2 ounces of cocaine from the shop, having brought the cocaine from his mobile home to consummate a prearranged sale. Both the trial court and the appellate court rejected Austin's argument that the forfeiture would violate his Eighth Amendment right to be protected from excessive fines. Austin appealed to the Supreme Court.

The government urged that civil forfeiture of real property is not a criminal punishment and, therefore, the government cannot be held to the strict requirements of criminal procedure when it confiscates real property. The Court rejected this argument, unanimously reversing the lower court. The Court found that "forfeiture generally and statutory *in rem* forfeiture in particular historically have been understood, at least in part, as punishment,"[42] thus repudiating the government's assertion that the Drug Act's forfeiture provisions are not punitive. The Court concluded that the forfeiture was a "payment to a sovereign as punishment for some offense...subject to the limitations of the Eighth Amendment's Excessive Fines Clause."[43]

The case of *James Daniel Good* also represents a step forward in restoring liberties trampled underfoot by a government motivated by civil forfeiture revenues. Four years after James Daniel Good was convicted, sentenced, and fined in a Hawaii state court for growing marijuana, the United States government seized his house and the 4 acres of land upon which it sits. Good received no prior notice of the seizure. Although the trial court upheld the seizure, the court of appeals reversed it, finding that the government violated Mr. Good's right to due process of law by not affording him notice and a hearing prior to the seizure.

Arguing before the Supreme Court, the government insisted that the due-process clause does not apply when the government seizes property for law enforcement purposes.[44] The Court did not buy this claim. In *James Daniel Good*, the Court reasoned that the government's asserted interests in seizing property—obtaining jurisdiction and preventing the loss or destruction of the property—were slight in the case of real property. The Court ruled that due process requires the government to give notice and a hearing to owners of real property before seizures because of (1) the high risk of error created by allowing government to seize property without adhering to the requirements of due process of law, and (2) the substantial interests citizens have in being secure in their homes.

Thus, in just two terms of the Court, substantial constitutional constraints have been placed on government's exercise of civil forfeiture authority. Civil forfeiture remains, however, a source of revenue for government as it wages its war on drugs. For example, although *James Daniel Good* requires notice and a hearing prior to seizure of real property, the burden remains upon property owners to prove their innocence. Failure to prove innocence at a preseizure hearing means that government may seize the property and liquidate it for revenue purposes. We believe that more can be done by the courts, under the Constitution, to further rein in government's use of civil forfeiture. Indeed, as we read the Constitution, more *must* be done.

At a minimum, civil forfeitures of real property should all be declared unconstitutional. The common law of England and the United States at the time of the Constitution's ratification did not provide for civil forfeiture of real properties; such forfeitures could be accomplished only following criminal convictions of the owners of real property. Unlike captured pirate ships and contraband goods, there is no chance that real property can stealthily escape jurisdiction before its owner is convicted. Consequently, the pragmatic rationale for allowing *in rem* seizures of personal property does not apply to real property. Because *in rem* forfeiture of real property was unheard of at the time the Constitution was ratified, the framers and ratifiers of the Constitution cannot plausibly be supposed to have intended to permit such forfeitures. Thus, any forfeitures of real property sought by government should be part of the explicit punishment sought in criminal proceedings.

Given the abuses that have marked civil forfeiture under the Drug Act, the Court might consider it wise to adopt an even more stringent approach to civil forfeiture. Under such an approach, the government would be barred from using civil procedures for the forfeiture of any property—real or personal—whenever (1) the property is forfeitable to the government because of its use in criminal wrongdoing, and (2) the government cannot prove that the property owner is beyond the personal jurisdiction of domestic courts. If the property owner is within the jurisdiction of domestic courts, then he or she should be duly accused, indicted, tried, and convicted before his or her property is forfeited to government. The protections of the criminal process are essential to safeguard innocent parties from government overreaching. If the owner is outside of domestic jurisdiction, the government must then, in good faith, attempt to notify the owner that his or her property temporarily (pending the outcome of a criminal trial) has been seized. If the owner then appears to wage a defense, a criminal conviction should be necessary before final forfeiture. In contrast, if the owner refuses to attend the trial, the property can then be forfeited in a civil action. In either case, however, the burden should be upon the government to prove wrongdoing by the owner, and not (as it is now) upon the owner to prove his or her innocence of any wrongdoing.

Given that one role of the courts is to protect citizens' constitutional rights from legislative legerdemain, the label attached by the legislature to the forfeiture should be of no consequence. In all cases, a court should ask, "Is this forfeiture punitive in purpose?" If the answer is no (that is, if the court finds that no punitive purpose is served by the forfeiture), the court should then ask, "Is the property contraband, or is it a legal good?" If it is contraband, then the government can constitutionally seize these goods and destroy them. But if the property is not contraband, absent a criminal conviction, a taking of private property has occurred, and under the Fifth Amendment, fair compensation must be paid to the dispossessed owner.[45]

When a court finds that the forfeiture is designed to be punitive, *all* procedural requirements of the criminal law should be met before the forfeiture is final. If the owner of the property is outside the court's jurisdiction, then fair notice to the defendant of the charges is necessary, as is a fair opportunity for defense. If the defendant fails to show for his or her trial after being notified (or after a reasonable attempt to notify has been made), then a conviction obtained *in absentia* permits forfeiture to the government of the defendant's property. The value of such forfeitures would still be limited, of course, by the excessive-fines clause of the Eighth Amendment.

## Conclusion

Although superficially a sin tax on undesirable behavior, civil forfeiture is more accurately described as a money tree for legislatures and law enforcement agencies. This tree is regularly shaken down for revenues by government. Such shakedowns, however, are precisely the kinds of government overreaching that the rule of law and constitutional protections are supposed to prevent. The Bill of Rights is intended to restrain government's scope of action in dealing with the criminally accused. To avoid these restraints, legislatures label their punitive actions "civil" rather than "criminal." For too long, courts have allowed government to escape constitutional fetters by this sleight of hand. Although the Supreme Court now grants less deference to legislative labels than in the past, civil forfeiture remains a viable source of revenue for government. As a matter of policy, complete abandonment of civil forfeiture (as opposed to criminal forfeiture) is appropriate. As a matter of constitutional law, civil forfeiture outside of its narrow historical confines of the maritime law ought to be struck down as unconstitutional.[46] When the government seeks revenues, it ought to secure these explicitly from uniform taxes levied upon the general populace; when the government seeks to punish criminals, it ought to do so within the guidelines of the Bill of Rights.

In this spirit, the Constitution, particularly the Bill of Rights, is usefully viewed as a sin tax on oppressive government. Tyrannical government was a sin well known to America's founding generation. They rebelled against a distant government that taxed without representation, refused jury trials to those accused of crimes, and, generally, denied rights essential to citizens of a free and prosperous nation. James Madison and his peers sought to check government by special-interest groups. To this end, the original Constitution and the Bill of Rights were designed to raise the costs of government tyranny.

Some portion of this constitutional sin tax is self-enforcing and self-sustaining; for example, the separation of executive from legislative powers increases the costs of enacting interest-group legislation. But other portions of this tax require active and ongoing enforcement by a constitutional tax collector: the courts. Courts sit in judgment on the legislative and executive branches, requiring these branches to adhere to their constitutionally prescribed roles. If the legislature or the executive attempts to make an end run around the Constitution, the courts are charged with stymieing such unconstitutional power grabs. By keeping the other branches within their constitutional boundaries, the judicial branch can enforce the Constitution's tax on overreaching government behavior.

The analogy is not perfect between ordinary selective taxes and the Constitution. Constitutional protections provide no public revenues. Nevertheless, to the extent that ordinary sin taxes are aimed at discouraging antisocial behavior, the Constitution surely is such a tax, for few behaviors are as antisocial and uncontrollable as actions by a government unchecked by meaningful constitutional restraints. The U.S. Constitution unquestionably was meant to impose such restraints. The courts have failed to realize the full potential of this document; they have allowed the legislative and executive branches to employ the label "civil forfeiture" as an artifice to elude clear constitutional prohibitions. We are encouraged by the recent trend of Supreme Court cases reining in civil forfeiture, but much work remains to be done toward the fuller restoration of citizens' constitutional rights.

## Notes

1. 21 U.S.C. § 881(a)(7) (1988).
2. Ibid.
3. *United States v. One Single Family Residence*, 683 F.Supp. 783 (S.D. Fla. 1988).
4. The Drug Act is not the only source of civil forfeiture provisions, but as a practical matter, civil forfeitures occur overwhelmingly in the context of the so-called war on drugs. In this chapter, we deal only with forfeitures initiated under the drug laws. We note, however, that the original health care bill President Clinton sent to Congress contained a civil forfeiture provision. Under the president's plan, the Department of Health and Human Services, as well as the attorney general, would be authorized to audit and evaluate physicians' practices. If the government finds that a physician committed a "federal health-care offense," that physician's personal property (e.g., office and laboratory equipment) could be seized without the physician ever being convicted of a crime. Such "offenses" are defined in the proposed act as knowingly falsifying or concealing a material fact in "any matter involving a...health plan." President Clinton's proposed Health Security Act (1993), § 5433. Money raised from these seizures would be earmarked for an antifraud account to finance additional investigations of such newly created "offenses." § 5432. See also *Dental Economics*, February 1994, 17; and Bradley A. Smith, "The Health Police Are Coming," *Wall Street Journal*, 16 December 1993, A-16.
5. Moreover, there are now constitutional bounds on the amount of such taxes. See *Department of Revenue of Montana v. Kurth Ranch, et al.*, 114 S.Ct. 1937 (1994).

6. See Boudreaux and Pritchard (1994). Alcohol prohibition in the United States was repealed in 1933 during the fiscal crisis confronting the Depression-era Congress. We argue that this repeal occurred—and occurred when it did—because the Great Depression substantially reduced incomes (and, hence, income tax revenues) and Congress was desperate for the funds available from taxing legally sold liquor.

7. Consequently, government gains a stake in the formally prohibited industry—an industry which, in the case of drugs, supplies hundreds of millions of dollars annually in revenue to government. In 1991 alone, federal civil forfeitures were valued at approximately $700 million (Benson, Rasmussen, and Sollars 1995). This figure rose to nearly $900 million in 1992 (*Sourcebook of Criminal Justice Statistics,* table 4.43, Bureau of Justice Statistics, 1992. See also Wollstein (1993). Of course, these civil forfeiture revenues are not listed as tax receipts in government budgets; nor do legislators call them taxes. Their formal label, however, cannot disguise their essential character.

8. And, as we discuss below, retention of civil forfeiture revenues causes these agencies to make inefficient law enforcement choices.

9. See Benson, Rasmussen, and Sollars (1995). Agencies' quest for forfeiture proceeds may also help explain support by law enforcement agencies for gun control (particularly bans on assault weapons): heavily armed drug dealers are better able to protect their properties from government officials than are unarmed or weakly armed dealers. But this speculation may be inaccurate. If gun control is effective in reducing the munitions of drug dealers, the profitability of dealing drugs may decline because turf protection will be more costly. In turn, reduced drug crime profitability might reduce the aggregate value of assets seizable through civil forfeiture. An alternative hypothesis is that law enforcement agencies support gun control because voters regard guns as substitutes for police protection services. When the number of guns possessed by law-abiding citizens is reduced, the demand for police services increases. This effect is especially plausible if gun control statutes reduce gun possession by criminals proportionately less than they reduce gun possession by noncriminals.

10. "Once the government demonstrates that probable cause exists, the burden of proof in a civil forfeiture proceeding shifts to the claimant [i.e., the property owner seeking the return of seized property] to establish by a preponderance of the evidence that the property is not subject to forfeiture." *United States v. A Single Family Residence,* 803 F.2d 625, 629 (11th Cir. 1986).

11. As we discuss below, insofar as government is excused from the inconvenience of abiding by the Constitution, members of the subgroup bearing the disproportionate burden of the civil forfeiture tax are not sufficiently likely to be criminals. It is precisely in such cases—in which majoritarian outcomes are likely to trample the rights of politically weak groups—that constitutional restraints on government are most important. The U.S. Constitution (especially the Bill of Rights) safeguards accused criminals from government overreaching, thus discouraging government from falsely prosecuting innocent people.

12. Much of the cost of civil forfeiture seizures ultimately falls on tenants and other lessees. A landlord who knows about the possibility of civil forfeiture understands that he faces some positive chance of losing his property to the government because of drug offenses committed by his tenants. This landlord will thus raise the rent. A form of "fiscal illusion" is thus created; fiscal illusion is rational ignorance about the full costs of government. As the costs of government become more and more detached from explicit tax payments (by, e.g., being

hidden in higher rental rates), fiscal illusion increases. Larger-than-optimal government is the consequence.

13. See Benson, Rasmusen, and Sollars (1995), citing evidence that increased enforcement of drug laws reduces police efforts to thwart nondrug violent and property crimes (resulting in an *increase* in these latter species of crimes). See also Barnett (1994), especially page 2596.

14. Recall that empirical evidence suggests that civil forfeiture proceeds add to the discretionary budgets of law enforcement agencies. See Benson, Rasmussen, and Sollars (1995, 22).

15. Although drug law enforcement would have no revenue advantage over other law enforcement activities, a bias causing excessive drug law enforcement may nevertheless exist insofar as drug-related arrests and seizures are more visible evidence of bureaucratic output than is, say, a drop in the number of burglaries. But even if such a "bureaucratic-output" bias exists, it is amplified when enforcement agencies are able to appropriate civil forfeiture loot.

16. See, e.g., Buchanan and Tullock (1962), McCormick and Tollison (1981), Buchanan and Tollison (1984), Mitchell and Simmons (1994), Lee and McKenzie (1987), and Mueller (1989).

17. See Miller, Shughart, and Tollison (1984). These authors argue that "[i]f regulatory administration is decentralized, with rules issued piecemeal by a variety of independent agencies, then concentrated interests will typically be more successful in inducing regulators to fashion their decisions to benefit them. In contrast, a centralized review process makes this outcome less likely" (p. 83). The reason centralization of regulatory policy making and review reduces public decision-making bias is that "centralization sums the individual welfare losses created by the regulatory bodies subject to its jurisdiction" (p. 86). A legislature, of course, is a more centralized evaluator of alternative law enforcement policies than are individual law enforcement agencies.

18. Characterizing drug use as a victimless crime can be challenged. Those who object to our characterization typically point to families and friends rendered distraught by drug abuse, lost productivity, and increased burdens on the health care system. While we do not deny that drug abuse causes genuine, deep, and often expensive tragedies, it remains, in our view, a victimless crime. Drug use is victimless in the significant sense that no one is physically coerced, defrauded, or blackmailed into acting against his or her will, or involuntarily stripped of property. This fact distinguishes drug use from crimes such as murder, rape, and burglary. See Barnett (1994, 2621): "[D]rug use is a victimless crime in the sense that it is conduct that does not physically interfere with the person or property of another." Also, Barnett persuasively argues (pp. 2621–25) that criminalizing noncoercive, nonfraudulent, and nonthieving activities actually *increases* social costs because victimless crimes have no complaining victims. Consequently, police must rely upon highly invasive techniques to detect such crimes, to apprehend their perpetrators, and to gather incriminating evidence. Constitutional protections from zealous law enforcement authorities are thereby seriously imperiled.

Another social cost of criminalizing victimless behavior is that valuable disapproving attitudes about criminal activity *with* victims become diluted:

> Criminalizing behavior that is commonly engaged in by a substantial segment of society inevitably debases the currency of criminal proscriptions. If a legal system declares that both drug use and robbery are reprehensible, it is

not only making a moral statement about drug use, it is making a moral statement about robbery. (Duke and Gross 1993, 106)

19. "The American People Talk about Drugs," poll conducted by the Drug Policy
Foundation, Washington, D.C., April 1990.

20. *NBC Nightly News* phone poll, 4 January 1994. Legalization was supported by
42,812 of the callers; 39,254 opposed it. Moreover, unlike violent and property
crimes, drug prohibitions are condemned by a number of prominent people. This
number includes former Secretary of State George Schulz, Baltimore Mayor Kurt
Schmoke, economist and Nobel laureate Milton Friedman, columnist William
Buckley, and the editors of the news magazine *The Economist*.

21. *In rem* cases typically have amusingly odd names, for example, *United States v.
One 1976 Mercedes Benz 280S, Serial No. 11602012072193*, 618 F.2d 453 (7th
Cir. 1980).

22. Act of August 6, 1861, 12 Stat. 319; and Act of July 17, 1862, 12 Stat. 589.

23. For a thorough review of the effects of crises—real and fabricated—on the growth
of government in the United States, see Higgs (1987).

24. *Miller v. United States*, 78 U.S. (11 Wall.) 268, 305 (1871): "The Constitution
confers upon Congress expressly power to declare war...and make rules respecting
capture on land and water. Upon the exercise of these powers no restrictions are
imposed. Of course the power to declare war involves the power to prosecute it
by all means and in any manner in which war may be legitimately prosecuted. It
therefore includes the right to seize and confiscate all property of an enemy and
to dispose of it at the will of the captor. This is and always has been an un-
doubted belligerent right."

25. See An Act imposing Taxes on distilled Spirits and Tobacco, and for other Purposes, 15 Stat. 125, 133 (20 July 1868).

26. 96 U.S. 395 (1877).

27. Ibid., pp. 396–97.

28. Ibid., p. 399.

29. Ibid.

30. It is interesting to note that real property is the largest single source of federal
drug-related civil forfeiture revenues. See "Sourcebook of Criminal Justice Statistics," table 4.43, Bureau of Justice Statistics, 1992.

31. 96 U.S. 395 (1877), p. 401.

32. 116 U.S. 436 (1886).

33. 116 U.S. 616, 633-34 (1886).

34. 161 U.S. 475 (1896).

35. *United States v. Regan*, 232 U.S. 37 (1914).

36. *Hepner v. United States*, 213 U.S. 103 (1909).

37. *United States v. One Assortment of 89 Firearms*, 465 U.S. 354, 361 (1984).

38. 448 U.S. 242 (1980).

39. 416 U.S. 663 (1974).

40. 416 U.S. 663, 689 (1974).

41. These cases are *Republic National Bank of Miami v. United States*, 113 S.Ct.
554 (1992); *United States v. 92 Buena Vista Ave.*, 113 S.Ct. 1126 (1993); *Austin
v. United States*, 113 S.Ct. 2801 (1993); and *United States v. James Daniel Good
Real Property*, 114 S.Ct. 492 (1993).

42. *Austin*, at 2806.

43. *Austin*, at 2812.

44. Brief for the United States in *James Daniel Good*, at 13.

45. On takings law in general, see Epstein (1985).

46. It would be incorrect to argue that *all* civil forfeiture should be declared unconstitutional. Civil forfeiture was well known to the founding generation and was clearly a part of the English common-law tradition handed down to the newly independent United States. Such forfeitures were limited to contraband and personal properties used in the commission of maritime-related offenses.

## References

Barnett, Randy E. 1994. "Bad Trip: Drug Prohibition and the Weakness of Public Policy." *Yale Law Journal* 103 (June): 2593–630.

Benson, Bruce L., David W. Rasmussen, and David L. Sollars. 1995. "Police Bureaucracies, Their Incentives, and the War on Drugs." *Public Choice* 83 (April): 21-45.

Boudreaux, Donald J., and A. C. Pritchard. 1994. "The Price of Prohibition." *Arizona Law Review* 36 (spring): 1–10.

Buchanan, James M., and Robert D. Tollison, eds. 1984. *The Theory of Public Choice II.* Ann Arbor: University of Michigan Press.

Buchanan, James M., and Gordon Tullock. 1962. *The Calculus of Consent: Logical Foundations of Constitutional Democracy.* Ann Arbor: University of Michigan Press.

Duke, Steven B., and Albert C. Gross. 1993. *America's Longest War: Rethinking Our Tragic Crusade against Drugs.* New York: G. P. Putnam's Sons.

Epstein, Richard A. 1985. *Takings: Private Property and the Power of Eminent Domain.* Cambridge: Harvard University Press.

Higgs, Robert. 1987. *Crisis and Leviathan.* New York: Oxford University Press.

Lee, Dwight R., and Richard B. McKenzie. 1987. *Regulating Government.* Lexington, Mass.: D. C. Heath.

McCormick, Robert E., and Robert D. Tollison. 1981. *Politicians, Legislation, and the Economy: An Inquiry into the Interest-Group Theory of Government.* Boston: Martinus Nijhoff.

Miller, James C. III, William F. Shughart II, and Robert D. Tollison. 1984. "A Note on Centralized Regulatory Review." *Public Choice* 43:83–88.

Mitchell, William C., and Randy T. Simmons. 1994. *Beyond Politics.* Boulder: Westview Press.

Mueller, Dennis C. 1989. *Public Choice II.* New York: Cambridge University Press.

Pritchard, Adam C. 1991. "Government Promises and Due Process: An Economic Analysis of the 'New Property,'" *Virginia Law Review* 77:1053–90.

Wollstein, Jarret B. 1993. "The Government's War on Property." *Freeman* 43 (July): 244–52.

# 16

# Excise Taxation in the Rent-Seeking Society

## Gordon Tullock

Long ago when I took my first and only course of economics from Henry Simons, he discussed what in those days were called "luxury taxes." This was long before anybody realized that cigarettes could cause lung cancer. The fundamental luxury taxes of the U.S. government, and indeed most other governments in those days, were taxes on cigarettes and alcohol. The taxes on cigarettes were particularly heavy.

Simons pointed out that the real reason for these taxes was that the people who consumed cigarettes did not regard them as a luxury. He pointed out that if you put a tax on potatoes, people will reduce their consumption of potatoes considerably, so the revenue derived from the tax might not be very great. If you put a tax on cigarettes, on the other hand, people will reduce their consumption of cigarettes only slightly. Hence, the net incidence of a tax on "luxuries" was a reduction in the production of "necessities," because the people consuming them had a different attitude toward what was necessary, and what was not, than did the legislators.

Simons thought that the legislators knew all of this, and that the basic reason they were using taxes on cigarettes, alcohol, and the like for raising revenue was simply that they knew the demand for them was very inelastic and, in fact, that consumption would be reduced only slightly. A tobacco tax might not even actually reduce the revenues of tobacco farmers, about which more will be said later. These taxes were very widely dispersed, the incidence in reduction of consumption of other things was very hard to trace, and the likelihood of various difficulties in the legislatures was low.

It should be pointed out that this was long ago, when taxes were generally much lighter than they are now and various religious influences were also stronger, so taxes on alcohol certainly were backed by a number of clergymen. There were even some who thought that smoking was sinful.

It seems likely that the elasticity of demand for cigarettes, alcohol, marijuana, cocaine, and so on still is quite low. Taxes on them, if left to them-

369

selves, would not reduce their consumption very much, but would reduce the consumption of other goods perhaps considerably. I think this is probably one of the reasons why such taxes are still favored by politicians, but there are others. That it is actually undesirable to have people smoking, drinking, and using illicit drugs is now quite widely believed. Except for the particular people who smoke or engage in other politically incorrect behaviors, there is no significant demand for lowering existing taxes or refraining from raising them.

There have been other developments, though, so it seems likely that there will be little revenue gained from raising excise taxes on cigarettes. It should be said that the tax increases that are being recommended are much lower than the ordinary taxes on cigarettes that one finds in most European countries.

The prospective revenue gains from taxes on cigarettes right now are low. The consumers of cigarettes not only are being bombarded with propaganda about the dangers of the cigarettes, but also are being seriously harassed in various ways. They are frequently compelled to spend considerable periods of time without smoking, which is likely to reduce addiction.

I recently took a nonstop airline trip from Hong Kong to Los Angeles, thirteen hours in the air on Cathay Pacific Airlines. Cathay Pacific is effectively, if not legally, completely free from any regulations since it dominates policy in Hong Kong, its home base. This flight was nonsmoking for the whole of the MD11 aircraft.

Further, most airports have restrictions under which smoking is permitted only in certain places, and on the average, the places where they permit smoking are rather unpleasant. The one in Tucson is a good example, but I have seen it elsewhere.

The combination of a campaign to reduce smoking by propaganda and a program of harassment of people who do smoke seems likely to move the demand curve for smoking sharply to the left. Even if the demand stays relatively inelastic in the price dimension, these other factors may sharply reduce total sales.

The tax increase might be taken by smokers as evidence that they will eventually be forced to stop, and that they may as well get it over with immediately. It is not at all unlikely that revenue from cigarette taxes will fall sharply whether the tax is increased or not, but surely increasing the tax is risky at the moment from the revenue standpoint.

From the revenue standpoint, there is another problem here. The price of tobacco has been held up for the benefit of tobacco farmers for many years. The system, like most agricultural price supports, involves restricting total production by reducing the amount of land that can be cultivated for that purpose. In fact, tobacco farmers regard their allotments—which are freely transferable within counties—as highly valuable pieces of capital. Any reduction in demand will hit them hard.

It seems fairly certain that a rise in the price of cigarettes as a result of the tax would sharply reduce the revenues that tobacco farmers can get—in essence, it would confiscate rents on their allotments. Thus, the effect on the final price of cigarettes would be less than one might expect if one ignored this aspect of the matter.

Since such a large part of the costs of raising tobacco is the capital value of the allotments, it is likely that the supply of tobacco, as opposed to tobacco products, is extremely inelastic over a considerable range of prices. This is the reason why the tobacco farmers, a well-organized political pressure group, are so much opposed to the tax.

But to return to the harassment of smokers, it is not by any means confined to governmental bodies.[1] Much private harassment is by people who claim they don't like smoke. These claims are, I assume, correct, but it used to be that people who didn't like smoke simply kept their mouths shut.

In essence, as has been said a number of times, the ownership of the air has changed from people who want to smoke to people who do not want to smell smoke. The federal government has taken steps to "prove" that secondhand smoke is a dangerous carcinogen. But even if you accept the bizarre statistical study supposedly demonstrating this, the calculated risk of death from cancer is utterly trivial. Further research may indicate that there is a greater risk, but it may also indicate that there is even less.

An amusing twist on this matter is that recent demographic studies have begun to indicate that smoking may prevent Alzheimer's disease. The studies currently are not conclusive. Indeed, they are rather like the studies linking cigarettes with cancer back in the early days, but it is intriguing that the people interested in public health are not immediately calling for larger studies. As a matter of fact, they are offering criticisms of these studies using exactly the same arguments that the tobacco lobby offered against the early studies supposedly showing that cancer is caused by smoking. But this is merely an amusing phenomenon; it doesn't prove anything.

As mentioned above, there is the problem of ownership of the air, which apparently once belonged to smokers and now belongs to nonsmokers. This is a very difficult problem, a type of externality that raises very broad issues. When I was in Taipei recently, I acquired what was either a mild case of flu or a very bad cold. It didn't immobilize me, and I went on to Hong Kong and the Pacific Rim meeting of the Western Economic Association. I attended panels, appeared on some, had meals with other members, and so on. It was almost certain that I was breathing out the virus of my illness, mild though it was. The health risk of my breath was much greater than the health risk that would have occurred had I been smoking.[2]

It could be argued that I should have been compelled to remain in some safe area. This could not have been my hotel room, because I would have left the virus for future occupants, but the hotel could maintain a set of special rooms for people who have diseases, just as they have smoking rooms. Needless to say, this is not what we do, but it is not very obvious that we shouldn't.

My personal opinion is that any mild externality, which my virus was, and which, in my opinion, secondhand smoke also is, should largely be ignored. But that is a personal opinion, and there is no strong argument one way or the other on the issue. I would recommend further research on the point, except that I can't think of any way of undertaking the research.

It appears to be an area where we must depend on political decisions, and where the political decision of necessity has a very large element of error. What we should have is further research. It is astonishing that some forty-five years after the association between lung cancer and smoking was first discovered, we still do not know what the physiological mechanism is.

It might be that there is some single constituent of smoke that can be removed, eliminating this problem. It is also possible that there is a single constituent of smoke that is a specific against Alzheimer's disease and could be given to people in the form of pills. It is also quite possible that the initial studies indicating that smoking protects against Alzheimer's disease are defective, as in 1950 it was possible that the studies showing a relationship between smoking and cancer were defective.

The propaganda and harassment of people who smoke, combined with the requirement that a good many of them spend considerable periods of time without smoking at all because of being in a no-smoking area,[3] are likely to reduce the demand for cigarettes. This will produce a lower demand, even if it remains inelastic.

In dealing with the fiscal aspects of a tax on smoking, you should pay attention to the expenses that smoking either imposes on or saves for the government. To begin with, consider the current, by no means certain, evidence that smoking is a specific against Alzheimer's disease. This is a very expensive illness, because a person who has it is not likely to die soon, but requires expensive custodial care.

The diseases caused by smoking, however, are cheap diseases. When you get lung cancer, the odds are very good that you will die and that the treatment given to you, while you are waiting to die, will be relatively inexpensive. On the other hand, if you do not get lung cancer and you live longer, the odds are that you will draw at length on Social Security funds, and that you will become eligible for very, very expensive treatments for one or more of the large number of ailments that afflict the elderly. The same can be said about the various heart problems that can be caused by smoking.

From the fiscal standpoint, then, it would appear that we would be wise to encourage smoking. Obviously, I realize that there are other arguments. After all, executing everybody at the age of sixty-five would also reduce the fiscal burden. Simply repealing the pension system and not paying for medical care of older people would do the same.

All of these examples show that fiscal arguments are not decisive in such matters; indeed, most people don't even like to think about them. If we do think about fiscal matters, it is clear that reducing the amount of smoking is hard on the government. It can increase expenses and reduce tax revenues.

Of course, we don't know whether the amount of smoking would fall solely from the propaganda and harassment even without a tax increase. If it would, then a tax increase might well generate additional revenue, because there would still be elements of inelasticity in the demand.

People do not think of the problem of tobacco smoking in terms of revenue. Indeed, the introduction of this consideration in the Clinton health care reform program changed the general discussion considerably. The basic issue nowadays is that a great many people want to try to help other people by forcing them to stop smoking, along with the issue of who owns the air, which involves a mild genuine externality.

Both of these questions are ones in which the economist can offer some help, but where the answers have to be based on noneconomic criteria. Thus I hope this chapter may be of some help in clarifying thinking about them, but I refrain from telling you what I think your answers should be.

### Notes

1. Cathay Pacific Airlines is not, of course, a governmental body, although it has great influence on the Hong Kong government.
2. I have never smoked at any time in my life.
3. The new building in which I teach at the University of Arizona, McClelland Hall, is a smoke-free building. However, there are some open porches, and you are permitted to go outside and smoke if you wish. Very few of our staff take advantage of the privilege.

# About the Editor

*William F. Shughart II* is Professor and holder of the P.M.B. Self, William King Self, and Henry C. Self Free Enterprise Chair in the Department of Economics and Finance at the University of Mississippi. He received his Ph.D. in economics from Texas A & M University, and he has taught at George Mason University, Clemson University, and the University of Arizona. Professor Shughart is Book Review Editor for the journals *Public Choice* and *Managerial and Decision Economics*. His books include *The Organization of Industry, Antitrust Policy and Interest-Group Politics, Modern Managerial Economics* (with W. Chappell and R. Cottle), and *The Causes and Consequences of Antitrust* (edited with F. McChesney), and he has been a contributor to numerous other books. He is the author of more than eighty articles and reviews for scholarly journals, and his commentaries have also appeared in the *Wall Street Journal, Regulation*, the *Pittsburgh Post-Gazette*, the *Washington Times*, the *Detroit Free Press*, the *Providence Journal-Bulletin*, and other publications.

# About the Contributors

*Gary M. Anderson* is Professor of Economics at California State University, Northridge. Professor Anderson received his Ph.D. in economics from George Mason University, and he is the author of the monographs *Fiscal Discipline in the States* and *The Political Economy of the Federal System*. Professor Anderson is a contributor to the books *Neoclassical Political Economy, Deficits, The Political Economy of Rent-Seeking, Predicting Politics, The Politics and Economics of User Charges and Earmarked Taxes, Adam Smith*, and *Pioneers in Economics*, and he is the author of nearly fifty scholarly articles in such journals as *Journal of Political Economy, History of Political Economy, Southern Economic Journal, Journal of Legal Studies, Journal of Law and Economics, Public Finance*, and *American Journal of Economics and Sociology*.

*Bruce L. Benson* is Distinguished Research Professor of Economics at Florida State University and Associate Editor of *Journal of Regional Science*. He received his Ph.D. from Texas A & M University, and he has taught at Pennsylvania State University and Montana State University. Professor Benson has been a recipient of Earhart, F. Leroy Hill, and Salvatori fellowships. His research interests focus on regulatory policy, legal institutions, and environmental systems. He is the author of more than eighty articles and reviews in scholarly journals and a contributor to twelve books, as well as co-author of *American Antitrust Laws in Theory and in Practice* (with M. Greenhut) and the author of *The Enterprise of Law* and the forthcoming Independent Institute books *Privatization in Criminal Justice* and *The Evolution of Law*.

*Donald J. Boudreaux* is Associate Professor of Legal Studies at Clemson University, having received his Ph.D. in economics from Auburn University and his J.D. from the University of Virginia. He is also a Research Fellow of the Independent Institute. Professor Boudreaux has taught at George Mason University, and his many scholarly articles have appeared in *Southern Economic Journal, Arizona Law Review, History of Political Economy, Public Finance Quarterly, Journal of Institutional and Theoretical Economics, Supreme Court Economic Review,* and *Constitutional Political Economy.* In addition, his writings appear in Reason, the *Washington Times,* the *Freeman,* and other popular publications.

*Thomas J. DiLorenzo* is Professor of Economics at Loyola College in Maryland, where he directs the Loyola Institute for Business and Economics Research. Professor DiLorenzo received his Ph.D. in economics from Virginia Polytechnic Institute and State University, and he is the author of the books *Underground Government, Destroying Democracy, Unfair Competition, Patterns of Corporate Philanthropy, Official Lies,* and *Unhealthy Charities.* Professor DiLorenzo has also authored more than fifty scholarly articles in such publications as *American Economic Review, Economic Inquiry, Southern Economic Journal, Journal of Labor Research, Public Choice,* and *International Review of Law and Economics,* and he is widely published in the *Wall Street Journal, Reader's Digest, USA Today,* and other popular publications.

*Robert B. Ekelund, Jr.,* is the Edward L. and Catherine H. Lowder Eminent Scholar in the Department of Economics at Auburn University. He received his Ph.D. in economics from Louisiana State University, and has taught at Texas A & M University and St. Mary's University. His books include: *Advertising and the Market Process* (with D. Saurman); *Economics; The Essentials of Money and Banking; The Evolution of Modern Demand Theory; A History of Economic Theory and Method* (with R. Hébert); *Intermediate Microeconomics; Macroeconomics; Managerial Economics;* and *Mercantilism as a Rent-Seeking Society* (with R. Tollison). Professor Ekelund has been First Vice President of the Southern Economic Association, Director of Graduate Programs in Economics at Texas A & M University, and Director of Graduate Programs in Economics at Auburn University. He is the author of more than one hundred articles and reviews in scholarly journals, plus such volumes as *The New Palgrave: A Dictionary of Economic Theory and Doctrine.*

*Paula A. Gant* is visiting Assistant Professor of Economics at the University of Louisville, having completed her Ph.D. at Auburn University on the effects of taxation and regulation of alcoholic beverages. She has been published in *Southern Economic Journal* and is co-author (with T. Beard and R. Saba) of the forthcoming "Estimation of Border-Crossing Demands: An Application to the Casual Smuggling of Alcohol."

*Adam Gifford, Jr.,* is Professor of Economics at California State University, Northridge. Professor Gifford received his Ph.D. in economics from the University of California, San Diego. He is co-author of the book *Public Economics* (with G. Santoni), and his scholarly articles and reviews have appeared in such journals as *Public Choice, Journal of Economic Behavior and Organization, Cato Journal, Quarterly Review of Economics and Business, Atlantic Economic Journal, American Economic Review, Southern Economic Journal, Journal of Economic Literature,* and *Journal of Law, Economics and Organization.*

*Randall G. Holcombe* is Professor of Economics at Florida State University. He received his Ph.D. in economics from Virginia Polytechnic Institute and State University, has taught at Auburn University and Texas A & M University, and is the recipient of the Ludwig von Mises Prize and the Georgescu-Roegen Prize. In addition to his book from the Independent Institute, *Writing Off Ideas,* he is the author of *Public Finance and the Political Process, An Economic Analysis of Democracy, Public Sector Economics, Economic Models and Methodology, The Economic Foundations of Government,* and *Public Policy and the Quality of Life.* He is also the author of more than one hundred articles and reviews in scholarly journals and a contributor to fourteen books.

*Bruce H. Kobayashi* is Associate Professor of Law at George Mason University School of Law. He has served as Senior Economist at the Federal Trade Commission, Senior Research Associate with the U.S. Sentencing Commission, Economist at the U.S. Department of Justice Antitrust Division, and Economic Associate with Economic Analysis Corporation. He received his Ph.D. in economics from the University of California, Los Angeles, and is the author of *Patent Licenses and the Incentive to Innovate.* Professor Kobayashi's articles have appeared in *Research in Law and Economics, Supreme Court Economic Review, Journal of Economic Behavior and Organization, International Review of Law and Economics,* and *Asian Economic Review.*

*Dwight R. Lee* is Professor of Economics and holder of the Ramsey Chair of Private Enterprise at the University of Georgia. Professor Lee received his Ph.D. in economics from the University of California, San Diego, and has taught at Washington University, George Mason University, Virginia Polytechnic Institute and State University, University of Colorado, San Diego State

College, and American Institute of Banking. His books include: *Economics in Our Time* (with R. McNown); *Microeconomics* (with F. Glahe); *Taxation and the Deficit Economy* (editor); *Regulating Government* (with R. McKenzie); *The Market Reader* (editor, with J. Doti); *Quicksilver Capital* (with R. McKenzie); and *Failure and Progress* (with R. McKenzie). He has also been a contributor to twenty-five other books and the author of more than 135 scholarly articles and reviews, and his popular articles have appeared in the *Washington Times,* the *Chicago Tribune,* the *Wall Street Journal,* the *St. Louis Post-Dispatch,* the *Atlanta Constitution, USA Today, Newsday, Journal of Commerce, Across the Board,* the *San Francisco Chronicle,* the *Christian Science Monitor,* and *Forbes.*

*Jonathan R. Macey* is J. DuPratt White Professor of Law and Director of the John M. Olin Program in Law and Economics at Cornell University. He received his J.D. from Yale Law School, and he is the author of *Banking Law and Regulation* (with G. Miller), *Costly Policies* (with G. Miller), *Insider Trading, An Introduction to Modern Financial Theory,* and *Third Party Legal Opinions.* Professor Macey has also taught at the Stockholm School of Economics, the University of Chicago, the University of Tokyo, the University of Virginia, and Emory University. He is a member of the Board of Arbitrators for the National Association of American Law Schools Section on Corporate Law, Board of Directors of The American Law and Economics Association, and American Law Institute. Professor Macey is the author of more than 120 articles in professional journals.

*Paul W. McCracken* is the Edmund Ezra Distinguished University Professor Emeritus of Business Administration, Economics and Public Policy at the University of Michigan, and formerly Chairman of the President's Council of Economic Advisers. Professor McCracken received his Ph.D. in economics from Harvard University, and he is the recipient of honorary degrees from William Penn College, Albion College, Berea College, Central Michigan University, and Northern Michigan University. He is a member of the Public Oversight Board of the AICPA, Chairman of the National Bureau of Economic Research, a member of the Harvard Graduate Society Council, and a member of the President's College of Berea College.

*Adam C. Pritchard* is an attorney with the Securities and Exchange Commission in Washington, D.C., and a Research Fellow of the Independent Institute. He received his M.S. in social thought from the University of Chicago and his J.D. from the University of Virginia. Mr. Pritchard clerked for Judge Harvey Wilkinson of the U.S. Court of Appeals, Fourth Circuit, and for the U.S. Solicitor General. His articles have appeared in *Virginia Law Review, Fordham Law Review, Arizona Law Review,* and *Supreme Court Economic Law Review.*

*David W. Rasmussen* is Professor of Economics and Policy Sciences and Director of the Policy Sciences Center at Florida State University. He has been a president of the Southern Regional Science Association and a recipient of the Medal for Achievement in Research on Regional Economics from the Academy of Sciences of the USSR. Professor Rasmussen received his Ph.D. in economics from Washington University, and his books include *Urban Economics, The Modern City, Economics: Principles and Applications, A Housing Strategy for the City of Detroit, Elements of Economics* (with C. Haworth), and *The Economics of a Drug War* (with B. Benson). He is the author of more than eighty articles and reviews in scholarly journals, and he is a member of the Editorial Board for *Government and Policy, Review of Regional Studies,* and *Governing Florida.*

*Mark Thornton* is Assistant Superintendent of the Alabama State Banking Department, and was formerly the O. P. Alford III Assistant Professor of Economics at Auburn University, where he received his Ph.D. in economics. He is the author of *The Economics of Prohibition* and a recipient of Salvatori, Earhart, F. Leroy Hill, and Ludwig von Mises fellowships. His many scholarly articles have appeared in *Review of Austrian Economics, International Review of Economics and Business, Social Science Quarterly, Journal of Institutional and Theoretical Economics, Journal of Economic Education, Atlantic Economic Journal, Southern Economic Review, Public Choice, Southern Business and Economic Journal,* and *Review of Social Economy.* Professor Thornton's articles have also appeared in the *Houston Chronicle,* the *Wall Street Journal,* the *Birmingham News,* the *Minneapolis-St. Paul Star Tribune,* the *Dallas Morning News, USA Today,* and other major newspapers.

*Gordon Tullock* is the Karl J. Eller Professor of Economics and Political Science at the University of Arizona and a member of the Board of Advisors for The Independent Institute. Professor Tullock received his J.D. from the University of Chicago Law School, and he is a past president of the Public Choice Society, Southern Economic Association, and Western Economic Association. His books include: *The Calculus of Consent* (with J. Buchanan); *The Politics of Bureaucracy; The Organization of Inquiry; Toward a Mathematics of Politics; Private Wants, Public Means; The Logic of the Law; The Social Dilemma; The New World of Economics* (with R. McKenzie); *Modern Political Economy* (with R. McKenzie); *Trials on Trial; Toward a Theory of the Rent-Seeking Society* (with J. Buchanan and R. Tollison); *The Economics of Wealth and Poverty; Autocracy; The Economics of Special Privilege and Rent Seeking; The Political Economy of Rent Seeking* (editor, with C. Rowley and R. Tollison); *Economic Hierarchies; Organization and the Structure of Production; The New Federalist; On the Trail of Homo Economicus; The Economics of Non-Human Societies; Social Choice Theory; Public Choice Theory; Intellectual Biography of Duncan Black;* and *Primer on Public Choice* (with G. Brady and A. Seldon). He is also the author of more than 400 articles and reviews.

*Richard Vedder* is Distinguished Professor of Economics and Faculty Associate, Contemporary History Institute, at Ohio University, and co-author (with L. Gallaway) of the award-winning Independent Institute book *Out of*

*Work: Unemployment and Government in Twentieth-Century America.* He received his Ph.D. in economics from the University of Illinois and has taught at the University of Colorado, Claremont Men's College, and MARA Institute of Technology. He is the author of *The American Economy in Historical Perspective;* co-author of *Poverty, Income Distribution, the Family and Public Policy* (with L. Gallaway); and co-editor of *Essays in Nineteenth-Century Economic History, Essays in the Economy of the Old Northwest,* and *Variations in Business and Economic History.* His numerous scholarly articles and reviews have appeared in such journals as *Agricultural History, Business History Review, Canadian Journal of Economics, Economic Inquiry, Economy and History, Explorations in Economic History, Growth and Change, Journal of Economic History, South African Journal of Economics, Public Choice,* and *Research in Economic History.*

*Richard E. Wagner* is the Holbert L. Harris Professor of Economics at George Mason University. Having received his Ph.D. in economics from the University of Virginia, Professor Wagner has taught at the University of California at Irvine, Tulane University, Virginia Polytechnic Institute and State University, Auburn University, and the University of Konstantz. His authored books and monongraphs include: *Balanced Budgets; Fiscal Reponsibility and the Constitution* (with R. Tollison); *The Consequences of Mr. Keynes* (with J. Buchanan and J. Burton); *Death and Taxes; Democracy in Deficit* (with J. Buchanan); *Economic Policy in a Liberal Democracy; The Economics of Smoking* (with R. Tollison); *The Federal Budget Process* (with J. Gwartney); *The Fiscal Organization of American Federalism; Inheritance and the State; Parchment, Guns and Constitutional Order; Public Debt in a Democratic Society* (with J. Buchanan); *The Public Economy; Public Finance; Smoking and the State; To Promote the General Welfare; Trade Protection in The United States* (with C. Rowley and W. Thorbecke); and *Who Benefits from WHO?* In addition, he is the editor of the books *Charging for Government, Fiscal Responsibility in Constitutional Democracy* (with J. Buchanan), *Government Aid to Private Schools, Perspectives on Tax Reform, Policy Analysis and Deductive Reasoning* (with Gordon Tullock), and *Public Choice and Constitutional Economics* (with J. Gwartney). He is the author of 100 articles and reviews in scholarly journals, and he is a contributor to more than forty scholarly journals.

*Brenda Yelvington* is a graduate research assistant completing her Ph.D. in accountancy at the University of Mississippi. A certified public acccountant, she received her M.B.A. from the University of Central Arkansas, has taught at the University of Arkansas, and has been an American Association Doctoral Consortium Fellow. She is a contributor to the books *Disorder and Harmony: 20th Century Perscpective on Accounting Theory* (A. Richardson, editor) and *Proceedings of the Southern Academy of Legal Studies in Business* (J. Norwood, editor), and her articles have been published in *The CPA Journal, Oil and Gas Tax Quarterly, Oklahoma Law Review,* and *Tax Advisor.*

# Index

Ability-to-pay principle, 18, 253
Absenteeism, 255, 244n11, 267n8
ACCRA. *See* American Chamber of Commerce Researchers Association
ACS. *See* American Cancer Society
Act Against Geneva (1727), 60
Act Against Spiritous Liquors (1736), 60
Adams, Charles, 32, 53n1, 76n2; on Jefferson/tax revolt, 63; on taxation, 58
Adams, Henry Carter, 33, 36, 53n4
Adams, John: tavern licenses and, 175
Adrian, Manuella: on alcohol consumption costs, 232–33, 235–36, 237
Ad valorem tax, 61, 120
Advocacy Institute, 130
Agency problem, confronting, 144
AHA. *See* American Heart Association
Airline tickets, excise tax on, 88, 101n7
Airport and Airway Trust Fund, 18, 50, 81, 82, 87 (table), 99; earmarked taxes and, 87–89
ALA. *See* American Lung Association
Alchian and Allen theorem, 15, 61, 67, 338n58
Alcohol: crime and, 65, 339n64; elasticity of demand for, 369; prices of, 260, 267n14; prohibition on, 152–55, 172; war on, 152–55, 188
Alcohol abuse, 241, 248, 257; corrective taxation and, 242; death and, 237, 238; economic costs of, 250; external costs of, 255; health care costs of, 236–37, 238–39, 265; income-earning potential and, 22; social costs of, 6, 235, 243, 250
Alcohol and Drug Problems Association, therapy programs and, 210

Alcohol consumption: absenteeism and, 244n11, 267n8; average yearly, 66 (table); dietary/binge, 192n3; external costs of, 267n9; lost-production costs of, 234–36; medical costs of, 23–24, 236–40, 241, 243, 256; private costs of, 256; Prohibition and, 67, 238, 244n13; reduction in, 66; social costs of, 24, 26–27n14, 228, 233 (table), 236, 240–44, 247, 248, 250, 254–58, 263–65; taxation and, 68, 175
Alcoholic beverages: cross-price elasticities between, 266; demand for, 249; market price for, 231, 232; monopoly on, 180; regulation of, 59–64; social cost of, 232–33, 250; taxation of, 59–64, 153, 154, 162n16, 228, 229, 229 (table), 231–33, 242, 250, 258, 265–66
Alcohol taxes, 6, 24–25, 37, 53, 58, 65, 254, 267nn10, 14, 303, 369; as corrective taxation, 231–34, 248; income tax and, 182; increase in, 153, 180, 247, 248, 258–64, 266; public-health perspective on, 247–48; regressiveness of, 25n1; revenue potential of, 40, 251; social-cost justification for, 6
Ali, Muhammad, 105
Alvarez, Miguel, 347–48
Alzheimer's disease, smoking and, 371, 372
American Association of University Women, Proposition 99 and, 124
American Bankers Insurance Company, Alvarez case and, 347–48
American Bar Association, drug therapy programs and, 210